THE TOLL ROADS
OF
BUCKINGHAMSHIRE

**The
Buckinghamshire
Archaeological
Society**

has members throughout the historic county of
Buckinghamshire, including Milton Keynes. Their interests,
despite the society's name, range across the spectrum of history,
archaeology, natural history and historic buildings.

The society supports the research, understanding and
preservation of the county's historic assets, publishes the annual
journal *Records of Buckinghamshire*, books and papers, and runs a
variety of lectures and outings on historic subjects.

- To learn more about the society's activities, see our website
  at www.bucksas.org.uk or visit our Library in the County
  Museum in Aylesbury. If you would like to join the society,
  see membership details inside the back of this book.

The Toll Roads of Buckinghamshire 1706 - 1881

WITH THEIR CONNECTIONS INTO NEIGHBOURING COUNTIES

The making of the modern main road network

By PETER GULLAND

Buckinghamshire Archaeological Society

First published September 2017
by the Buckinghamshire. Archaeological Society,
County Museum, Church Street, Aylesbury,
Buckinghamshire HP20 2QP, UK.
Website: www.bucksas.org.uk

ISBN 978-0-9957177-3-2

A catalogue record for this book is available from the British Library.

Index compiled by Diana Gulland.
Maps drawn by Peter Gulland.
Designed and typeset by Peter Marsden.
Printed and bound by BookPrintingUK, Peterborough, England.

Contents

List of Illustrations

'Thumb-nail' maps showing the position of each turnpike road in Buckinghamshire appear on the first page of each road's entry between pages 63 and 289.

The Author

Peter Gulland, BSc, DipTP, a retired town planner, has been a member of the Buckinghamshire Archaeological Society for some forty years, during which he served on the society's Council for two periods in the 1980s. His main history interest has been in the events which formed the landscapes which we see around us today. This was illustrated, for example, by his article in the society's journal *'Records of Buckinghamshire', volume 43* (2003), on the effects of enclosing open fields in the parish of Aston Sandford. Within this topic he has been particularly focussed on the evolution of the network of paths, tracks, and roads on which people have moved around over the centuries.

The chance unearthing of an unusual milestone which had been buried in a back garden resulted in his being asked to write a note on the discovery in *'Records of Buckinghamshire', volume 48* (2008). His research to produce that note made him aware of how little detailed information about Buckinghamshire's turnpike roads was easily available. This started a project which was to run for eight years to gather the material for this book.

Peter, who has lived in Haddenham in Buckinghamshire for nearly fifty years, has combined his fieldwork on the routes of old roads with helping in the maintenance of public footpaths and bridleways in the Vale of Aylesbury. He has also enjoyed leading groups on walks to explore historic landscape features and, in conjunction with his wife Diana, has written five books of self-guided walks to see local history in north Buckinghamshire.

Acknowledgements

The research for this book involved many visits to places which were once part of the turnpike road network to see the results of the turnpike trustees' work. But most information has been gathered in the relevant record offices and local study centres where the friendly and proactive assistance of the staff has made my visits to their search rooms a real pleasure. To the past and present teams in the offices listed below I extend my sincere thanks for their help and for the interest they have taken in my project:

Bedfordshire Archives Service
Centre for Buckinghamshire Studies
Hertfordshire Archives and Local Studies
London Metropolitan Archives
Northamptonshire Record Office
Oxfordshire History Centre
Parliamentary Archives
Reading Borough Libraries and Local Studies

My wife, Diana, has created the index. She has also been my second pair of eyes when out searching for clues to the routes of abandoned sections of road, the sites of toll houses and the 'more difficult to find' milestones. To her I owe a huge 'thank you'.

I also thank Peter Marsden, Chair of the Buckinghamshire Archaeological Society, for his encouragement in this project over several years and for his enormous help in the publication stage of this book.

Peter Gulland
July 2017

Author's
Introduction

A BRIEF GLOSSARY

A toll road   is any road whose use is regulated by the payment of a toll by users.

A turnpike   originally referred to soldiers' use of a military pike to block a road, track or path as a means of controlling travellers. This could be 'turned' away to allow people to pass. The word 'turnpike' then became a standard term for any bar or gate placed across the road to control its use.

A turnpike road   is therefore a road controlled by turnpike gates and bars, usually to collect tolls.

Turnpike Trusts   were set up in the eighteenth and nineteenth centuries to maintain and improve sections of the public highway in return for the right to collect tolls.

A turnpike gate   was a gate set across the highway to control access and collect tolls.

A side bar   was a bar set across a junction with a side road to control access and collect tolls on the side road. Usually a pivoted wooden bar, it could be a gate or even a chain.

MEASURES

£ s d   Pounds, shillings and pence were the British currency in use before 1971, when replaced by the decimal currency of pounds and pence. Before 1971 a pound (£1) was made up of 20 shillings (20s), and each shilling made up of 12 pence (12d). An 'old pound' therefore contained 240 'old pence'. All values in this book are given in the form '£1 0s 0d'.

Calculations by the Bank of England indicate that £1 in 1706, when the first turnpike trust in this book was set up, was worth the equivalent of £219 in 2016.

Miles and yards   Miles and yards were standard measures of length during the 'turnpike era', with 1,760 yards to the mile. In metric terms, one mile = 1.6 kilometres and one yard = 0.91 of a metre.

Weights   Tolls for wagons could be determined by weight, using 'weighing engines' which measured in tons and 'hundredweights', one ton being 20 hundredweight ('cwt'). In metric terms, one ton = 1,016 kilograms.

Dates   Many dates in the records of the turnpike trusts are given in the form '1824/25'. This indicates the start and end years of a trust's letting of its turnpike gates and is used where calendar year financial data has not been found.

Key Facts about turnpike roads

When?

The first turnpike trust in Buckinghamshire and England to be appointed under a private Act of Parliament was set up in 1706. The last to operate in Buckinghamshire was wound up in 1881; with the last at work in the United Kingdom 'disturnpiked', meaning they became free of tolls, on Anglesey in North Wales in 1895.

How widespread were turnpike roads?

During the turnpike era these trusts selected 20 per cent of the English and Welsh public road network to become turnpike roads. At their peak in the late 1830s there were 231½ miles of turnpike road in Buckinghamshire.

How were turnpike trusts set up?

Groups of landed, professional, and business gentlemen formed private trusts, each of which obtained an Act of Parliament to take over part of a public main road in their locality for a limited period, with the object of improving it .

Who paid for the turnpike system?

Private individuals, including some trustees, loaned money to start the trust and to carry out major improvements. Tolls collected from road users at turnpike gates paid for the day-to-day maintenance of the road on which the gate was situated and for interest on the loans.

What did the trusts do?

In their early days turnpike trusts simply continued the work of the parish surveyors who preceded them by making superficial repairs to the surface of roads, but they made an immediate improvement by repairing their road more often.

From early in the nineteenth century turnpike roads began to be rebuilt in depth to make them the first network of roads capable of bearing heavy loads which had been seen in Britain since the Roman military engineers stopped work in the fourth century.[1] At the same time trusts widened their roads, eased steep hills, and cut out sharp bends. This led to a significant increase in the speed of coach travel and in the weight carried in wagons.

How long were individual turnpike roads?

Although main roads were part of a national network, and therefore sometimes of considerable length, individual turnpike trusts only adopted relatively short sections of road. The average length controlled by a Buckinghamshire trust was just under eighteen miles.

How many toll gates were there?

At the peak of the turnpike era in 1836 there were 42 toll gates across main roads in Buckinghamshire, giving an average 5½ miles between gates across the turnpike road. In the same year there were 23 others, called side bars, or chains, across turnings off turnpike roads in Buckinghamshire.

Were turnpike roads newly built roads?

In Buckinghamshire some 10 per cent of the peak turnpike road mileage, in 1838-65, had been built from scratch by or on behalf of turnpike trusts.

What became of them?

When the A, B and C classification of roads was introduced in 1919, 78 per cent of the initial mileage of A-class roads in Buckinghamshire had formerly been turnpike roads.

The area covered by this book

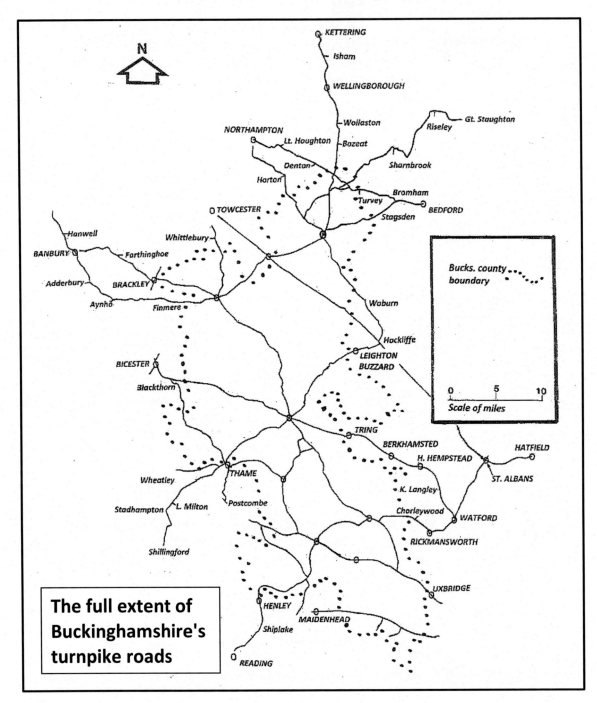

FIGURE 1

The territory covered in this book goes well beyond Buckinghamshire's borders in all directions because most turnpike trusts adopted lengths of road between significant towns, regardless of whether this meant crossing county boundaries. As a result, the story of the trusts which controlled roads in Buckinghamshire would be distorted if we only looked at what they did within this county. Our roads stretched from Reading in the south and Hatfield in the east to Banbury in the west and Kettering in the north.

Why study turnpike roads?

Inland transport in Britain was transformed in the eighteenth and nineteenth centuries as main roads were improved, canals dug, and railways built. Much has been written at the general level about the economic and social benefits for the country at large from this revolution, but the picture is not uniform at the local level.

There is a huge literature on nearly every canal and railway line in Britain, but studies of the history of individual main roads are comparatively rare; roads tend to be taken for granted. This is a pity because the rise and fall in importance of individual roads reflected the fortunes of markets and towns throughout history, and the 'turnpiking' of main roads was the most significant general event in highway development between the building of the Roman military roads and the dawn of the motorway era. It was also the first local legal event in the long history of most of the roads which were to be 'turnpiked'.

Turnpiking led to a revolution in the volume and style of personal travel in the era of the stage coach and enabled major growth in general trade in ever-larger road wagons.

Some local histories ignore the fact that the main roads crossing their study area have any history at all, or confine comment to the observation that a main road 'was turnpiked' in the eighteenth or nineteenth centuries - without saying what the 'turnpikers' actually did. Other authors describe a turnpike road as having been 'built', when what they meant in most cases was that a turnpike trust had been formed to take over and improve a road that was already in existence.

The scarcity of works on the history of individual turnpike roads probably has a simple explanation. Canals and railways had an opening date, a name, some distinctive architecture and in some cases a closing date. In contrast, those main roads which were selected for turnpiking were <u>chosen</u> from parallel and duplicating existing routes and not <u>created</u> by the turnpike trusts; they thus lack immediacy for researchers. And after the trusts were wound up their toll gates, side bars, and many of their distinctive toll houses, were dismantled and their roads became numbered parts of our modern main road network, their names forgotten.

The introduction, in 1919, of the A, B, and C road classification saw chains of formerly independent and differently named turnpike roads subsumed into single anonymous A-class identities. For instance the highway spine of Buckinghamshire, the A413, was constituted from the roads of three formerly independent Buckinghamshire trusts, each with its own name.

But even if their names were forgotten, the firm condition of former turnpike roads lived on in 1919, when 78 per cent of the initial mileage selected to be A-class roads in Buckinghamshire had formerly been turnpike roads.

This book seeks to provide background for researchers by identifying which roads in Buckinghamshire were turnpiked and how the turnpike era changed them. It also tries to give a flavour of the work of trustees, officers, and the men who worked on the road.

Part One
The work of the Turnpike Trusts

1:
The beginnings of the turnpike trusts

Growing trade needed larger vehicles and faster personal travel

The growth of trade in England has been almost continuous since the late fifteenth century, and the need to transport the goods on which that trade was based has grown in most years ever since. When not carried by water, this trade initially travelled on the backs of packhorses in loads of little more than two hundredweight per animal, or in two-wheeled carts where road conditions allowed.[2]

Initially trade grew by lengthening the gangs of packhorses and increasing the number of gangs and of carts. However during the seventeenth century it became more and more obvious that trade could continue to grow only if packhorses and carts could be replaced by four-wheeled wagons, each of which could carry one and a half tons. So carts began to be replaced by wagons during that century, but only on the roads which could support wagon weights, while packhorses continued widely in use on less substantial roads until the mid-eighteenth century.[3]

The seventeenth century also saw the slow growth of travel by coach but this, too, was restricted to the limited mileage of better roads to protect passengers from painful jolting.

How were road improvements to be achieved?

This expansion of carrying capacity was stifled as long as main roads were looked after unenthusiastically by the parishes in which they lay, under a maintenance system introduced in 1555. The roads inherited from the Middle Ages consisted of public rights of way over the soft natural land surface such as clay or sand with ruts intermittently filled with stones. They lacked foundations, and, in many cases, their surfaces were not solid enough to bear the increasing weight of wagons.

Parishes lacked the knowledge, finance, or motivation to improve them and some actively resisted the arrival of wheeled traffic because of the damage it did to the road. On the Hockliffe and Woburn Turnpike Trust's road Battlesden parish in Bedfordshire insisted in 1728 that it was only liable to maintain a causeway for the historic traffic of 'horses and other cattle' which were not drawing coaches, carts, or carriages.

This attitude developed against a background where parish expenditure was becoming dominated by support for the poor, as population grew in the seventeenth and eighteenth centuries – and highway maintenance was pushed to the bottom of parish priorities. It was painfully obvious that not enough was being spent on main roads.

From 1563 Justices of the Peace had power to fine parishes whose roads were in poor condition, but this was usually a reaction long after this had started to inconvenience travellers. The problem was how to raise money and ring-fence it to main roads in order to improve them to bear the growing weight of expanding long-distance coach and wagon traffic.

The precedent was already there. Medieval bridges over wider rivers were maintained by many varied local organisations. Since the thirteenth century travellers in England had been paying tolls when they crossed these bridges. The organisation that collected these tolls then applied the income to maintaining the bridge.

Several attempts were made in the seventeenth century to apply this system for maintaining bridges to maintaining main roads, but what worked well for a short structure with access only at its ends – so that all users could easily be charged for crossing – did not work for twenty miles of road with numerous access points.

The sought-after solution was to combine adequate toll charges with the minimum number of places at which they were to be collected. Too many toll gates across the road could result in income largely going on the cost of toll collection, and could deflect road users onto other routes. Experiments controlled by Justices of the Peace, such as that in Hertfordshire in 1663, did not result in a system which produced enough income or effective control of work on the road.

1706: First private turnpike trust formed

This all changed in 1706, when a group of 32 gentlemen in Bedfordshire and Buckinghamshire set up the first turnpike trust in England that was independent of the justices. They proposed to take over and improve twelve miles of the Holyhead Road – formerly the Roman Watling Street and now part of the A5 – from Fornhill, near Hockliffe in Bedfordshire, to Stony Stratford in Buckinghamshire.

This was an undulating stretch of road, with short, steep hills and severely muddy patches in the intervening dips, particularly at its southern end. It carried heavy traffic between London and the north-west, so was the subject of constant complaints. And though only twelve miles in length it was the responsibility of twelve separate parishes.

The 32 trustees put up the necessary capital themselves as loans at a fixed rate of interest and obtained an Act of Parliament which authorised them to put gates across 'their' road in order to levy tolls on the users. The tolls were to be applied to repairing, maintaining, and improving that road, and their powers to do this were to last for 21 years, because a public road could not be put permanently under private management.

Most later trusts applied to Parliament for a fresh Act towards the end of this 21-year term, and repeated the process several times. The longest-lived trust in Buckinghamshire, for instance, the Wendover and Buckingham, lasted for 157 years. After 1834 Parliament simplified the procedure by passing a Turnpike Act Continuance Act every year so that trusts whose acts were expiring could have their cases processed together.

The multiplication of turnpike trusts between 1706 and 1836

The first turnpike trust in Buckinghamshire, the Hockliffe and Stony Stratford, actually got off to a disastrous start due to the inexperience of trustees, leading to gross mismanagement of their road improvements. The trust was soon unable to repay its debts *(see Road number1 in Part Two)*.

In spite of this, the trustees' concept of how to finance a turnpike road soon began to be copied all over England. The amount of money available to lend was initially suppressed by the banking crisis after the South Sea Company's investment 'Bubble' burst in 1720, but after the 1730s money became available for turnpike trusts to be founded in increasing numbers.

A glance at a national map of turnpike roads will identify a line running from Leeds to Southampton which separates the well-spaced turnpike roads of eastern England, including Buckinghamshire. from the much denser network of the West Midlands and Welsh borders. The reason for this contrast is that turnpike trusts in the east took over routes linking towns and ignored lesser roads between them, whereas trusts further west were formed to turnpike all main roads radiating from a particular town. Since the turnpike network was not planned it is difficult to explain why the two areas developed so differently.

By the time the last trust was formed (in Sussex in 1836[4]) nearly 20 per cent of the English and Welsh public road network – 22,000 miles out of 125,000 – had been taken over and improved by 1,116 turnpike trusts which had erected 7,796 toll gates and side bars.[5] In Buckinghamshire the system reached its peak mileage in 1836, by which year there were 231½ miles of turnpike road in the county controlled by 24 trusts operating 42 main gates, 26 side bars, and seven weighing engines.

How the turnpike road network was selected

In the absence of any national coordination, the turnpiking of main roads spread haphazardly through England and Wales. Initially this created situations in which isolated sections of trunk route, for example between Wendover and Buckingham, were being improved as turnpike roads while miles of road at each end were not.

Nevertheless, certain trends can be seen, with roads radiating from London turnpiked in the first half of the eighteenth century, while cross-country routes which linked these radials followed later in that century and multiplied in the early nineteenth century.

Among the first roads in Buckinghamshire to be taken over by turnpike trusts were the four great trunk routes across it:
- The London to High Wycombe to Oxford route was largely turnpiked by 1719;
- London to Slough to Bath by 1728;
- London to Wendover to Buckingham to Birmingham by 1744;
- London to Dunstable to Stony Stratford to Birmingham by 1745.

However each of these trunk routes had a section of road that had still not been turnpiked by 1750.

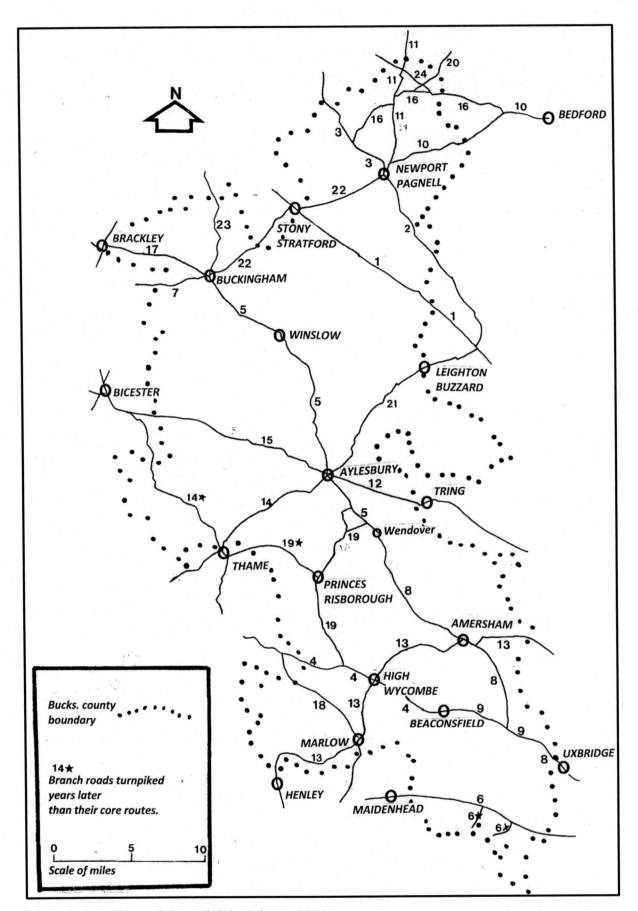

FIGURE 2: **Turnpike roads in Buckinghamshire in 1836.**
These are numbered 1-24 in the order in which they obtained their first Acts of Parliament – with number 1, the Hockliffe and Stratford, in 1706. The same numbers are used throughout this book.

This was a pivotal time in the evolution of our modern road network. Until the eighteenth century most inter-urban routes consisted of general corridors of travel, often with parallel alternative roads, one of which was usually recognised as the principal route.

From 1706 onwards, however, turnpike trustees were deciding which of these alternatives had the most potential for cost-effective improvement. Those which were not selected, such as an early version of the A40 Oxford road through the high Chilterns via Radnage *(see Road number 4 in Part Two of this book)*, declined into lanes and bridleways, while others such as the future A4010 route between Aylesbury and Princes Risborough were brought from relative obscurity and would later become 21st-century trunk routes.

While making these local decisions on which parts of the medieval main road network to adopt and develop in the eighteenth and nineteenth centuries, unelected groups of turnpike trustees were unknowingly selecting what would become the strategic national A-class road network of the twentieth century. The importance of these decisions by the turnpike trusts cannot be overemphasised.

From late in the eighteenth century the emphasis began to change from improving only the roads used by obvious existing flows of traffic to creating new travel opportunities. Trusts began to upgrade roads linking towns which so far had not been well connected, such as Aylesbury and Princes Risborough.

Sadly some of these new links were triumphs of optimism over commercial potential and roads such as Marlow to Stokenchurch (turnpiked in 1791), Great Staughton to Lavendon (1802), Buckingham to Towcester in Northamptonshire (1824), and Thame in Oxfordshire to Princes Risborough (1825) were taken over by trusts with the best intentions but rapidly became financial liabilities.

Other bodies maintaining main roads

Toll collection by the organisations that built or maintained medieval bridges has already been mentioned. Similar proprietary bodies came to be responsible for the upkeep of the principal streets in some towns, and this could pose a problem for some turnpike trusts. Town toll gates and tolls for short lengths of road which were part of longer turnpike roads made an unwelcome addition for road-users to the tolls of turnpike trusts.

After 1801 Stony Stratford's Bridge and Street Commissioners were responsible for maintaining that part of the future A5 which formed the High Street, the bridge over the River Ouse, and the causeway linking them, under an Act of Parliament which superseded a tangle of earlier charities.[6] This body formed a buffer between the turnpike trusts to north and south of the town, but did not start to charge tolls until 1835.

At Newport Pagnell turnpike control of the road from Northampton ended on the north side of North Bridge. That bridge, Tickford Bridge on the other side of town, and the streets between them were controlled by the town trustees who had obtained an Act in 1809 which enabled them to collect tolls

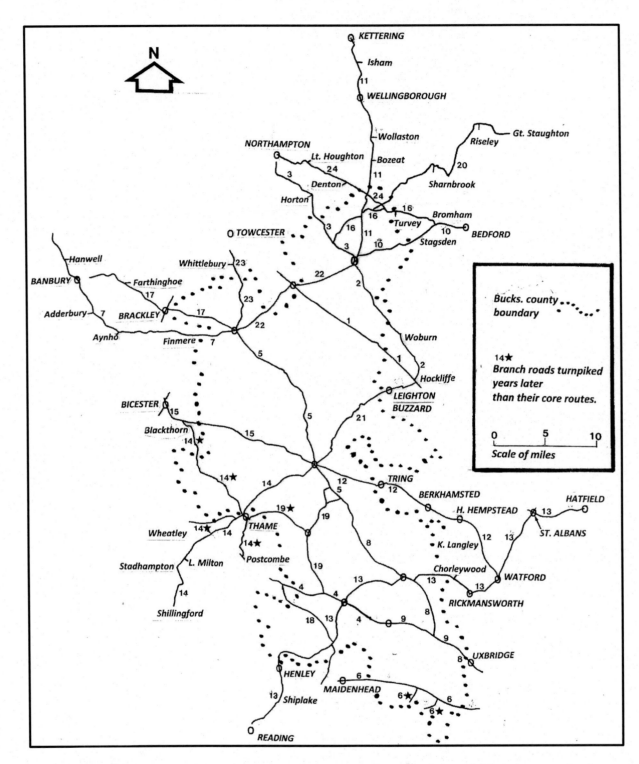

FIGURE 3: **The continuations of turnpike roads from Buckinghamshire into neighbouring counties in 1836, showing key place names outside Buckinghamshire.**

The numbers 1-24 for the county's 24 turnpike roads is used consistently throughout this book. Each of the 24 sections in Part Two of the book is dedicated to an individual road and starts with a smaller map showing its individual route and location within the county.

to fund the rebuilding and maintenance of their bridges and streets. The fine toll house which still stands on North Bridge was built in 1810 and was operated by the town trustees.

At the other end of the county the Reading and Hatfield Trust's 1859 Act prevented it from spending money on maintaining roads within the towns of Henley, Marlow, High Wycombe, Amersham, Rickmansworth, Watford and St Albans, but none of these towns charged tolls on traffic.

Turnpike roads and the enclosure of open fields	In England as a whole the peak period for authorising new turnpike trusts, 1750-1770, was closely followed by the peak period for enclosure of the remaining open-field parishes as improved roads made markets more accessible. This period of enclosure produced the chequerboard landscape of rectangular, hedged fields which is so familiar in the Midlands north of the Chiltern Hills today.

In many such parishes the process of bundling the acreage of each farmer's scattered holdings in the open fields into a compact block of land in the newly enclosed fields led to a major rearrangement of the parish's road network. However these changes usually excluded any turnpike road which crossed the parish because this road was already administered under an Act of Parliament. The parish's own enclosure Act usually forbade any interference with the alignment of the turnpike road unless approved by a special meeting of turnpike trustees.

In the enclosure of Haddenham parish, for example, virtually all old roads except the village streets and the turnpike road were ploughed up and replaced by a new, coarser, network of straight roads of uniform width. The result is that on the map of Haddenham today the winding medieval course followed by the turnpike road contrasts with the straight enclosure roads laid out in the rest of the parish in 1833.

Matters became complicated at Thame in Oxfordshire when the open fields were enclosed under an Act of 1823 and the Risborough Road Trust then obtained an Act to build a largely-new branch road from Princes Risborough to Thame two years later in 1825. The route of the new road was therefore not protected by Thame's enclosure Act and the road's trustees had to build it through a landscape in upheaval, as Thame's new enclosed fields were laid out. Nearly four years of friction between turnpike trustees and some of Thame's farmers followed before the road was completed in 1830.[7]

2:
Routine road maintenance by the trusts

Getting started with a road repair gang

The first few meetings of each trust were dominated by swearing in trustees, electing a clerk, treasurer and surveyor, agreeing where to erect toll gates and toll houses, and surveying the road itself to identify sections which needed widening or were in urgent need of repair. A team of labourers then had to be engaged to carry out routine maintenance.

The size of these teams varied but could be surprisingly large. The Risborough Road Trust, for example, was employing between 16 and 22 men in the financial year 1795/96 on a road that was at that time only thirteen miles long.[8] Taking an 1811 example from the Beaconsfield and Stokenchurch Trust,[9] road men typically worked from 6am to 4pm in summer, or from dawn to 4pm in winter, six days a week, often for between ten and twelve shillings a week.

Concern for the welfare of the labourers is not prominent in the trusts' records, although acts of kindness by trustees may be disguised under other, inscrutable, headings. In one unambiguous minute book entry in 1758,[10] the Colnbrook Trust allowed Joseph Parfect, a labourer with wife and children, seven shillings a week until the trust's next meeting in consideration of his being disabled by a fall of gravel.

For equipment, the 25½-mile Sparrows Herne Trust started work in 1762 with two ploughs (for levelling the road surface), sixteen wheelbarrows, forty pickaxes, forty iron shovels, three ballast screens, two 10ft rods, and two lines with iron reels.[11]

The use of 'Statute labour'

Throughout most of the turnpike era every parish was legally responsible for the maintenance of all public highways within its boundaries, and that included any length of turnpike road within the parish. Road maintenance was carried out by 'statute labour', under which owners or occupiers of land worth £50 a year or more were obliged to provide a cart, horses, tools, and two men for six days' work each year – while all other men in the parish had to labour for six days on the roads unpaid.[12]

In practice most statute labour was performed on the minor roads of the parish and some turnpike trusts hired their own labourers for work on their road in order to have better control. Nevertheless, the trusts were entitled to call on the parishes to provide a few (typically two or three) days' statute labour on the turnpike road under the direction of the trust's surveyor. While notoriously inefficient, this brief influx of labourers could be useful for dealing with repair backlogs or major tasks.

Every new trust started by obtaining from surveyors of the parishes along its road a list of who in each parish was liable to carry out unpaid statute labour on the turnpike road, and whether such duty was to be performed by manual labour or the provision of carts and teams of horses. Most trusts obtained updated lists annually.

In 1835 statute labour was abolished and replaced by a system of parochial rates,[13] so from that year the trusts had to pay for all work done on the turnpike road by the parishes.

Road repairs and gravel digging

Turnpike trusts initially worked as the parish surveyors they replaced had done, by continuing to patch, level and resurface their roads in the time-honoured fashion. As newcomers to road maintenance many of the trustees knew no better.

The important difference was that, unlike the parishes which intermittently patched all the highways within their boundaries, each trust's work was focussed solely on one main road and was carried out more regularly. This meant that pot-holes and the triple ruts in turnpike roads – two wheel ruts with the 'horse way' between them – began to be filled before they became impassably deep.

This maintenance was an unending battle by the trust's surveyor and his labourers to prevent the disintegration of the surface of their road. Nowhere was this more acute than on the heavily-trafficked Bath Road, which probably explains why the Colnbrook Trust's minutes in the 1770s contain more detail about this routine work than do those of most other trusts.

Every January or February the Colnbrook Trust's surveyor inspected the whole road to assess the quantity of gravel which would be needed for maintenance during the coming year. Contracts were then let for the annual digging, sifting, loading and carting of gravel from pits near the road to be dropped beside it in piles where repair work was needed. Some gravel then lay on the roadside for weeks before it was actually needed and there was a sporadic, but repetitive, complaint by several trusts that some gravel had been illegally removed before the work team got to it.

The digging of the all-essential gravel was a source of endless friction between turnpike trusts and local landowners. Trusts were empowered by their Acts to dig gravel or stone for road repair from common land or private fields in parishes that the road passed through. The extent of that digging was illustrated by a landowner at Weedon, north of Aylesbury, who complained in 1789 about the manner in which the Wendover and Buckingham Trust had excavated gravel from more than two acres of his land. Sometimes the local geology meant that there was no accessible gravel near where road repairs were contemplated and surveyors had to dig for it some way away, with resultant extra cartage costs.

When gravel was found the owner of private land was paid for the gravel and compensated for any damage to his land. Numerous, almost routine, damage claims from landowners suggest poor supervision by surveyors, but were probably a widely-understood mechanism for increasing the payment for gravel taken. No payment was made for gravel taken from common land, but the site had to be made safe after digging.

The surveyors, however, were not blameless. Doubtless prompted by past experience, the Whitchurch enclosure award of 1771 allocated land beside Hurdlesgrove Hill, near Dunton, for gravel digging, but in 1800 the Wendover and Buckingham Trust's minutes recorded complaints that surveyors had been straying outside their allotted area in the parish in the search for gravel.

How a road should be formed – new ideas in the early 19th century

By late in the eighteenth century there was still no concept of completely rebuilding a road in depth to give it foundations which would support the surface layers. However trusts had come to understand that deeper surface layers gave a better ride for passengers and goods alike, cushioning any variations in the subsoil or underlying rock. When the trustees of the Banbury and Brackley turnpike road started work in 1791 they specified that it should be given a consistent width of 24ft between hedges "...16ft whereof to be stoned twelve inches deep where the ground is tender, and nine inches deep where the soil is stony and firm..."[14]

Within twenty years Thomas Telford had shown that there was a limit to the improvement which could be achieved by simply increasing the thickness of stones on the road. In his improvements to the Holyhead Road he had levelled the old road surface by ploughing it, then laid a base course of large stones placed by hand, with raised kerb stones at the sides to support a camber which he created for drainage. These were then covered with a layer of packed broken stone, kept in place by the kerb stones, and topped by a wearing course of gravel. To complement the camber he dug side ditches to drain water away and encourage the road to dry out.[15]

With growing experience in road repair the trusts were now ready to switch to Telford's principles, but found his hand-placed foundation and flanking ditches too labour-intensive. They therefore tended to follow the less expensive system employed by John Loudon McAdam, surveyor to the Bristol Turnpike Trust. He also levelled the old road surface by ploughing it, but omitted Telford's hand-placed foundation and covered the levelled surface with up to 15 inches of stone compacted in layers graded in size from large at bottom. McAdam also cambered the road surface to improve drainage but relied on gutters rather than ditches to carry the water away.

Today both methods sound so obvious that it is difficult to grasp what a great leap forward they represented at the time.

As the 18th century progressed, road users began to appreciate the results of turnpike trusts concentrating their work on just one road, but, as today, local residents had to suffer while the work was carried out. Writing in 1791 as the Bromham and Olney Trust began work in his village, Turvey in Bedfordshire, John Higgins told his brother: "...Mr. Parker has begun the new turnpike through the village and they have pushed up the carriageway so that we see a great many stones and wheelbarrows with dirt and pickaxes and spades..."[16]

While there was often general disquiet at the introduction of turnpike tolls, those who could afford them saw turnpiking as progress. Writing in 1824, immediately after the road through his village had been turnpiked, the Vicar of Lillingstone Dayrell said: "...we now have, on the Macadamising plan, an excellent road .... Our new road is much admired and reckoned not only of great utility, but an ornament to our vicinity."[17]

Repairs to bridges

Repairs to bridges were a particular headache in the early years of most trusts. For many minor bridges this was due to arrangements going back into the mists of time by which counties, parishes, and the owners or occupiers of specific pieces of land had 'maintained' individual bridges to varying standards. When turnpike trusts came on the scene, some private bridge maintainers could not be traced, others were unwilling to continue their work on a bridge which was likely to see traffic increased by the trust, and some could no longer afford to do so.

Several trusts spent time and energy in trying to persuade the relevant people to honour their commitments, often without success but always with delays in rebuilding the relevant bridge. When, for example, Rowsham Bridge over the River Thame east of Aylesbury was found to be 'seriously decayed' in 1810, it took the newly-formed Aylesbury and Hockliffe Trust until 1813 to discover whether Buckinghamshire county or Hulcott parish was responsible for rebuilding it. This did not produce the required action so, after further exchanges in 1820,[18] the trust finally rebuilt the bridge itself in 1825 at a cost of £60.[19]

Keeping the dust down

While some trusts struggled to keep up with routine maintenance, five trusts on the principal and most profitable roads in the south of Buckinghamshire had more sophisticated concerns. Dust from stones crushed by passing wheels was a constant problem in the summer months for travellers and residents alike. An 1823 advert for an Amersham coaching inn extolled the route on which it lay by saying that "...the fifteen miles from Uxbridge to London are now cleansed from dust by constant watering".[20]

Early efforts to lay the dust were laborious. This involved first using buckets to fill water carts with water from streams. The Beaconsfield and Stokenchurch Trust's 1736 and 1794 Acts appear to authorise sourcing water in this way from the River Wye, after compensating those, such as millers, who owned the water.

From the 1760s wells began to be sunk and water pumps erected beside trunk roads near London to make water collection easier. However the Colnbrook Trust, responsible for part of the Bath Road, now the A4, did not do this until 1827, erecting pumps at one-mile intervals and providing water carts with which, from mid-March to mid-September, contractors could "...keep the said Roads damp so as effectually to prevent all inconvenience from dust to the entire satisfaction of the Surveyor...."[21]

However the Red Hill and Beaconsfield Trust, whose turnpike road was part of the Oxford Road, now the A40, watered the whole of its road from some

time after 1823, and the Sparrows Herne Trust (now the A41) started in 1827, but only at its Watford end.

Two examples of the Colnbrook Trust's massive turnpike water pumps can still be seen on the Bath Road at Longford and Poyle. Their unusual height was needed to position their spouts above the water carts which patrolled the road.

Dealing with obstructions

People in the eighteenth century had a more relaxed attitude to the appropriation of parts of the highway than we are used to today. All turnpike trusts therefore had to spend time and effort in stopping the use of the highway verge for vegetable gardens or the storage of dung, and they even had to remove unauthorised buildings.

In 1794 it was reported to the Wendover and Buckingham Trust that a house had been built on the highway verge between Holman's Bridge Gate and the edge of Aylesbury town.[22] This probably only meant that a house which was under construction beside the road had encroached marginally on highway land, but the trust had to come down heavily on such incursions in case they expanded further.

In 1830 the Risborough Road's surveyor was ordered to remove 'gardens and encroachments' from the roadside verge between North Lee and the World's End, north of Wendover. It took until 1834 to remove them all, but in the meantime trustees had become concerned that the person who had planted a hedge on the verge at Great Kimble might be going to put up a building behind it. Furthermore, dung heaps had appeared beside the road at Monks Risborough.[23]

3:
Alterations to the highway

When trusts first took control of their roads they were mainly preoccupied with improving the surface, digging drainage ditches, widening pinch points, and rebuilding bridges. For a short period in the 1760s, and more widely after about 1800, they began to expand their work by widening longer sections of road, easing gradients, and even building completely new lengths of road. This work came to a peak of activity in the 1820s and early 1830s before suddenly coming to a stop as the railway era dawned.

Widening the road

The widths of medieval highways varied from broad expanses to narrow defiles in which wheeled traffic going in opposite directions could not pass. From the outset turnpike trusts set out to replace this variety with a uniform distance between the boundary hedges. This could be as little as the 24ft provided by the Banbury and Brackley Trust in 1791 or the 36ft on the Hockliffe and Woburn Trust in 1728, but increasingly it was set at 40ft or 60ft. That such improvements were viewed as being in the public interest in the turnpike era is shown by the number of cases in which owners of land adjoining the road gave the trust the strip of their land needed to widen the road.

In turnpike days about half of the total width between highway boundaries was left as broad grass verges to allow animals driven on the hoof to graze while keeping them out of the way of wheeled traffic on the metalled central strip. This has enabled a lot of carriageway widening in our motor age to be done without the need to acquire more land from adjoining owners.

As the narrow sections of turnpike roads were eliminated in the eighteenth and nineteenth centuries, it became possible for coaches and wagons to pass each other while being drawn by horses in pairs controlled by a driver riding on the vehicle. For wagons this replaced the previous less efficient arrangement where they had been drawn by five or six horses in line, with their driver walking or riding beside them. Allowing horses to work in pairs increased their pulling power so that, early in the nineteenth century, wagons carrying up to four tons, and finally six tons, could be drawn by up to four pairs of horses.[24]

Reducing the steepness of hills

The trusts' improvements in quality of road surface from the late eighteenth century onwards encouraged, predictably, the use of bigger and heavier stage coaches and wagons. These larger vehicles, in turn, made hills into more noticeable obstacles – because even moderate gradients hugely increased the work level for horses.

Trusts which had steep hills on their roads thus found themselves under pressure in the 1810s and 1820s to ease gradients, and this led, mainly in the 1820s, to a spate of hill lowering. This was typically carried out by straightening the road, excavating the upper end of the hill into a cutting, and using the resultant spoil to build up the lower end on to an embankment, thereby lengthening the hill and reducing its average gradient.

Good examples are Tring Hill at Aston Clinton on today's A41, where the cutting was later nearly doubled in width in 1975, White Hill at Holtspur on the A40, and Old Dashwood Hill further west on the A40 between Piddington and Studley Green. On the last of these the original pre-turnpike hill was abandoned altogether and today it is a public footpath *(see Road number 4 in Part Two of this book)*. The original Dashwood Hill is worth walking to experience just how narrow and unevenly-graded main road hills could be in the early days of the turnpike era *(see figure 21)*.

Cutting out detours   Elsewhere routes were shortened by bypassing meandering sections. The Sparrows Herne Trust built 3½ miles of new road in various places between 1810 and 1827. The longest of these was a new, more direct road into Aylesbury – the present High Street and part of Tring Road – which was built in 1826 and stretched for one mile from Adams Garage at Oakfield Road into Market Square

FIGURE 5: **Tring Hill cutting, excavated in 1825 by the Sparrows Herne Turnpike Trust.**
This photograph was taken before its widening in 1975.

PHOTOGRAPH BY PETER GULLAND.

Just to the south, the Risborough Road Trust (today's A4010) built five 'cut offs' between Stoke Mandeville and West Wycombe to eliminate indirect sections of its road. Historically more important were the bypasses to Westbury, built between 1792 and 1814, Chenies, before 1812, and Little Missenden in financial year 1828/29. These were the first new roads to bypass any settlement in Buckinghamshire

The willingness of some landowners to donate narrow strips of land to trusts to facilitate road widening has already been mentioned, and can partly be attributed to the fact that road widening benefitted the public without significantly interfering with the working of the land. In contrast there were several cases in which landowners opposed schemes to build completely new lengths of road across their estates where blocks of land could be cut off. The Kettering and Newport Pagnell Trust's road was blighted by a series of sharp bends at Warrington, north of Olney. The trust applied to Lord Dartmouth in 1802 for land on which to build a straight road through the bends, but he refused, and the bends stayed until bypassed by Buckinghamshire County Council in the 1970s.

Major diversions to avoid wet ground

The intention of the trusts was to improve the structure and surface of the main roads that they took over. However there were several cases in and adjoining Buckinghamshire where they decided that the route already in use was too difficult to improve. This was usually because it was too boggy to drain properly. So they diverted the turnpike road to the route that we use today, which is usually on higher ground.

A lengthy example of such a change is on the older original road between Aylesbury and Buckingham, where the existing road was low-lying and seasonally muddy between North Marston and Hogshaw. Early in the eighteenth century traffic appears to have moved away from this route to a 14½-mile long string of existing minor roads which ran parallel to the old road on higher and drier ground to the east.

When the Wendover and Buckingham Trust obtained its first Act in 1721 it seems to have followed the traffic, taking this higher preferred route as its turnpike road. As a result this is now the A413 main road between Aylesbury and Buckingham. The older route fell into disuse, and part of it today has since ceased to be a road altogether.

A shorter example is the old road between Princes Risborough and Thame which went through low-lying soft ground east of Towersey. This was bypassed by building a largely-new route on higher and drier ground to the north between 1825 and 1830. This is now the A4129, probably the last significant new main road to be built in Buckinghamshire for a century.

The total length of newly built road

By 1836, the peak year of the turnpike era, 24 miles or just over 10 per cent of the turnpike road network in Buckinghamshire had been new-built by the trusts or, in a few cases, by landowners and enclosure commissioners working on trusts' behalf. This total excludes the 14½-mile diversion of the road between Aylesbury and Buckingham because it used existing minor roads and did not involve any new road-building. Although isolated cases of

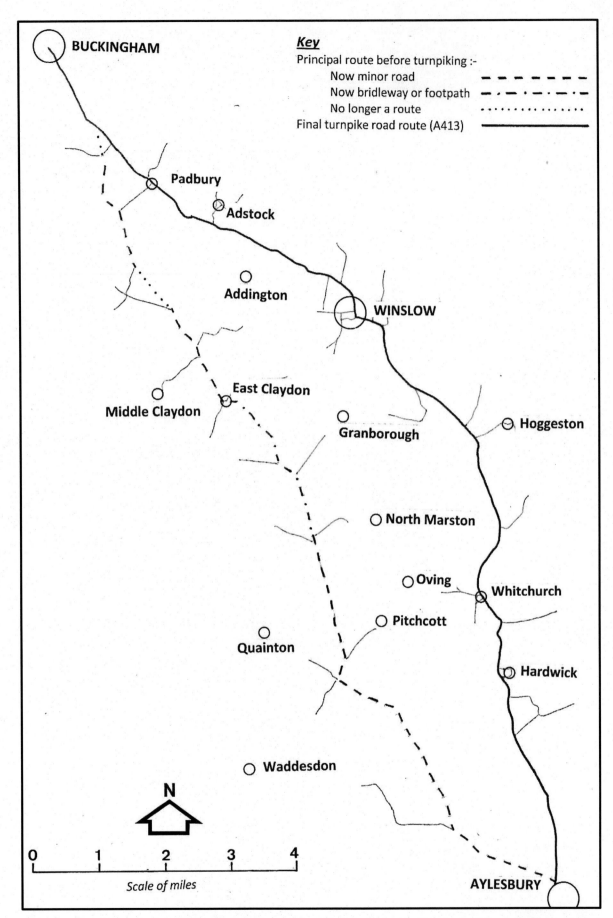

FIGURE 6: **The older road between Aylesbury and Buckingham**, shown as a dashed line, and to its right the 1721 turnpike road, an upgrading of minor roads that has become today's A413.

new-build started in the 1760s, the majority was carried out in the years 1800-1830, particularly in the 1820s.

The effect of widening roads, easing gradients, and building new sections is most obvious today on a route such as that between Buckingham and Banbury. The A422 twists and turns on sharp gradients and bends between Buckingham and Westbury on a section where the trust did not improve the alignment. But west of Westbury the A422 has easy gradients and gentle curves through Brackley to Farthinghoe in Northamptonshire – because here the trust replaced the old route with a completely new one.

A few other sections of turnpike roads in and adjoining Buckinghamshire, such as Buckingham to Whittlebury, again in Northamptonshire, Marlow to Henley, and Newport Pagnell to Northampton, have not been significantly realigned either as turnpike roads or in the improvements since the 1950s. These preserve much of the character of roads of the early turnpike era, with their frequent bends and changes of gradient as their narrow carriageways twist between enclosing hedgerows. In complete contrast, the comprehensive widening, straightening, and diverting of the Kettering and Newport Pagnell Trust's road as the A509 since the 1960s has virtually obliterated the road's turnpike era character.

4:
Erecting milestones and mileposts

The need for mile-markers

We tend to use the word 'milestones' today, but mile-markers were not always stone; they could be wooden boards or iron posts. The first turnpike milestones in England were erected voluntarily on the Cambridge and Fowlmere Turnpike Trust, the modern B1368, in financial year 1725/26.[25] But as the spread of turnpike roads encouraged a growth in travel milestones became a 'must'.

Stage coaches advertised fixed fares between towns but charged a rate per mile for what were quaintly called 'short passengers', who were making a local journey from their village to a nearby town. Independent travellers hiring post-horses and post-chaises from posting inns were also charged by the mile. Passengers and post-horse riders therefore needed unbiased verification of the number of miles they were paying for, and stage coach drivers were helped in keeping to their exacting schedules by noting progress past milestones.

In recognition of this Parliament imposed a requirement to erect milestones or mileposts in many individual turnpike Acts passed after 1744, then made this a general requirement in the General Turnpike Act of 1766 *(7 Geo.III, c.40)*.

Some trusts clearly turned a blind eye to the 1766 Act, because several subsequent turnpike renewal Acts continued to require mile-markers to be erected. The Aylesbury and Shillingford Trust, for example, obtained its initial Act in 1770 and when it came to renew this in 1791 the new Act implied that the trust had so far failed to erect milestones and ordered it to do so. By 1813 the Ordnance Survey recorded that this had been done.

The materials and orientation of mile-markers

The first mile-markers were wooden, prone to rotting, and were quickly replaced on most turnpike roads by milestones, although most of the Sparrows Herne Trust's mileposts were still wooden until 1826.

The earliest milestones were roughly square in plan, with only one inscribed face and with that face aligned parallel to the road. They had incised lettering and displayed Roman numerals. Difficulty in reading long Roman numbers such as XXXVIII when passing them quickly led to milestones being reset diagonally to the road with two inscribed faces, one of them facing towards each direction of oncoming traffic. In addition, cast iron plates with raised lettering were attached to some stones from about 1750 to further improve legibility, and eventually Arabic numerals replaced Roman from the 1770s.

The Colnbrook Trust's Bath Road, now the A4, still has an almost complete set of milestones which illustrate parts of this evolution. Its stones were

FIGURE 7:
The turnpike road south from Buckingham to Padbury, with milestones 54 and 56 marked, on Thomas Jefferys' map of 1770.

originally installed in 1741 with one face parallel to the road; that face was inscribed with destinations in difficult-to-read lower case lettering and Roman numerals. In the nineteenth century the same stones were made more legible by being lifted and reset to stand diagonally to the road, with two faces inscribed with capital letters and Arabic numerals. Although it was intended that the original inscriptions would be obliterated, a few of these stones still carry some of this older lettering on the rear faces.

Legibility reached its peak with the arrival, in about 1810, of mass-produced cast-iron mileposts made to standard designs, painted white with raised black lettering on two faces which obliquely faced oncoming traffic.

In Buckinghamshire the most obviously standard design probably dates from the 1880s or 1890s, just after the end of the turnpike era. This consists of a plain steel pressing with two smooth, white-painted faces on to which destinations and mileages were painted in black. These are called 'Buckinghamshire Pressings' by the Milestone Society, and appear to have been commissioned by the new highway authorities – the county or district councils – to replace damaged or worn out mile markers on any of the former turnpike roads that they had inherited. They were also installed on one or two roads which had never been turnpiked, most notably the cross-country route between Brill and Buckingham via Grendon Underwood. While isolated Buckinghamshire Pressings can be found in mid and south Buckinghamshire, most are in the north of the county and several have been found in poor condition due to traffic accidents and heavy rusting at ground level.

Which side of the road?

One would have expected mile markers to be placed consistently on one side of the road to enable travellers to be able to spot them, but this was not always the case. The Wendover and Oak Lane Trust placed consecutive milestones on alternate sides of their section of today's A413. On the Oxford road, now the A40, the Red Hill Trust placed all its milestones on the north side of the road while the next trust to the west, the Beaconsfield and Stokenchurch, placed its stones on the south side. Coachmen doubtless became used to these idiosyncrasies, but infrequent travellers could have gone for miles without spotting a milestone.

'Moving milestones'

Mile markers did not necessarily stay in one place throughout the life of a trust. As the turnpike era proceeded several trusts shortened parts of their routes by cutting out indirect sections of road. This meant that the existing milestones began to overstate distances.

On roads radiating from London it is noticeable, if one compares old maps of different dates, that turnpike trusts reacted to road shortening by moving their milestones further from London as the road distance from it decreased. An extreme example in Buckinghamshire was the Bicester and Aylesbury Trust *(see Road number 15 in Part Two)*, where the change may have been made to improve the attractiveness of its route. The trust switched its calculation of the mileage between Aylesbury and London from a route via Uxbridge to one via Watford which was two miles shorter. To reflect this the trust apparently moved each of its existing milestones two miles further from London – to avoid the need to renumber them – and cut two new ones for the Aylesbury end of its road.

Mile markers and the Second World War

On 30 May 1940, when Britain faced the possibility of a German invasion, the Minister of Transport instructed highway authorities to remove direction signs which could help an invading enemy.[26] While signposts and town or village name boards were extensively uprooted and put into store, the picture is less clear with mile markers.

It is on record that some counties definitely did uproot or bury mileposts, many of which were not returned to their rightful places after the war. In Buckinghamshire it is noticeable that several turnpike roads which cross the county boundary have mile markers in place in Buckinghamshire but not in the adjoining county. This suggests that either Buckinghamshire did not have enough staff to remove milestones in 1940, or that it was uncommonly diligent in returning them to the roadside after the war.

Whichever is the truth, today Buckinghamshire still has some 116 out of its peak number of about 230 mile markers in place while, probably as a result of the war, neighbouring Bedfordshire has about fifteen and Northamptonshire about 32.

Unusual mile markers

Every now and then an unusual milepost was erected as a feature rather than as a practical marker of distance. In 1752 Sir Francis Dashwood erected an obelisk called The Pedestal at West Wycombe to mark the completion of his rebuilding of a short section of the London to Oxford turnpike road and inscribed it with esoteric destinations such as 'The City' and 'The University' *(see Road number 4 in Part Two)*. In Great Marlow the Reading and Hatfield Trust graced the top of the High Street with an obelisk carrying a more predictable set of local destinations, but including Bath, which was 80 miles away *(see Road number 13 in Part Two)*.

Boundary markers

Boundary markers were rare and were presumably only set up where a dispute with adjoining landowners was expected or experienced. Only one trust with a road in Buckinghamshire – the Sparrows Herne Trust – had to resort to such measures. At three places in Hertfordshire at Tring, Berkhamsted and Watford the trust placed a small cast-iron marker inscribed with its name to indicate the boundary of the highway *(see Road number 12 in Part Two)*.

5:
Financing the work of the trusts

Raising money from investors

Toll income paid for the maintenance of the road, the cost of collecting tolls, and the salaries of the trust's officers. Any money left over was put towards paying interest to the trust's creditors.

But toll income was obviously not available to get the trust started, and it was usually insufficient to fund major improvements such as building sections of new road. For these it was necessary for the trustees to advertise in local newspapers to raise money in the form of loans. These were usually issued in the form of fixed-rate bonds, typically paying interest at 4 or 5 per cent a year. Such loans were held against the security of future toll income. From the 1730s investment in turnpike roads was popular but after 1760 canal construction increasingly provided a rival attraction for investors.

Uniquely in Buckinghamshire the Colnbrook Trust had only one creditor at a time until the 1820s. Others typically had between ten and twenty, most of them living fairly close to the trust's road, some making repeat loans to the same trust when its finances became stretched. The size of loans ranged from a few at £10 or less to an even smaller number between £1,000 and £1,600. This indicates a very small group of people with sizeable disposable incomes. The great majority were between £120 and £300 – the equivalent of, say, between £20,000 and £50,000 at today's values.[27]

Such loans were essential for the trust to do its work, but proved to be poor investments when some trusts found themselves unable to pay interest for years at a time. The Northampton and Cold Brayfield Trust got into this situation and found itself in 1850 with annual toll income of about £500 and unpaid interest standing at £3656. In 1852 its creditors were asked to accept a reduction in the rate of interest to 1 per cent and, either through public spiritedness or acceptance of the inevitable, they agreed.

Raising money from tolls

One of the first actions of each new trust was to erect toll gates at strategic points and, in the early years of the turnpike era, to employ people at between ten and twenty five shillings per week[28] to live beside the gate and collect the tolls. By the 1770s trusts were finding the hassle of directly employing gatekeepers was too much and began to employ contractors to act as middle men, usually for a year at a time. These collected the toll gate takings once a week and, after paying their monthly rent instalments to the trust, kept the residue as their commission.

FIGURE 8: **Contrasting styles of inviting loans in 'The Bucks Gazette' of 2 July 1825.** The first is to finance the Risborough Road Trust's new road from Princes Risborough to Thame, while the second is for the Sparrows Herne Trust's new road on the approach to Aylesbury and the easing of the gradient on Tring Hill.

BY KIND PERMISSION OF THE CENTRE FOR BUCKINGHAMSHIRE STUDIES.

MONEY WANTED.

THE Commissioners acting under and by virtue of an Act of Parliament passed in the present Session, entituled " An Act for more effectually repairing and improving certain Roads passing through Princes Risborough, in the county of Buckingham, and communicating with Aylesbury and Great Marlow, in the said county, and Thame, in the county of Oxford," are desirous of BORROWING £3000., for the purposes of the said Act, to be secured by way of Mortgage on the Toll, on the said Roads, with interest, after the rate of £4. per cent. per annum, according to the provisions of the said Act, in sums of not less than £50. each, the interest to be payable half yearly.

The money will be required at Midsummer next; and all persons willing to advance any portion of the said sum are requested forthwith to send letters stating the amount to the office of Messrs. Fell and Prickett, solicitors, Aylesbury.

GEORGE FELL, Clerk to the Commissioners.

Aylesbury, June 8th, 1825.

SPARROW'S HERNE TURNPIKE.

MONEY ON TURNPIKE TOLLS.

THE Trustees of the Turnpike Road leading from Sparrow's Herne, on Bushey Heath, through Watford, Berkhamsted St. Peter, and Tring, in the county of Hertford, to Walton, near Aylesbury, in the county of Buckingham, having occasion to take up at interest TEN THOUSAND POUNDS for Improvements going on and projected on the said Road; any persons who may be disposed to advance money at four per cent. on security of the Tolls, are requested to signify the same to us for the information of the Trustees, specifying the amount they will lend on the above terms, and the period at which they will advance it, the whole not being immediately required.

Particulars of the Revenues of the Trust may be had on application to us. By order of the Trustees.

GROVER and SMITH, Solicitors, Hemel Hempsted.

June 13th, 1825.

By the early nineteenth century several of these contractors in Buckinghamshire were giving toll houses as their home addresses but these were probably 'business addresses' because they clearly could not have travelled regularly to collect toll takings at other gates if they were actually the gate keeper at the address given.

Once trusts had begun to employ contractors they would advertise each year in the local newspapers to invite prospective contractors to attend a trust meeting and bid for the lease of one or more gates for the next year. Until the 1840s these adverts usually gave the net amount made at each gate during the preceding year, but in the last years of the trusts often only the total income for all of the trust's gates was advertised. Either way, these statements are of great value to the highway historian because they show the changing financial health of each trust over the years.

At gate-letting meetings trustees would lay on refreshments to encourage attendance, typically at the rate of one guinea per gate. In the 1790s and 1800s the Newport Pagnell Trust routinely advertised its toll gate auctions

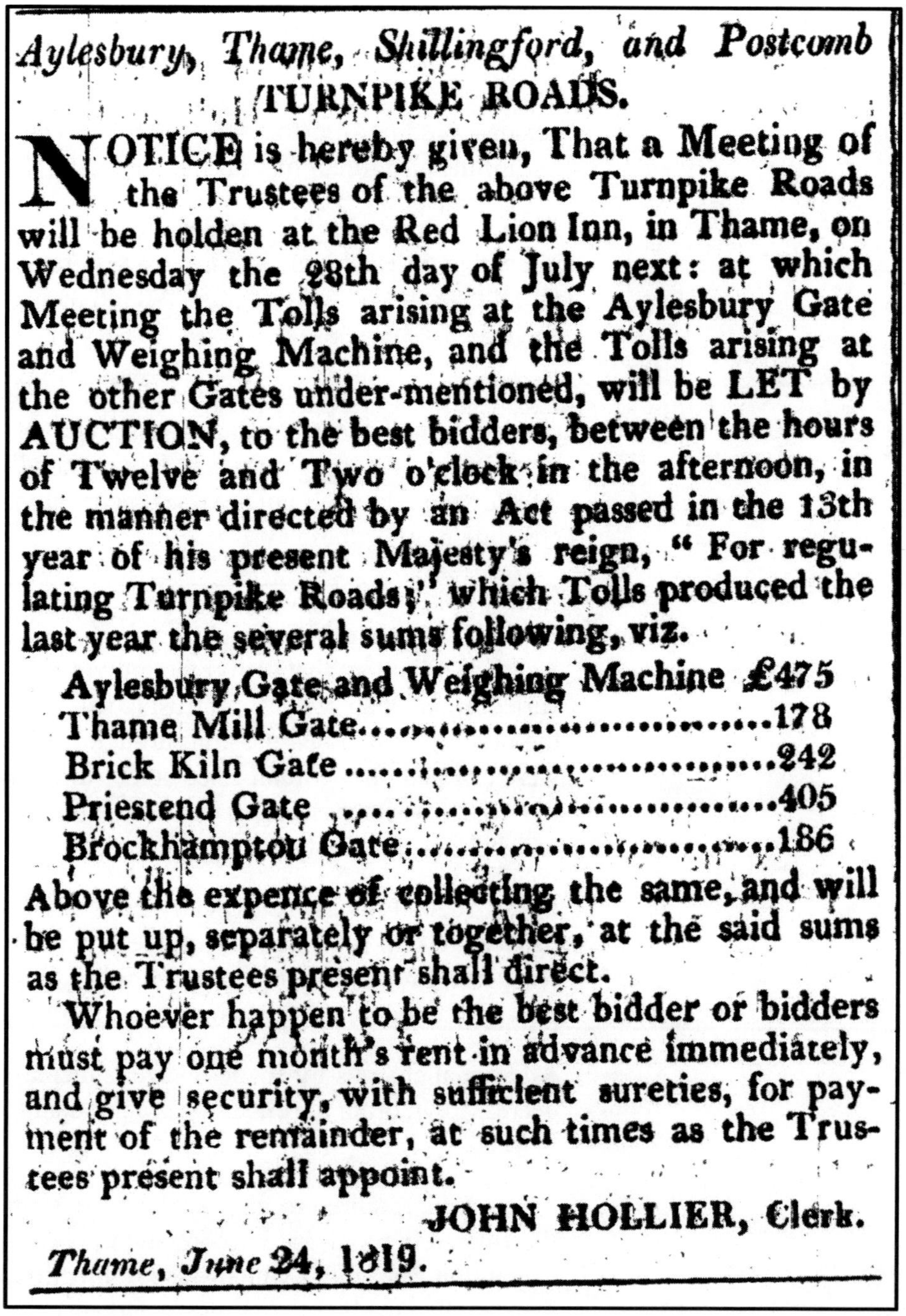

Aylesbury, Thame, Shillingford, and Postcomb
TURNPIKE ROADS.

NOTICE is hereby given, That a Meeting of the Trustees of the above Turnpike Roads will be holden at the Red Lion Inn, in Thame, on Wednesday the 28th day of July next: at which Meeting the Tolls arising at the Aylesbury Gate and Weighing Machine, and the Tolls arising at the other Gates under-mentioned, will be LET by AUCTION, to the best bidders, between the hours of Twelve and Two o'clock in the afternoon, in the manner directed by an Act passed in the 13th year of his present Majesty's reign, "For regulating Turnpike Roads;" which Tolls produced the last year the several sums following, viz.

Aylesbury Gate and Weighing Machine	£475
Thame Mill Gate	178
Brick Kiln Gate	242
Priestend Gate	405
Brockhamptou Gate	186

Above the expence of collecting the same, and will be put up, separately or together, at the said sums as the Trustees present shall direct.

Whoever happen to be the best bidder or bidders must pay one month's rent in advance immediately, and give security, with sufficient sureties, for payment of the remainder, at such times as the Trustees present shall appoint.

JOHN HOLLIER, Clerk.

Thame, June 24, 1819.

FIGURE 9: **An advertisement for contractors to collect the tolls** for the Aylesbury, Thame and Shillingford Trust, which appeared in 'Jackson's Oxford Journal' on 26 June 1819. From late in the eighteenth century these adverts came to have a highly standardised text and layout but, after the late 1830s, details of individual gates were often replaced by single totals of income for the whole trust.

as from 11am to 2pm, with "Dinner to be on the table at two o'clock".[29] However, the process had become ethically complicated at the Bromham and Olney Trust by 1844, when trustees debated the propriety of their giving presents to the bidders for the tolls.

Trusts were able to profit where there was competition to lease busy gates. For many other gates only one bidder appeared, often due to collusion among the contractors,[30] and he was able to state his terms. However where there was bidding the newspaper adverts sometimes revealed background colour. In 1792 the Reading and Hatfield Trust had to warn that 'neither of the present renters of the tolls will be permitted to bid unless they first pay all their arrears of rent'.[31]

And in 1801 an outbreak of smallpox in Aylesbury led to a reduction in travellers paying tolls so, in order to attract bidders, the Wendover and Buckingham Trust agreed 'to pay two guineas towards the expenses of persons bidding for the tolls at the [Walton] turnpike gate, and also 19 shillings for liquor had during the bidding'.[32]

Once a contractor had been selected he paid monthly instalments of his total bid which, in Buckinghamshire in 1836, ranged from £91 to £4,028 a year for all the gates of any one trust. All toll income in excess of his instalments and expenses was his.

The mid-1860s saw an unexpected overlap between the dying eighteenth-century turnpike system and a harbinger of the twentieth century. The turnpike trusts on the future A40 found a small additional source of revenue by allowing telegraph poles to be erected along the verge of their road, and charging rent for these.[33]

Toll tariffs and general examptions

The tolls and charges for such items as overweight wagons were set by the Acts of Parliament that set up the individual trusts. Tolls and other charges varied by small amounts from trust to trust. All scales of tolls were based on the number of animals passing through the gate, so coaches, for example, were charged on the number of horses drawing them, not on the weight of the coach or its passenger capacity, although horse power and carriage weight were obviously linked.

In the 1830s tolls could typically be 1½d or 2d for a horse and rider and between 8d and 1s 1½d for a carriage drawn by two horses, while pedestrians went free. Problems could arise from trying to count herds of cattle, sheep, pigs and so on which were charged by the score.

Additional charges for loaded wagons increased as the width of wheel rim decreased, in order to reflect the greater damage done to the road by narrow wheels.

Trusts were required to display the basic tariff on a board at each gate but the rules left room for interpretation. There was, for example, a general exemption from toll – which was not mentioned on most boards – for local people going to church on Sunday. However as late as 1865 the toll collector at the New Road Gate in Aylesbury was charged with demanding toll from a Methodist preacher on a Sunday.

6:
Toll gates, side bars and weighing engines

The first and last toll gates

The earliest toll gates on turnpike roads which had any part of their mileage in Buckinghamshire were put up in 1706 in Bedfordshire, one at Fornhill near Hockliffe on the Hockliffe and Stony Stratford Road, and the other at Woburn on the Hockliffe and Woburn Road *(see Roads numbers 1 and 2 in Part Two)*. The Fornhill gate was almost certainly the first toll gate <u>for a private trust</u> in England. The first gate to be erected in Buckinghamshire itself was in 1709 on the Newport Pagnell Trust's road at Eakley Lanes, a tiny hamlet near the Buckinghamshire–Northamptonshire border just east of Salcey Forest.

All three of these ground-breaking gates were found to be inconveniently placed and were resited later in the eighteenth century. Today there is no trace of them or their toll houses.

The last toll gates in operation in Buckinghamshire were those on the Reading and Hatfield Trust's road and these were removed late in 1881 *(see Road number 13 in Part Two)*.

The design and distribution of toll gates

In 1836, at the height of the turnpike era, there were 42 toll gates across main roads and 26 side bars across side turnings within Buckinghamshire *(see figure 10)*. Several writers claim that the very earliest gates across turnpike roads consisted of a single horizontal bar pivoted from a vertical post on the verge and swung across the road to open or close it. This would have perpetuated the traditional military way of controlling road traffic.

The present author has not found any evidence for a single bar being used for gates across the main road, but there are clear references to side bars having this design *(see 'Side bars' below)*. The available information points to main roads in Buckinghamshire always being closed by a single five-barred gate which could be locked across the carriageway, with a small pedestrian gate beside it which did not need to be locked because pedestrians did not pay a toll. At their peak in 1836, turnpike roads in Buckinghamshire had an average of one toll gate across them every 5½ miles.

The earliest trusts with roads in Buckinghamshire were also the busiest, but found that they could raise adequate toll income with only one or two toll gates across their roads. Several of these, such as the Beaconsfield and Stokenchurch Trust and the Colnbrook Trust, managed with only one gate for up to a century. By the late eighteenth century, however, the roads being adopted for turnpiking were less important and less profitable, so the trusts being formed to take them over took the precaution of starting work with three and sometimes four gates.

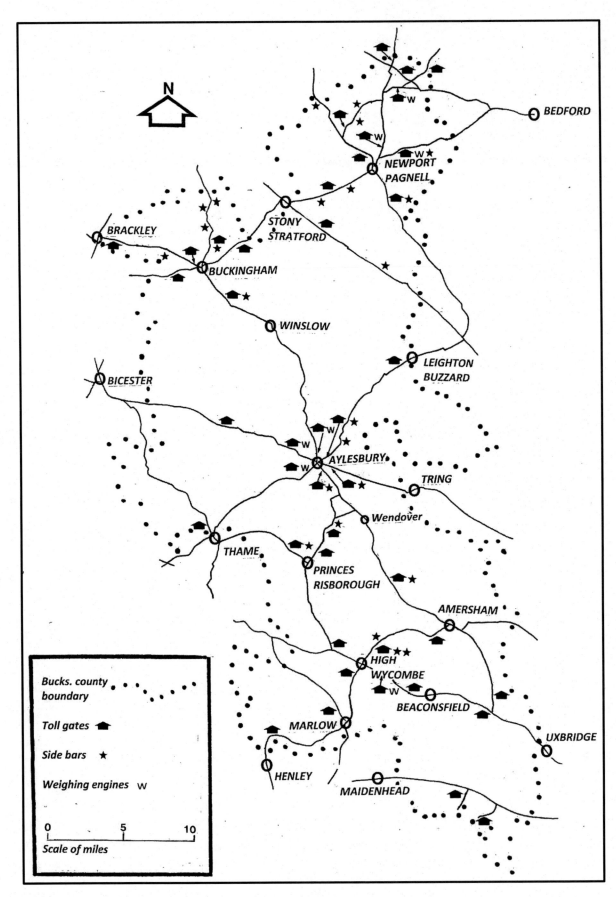

FIGURE 10: **Toll gates, side bars, and weighing engines in Buckinghamshire in 1836**, at the peak of the turnpike era, showing gates predominantly encircling the main towns.

Toll evasion was a concern from the start of the turnpike era, but seems to have been accepted to a certain degree as long as trust incomes were rising. After the railway era had started in 1838 and income began to fall rapidly on most trusts there was a general tendency to erect additional gates in order to catch toll evaders who had previously been tacitly ignored.

The siting of toll gates

Toll gates were sited where traffic was highest and where there were the fewest opportunities to avoid paying tolls by using minor roads which did not go through the gate. Most were therefore sited on approaches to towns or at isolated locations. Aylesbury is an example of the first, being ringed by six gates. Westcott on the Bicester and Aylesbury road, where there were no convenient byroads on which to bypass the gate, is an example of the second.

Because the boundaries between trusts were often in towns, this meant that travellers might have to pay to enter *and* then to leave a town that they passed through, if they entered on one trust's road and left on that of another.

As the turnpike era proceeded the map of toll gates slowly changed as toll evaders first found ways of bypassing gates and the trusts then moved their gates to block the loopholes, in an endless game of cat and mouse. As a result, although there were 42 toll gates across main roads within Buckinghamshire in 1836, these gates had stood in no fewer than 77 different locations at one time or another during the existence of the trusts

There was constant pressure from townspeople to keep gates as far as possible outside town boundaries so as to minimise inconvenience to their daily business. The Banbury and Brackley Trust, for example, was prevented by its originating Act in 1791 from having a gate within Brackley town, and was obliged by its renewal Act in 1851 to move its Buckingham Gate further out of town towards Radclive so that traffic from the town on to Stowe Avenue would not be tolled.

Side bars

As already mentioned, toll income suffered where travellers were able to turn off the main road on to minor roads for a mile or so in order to avoid a turnpike gate. Although travel might be considerably less comfortable on the minor road many road users were prepared to put up with this for a short distance to save on tolls.

From the early 19th century the trusts' solution was to identify the most-used exit points and put barriers across them. These barriers were usually called side bars, but were sometimes described as side gates or check gates. Because this involved putting an obstruction across roads which were not covered by the turnpike trust's Act, Parliamentary approval was needed, and this was given nationally in 1741.[34.] By 1836 there were 26 side bars in Buckinghamshire.

Buckinghamshire's first side bars appeared in the 1780s to offset rising maintenance costs caused by increasing traffic. They became more numerous from the 1820s to the 1850s, initially to help pay for the growing amount of road rebuilding carried on as the turnpike era peaked in the 1820s and 1830s. With the start of the Railway Era at the end of the 1830s the need for road improvement suddenly ended but the trusts then faced a cash flow problem which was tackled, ultimately unsuccessfully, by putting up more main gates and side bars to reduce toll evasion.

We may deduce from the fact that these barriers tended to be called 'side bars' that the earliest examples, at least, adopted the old military idea of a horizontal bar pivoted on a vertical post to swing across the side road. Such a structure would have cost less than a conventional five-barred gate plus pedestrian gate and would have been in tune with the fragile economics of side bars.

However once into the nineteenth century there was an increasing number of references to chains, suggesting a move to the even cheaper solution of simply hanging a chain across the side road between two posts. Minimising the cost of providing side bars was helped by most of them having only a kiosk – sometimes called a "wooden watching box" – without any domestic accommodation, instead of a habitable cottage to shelter the toll collector.

The economics of operating side bars are highly questionable, but difficult to establish because virtually all of them were included with a nearby main gate when let to toll contractors. Details of the side bar's toll income were then hidden in reports for the contract as a whole.

What is obvious is that some side bars were across turnings with so little likely traffic that they seem to have originated from trustee paranoia about potential toll evasion rather than a rational comparison of toll collectors' wages with likely toll income.

For most of its short life the Buckingham and Towcester Trust had two gates across the main road and five side bars, one of which apparently controlled a traffic flow so obscure that it is difficult to relate its advertised name to any likely location. The economics of side bars may sometimes have been dealt with by gatekeepers putting members of their family to watch them. The minute book of the Bromham and Olney Trust[35] offers a clue: there the Stevington and Stagsden side bars were 170 yards apart but apparently they were manned by one toll collector for at least their last seven years!

An unusual extension of side bar operation was made by the Reading and Hatfield Trust in Great Marlow. Here it placed its Aggleton Green side bar across what is now called Station Road, a ¼ mile south of the trust's main gate on Chapel Street, and not on a turning off the turnpike road. While this was clearly to deter travellers from High Wycombe from deviating via Bobmore Lane and Newtown Road to avoid the Chapel Street Gate, the siting of a side bar so far off the road maintained by the trust was legally interesting.

Due to their simple structure side bars have vanished almost without trace. At Longwick the street name 'Bar Lane' and its nameplate still commemorate the side bar which controlled entrance to the lane that had been known as Owlswick Road before the turnpike era. It was there from 1832 to 1871 to ensure that travellers between Thame and Princes Risborough did not divert via Owlswick to avoid paying the toll at the main gate in Longwick village.

Weighing engines

As wagons became heavier and did more damage to road surfaces Parliament reacted initially by encouraging the fitting of broader wheels to wagons – in the hope that these would roll the road flat. However on early turnpike roads which had been resurfaced but not rebuilt in depth broad wheels had the opposite effect, throwing up ridges of displaced road surface on either side of the wheel rut.

Attention then turned to putting national maxima on the laden weight of wagons on the public highway. The General Turnpike Act of 1741 set a new limit of three tons, and introduced powers for turnpike trusts to weigh laden wagons and carts if they suspected that this was being exceeded. The limit was increased to six tons in 1765.[36]

This *authority* to weigh was increased to a *requirement* in respect of roads within 30 miles of London by an Act of 1751 *(24 Geo. II, c.43)*. The southern one-third of Buckinghamshire was covered by this Act, but there was no obvious response from the seven trusts that were affected. Only one of them had a weighing engine at the time and more than 60 years passed before engines were installed by any of the other six.

The weighing engines which initially appeared at the side of the road were cumbersome structures, made of heavy timber, which lifted the whole wagon off the road in order to weigh it on the principle of a giant set of scales.[37] They were built on site by craftsmen and occupied too much of the trustees' time because of frequent mechanical failures and disputes with wagoners over the accuracy of the gauges.

In 1775 the Newport Pagnell Trust felt obliged to allow excess weight of three hundredweight from the beginning of November to the end of March to compensate for mud on wagons and in 1781 the trust's minute book complained that "...the weighing machine ... is become uncertain and out of repair and almost useless."[38] The minutes of several other trusts record difficulties in getting the original builders of their machines to return and service them.

It is probably no coincidence that three Buckinghamshire trusts which were earliest to obtain engines in the 1770s – the Newport Pagnell, the Hockliffe and Woburn and the Hockliffe and Stony Stratford trusts – were near neighbours who could observe each other's progress. When the adjoining Aylesbury and Hockliffe Trust acquired two weighing engines in 1814, they were built by Mr Shepherd of Woburn, who had done the maintenance on the engines at Two Mile Ash Gate on the Hockliffe and Stratford Trust in 1804 and at Woburn in 1809. Elsewhere the only concentration of weighing engines in Buckinghamshire was around Aylesbury, where four out of the five trusts with roads into the town had engines beside their toll gates at some time in their histories.

In 1808 continuing concern with the damage being done to the county's roads by overladen wagons led Aylesbury Quarter Sessions to urge all trusts in Buckinghamshire to install weighing engines.[39] However, possibly as a result of these maintenance problems and in spite of the fact that fines paid for overweight vehicles brought in increased revenue, only thirteen of the 24 trusts with roads in Buckinghamshire had a weighing engine at any time in their existence *(see Appendix B)*. Twelve of these had one engine, and only the Aylesbury and Hockliffe Trust had one at each end of its road.

By the early nineteenth century weighing machines consisted of metal platforms flush with the road surface, resembling modern weighbridges, on to which wagons could be hauled. Despite this improved technology the 1835 General Turnpike Act abolished the weight limit regulations.[40] By then several trusts had disposed of their weighing machines, though at least four kept theirs until they were wound up.

7:
Accommodation for toll gate keepers

From "wooden watch box" to cottage

Tollgate keepers needed shelter from the elements. In the early years, when there was uncertainty as to whether a trust would last for the initial 21 years granted by Parliament, some shelters were little more than simple wooden kiosks, described as "wooden watch boxes" by some trusts. Such kiosks also resulted from the early uncertainty as to whether the initial siting of the gates was the best for toll collection, or whether the gate would have to be moved.

Once concerns about the long-term future of the toll gate were resolved, proper cottages were built for the toll collector and his family. This is illusrated by two large-scale maps of Lavendon in north Buckinghamshire. In 1801 at the Lavendon Mill gate on the Bromham and Olney Turnpike Road there was only a small kiosk beside the gate,[41] but by 1856 there was a rectangular cottage on the road's northern verge.[42]

The popular image of a toll house is a distinctive single-storey building with a hexagonal or octagonal ground plan with a front porch or projecting day room from whose side windows the gatekeeper can see approaching toll-payers even in bad weather.

Figure 11:
This toll house was built at Padbury in 1828 by the Wendover and Buckingham Trust after it had rerouted the road. The ground-floor plan and front elevation show the angled front windows through which approaching traffic could be seen by the gatekeeper.

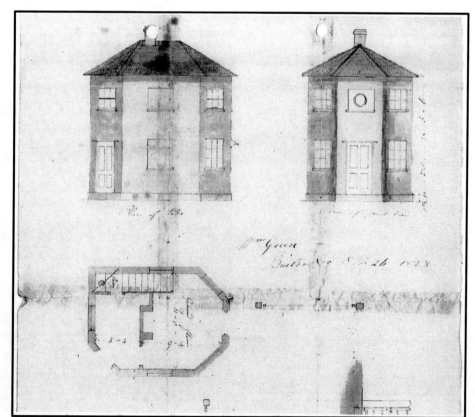

A fine example of this is the Beaconsfield and Stokenchurch Trust's toll cottage which formerly stood in High Wycombe but has been dismantled and superbly rebuilt in the Chilterns Open Air Museum. The Wendover and Buckingham Trust's building at Padbury, near Buckingham, was a two-storey variation of the type.

The few toll cottages for which records have survived in Buckinghamshire, however, are mostly simple two- or three-roomed cottages in a local vernacular style with a rectangular ground plan and a projecting porch.

Almost all toll cottages outside town centres had a garden attached to them and this provision for growing food was regarded as part of the gate keeper's wages. In 1816 the Sparrows Herne trustees, when seeking a gatekeeper for their New Ground Gate between Tring and Northchurch in Hertfordshire, agreed that the post was suitable only for a single man or childless couple because the cottage's garden was too small to support a family.[43]

Toll cottages built on private property

About half of the 42 tollhouses in use in Buckinghamshire in 1836 stood on a small area of private land outside but bordering the highway boundary. This plot had either been purchased by or given to the trust and the house built there beside the toll gate usually had a porch or bow front projecting on to the highway verge as a covered lookout place for the gatekeeper.

When the trusts were wound up between the 1860s and 1880s these pockets of private land were often sold back to their previous owners or auctioned, with the proceeds of sale helping to balance the trusts' closing accounts. Sometimes they continued as the home of the last gatekeeper.

FIGURE 12:
A former toll cottage at Great Missenden, probably dating from 1828, when the of the Wendover and Oak Lane Trust moved its gate southwards into the village.

PHOTOGRAPH BY DIANA GULLAND.

A significant number of the toll houses built on private land survived at first because they became private houses. Road widening in the 1930s then removed some, and more went when pressure for redevelopment grew in the 1970s and 1980s. Today only two survive on their original sites on private land in Buckinghamshire, at Great Missenden and Lavendon (Snelson Gate). A third, from High Wycombe, survives in the Chilterns Open Air Museum, but not on its original site. Two other buildings – at Sherington Bridge, north of Newport Pagnell, and Little Kimble, south of Aylesbury – <u>may</u> incorporate the toll cottage in their present structure *(see roads numbers 11 and 19 in Part Two for details)*.

In one or two places local folk lore identifies existing houses as former toll cottages, but without supporting evidence. For example several local histories identify number 2 Stoke Road, a terraced Victorian cottage in Walton on the south side of Aylesbury, near the junction of Stoke and Wendover Roads, as a toll keeper's house. However, the Ordnance Survey first edition 25-inch scale map of 1880 clearly shows a substantial toll house, labelled 'Walton TP' standing nearby on the opposite side of the road. A more likely explanation is that the terraced cottage was one in which a relief toll gate keeper lived.

Toll cottages built on the highway verge	The other half of the county's 42 tollgate cottages and all side bar kiosks existing in 1836 were built on the highway verge under the authority of each trust's Act of Parliament. They usually had a small garden plot on the verge beside them, but sometimes the garden was on land purchased from the owner of the adjoining field. Where the garden was on the highway verge the Act usually restricted it to one-eighth of an acre.

However once trusts started to be wound up after 1864, the expiry of their Act ended their authority to keep the house and garden on the highway verge. After legislation in 1871, part of the winding-up process was to demolish any toll house which stood on highway land and to return its site and that of any roadside garden to highway use, usually as part of the verge.

For a variety of reasons this requirement was not always complied with at the time, but all toll houses on the highway verge in Buckinghamshire have gone now, the last survivors removed by twentieth-century road widening.

8:
The operation of toll gates

The toll gate keeper's day

In their day turnpike gate keepers – or 'pikers' as they were known[44] – had a poor public image which could have been caused partly by the extremely long hours of duty.

In big towns and on the busier roads the gates were manned 24 hours a day and accordingly had two gate keepers, plus a reserve. Some of these gates therefore had two toll houses. At Colnbrook Gate on the heavily-trafficked Bath Road, for example, two gatekeepers occupied toll houses facing each other at the gate, while a 'supernumerary' gatekeeper was employed to go on duty when either of the two 'regular' pikers was sick or could not attend.[45]

A more complicated arrangement was made in 1762 on the Sparrows Herne Trust road, another busy trunk road, after it had been decided that its two gates north and south of Watford would remain open for traffic day and night. For this three gatekeepers were to rotate between the two gates.[46]

At less busy gates the toll collector lived on the job without a deputy to relieve him or her, unlocking the gate when traffic started to flow in the morning and on duty until it was padlocked for the night. These long hours could test the temper of characters like the Aylesbury and Shillingford

FIGURE 13:
Scene at a toll gate from a contemporary drawing.

IMAGE BY COURTESY OF LUTON CULTURE

Trust's gate keeper who was found guilty of a 'misdemeanour' at Aylesbury in 1805.[47] His offence was to lock his gate for the night at 11pm instead of the advertised midnight – and then tell a traveller arriving at 11.20pm that he could stay there all night for all that the gate keeper cared.

Of course there was also provocation from travellers such as John Williams, a drover, who, in 1732, assaulted William Scotcher, gatekeeper at the Colnbrook Gate, after presenting three forged toll tickets worth three shillings.[48]

Such events could have led one of the Sparrows Herne Trust's gatekeepers at Watford in 1766 to have "often been in liquor on his duty".[49] On the same trust in 1809 the Reverend Dupré complained that the toll collector at the New Ground Gate near Tring "had been guilty of misconduct and misbehaviour... by refusing to give him good money in change on his payment of the toll... and by using abusive language".[50]

This sort of confrontation had already led to the 1796 requirement for all gatekeepers to clearly display their name at their toll gate.

Charles Dickens caught the atmosphere perfectly in 'Pickwick Papers' when Mr Weller senior explained that "...they're all of 'em men as has met with some disappointment in life, ... consequent of which they retires from the world, and shuts themselves up in pikes; partly with a view to being solitary, and partly to revenge themselves on mankind by taking tolls."

On overnight mail-coach routes such as Watling Street or the Oxford Road pikers expected to be called out to open the gate for the passage of coaches at tightly regulated times. For other late-night travellers, a knock on the toll house door was needed to rouse the piker, who had to get out of bed, dress, take the toll and issue a ticket, before unlocking the gate.[51]

The time lost in this ritual was a strong deterrent to night travel, and its inconvenience to gate keepers could explain several complaints from trusts about their gates being left open all night "through carelessness". In 1771 Benjamin Harvey, one of the Colnbrook Trust's resident gatekeepers, was sacked after leaving the gate open on several nights, thereby enabling carriages to pass through toll free.[52]

Whether or not a gate was manned all night, it was necessary for it to be lit during hours of darkness so that toll collectors and travellers could see what they were doing. Initially lamps were doubtless lit by oil but by at least the 1860s some lamps in urban areas such as Aylesbury were lit by gas from half an hour after sunset until daybreak.

While gatekeepers had to be constantly vigilant against dishonesty by travellers, trustees had to constantly watch the gatekeepers, some of whom were not averse to pocketing tolls without issuing tickets. A more audacious scam was uncovered by the Sparrows Herne trustees in 1818, when they found that the toll boards at all four of their gates had been altered without authority to raise the toll for sheep and swine from 2½d to 5d per score of animals, with the proceeds from the new rates going to the gatekeepers.[53] A month after this deception had been uncovered one of the trust's gatekeepers at Watford was dismissed for assaulting the surveyor in an incident which may have been linked to its discovery of the scam.

Toll gate tickets exempting payment at some other gates

Travellers paid once a day to pass through the first gate they came to on each trust's road. After that payment they could pass through that same gate any number of times during the rest of the same day. The ticket, which had to be issued in receipt for a toll, also entitled the traveller to pass without paying through any other gates on the same trust's road which were named on the ticket.

If a trust's road was short the ticket was often a pass for all gates along it. An extreme exception to this was the Reading and Hatfield Trust, which controlled the longest road with any part in Buckinghamshire. For many years it allowed one ticket to pass all gates in its 54 miles. But from 1859, as finances became tighter, a journey from end to end of the trust's road would have involved buying tickets at three different gates.

Local travellers knew well the names and locations of their local gates, and which gates' tickets gave exemption from tolls at which other gates. However, the system was trying for long-distance travellers, who might lose track of how many gates they were allowed to pass toll-free with the toll ticket that they were currently carrying. Here again there was potential for friction with the gate keeper.

Toll gate tickets were issued in huge numbers but were clearly not considered to be collectable because only a tiny number have survived.

FIGURE 14:
A ticket issued for the toll paid in 1854 at the Hickliffe and Stony Stratford Trust's Hockliffe Gate, with advice that no further payment would be needed at the Fenny Stratford side bar. (This image is more than twice the size of the original).

IMAGE BY COURTESY OF LUTON CULTURE

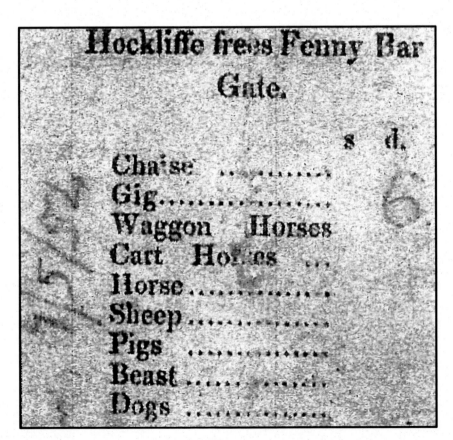

Toll evasion   Evading payment of tolls was almost viewed as socially acceptable. In 1729 the Colnbrook Trust bemoaned that some people were routinely passing their gate without paying.[54] Earlier, in 1719, the Beaconsfield and Stokenchurch Trust's Act[55] included a penalty for anyone convicted of going over private land to avoid a toll gate, or for landowners who acquiesced in such behaviour. This was widely repeated in other trust Acts, but public sympathy with offenders could make it difficult to obtain a conviction.

For a short time in the 1860s the Wendover and Oak Lane Trust positioned a toll gate in the village of Chalfont St Peter, beside the 'Greyhound' inn. However the inn's landlord soon began to allow people to go through his courtyard to avoid the toll gate. When he was charged with this offence in 1865, he was acquitted by Beaconsfield Petty Sessions.[56] The trustees removed the gate soon afterwards.

In 1846 the Sparrows Herne Trust was becoming concerned that people were parking their carriages on the turnpike road on the Bushey side of Watford Gate and then walking, for free, through the gate to conduct their business in Watford.[57]

In the nineteenth century several trusts, most noticeably the Buckingham and Towcester, combatted toll evasion with an almost obsessive wish to erect side bars across minor turnings off the turnpike road which were being used to bypass toll gates *(see Road number 23 in Part Two).*

A modern practice of giving an unexpired car parking ticket to strangers has its origins as early as 1740 when the Hockliffe and Stratford Trust introduced a ten-shilling fine for travellers who, having a ticket for the toll they had paid, proceeded to pass that ticket to another traveller to enable them to avoid paying toll. Interestingly the fine was to be divided, with half of its value going to the informer and half to the repair of the road).

Robberies   Toll contractors needed to collect toll takings from their gatekeepers regularly in order to pay their monthly instalments to the trust's treasurer. In spite of this the amount of money believed by local people to be held in toll houses made them the occasional target of robberies, and these sometimes ended in murder. In 1822 at Weston Gate on the Sparrows Herne Trust just outside Aylesbury, the keeper and his wife were murdered one night for £5. The trust responded by equipping each of its toll houses with a pistol with fixed bayonet, an alarm bell, and a rattle, but its minute books did not record any of this equipment being used in anger. Other toll house robberies included one at Padbury on the Wendover and Buckingham road in 1825, and one at Terrick on the Risborough Road Trust in 1850 *(for details see entries for Roads numbers 5 and 19 in Part Two).*

The murder of Joseph Pierce while on night duty at Colnbrook Gate on the Bath Road in 1781 gives a rare insight into the social responsibility felt by trustees. His widow Hester was left 'in poor circumstances' and facing eviction from the toll house to make way for the replacement gatekeeper, but it was agreed to give her £5 immediately, then £5 a quarter "during the pleasure of the trustees".[58]

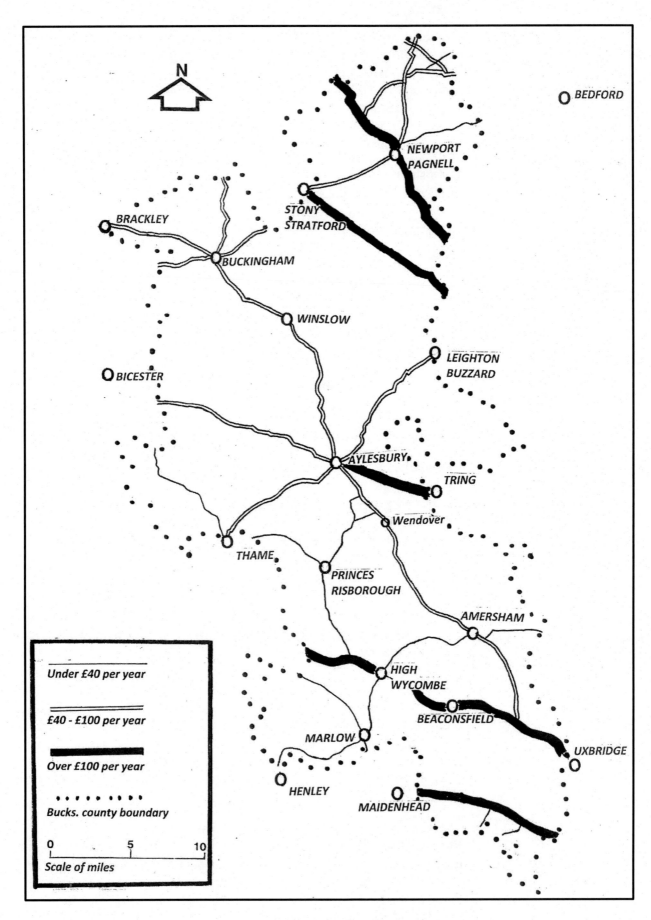

FIGURE 15: Toll income per mile on turnpike roads in Buckinghamshire in 1836.

9:
Levels of traffic reflected by toll receipts

While tolls are a crude measure of traffic flow, toll receipts, when related to the mileage controlled by the trust, give a rough comparison of the volume of traffic on each road.

Predictably the heaviest traffic in Buckinghamshire *(roads shown bold on the figure 15)* was on the five trunk roads radiating from London, three of which have now been superseded by the M1 and M4 motorways. Highest annual income from tolls in the county in 1836 was £251 16s 0d. per mile on the Hockliffe and Stony Stratford Trust, which had once been part of the Roman Watling Street and after the turnpike era became part of the A5. This was closely followed by the £248 12s 0d per mile taken on the Beaconsfield and Stokenchurch Road, part of the road to Oxford and beyond, now the A40, and £236 18s 0d per year on the Colnbrook Trust Road, the road to Bath and later the main A4 route to the west.

Next were the main roads radiating from Aylesbury, Buckingham, and Newport Pagnell *(roads shown as double lines on the map)* which provided the basic framework for travel within Buckinghamshire but which only saw traffic levels between one-quarter and one-third of those on the radial roads. With the exception of the Sparrows Herne Trust, now the A41, at £134 18s 0d per mile all of these had income between £39 and £83 per mile in 1836, and have retained their importance as main roads.

The least busy *(roads shown as a single line on the map)* were a scatter of five roads which maybe should not have been turnpiked. The Great Marlow and Stokenchurch Trust had the lowest annual income in Buckinghamshire at £11 8s 0d per mile in 1836. It earned less than 5 per cent of the Hockliffe and Stony Stratford Trust's income. Its promoters presumably misjudged the number of people wanting to go from Marlow to Oxford as opposed to Wycombe, Aylesbury, and London.

Next least successful was the Thame branch of the Risborough Road Trust. This was intended to link two towns which even today seem to have little in common, and back in 1836 it had a total annual toll income of £20 2s 0d per mile. Most of the least-busy turnpike roads tend to remain minor routes today: the Great Staughton and Lavendon Trust's road is entirely C-class. Only the Bedford and Newport Trust's road and the Aylesbury to West Wycombe section of the Risborough Road have developed into traffic arteries in more recent times.

10:
The origin of the word 'turnpike'

The name 'turnpike' originally referred to a military form of barrier used to control traffic at check points. Initially this was simply a soldier's pikestaff suspended from a roadside tree or post to form a horizontally-swinging pole. The pole, or pike, was turned aside to let people pass after they had been cleared by the sentries,[59] hence the name 'turnpike'. In due course the military formalised the simple suspended pikestaff by producing a more substantial horizontal counterbalanced beam which was pivoted to swing horizontally across the road.

During the English Civil War Aylesbury's Parliamentary garrison controlled the roads into the town with turnpikes.[60] This was more than 70 years before the turnpike trusts began to create their ring of gates around the town, some of which might well have been on the same sites as their military predecessors.

This military precedent was clearly in the minds of the earliest trustees when they named the first barriers at which tolls were to be collected, and early turnpike Acts refer to the erection of 'turnpikes or gates'.

This author has not found any evidence that military-style turnpikes were <u>actually</u> erected across main roads by turnpike trusts, but there were many examples of the horizontally-swinging pole, called side bars, across side turnings.[61] Any that did appear on main roads must have been quickly superseded by the conventional five-barred gates, with side gates for pedestrians, which became a familiar sight on the turnpike road network. However the name stuck, and the term 'turnpike' soon came to refer to the whole road controlled by a trust, as well as to the gates at which tolls were taken.

11:
The workings of the turnpike trusts

The length of road controlled by turnpike trusts in Buckinghamshire

The turnpike roads which were operating in Buckinghamshire in 1836 at the peak of the turnpike era are shown in *Figure 2*. There were 24 trusts which had all or part of their roads within the borders of the county in that year. Only three were wholly within the county.

With one major exception, the 54-mile Reading and Hatfield Trust, most trusts working in Buckinghamshire were responsible for fairly short lengths of road. The average length controlled, inside and outside the county, was only just under eighteen miles. Nearly two-thirds of trusts controlled only between seven and sixteen miles.

As a result the level of tolls and the list of exemptions from payment granted by toll tickets *(see above)* could change frequently in the course of a journey as the traveller passed from one trust to another, to the confusion of long-distance travellers. However as far as the state of the road was concerned, nearly eighteen miles on a road maintained to a consistent standard was an improvement on the pre-turnpike situation in which the condition of the road changed for better or worse with every parish crossed by the traveller's journey.

Trustees

Trustees were charged with carrying out the terms of their Act of Parliament without payment or reimbursement of expenses, and many turnpike Acts listed their names. For trusts with roads in Buckinghamshire the number of trustees listed in their first Act ranged from 32 to 210, but again with the major exception of the completely atypical Reading and Hatfield Trust which listed 505.

Trustees were predominantly landed, professional, or business gentlemen, a noticeable number of whom took part in many local activities and seemed to regard being a turnpike trustee as part of their responsibilities in society. As a result the same names often occur in the lists of more than one trust.

From 1726 some trusts required trustees to own property yielding £100 a year and from 1773 a property qualification became mandatory for all turnpike trusts.[62] This requirement effectively narrowed the number of people who were eligible to run a trust to those like the "gentlemen of consequence and respectability" who had decided to form the Buckingham and Newport Pagnell Trust in 1814,[63] but some tradesmen also managed to qualify.

Trustees typically lived in or near a parish which their trust's road served, or were relatively frequent users of the road from a little further afield. They had a personal interest in the state of 'their' road. Only a few of them loaned money to the trust but more of them reported defects in the road to the surveyor and reminded him if these were not rectified. This made a great improvement compared to the pre-turnpike reaction to problems by the parishes. Unfortunately, however well-connected the trustees were, many had little or no experience of maintaining a main road until they became trustees, and therefore had to learn on the job.

Meetings of trustees to manage their road

In theory members of each trust met roughly quarterly to approve their officers' accounts, receive reports from the officers, consider matters raised by the travelling public and the tollgate keepers, and to plan maintenance work and improvements to the road. Once a year they auctioned the leases of their tollgates to the highest bidder.

Meetings were held in a hired private room at an inn on their road and trustees were summoned to it by adverts placed in local newspapers and by letters sent by the clerk. Some trusts varied their venues in order to share out the travelling for trustees: the Aylesbury and Hockliffe, for example, alternated between Aylesbury and Leighton Buzzard throughout its life. Others, such as the Sparrows Herne Trust, stuck to the same town, sometimes even the same inn – in its case the 'King's Arms' at Berkhamsted – for decades.

Meetings were often preceded or rounded off with a lunch. A fortunately rare event occurred before a 1773 trust meeting when members of the Colnbrook Trust consumed verdigris from a poorly-washed copper soup vessel; ten were taken ill and five died shortly afterwards.

Getting trustees to attend these meetings was a constant headache, as five years in the life of the Risborough Road Trust illustrates. Its trustees, who numbered 180 on paper in 1825, met every one to two months during the construction phase of their Thame branch between 1825 and 1830 and less frequently after 1830.

During those five years only 45 of the 180 actually attended any meetings, and only about ten trustees attended with any regularity. Actual average attendance at Risborough Road Trust meetings at that time was 5.6 trustees, of whom four – a rector, a miller, and two local landowners – were the most consistent and so dominated business. The two landowners, Sir Scrope Bernard-Morland and John Grubb, between them chaired 84 out of 106 meetings during the construction of the branch road to Thame and thus established an almost-patriarchal control of the trust's affairs.

This was a pattern of attendance repeated in many trusts. Most trustees regarding their involvement as ending at giving moral or financial support. However when even the faithful few failed to attend, decisions on expenditure could not be made and the work of the trust suffered. This was illustrated in 1772 in a newspaper notice by the two-year-old Aylesbury and Shillingford Trust summoning trustees to a meeting in which the clerk stated the obvious "...as there is much business to be done, it is hoped that such gentlemen who can, will attend".

Between 1804 and 1817 the Kettering and Newport Pagnell Trust did not meet at all in some years and at one point accounts had not been examined for five years. Only after 25 new trustees had been appointed in 1818 was new life injected. The Sparrows Herne Trust reacted to having many of its meetings adjourned for lack of a quorum in the 1770s and 1790s by reducing its quorum from nine trustees to five in 1803, and by 1852 the Red Hill Trust's quorum was down to three.

Every now and then a contentious issue arose – often the appointment of a new officer or gate keeper – and a routine trust meeting would suddenly be swamped with trustees who may not have attended before, and who disappeared as soon as the issue was settled.

The Aylesbury and Hockliffe Trust normally saw betwen five and eleven trustees at its meetings, but suddenly 23, 26, and then 44 appeared at three consecutive meetings in 1812 after the 'hard core' of trustees had agreed to erect two additional side bars at Linslade. At the third of these meetings fifteen men became trustees at the start of the meeting and their votes doubtless helped to overturn the earlier decision to erect the side bars.

Officers Trustees were served by a clerk, a treasurer, and one or more surveyors. The clerk and treasurer were usually local solicitors, and often one person combining both offices until Parliament banned the practice with the General Turnpike Act of 1823.

Clerks in particular held their posts for many years. On the Aylesbury and Shillingford Trust, father and son solicitors from Thame, confusingly both called John Hollier, served as clerk one after the other from 1791 until 1856. Meanwhile Aylesbury solicitor James James, his son and grandson – both also called James James – served as clerk to the Bicester and Aylesbury Trust from 1825 until it was wound up in 1874. In 1806 William Hayton, of Ivinghoe, was presented with a piece of plate worth 100 guineas on his retirement after having been clerk and treasurer to the Sparrows Herne Trust for 44 years without remuneration. This last example, it must be said, was unusual!

Several clerks served more than one trust, which led at times to two or more trusts meeting on the same day at the same inn. While this may have put pressure on trustees to debate efficiently and finish their business to a timetable, complications could arise, such as on the day when two trustees who were not part of the Bedford and Newport Pagnell Trust inadvertently took part in the election of its surveyor.

On many trusts the fees of officers remained the same for decades. In the peak turnpike year of 1836 most clerks of trusts in Buckinghamshire were paid between £15 and £30 per year. This was basically for arranging trustees' meetings and taking the minutes at them. They were paid separately for obtaining and renewing the trust's Acts of Parliament.

From time to time most trusts exploded over a local issue, creating considerable unexpected work for the clerk. As at that time an unskilled labourer was earning between £23 and £31 a year, and a skilled man up to

£44, it would seem that local firms of solicitors saw this work more as a public duty than as a serious source of income.

Most turnpike trust treasurers in Buckinghamshire were being paid between £10 and £25 a year in 1836. Surveyors tended to receive higher fees, mostly between £30 and £105 a year in Buckinghamshire that year, recognising that they were more actively involved in the trust's work, superintending the road men, checking on deliveries of road-mending materials, and inspecting reported defects on the road. Surveyors had greater variations of salary between trusts, largely reflecting the volume of traffic on each trust's road. Thus the busy Colnbrook Trust on the Bath Road paid its Surveyor £80 a year in 1836, while the lightly-trafficked Bromham and Olney Trust paid £35.

Some of the poorer trusts saved money by paying low fees or combining officer roles. The Great Marlow and Stokenchurch Trust did both by paying its clerk a nominal five guineas a year in 1836 and by not having a treasurer or surveyor. It is likely that these services were provided for them by the closely-related Reading and Hatfield Trust, but no documentation has been found to indicate what the arrangement actually was.

The somewhat-more-profitable Aylesbury and Hockliffe Trust dispensed with the services of a surveyor in 1825 after nearby landowners had sought a reduction in tolls by claiming that the road was in good enough condition and implying that any surveyor would find work to do regardless of need. Twelve years later the state of the road had deteriorated to the point at which the trust was obliged to engage a surveyor again.

There were a number of cases of two or more men sharing one post for a few years where the fee for one person was simply divided equally between them. On the Bromham and Olney Trust, for example, two solicitors were sharing the clerk's fee of £15 in 1838, but by 1840 only one of them remained, receiving the whole £15.

In contrast, some trusts with busier roads in the south of the county, such as the Beaconsfield and Stokenchurch, Red Hill and Sparrows Herne, tried in the nineteenth century to bring the highest standards to their road maintenance by hiring national figures such as Sir James McAdam as superintending surveyors. These men advised the trust's own surveyor, but the added cost of their help was quickly dispensed with when the high days of turnpike travel ended in the 1840s.

Incompetence and corruption

Turnpike trusts were not immune from wasting money as a result of hiring officers who were not up to the job. It seems that in 1780 the Newport Pagnell Trust engaged Thomas Roe junior as surveyor for their northern division mainly on the grounds that his deceased father had held the post for the previous five years. Their minutes[64] show that the trustees quickly realised that their new surveyor knew little about road maintenance and began to give him embarrassingly basic advice on how to do it. After two years this became too much and Roe junior resigned, leaving the trust with several years' work to get the road back into acceptable condition.

The nearby Kettering and Newport Pagnell Trust had a run of problems with its officers in the 1830s and 1840s, during which they eventually dismissed their surveyor for incompetence in 1836, but did not go to the same lengths as the Newport Trust to get rid of him.[65]

Several trusts' minute books record trustees' concern at inadequate accounting for money spent by their surveyors and at other problems which arose because surveyors were not giving the road and its workforce their full attention. Examples of this in the Colnbrook Trust in 1727 and 1779-81 and the Beaconsfield and Stokenchurch Trust in 1811 suffice to make the point *(for details see the sections below on Roads numbers 6 and 4 in Part Two)*.

Trusts seemed to have a resigned acceptance that some gatekeepers might pocket some short-distance tolls without issuing tickets, and that others might abscond with the takings, but there was greater concern when a trust officer failed to live up to perceived standards. One of the Kettering and Newport Pagnell Trust's treasurers died in office in 1834, and, while going through his papers, his executors found that he had borrowed £498 of the trust's money, which represented nearly half of its annual toll earnings.[66]

Even when there was no suggestion of impropriety, problems arose when treasurers kept trust money in their private accounts. A treasurer of the Colnbrook Trust died in 1766 with some of the trust's funds in his own account and the trustees had great difficulty in recovering their £772 from his executors.[67]

In the 1840s corruption and incompetence came together in the Kettering and Newport Trust when Daniel Bradshaw, the surveyor, was initially warned for submitting "extravagant expenses". By 1847 trustees decided that he was "an inefficient surveyor [who] does not duly attend to the interests of the Road" and did not renew his contract.[68]

At a more subtle level some trustees gained advantage when their trusts promoted new sections of road. At Little Kimble, on the Risborough Road, trustee Sir Scrope Bernard-Morland assembled an estate in the 1790s with the intention of building a mansion in an area of parkland which was cut through by the Upper Icknield Way. In its 1795 Act the Risborough Road Trust introduced plans to divert this on to a newly built section of road – today's Ellesborough Road – which would have been outside the park. The new road was built by the trust between 1797 and 1805, even though it was not part of its turnpike road, but in the event Sir Scrope Bernard-Morland's mansion never materialised.

The move to reduce the number of trusts

By the 1830s there was a groundswell of national opinion that turnpike trusts should be combined to make larger, more efficient operating units. Legislation to encourage mergers by making the process easier was passed in 1849-50, but by then most trusts were in decline and enthusiasm for such action was passing.

The roads of the Banbury and Brackley Trust *(Road number 17 in Part Two)* and the Towcester and Weston-on-the-Green Trust crossed in Brackley and the two trusts became one in 1851, but this was the only full-scale example of such rationalisation for a trust with a road in Buckinghamshire. A less far-reaching move concerned the Great Staughton and Lavendon Trust *(Road number 20 in Part Two)*, which operated as two nominally independent districts until 1855, when it merged them to make economies by having a single management structure. In 1852 Parliament had contemplated the merging of the Red Hill and Wendover and Oak Lane Trusts, but nothing had happened by the time they were wound up in 1867.

| **Parliament's involvement in the running of the turnpike trusts** | Government involvement with the trusts during the first half-century of the turnpike era was largely limited to reacting to applications for Acts under which trusts could adopt their chosen lengths of road. But as the number of trusts grew the impact of these Acts on the parliamentary workload became significant; the 'Turnpike Mania' of 1751-1772 saw more than a third of the final total of trusts make their first applications for Acts of Parliament and this seems to have galvanised Westminster into action. |

The General Turnpike Act of 1772-3 *(13 Geo.III, c.84)* was the first major attempt to introduce national standards for the trusts, and it remained the basis of turnpike legislation for fifty years. Thereafter the General Turnpike Act of 1822 *(3 Geo.IV, c.126)* required trusts to standardise their procedures and accounting methods. It began the move towards transparency with an obligation on trusts to deposit a copy of their annual accounts with the Clerk of the Peace for each of the counties in which the trust's road lay.[69] An Act of 1833 *(3,4 Will.IV, c.80)* saw further refinement in the way in which these accounts were to be presented.

Unfortunately some of the less efficient trusts failed, from time to time, to submit their accounts and the authorities were dilatory in chasing them up. As a result, what *should* be a full record of accounts from each trust from 1827 onwards has numerous gaps and these get greater after the 1850s as enthusiasm for running the trusts waned.

Among those operating in Buckinghamshire, the only returns submitted by the Banbury and Brackley Trust *(Road number 17 in Part Two)*, were for 1853 and 1854,[70] when it was preparing to merge with the Towcester and Weston-on-the-Green Trust.

12:
The impact and legacy of turnpike roads

The growth and acceleration of wagon and stage coach services

The work of the turnpike trusts in making the surface of our main highways firmer on layered foundations in the late eighteenth and early nineteenth centuries brought those roads up to the highest standard seen in Britain since the days of the Roman legions. This opened the way for wagons to increase in number – but not speed, which continued to average two miles per hour – and to be enlarged until they could carry six tons in the late eighteenth century.[71]

This in turn brought to an end the use of packhorses for long-distance transport by the mid eighteenth century.

While the earliest stagecoach services had been started in the 1650s,[72] these were isolated, slow and infrequent precursors of the network which was to follow. Most stagecoach services tended to be started <u>after</u> the majority of their route had been turnpiked and improved. However whether or not their route had been turnpiked, it is noticeable that coach speeds did not increase significantly until after the 1752 introduction of steel springs which cushioned passengers more effectively against the jolts from irregularly surfaced roads.

Once coaches' suspension enabled them to go faster, the pressure was on the turnpike trusts to provide suitable road surfaces to permit that speed. It is no coincidence that the prestige network of steel-sprung mail coaches radiating from London was not inaugurated until 1784, by which year great lengths of the trunk roads from the capital had been improved by turnpike trusts.

After that year other stagecoach services accelerated noticeably so that by the end of the eighteenth century turnpike roads were becoming synonymous with fast passenger travel, for example 9-10 miles per hour, rising to 12 mph at their peak in the 1830s.

Using the Sparrow's Herne Trust road as an example, an Aylesbury to London stage coach took a day for the journey in the 1730s and five hours in 1821. Turnpiking also allowed stagecoach loads to grow: the earliest coaches had carried six passengers but by the 1830s they were carrying up to fourteen.

The effect of railway building

At the start of the nineteenth century road travel was improving and accelerating so noticeably that the hesitant experiments with steam locomotives on rails were not considered to be a threat to highly developed stage coach services.

By the 1830s turnpike roads had reached their peak of extent and efficiency. However railway technology advanced quickly and after 1838 the rapid spread of railways drained many main roads of traffic and thus drained the trusts of toll revenue.

The drop in toll income was most noticeable on the high-earning radial routes from London, which faced the earliest competition from the new main-line railways. Thus on the Bath Road the Colnbrook Trust's annual toll income fell from £4,028 in 1836 to £793 in 1859. In contrast, on a cross-country route without main-line rail competition the Buckingham and Newport Pagnell Trust's more modest toll income rose from £447 in 1835 to £983 in 1846 because of its new role as a feeder to the London and Birmingham Railway at Wolverton.

But the new technology also diverted money available for investment from roads to more profitable railways, so that few trusts were able to contemplate any further capital works, and no more new trusts were formed. There was a scheme in 1841 to turnpike the road from Bletchley Station to Newport Pagnell, with a branch to Kempston, for Bedford, to form feeders to the new railway at Bletchley. But by 1846 the Bletchley to Bedford railway line was open, and this killed the chance of a turnpike trust raising money to follow the same route.

As each railway line opened, road traffic flows abandoned their historic routes and began to focus on short routes radiating from railway stations. Often this took them along lesser roads which had never been turnpiked, leaving turnpike roads empty. A couple of Buckinghamshire trusts contemplated placing side bars across new station approach roads – such as Station Road, Winslow, in 1854 – to catch rail traffic which would not pass a toll gate but, faced with strong resentment, neither persevered with the idea.

By the early 1850s the main activity of turnpike trusts had become the collection of tolls in order to carry out minimal maintenance and to repay the money loaned to them. Having borrowed the money easily in an era when toll income was rising, some trusts had the greatest difficulty in making repayments when toll income began to fall in the 1840s.

Some investors had been waiting decades for repayment and had received no interest for years. Probably due to fatalistic realism, most seemed to uncomplainingly accept measures by the trusts such as cutting their mortgage interest rates and even extinguishing arrears of interest. At the same time some trusts reduced the number of their officers by combining posts, sometimes reducing the fees of those who remained, as well as putting tough limits on the amount that their surveyor could spend on day-to-day work.

The winding up of trusts after 1864 In 1864 Parliament decided that, with road traffic dwindling and trust-financed road improvements at an end, the continued presence of turnpike gates had become a pointless burden on traffic. As many trusts were also deeply in debt, it proposed that turnpike trusts should be wound up once they had repaid their creditors. Management of their roads should then be passed to the local highway boards, and these were themselves to be absorbed by the new county councils in about 1890.

After taking 130 years to build up to their peak, turnpike trusts faded away in the next thirty. In Buckinghamshire, the Wendover and Oak Lane Trust was the first to be wound up (in 1866), and the Reading and Hatfield the last (in 1881).[73] Nationally, a trust on Anglesey was the last to go, in 1895.

FIGURE 16:
Total mileage of turnpike roads in Buckinghamshire year by year, illustrating the sudden end of an era.

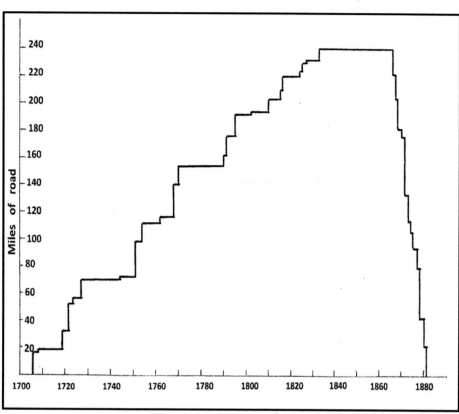

The legacy of the turnpike trusts in today's road network

The eighteenth and nineteenth centuries saw a major investment in the transport infrastructure of England. The turnpike roads, canals, and railways resulting from that era provided a large part of the transport network that we still use today. The most obvious legacies of the turnpike trusts are the roads themselves, most of which in Buckinghamshire remain in use as main roads today.

Main roads became A-class roads in 1919-23. In 1919 the Ministry of Transport introduced the now-familiar A, B, and C classification. While this was to provide the ministry with a basis for allocating future levels of investment in roads, it was also useful for the many new motorists whose only previous travel experience had been by train, and who were thus uncertain as to which roads were maintained as main roads.

There was continuity between turnpike roads and A-class roads. When the A-class road network for Buckinghamshire emerged in 1919-23, nearly forty years after the winding-up of the turnpike system, that network inherited 80 per cent of its 277 route miles from the turnpike trusts. The 20 per cent of A-class mileage which had not been turnpike roads was all in the Chiltern

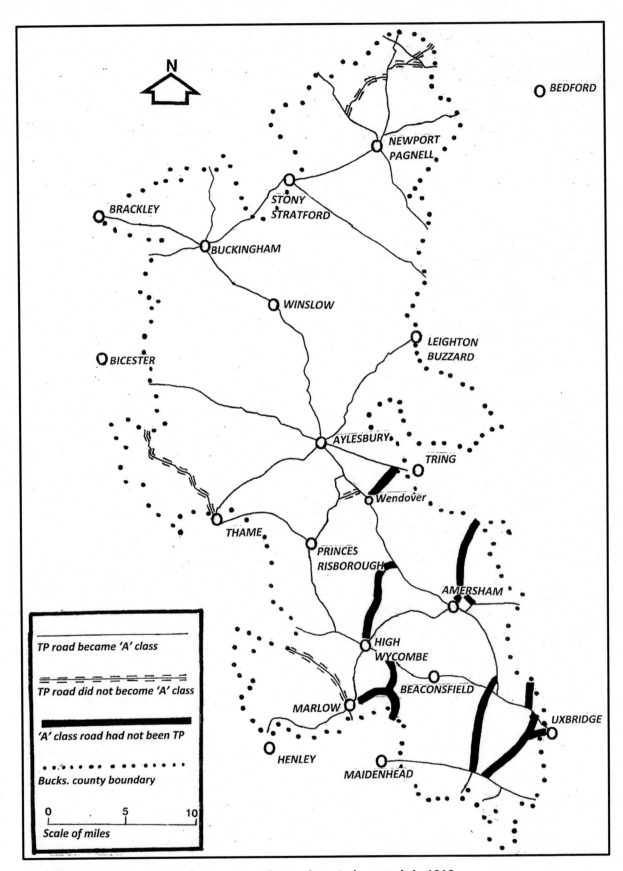

FIGURE 17: Continuity from former turnpike roads to A class roads in 1919.
In the key 'TP' means a former turnpike road. Most turnpike roads became A-class roads, while the additional A-class roads were in the Chilterns.

Key on map:

TP road became 'A' class

TP road did not become 'A' class

'A' class road had not been TP

Bucks. county boundary

0   5   10
Scale of miles

Place labels: BEDFORD, NEWPORT PAGNELL, STONY STRATFORD, BRACKLEY, BUCKINGHAM, WINSLOW, LEIGHTON BUZZARD, BICESTER, AYLESBURY, TRING, Wendover, THAME, PRINCES RISBOROUGH, AMERSHAM, HIGH WYCOMBE, BEACONSFIELD, MARLOW, UXBRIDGE, HENLEY, MAIDENHEAD

Hills, where it formed links between former turnpike roads, all of which had paralleled each other in the valleys, without being connected.

Since the 1960s there have been many changes to the A-class network, so while a modern A class road is still likely to have had a turnpike road as its ancestor, the relationship between the two is less strong today than it was in 1919. As a rule of thumb former turnpike roads can be identified by the intermittent survival of the milestones or mileposts which once lined them.

Recognising former turnpike roads

In Buckinghamshire there are only three exceptions to this rule, of which the most obvious is the chain of C-class roads from Brill via Grendon Underwood to Buckingham which was never turnpiked, yet was given mileposts by the new highway authorities after the turnpike era.

In some counties the situation is very different. As the result of Second World War removals several counties have few milemarkers surviving today. At the other extreme Cornwall has 280 turnpike milestones and 380 non-turnpike stones[74] and Norfolk has 193 put in place by turnpike trusts and 165 by others.[75]

Milestones and mileposts

Buckinghamshire retains a representative selection of milestones and mileposts at some 116 sites, out of an estimated 230 original sites, in spite of the recent spate of thefts, apparently to embellish private gardens. This compares with an estimated 66 surviving mile markers in Warwickshire, 32 in Northamptonshire, and fifteen in Bedfordshire.

Tollgate keepers' cottages

Only two definitely-identified toll cottages survive in their original positions in Buckinghamshire, and this is a pale shadow of the survival rate in some counties. The Buckinghamshire pair are at Great Missenden and Lavendon, and there are possibly two more at Sherington Bridge and Little Kimble *(see Roads numbers 8, 11, 19 and 20 in Part Two).*

Part Two
The individual histories of Buckinghamshire's Turnpike Trusts

There were 24 turnpike trusts in Buckinghamshire, spanning 175 years. The first was set up by Act of Parliament in 1706 and the last was wound up in 1881. As you would expect over such a long period, their experiences differed considerably.

The earliest stepped forward with enthusiasm, keen to solve the problems of road communication caused by parochial divisions and poor surface maintenance, but with lack of experience. Some learned quickly, others failed. A hundred years later the last trusts on the scene found things very different. They could benefit from their predecessors' experience and from improved road technology, but roads now faced competition from an established canal system. And more was to come: Buckinghamshire's last turnpike trust was set up in 1827, just two years before the Rainhill Locomotive Trials opened up the railway age.

Notes on the entries for individual trusts

Part Two of this book looks individually at each of the 24 turnpike trusts which had roads in Buckinghamshire.

- The Trusts are **numbered and listed** in the order in which they began work. All of their roads are shown and indicated by number on the map in *Figure 2,* while a 'thumb-nail' map of each individual route appears on the map at the start of each road's entry.

- For each trust the **towns, villages and toll gates** through which their road passed are generally listed in the order indicated by the trust's title – for example east to west for the Bedford and Newport Pagnell Trust, south-east to north-west for the Beaconsfield and Stokenchurch. The same order is used for toll gates, road maintenance and road improvements.

- The intention was to give **toll gate income** for all gates in 1836, the peak year of the turnpike era, to enable easy comparison between trusts. Where figures for 1836 are not available, the nearest appropriate date has been used, though that invalidates direct comparison.

- The entries for **trustees and officers of each trust** do not pretend to be comprehensive and, for trustee chairmen, only intend to highlight those who made a noticeable impact on their trust. Trust clerks are given some prominence because of their influence on where and how often trust meetings were held.

Buckinghamshire's Turnpike Trusts by year

Road 1:
The Hockliffe and Stratford Turnpike Road 1706

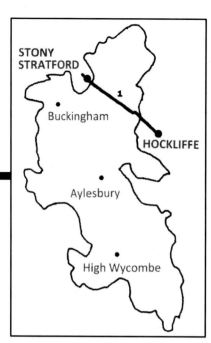

Identifying the road's route

This follows today's A5 north from Hockliffe in Bedfordshire, ignores the modern bypass to go through Little Brickhill to the A4146 roundabout south of Milton Keynes. The route then follows the C-class road known as V4 Watling Street to Stony Stratford.

Historic background

As it strides across the landscape, with long straight stretches joined by gentle bends, Watling Street (the present A5 and Milton Keynes V4) is everyone's idea of a Roman military road. Laid out by Roman engineers in the first century AD to link Dover and London with Wroxeter near Shrewsbury, the route has probably been in continuous use ever since as a major link between south-east and north-west England. This importance made the former Watling Street an early candidate for improvement when the turnpike era began. Indeed in 1706 this section between Fornhill, near Hockliffe, and Stony Stratford became the first piece of main road in England to be taken over by a private body of trustees.

Doubtless suffering from being a pioneer, the trust's early years were not successful *(see "Maintenance of the road" below)* and it was moribund by 1737. In 1740 a new Act, new officers, and mainly new trustees gave it a fresh start and the accumulated backlog of maintenance was attacked. Even with this effort the road remained below the expected standard and continued to attract complaints about its poor surface until the end of the century.

The route acquired added significance when Parliament, after passing the Act of Union with Ireland in 1801, voted funds to improve the London to Holyhead road as the main link between London and Dublin. Thomas Telford was commissioned to superintend the work. After a survey of the whole route in 1810-11, he decided that the existing road between London and Shrewsbury should be upgraded by the turnpike trusts which already controlled it, while he built a largely-new road between Shrewsbury and Holyhead.

This project became the first government-financed road improvement scheme in England and, by 1828, the Hockliffe and Stratford Trust was effectively a local division of the Holyhead Road.

The limits of the Trust's road

The original south-eastern end of the trust's responsibilities was stated in its 1706 Act to be at Fornhill (today Fourne Hill Farm) nearly 1½ miles north-west of Hockliffe.[76] This hilltop location at the corner of four Bedfordshire parishes (Battlesden, Heath and Reach, Hockliffe, and Potsgrove) had no community resident on the road and nothing else to suggest why it was chosen in preference to the village of Hockliffe as the end point of the trust's control.

When in 1710 the Puddle Hill Trust was formed to improve the next section of road south-eastwards to Dunstable, its trustees chose the crossroads in the middle of Hockliffe as their north-western limit, leaving 1½ miles of unturnpiked road between there and Fornhill.

In a strange attempt to remedy this, the Hocklffe and Stratford Trust's replacement Act in 1740 extended their control to the 'King's Arms' public house at the north-western end of Hockliffe village, leaving ¼ mile of unimproved road between the two trusts. Eventually in 1753 the Puddle Hill Trust adopted the intervening gap by extending their control to the 'King's Arms'.

The north-western end of the trust's control was always at the south-eastern end of Stony Stratford High Street. The road through the town was maintained, rather ineffectively, by various charities until 1801, when the town's bridge and street commissioners took it over.

Its length and maintenance districts

After its extension in 1740 the trust's road was 14 miles long, of which 10½ miles were in Buckinghamshire and the rest was in Bedfordshire.

From 1706 until the 1770s the road was divided for maintenance purposes into two districts which met at the north end of Fenny Stratford. Each district had its own surveyor until the 1770s, after which one man supervised the whole road.

The initial Act of Parliament

6 Anne c.4 (1706) came into effect on 1 May 1707 and 'turnpiked' the road from Fornhill (1½ miles north-west of Hockliffe) to Stony Stratford for a period of 21 years until 1 May 1728.

Continuation Acts

9 Anne c.35 (1709) extended the period covered by the 1706 Act from 1728 until 1737 in order to give more time for toll income to pay off the first loans raised by the trust.

The expiry of this Act in 1737 was followed by a two-year hiatus while the trust's future management was debated; it is not clear whether the trust ceased work during those two years, or continued to collect tolls without the benefit of Parliamentary authority to do so. *(See 'Financial Matters' below for reasons for this).*

13 Geo.II, c.9 (1740) restarted the trust and extended its control south-eastwards to the edge of Hockliffe village. The trust's powers were further extended by:**27 Geo.II, c.21 (1754), 26 Geo.III, c.143 (1786),** and **49 Geo.III, c.16, (1809).**

55 Geo.III, c.152, (1815) set up the government's Holyhead Road Commission and provided finance for the whole London to Holyhead road improvement. It also unified toll charges throughout the trusts which now found themselves part of the Holyhead Road project.

11 Geo.IV, c.83 (1830) was the last renewal Act specifically for the Hockliffe and Stratford Trust.

3-4 Will.IV, c.43 (1833) was a multi-trust Act for the general improvement of the Holyhead Road.

Control of the Trust:
TRUSTEES

The initial 32 trustees got off to a bad start, with debts mounting rapidly, and pressure from creditors who were more concerned with their annual interest payments than in repairing the road *(see 'Financial Matters' below)*. While facts are sketchy, it seems that there was a hiatus in 1738-40 during which the number of trustees rose to 85. This enabled new men with a greater commitment to maintaining the road to replace or outnumber the original trustees who favoured the creditors. Only then did the trust obtain a new Act.

After 1740 the chairmanship of trust meetings was shared quite widely, although Great Brickhill landowner P D P Duncombe was a regular chairman for more than 20 years in the 1830s and 1840s. A relative of his, Henry Barton of the same parish, was chairman for 15 years in the 1850s and 1860s.

CLERKS

All the trust's known clerks were Stony Stratford solicitors. Edward Bloxham was clerk for at least 36 years from 1740, followed by Thomas Ewesdin from at least 1790 to at least 1805. Next was J F Congreve, who held the post from at least 1812 to 1858. For much of that time, 1823-54, he was also clerk to the Buckingham and Newport Pagnell Trust, which also met at Stony Stratford. His successor at the Hockliffe and Stratford Trust after 1859, was Edward Harris, who was its last clerk.

TREASURERS

After electing treasurers annually until 1753 the trust thereafter employed a small number of men for long periods. Most notable of these was John Oliver, who was appointed in 1806 and who owned a private bank in Stony Stratford from the 1820s. When his bank failed in 1843 he was obliged to resign as the trust's treasurer.

SURVEYORS

There were two surveyors, one for each district *(see 'Its length and maintenance districts' above)*, until the districts were merged in the 1770s and one man took over on the combined salary of his two predecessors.

MEETINGS OF THE TRUSTEES

In its early years the trust varied its meetings between ten inns in Fenny Stratford, Little Brickhill, Loughton and Stony Stratford, although they mainly favoured The Talbot at Loughton. After the 1770s meetings settled on the 'George Inn' at Little Brickhill, augmented by the 'Cock Inn' at Stony Stratford from the 1790s. When the 'George Inn' closed in 1845 the landlord stayed on as a farmer and the trustees initially continued to meet under his roof, now in a private farmhouse, until 1852. They then concentrated their remaining meetings at the 'Cock Inn' at Stony Stratford.

'The George' had been Little Brickhill's largest coaching inn until the end of the coaching era in the 1840s, whereupon it became a farm which, renamed as Home Farm, has today been reduced in size and stands opposite the 'Old Green Man' in the middle of the village. The present 'George Inn' dates from the twentieth century).

Maintenance of the road	With little experience of road improvement, the trust had a disastrous start in 1707 as it set out to upgrade the road by covering the old surface with a good layer of broken stone. There was little supervision of the contractors who dug the stone and carted it to the work sites along the road, nor of the labourers who were meant to spread and level it. In short the surveyors "... suffered the country people to work in different parts of the said road in what numbers and what manner they pleased..."[77]

Such indiscipline produced a road surface of poor and variable quality and led to the trust being seriously in debt as early as 1709 *(see 'Financial Matters' below)*. The next thirty years were so dominated by financial worries rather than by road repairs that, by 1737, the Hockliffe and Stratford section was said to be the most notoriously ruined part of the London to Chester road.[78]

After what amounted to a relaunch of the trust in 1740 it began to receive loans again, but had to advertise for more in 1744 in order to accelerate the rate of repair of the road. Tellingly it was agreed in 1740 not to employ any road labourers who kept an alehouse, and in 1744 the two surveyors were reminded that they should be present in their respective districts of the road for four days each week in order to supervise the labourers.[79]

Improvements to the road	By the end of the eighteenth century the trust was better managed. From 1758 the condition of its road had improved sufficiently for it to be able to progress to limited local widenings of the road, especially in and around Little Brickhill and Fenny Stratford. However, serious improvement of the road did not replace patching and filling until between 1815 and 1830 when the Government-backed upgrading of the whole Holyhead Road under Thomas Telford's supervision got going.

Individual improvements are listed from south to north:

HILLS BETWEEN HOCKLIFFE AND FENNY STRATFORD	In the early 1820s, partly funded by a £7,000 Government loan,[80] the severity of the gradients on the succession of short hills in the undulating country between Hockliffe and Fenny Stratford was eased by digging cuttings through their summits, then using the excavated spoil to build low embankments across the intervening valleys.[81] Today these works are most noticeable in the 10-15ft deep cuttings which lower the five summits between Hockliffe and Little Brickhill.

They are also seen in a short cutting running south-east from the church in Little Brickhill village, and in the 4ft lowering of Fenny Stratford High Street between Aylesbury Street and Victoria Road, where the raised pavement on the north-east side of the road shows how much the carriageway was lowered.

Less obvious today is the ½-mile of new road on the north side of Model Farm at the west end of Little Brickhill village. This new road section was built in 1822-23 to provide an easier, smoother gradient to replace the original hill which lay on the south side of Model Farm. The narrow, grassy hollow way of the old road is still visible in a field at its upper end. (The Little Brickhill bypass was built in the 1990s).

FENNY STRATFORD	In about 1800, during the construction of the Grand Union Canal, about ¼ mile of the turnpike road was replaced by the present straight route, on the south-west side of the original route, between the crossings of the River Ouzel and the canal. This allowed the road to be raised on to an embankment to cross the new bridge over the canal. Disconnected parts of the original route survive as private access ways north-east of the modern road.

BETWEEN FENNY STRATFORD AND STONY STRATFORD	Shortly after 1828 the trust eased the gradient on Rickley Hill – now just west of the Denbigh Hall railway bridge – by digging a cutting through it. Today this cutting is barely noticeable, probably due to its having been incorporated into Milton Keynes city landscaping.

A similar cutting was dug in about 1824 to ease the gradient of Crown Hill near Loughton, and again the trust's earthworks have been obscured by twentieth-century road widening and landscaping.

Toll gates and tollhouses	Details of the trust's toll gates in the early years are scarce, but writers including Daniel Defoe[82] suggest that until 1738 it only had one, which was Bedfordshire's and England's first toll gate to be put up by a private turnpike trust. If this was the only toll collection point on 14 miles of road it might partly explain the trust's cash flow problems in the early days, but a few other trusts in Bucks. managed successfully for many years with only one gate.

The trust's financial problems came to a head in 1738-40, when operations appear to have ceased, in which case no tolls would have been collected. After 1740 the trust had two gates in use until the early 1800s, when a third was added.

HOCKLIFFE GATE 1706-1867	*Sample annual toll income: £1,357.10s.0d in financial year 1832/33.*

The Hockliffe toll gate was probably in use at Fornhill between 1706 and 1738, and was certainly in use between 1740 and 1867, first at Fornhill then at Hockliffe Hill. The south-eastern end of the trust's responsibilities was originally at Fornhill on the second summit north-west of Hockliffe – and the trust's minutes for 9 April 1740[83] suggest that this was where its first toll gate stood before the hiatus in 1738. The trust's 1740 Act extended its responsibilities for 1¼ miles from Fornhill to the edge of Hockliffe village and the same minutes record agreement to erect two toll gates, one near

Stony Stratford and the other "near the parish of Hockliffe where a gate lately was erected".

This 1706 gate cannot actually have been within Hockliffe parish before 1740 because that would have been on a section of road beyond the trust's control. This all points to this first gate being on the summit at Fornhill *(at grid reference SP 953 285)*, due north of Fourne Hill Farm and only 500 yards outside (and thus 'near') the Hockliffe parish boundary. Over the following decades the records of toll collection here consistently ignored the place name Fornhill and assigned the takings to Hockliffe, but this was presumably because the latter place was more widely known.

In 1740 a toll house was built at Fornhill at a cost of £29 but was not completed in time for the start of toll collection at the new gate, which was probably on 22 October 1740. Thomas Nutting,the first toll collector, was therefore billeted in a rented house in Hockliffe with a 1¼-mile walk to work until the toll house was ready.

However by the time of Bryant's map of Bedfordshire in 1825 the gate had been moved and was now in Hockliffe parish, on the summit of Hockliffe Hill, the first hill north-west of the village *(at grid reference SP 966 274)*, with the toll house and its garden on the north-east side of the road. No written record of the move has been found, but a likely date for it would have been in the early 1820s when the trust was lowering the summits of the hills between Hockliffe and Little Brickhill by digging cuttings through them.

The site of the Fornhill toll house would have been obliterated when the cutting, which today is at least ten feet deep, was dug there, so it is likely that the cutting through Hockliffe Hill was dug first, with a widening on its summit to accommodate a new toll house, whereupon the gate was moved to its new site.

The new toll house survived in private use after the trust was wound up, but appears to have been demolished in the 1950s. Today its site at the summit of Hockliffe Hill is indicated by a tree-covered platform excavated out of the north-eastern cutting side, with a short, signposted, parking lay-by in front of it.

FENNY STRATFORD GATE
from about 1814 to 1854

Sample annual toll income: £322 in financial year 1832-33.

The Fenny Stratford gate was in use from around 1814 until at least 1854, latterly as a side bar. The gate was located at the Galley Lane crossroads half a mile south-east of the bridge over the River Ouzel at Fenny Stratford. This is now the southern corner of the roundabout junction of the A5 and A4146.

It was called Fenny Stratford Gate when it came into use around 1814, but began to be called Fenny Stratford Bar in 1824, which probably indicates that the gate had stood across the main road until 1824, but was then moved to stand across one of the side roads for the rest of its working life, which would explain its relatively low toll income.

The toll cottage, on the south side of the main road, initially continued in use as a private dwelling but was demolished before 1880. Its site was used in 1933 for road widening.

TWO-MILE ASH GATE **1740-1867**	*Sample annual toll income: £1,547.10s.0d in financial year 1832/33.* This was erected in what was then open countryside but which is now within the built-up area of Milton Keynes. Located two miles south-east of Stony Stratford it stood on the summit of a gentle hill rising south-east from a bridge over a stream *(at grid reference SP 816 383)*. An isolated pair of cottages which already existed at the site on opposite sides of the road were rented as its toll house and outbuilding from 1740 until some time after 1790. Toll collection here began on 22 October 1740. By 1831 the cottages had been replaced by a purpose-built toll cottage on the south-west side of the road. This had a central projecting bay, which gave the gatekeeper views along the road. It had been demolished by 1880 and today its site is part of a wide highway verge.
STONY STRATFORD **GATE** **1835-1857**	This gate was at the north-west end of Stony Stratford's High Street and was operated by the Stony Stratford Bridge and Street Commissioners to recoup the cost of rebuilding Old Stratford Bridge over the River Great Ouse around 1837. At no time were Stony Stratford High Street or the toll gate the responsibility of the Hockliffe and Stratford Trust.
Weighing engine	A weighing engine was built at a cost of £60 beside Two-Mile Ash Gate by Thomas and Abraham Curtis, carpenters of Warwick, who undertook to keep it in repair for 20 years for an annual retainer of two guineas. It came into use on 31 October 1774, from which day the gatekeeper – who was already on 10s 6d. per week wages – was allowed an extra five shillings a week for weighing carriages. The engine was in use until at least 1815, but had gone by 1831.
Milestones	A milestone or milepost marking 41 miles to London was recorded on a 1731 estate map[84] at the Sheep Lane crossroads in Potsgrove parish in Bedfordshire. Whether or not this was an isolated feature or part of an earlier set of milemarkers is not known, but after 1740 the revitalised trust surveyed its road in 1744 and put up new milestones in 1745 at a cost of one guinea each. Mileages on the 1745 series of milestones read from 38 miles to London immediately north-west of Hockliffe to 52 miles on the south-eastern edge of Stony Stratford. Some of these were replaced by milestones made to a standard design introduced by Telford for use throughout the length of the Holyhead Road and installed on this section between 1830 and 1840. Telford's stone slabs with rectangular cross section and gable top originally had an iron plate carrying raised capital lettering attached to their front faces. The original plates have been lost but within Milton Keynes the stones have been turned round and alloy replica plates have been attached. The southernmost three stones (all in Bedfordshire) and one at Stony Stratford are missing, but the

remaining eleven are still in place, five of the Telford design, five with flat tops which possibly date from 1745, and one concrete replacement.

As a result of re-measuring and road straightening further south, the distance to London was reduced by half a mile between 1814 and 1834, and by another half mile after 1834. It appears from contemporary maps that all fifteen milestones were twice moved a half mile north-westwards, further from London, to reflect this.

Financial matters

Failure to control costs in its earliest years *(see 'Maintenance of the road' above)* led the trust into £6,484 of debt to contractors and labourers, probably as early as 1709. A dozen or more individuals then purchased many of these debts at discounts between 30 and 40 per cent in order to receive a steady 6 per cent annual interest from the trust. These new creditors exerted pressure on trustees to keep paying the annual interest out of the tolls, sometimes in preference to spending toll income on the road. It was alleged[85] that in some years no road repairs were done.

By about 1729 matters came to a head and interest payments were stopped in order to get work done on the road. This prompted several of the external creditors to become trustees with the intention of doubling the tolls so as to resume interest payments. Meanwhile road users wanted the trust to be abandoned so they would no longer have to pay tolls to use a poorly-maintained road.

By the time that its 1709 Act expired in 1737 the trust was still more than £6,000 in debt, interest on that debt had not been paid for seven years, and its road was still in poor condition.

This was in spite of £1,900 spent on repairs in 1734-37. Detractors suspected that costs had been inflated through fraud by contractors. When the dust settled on the debates of 1738-40 the trust's powers were renewed in 1740 with the number of trustees more than doubled, presumably in order to swamp the vociferous group of 'creditor trustees'.

The year 1740 marked the start of the trust's slow climb out of debt, which was down to £800 by 1786, although it was to rise again in the 1820s and 1830s when the general reconstruction of the Holyhead Road was in progress. This was paid for by some £7,000 of government loans on top of the £1,200 of private loans already held.

1867: The Trust wound up

One of the first trunk railways in England – the London and Birmingham – was opened parallel to the Holyhead Road from 1838 and the Hockliffe and Stratford Trust immediately suffered a huge loss of income. Traffic deserted to the railway en masse and tolls plummeted from a peak of £3,622 a year in 1838 to £1,318 in 1839 and only £234 in 1858.

By 1841 there simply was not enough income to support road maintenance, though the trust's debt was by then only around £150. When Parliament decided in 1864 that turnpike trusts should end their work, the Hockliffe and Stratford jumped at the chance to get out while its debt was at a low level. The trust immediately applied to Parliament to be wound up.

Perhaps because of the number of other applications the trust was unsuccessful in 1864, 1865, and 1866, but by the Act of **30/31 Vic. c.121 (1867)**, it became one of the first trusts in Buckinghamshire to close. It stopped work on 1 November 1867.

Road 2:
The Hockliffe and Woburn Turnpike Road 1706

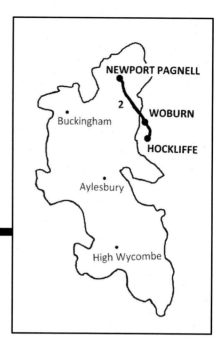

Identifying the road's route

The original route follows today's A4012 from Hockliffe to Woburn; then its later extension first follows the modern A5130 Woburn to Broughton in Milton Keynes. The route then follows ¼ mile of disused road at Broughton between the A5130 at Manor House and the junction of the A509 with the M1 motorway. From there the route follows the A509 to Newport Stables; then the B526 to Newport Pagnell.

Historic background

In the turnpike era this road, together with its pair of continuations north of Newport Pagnell, *(see Roads numbers. 3 and 11 below)* became part of a new link between London, Northampton, and the East Midlands. In the Middle Ages traffic for the East Midlands had followed the future A6 via Bedford or had left London on the Holyhead Road (later the A5) and forked right at Stony Stratford to head for Northampton.

This was still the usual route at the start of the seventeenth century. However as trade and traffic grew during that century an additional route midway between the two historic trunk routes began to be used, and this was developed by turnpike trusts in the eighteenth century. Thus in turnpike days Hockliffe in Bedfordshire replaced Stony Stratford as the parting of the ways. Traffic now turned right at Hockliffe to go via Woburn and Newport Pagnell to Northampton and the East Midlands.

In the twentieth century the building of the M1 motorway and the road network of Milton Keynes have robbed this route of its historic function and today the former turnpike road survives as a string of local main roads in place of the regional route that the turnpike trusts had made it.

The limits of the trust's road

The trust was responsible from the crossroads at Hockliffe, east of Leighton Buzzard, through Woburn to the east end of Tickford Bridge in Newport Pagnell.

Its length and maintenance districts

After extension in 1728, the trust's road was 12½ miles long, of which 6½ miles were in Buckinghamshire and the rest in Bedfordshire.

The original short section from Hockliffe to Woburn was administered by two joint surveyors. After the extension of trust control from Woburn to

Newport Pagnell in 1728, each man superintended one half of the longer road, the southern or Lower Division being based at Woburn while the northern or Upper Division was based at Broughton. (It will be noticed that in altitude above sea level the 'Lower' Division was considerably higher than the Upper!).

From 1759 to 1771 the two divisions were merged under one surveyor, only to revert to having two again after a few years. Finally, faced with declining traffic in 1840, trustees agreed to make do with one surveyor.

Initial Act of Parliament	**6 Anne c.13 (1706)** 'turnpiked' the road from Hockliffe to Woburn.
Continuation Acts	**1 Geo. II, c.10 (1728)** extended the trust's control northwards from Woburn to Newport Pagnell. The trust's powers were subsequently renewed by **16 Geo.II, c.4 (1742), 20 Geo.III, c.68, (1780), 40 Geo.III, c.67 (1800)**, and **2 Geo.IV, c.85 (1821)**. The 1821 Act also authorised the diversion of more than two miles of the road at Hockliffe.
Control of the Trust: CLERKS	William Harrison of Leighton Buzzard was possibly the first of the trust's clerks; as he was recorded in post in 1728 and replaced in 1729 by Thomas Howard of Dunstable. Howard was replaced in 1740 by Thomas Cawns of Bedford, who in turn was followed by Dixie Gregory of Bedford in 1750. Gregory died in office in 1767 and was superseded by John Rotherham of Eversholt in Bedfordshire. Samuel Davis of Ampthill was in post by 1818 and remained there until 1843, succeeded by John Green of Woburn. This trust was unusual in that only one of its clerks actually lived on the road.
SURVEYORS	There were two surveyors from 1706 until 1759, when the road's two divisions were merged under one surveyor. In 1771 this reverted to two surveyors, only to be reduced to one in 1840 as a result of a decline in traffic. At least two surveyors came under a cloud. The first was John Greaves of Broughton, who was suspected of mishandling toll income in 1759. William Page of Wavendon, surveyor for the Upper Division, was dismissed in 1782 for failing to properly supervise the work on the road in his division.
MEETINGS OF THE TRUSTEES	'The George Inn' at Woburn (later called the 'Bedford Arms', and now 'The Woburn Hotel') was the trust's principal meeting place in the eighteenth century and again from about 1823 until the trust was wound up. During the first twenty years of the nineteenth century meetings moved between 'The Magpie Inn' in Woburn (now 'The Magpies') and 'The Cock' and 'The Swan' in Woburn Sands.

Maintenance of the road

In its early years the trust had a lot of trouble with Hockliffe Lane, which was the first two miles of the road north-east of Hockliffe village. In 1728 its second Act of Parliament recorded that this section of road was in such bad condition that traffic was deviating from it over the lands of the Manor of Battlesden.

The 1728 Act therefore required the trust to clarify where the road lay by staking out the lane's boundaries, up to 12 yards apart, and then to make it passable to traffic which in 1728 meant spreading a lot of stone on its surface. Battlesden's lord of the manor, who seems to have been the main complainant, was then required by the Act to ditch, hedge, and fence the repaired lane so as to keep traffic off his land.

This appears to have dealt with the immediate complaints but this section also suffered from flooding at the edge of Hockliffe village, followed by a difficult ascent of Battlesden Hill – problems not solved until a century later.

Improvements to the road: AT HOCKLIFFE

In 1772-73 the bridge over the Clipstone Brook, just outside Hockliffe, was rebuilt with three arches and the road between the bridge and Watling Street raised on to a short causeway to reduce the risk of flooding.

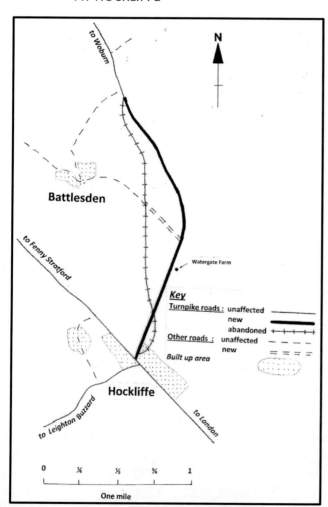

FIGURE 18: **The diversion of the Hockliffe and Woburn turnpike** road between Hockliffe and Battlesden Hill.

Between 1827 and 1833 this work was made redundant when the trust built more than two miles of entirely new road (the modern A4012) from Hockliffe to the second Battlesden turn *(at grid reference SP 970 296)*. This included a short link between old and new routes and cost £3,767.[86]

The new route started from Hockliffe with more than half a mile of dead-straight road on an embankment which today varies in height up to 12ft in order to make a smooth, consistent, gradient. This skirts the lower slopes of Battlesden Hill, whereas the medieval route went over it, and has a summit (in a shallow cutting) 45ft. below the old summit.

The first ¼ mile of the new road from the Watling Street junction is west of the old road wih a two-arched bridge built in 1827-33 over the Clipstone Brook. The rest of the new road is up to ¼ mile on the east side.

The Ordnance Survey's map of 1834 shows the new road complete and the old road still in place, with milestones 38 and 39 still beside it waiting to be resited. The route of the old road was sold in 1836 and its course is no longer even a footpath. All that remains of it is a dip in the modern road where the old road crossed from one side to the other.

WOBURN TO WOBURN SANDS	The road's steep one-mile-long climb and descent, known as The Sand Hill, over the 80ft-high Aspley Heath ridge between Woburn and Woburn Sands occupied the minds of the trustees for more than fifty years. A half mile-long section of cutting over the original summit, known as The Packhorse Road, was replaced by the present route shortly before 1768 because its cutting was too narrow for coaches and wagons to pass each other. The old course, up to 200 yards east of the modern road, has been obliterated by subsequent sand quarrying and rubbish tipping.

In 1770 the trustees began discussions about ways of easing the gradient of their new road. Work actually started in 1770 but was suspended in 1771 and reconsidered in 1788, 1797 and 1804. Finally in 1824-25 the road was lowered into a 20ft-deep cutting at its summit with shallower cuttings on parts of both approach hills. Most of the resulting spoil was used to build embankments at both lower ends of the hill, to lengthen the climbs, and thus reduce their gradients. Some of the excavated material went to fill in the disused cutting of the Packhorse Road.[87]

Later quarrying beside the modern road has largely removed the sides of the summit cutting, but the 1824-25 embankments and cuttings are still visible at lower levels on both approach slopes.

WAVENDON AND BROUGHTON	On the boundary between these parishes, Kingston Bridge was built over the Crawley Brook in 1759, presumably replacing a ford.

BROUGHTON BY-PASS	In 1820 the trustees resolved to build a ¾-mile by-pass on the north-east side of Broughton village.[88] The trust did not go ahead with this, but the by-pass was finally built by the county council in the 1960s on roughly the same line as the 1820 scheme, though a little shorter than the 1820 proposal.

NEWPORT PAGNELL	In 1812 the trust lowered and straightened a short length, probably no more than a quarter of a mile, of what is now Tickford Street in Newport Pagnell.

Toll gates and tollhouses	The trust started work with one gate across its road in 1706, and added a second in 1728 when turnpike control was extended from Woburn to Newport Pagnell; both gates were resited once during the life of the trust. A third gate across the road at Woburn Sands was added late in the turnpike era, and side bars were put up in 1779 and 1840.

WOBURN GATE 1706-1877	*Sample annual toll income from this gate: £1,265 in 1835.*

A gate was erected in Woburn when the trust started work in 1706. As Woburn was the northern end of the turnpike road until 1728 this gate must have been on the south side of the village, but its precise location is not known. The gate was moved in 1738, possibly only a short distance to a position one mile south of the village and about 300 yards north of the turning to Potsgrove. Here it stood in front of the long wall bounding Woburn Park *(at grid reference SP 956 317).*

The Duke of Bedford paid for the building of the new tollhouse, possibly in order to control its appearance in view of its prominent location near an entrance to Woburn Park. He then rented it to the trust for £3 a year.

WOBURN SANDS GATE
1832-33 AND 1856-77

No separate records of tolls has been found for this site.

In the financial year 1832/33 a gate was erected in Woburn Sands near the 'Weathercock Inn', at the junction with Weathercock Lane. It clearly had a short life because the trust's minutes did not mention it after 1833. Later, when the trustees came to discuss and decide against erecting a gate at Woburn Sands in 1846, the fact that there had been one there earlier was not even mentioned.[88]

Possibly prompted by growing traffic to and from Woburn Sands railway station, which had opened in 1846, a new gate with a toll house standing on the highway verge was finally put up in 1856. It was on a fresh site about 100 yards north of the 'Weathercock Inn', near the southern tip of today's recreation ground.[89] This prompted a flurry of unsuccessful requests for toll reductions for coal carts coming from the railway station.

BROUGHTON GATE
1728-1840

Sample annual toll income for the Broughton Gate, which probably included Milton Lane side bar: £1,350 in 1835.

Tolls were collected on the main road at Broughton from 1728, the year in which the trust's control was extended from Woburn to Newport Pagnell.[90] The gate was at the southern end of Broughton village, at the junction of the turnpike road with Milton Lane – now Milton Road *(at grid reference SP 896 399)*. Its site is now lost under the realigned junction between London Road and Tanfield Lane; (the Broughton village by-pass was not built until the 1960s).

Initially the toll cottage was rented for £3 a year, so was presumably a building which pre-dated the turnpike trust. It stood on the west side of the junction. By 1825 a toll house with an octagonal ground plan stood in the angle between the converging roads.[91]

It is not clear when a side bar was placed across Milton Lane (see also below) beside the gate on the main road. However, in 1840 the main gate was removed and replaced by a new one more than two miles to the north at Tickford *(see also below),* leaving the octagonal toll house to watch over the side bar across Milton Lane.

In 1820 the trust produced a map of its road,[92] which showed the Milton Lane side bar in place but the main gate removed to the north end of Broughton village *(at grid reference SP 895 403)*. This is now a disused piece of road between the A5130 and the A509 junction with the M1. In the absence of any other evidence for a toll gate on this site the author believes that this map showed a proposed move which was not carried out.

In spite of its name, 'Tollgate House', which stands on the corner of Newport Road and the turning to Brooklands Farm some 250 yards south-east of the site of the gate, is unlikely to have been associated with the turnpike trust.

MILTON LANE SIDE BAR
from at least 1779 to at least 1856

Toll records for this bar over the side road of Milton Lane were included first with Broughton Gate, later with Tickford Gate.

Cartographic evidence[91] suggests that this side bar to Broughton Gate could have been in use as early as 1779, but there is little mention of it until the main gate adjoining it at Broughton was closed in 1840. As stated above the first toll cottage here was on the west side of the junction but, by 1825, this had been replaced by one between the converging roads.

TICKFORD GATE AND CALDECOT SIDE BAR
1840-1877

Sample annual toll income, which included Milton Lane and Caldecot side bars: £618 in the financial year 1842/43.

The main gate at Broughton was moved to Tickford in 1840. The new toll gate and cottage were erected just south-east of Newport Pagnell at the junction of Tickford Street and North Crawley Road, with the gate placed across Tickford Street north of the junction.

By 28 October 1840 the toll gate and its cottage had been completed at a cost of £108.10.0d. and James Baker, the Broughton gatekeeper, was ordered to move to occupy the new cottage and take over Tickford Gate.

Baker was also told to collect the tolls at a new side bar, which had also been erected in 1840, across Caldecot Lane, the side turning to the mill on the River Ouzel 500 yards south of Tickford Gate. Initially the trust intended to build a toll house at the side bar too, but there is no record of this having happened, so we must assume that a kiosk sheltered whoever Baker hired to collect the tolls there. There was no way in which Baker himself could have attended both gates with over a quarter of a mile between them.

TICKFORD BRIDGE GATE

The toll collector's house with a plaque reading 'Toll House 1810' and standing immediately east of Tickford Bridge belonged to the trustees of the Newport Pagnell Bridges and not to the turnpike trust, whose road terminated at the east end of the bridge.

The bridge trustees were responsible, under an Act of 1809 for the rebuilding of the town's Middle, North and Tickford Bridges and maintenance of the streets linking them. Tolls were taken at the bridge gate here from 1810 to 1826 to recover the cost of rebuilding these.

Weighing engine

A weighing engine was installed beside Woburn toll gate in 1774 and remained in use until sold in 1834. It was constructed of heavy timbers and operated by lifting wagons bodily off the ground on a balance arm so that their weight could be measured by weights attached to the opposite end of the arm. The man who built it, a Mr Edgell, undertook to maintain it in working order for its first two years.

Milestones and mileposts

The trust agreed in 1743 to erect 12 milestones, of which four were to double as mounting blocks. By 1766 these, plus an extra one, were recorded as running from the 38th mile from London at Hockliffe to the 50th near Caldecot Mill, Newport Pagnell.

In 1830 it was decided to resite them all a quarter of a mile northwards in order to reflect a reduction in mileage to London shown on stones along Watling Street. In 1835 a complete set of new, presumably cast-iron, mileposts was ordered for the road and these were placed a few yards from the stones that they replaced in order to reflect the Post Office's official measurement of the distance from London.

Today there are no milestones or posts surviving on the section of road within Bedfordshire, while in Buckinghamshire the five surviving milemarkers are metal mileposts in two designs. Those at Woburn Sands, Wavendon and Tickford have narrow cast-iron posts of unusual design made by Grundy & Co. of Northampton, probably dating from 1835. However those found at Caldecot Mill and south of Broughton are larger, round-topped pressed-steel posts without raised lettering known as 'Bucks Pressings'. These postdate the turnpike era so are assumed to be late nineteenth or early twentieth-century replacements for damaged 1835 mileposts.

1877: The Trust wound up

The opening of the London and Birmingham Railway in 1838 had an immediate but indirect effect on traffic on the Hockliffe & Woburn road, and the trust's toll income was more than halved between 1835 and 1842.

In a brave attempt to attract traffic back by improving its road, the trust advertised for the investment of £4,500 in 1840,[95] but the opening of a London and East Midlands line by the Midland Railway in 1857 took further traffic from the road – and the last straw came when the Midland opened its shortened line between Bedford and St. Pancras in 1868.

The trust first applied to be wound up in 1872 but, because it was then still in debt, **36/37 Vic. c.90 (1873)** authorised its continuation until 1 November 1877 to enable those debts to be paid off before closure.

Road 3:
The Newport Pagnell
Turnpike Road 1709

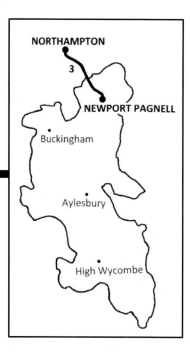

Identifying the road's route

The route follows today's B526 road, formerly the A50, from Newport Pagnell to Queen Eleanor Interchange in the suburbs of Northampton, then the A508 into Northampton. The construction of the modern interchange obliterated more than a quarter of a mile of the historic route of this road.

Historic background

This was a continuation of the highway from Hockliffe through Woburn to Newport Pagnell *(see road number 2 above)*, becoming part of a third route from London to the East Midlands running midway between the historic A5 and A6 routes. It was needed as traffic volume grew, probably during the late seventeenth century.

Although beyond the scope of this book, there are strong indications that in the years leading up to turnpiking the main traffic flow on this route went from Newport Pagnell to Horton in Northamptonshire, then due north to Kettering, bypassing Northampton, as an alternative route to today's A509.

In the twentieth century the building of the M1 motorway removed this turnpike road's role that had been built up in the previous two centuries so that today it has been largely downgraded to B-class status. As a result it saw few twentieth century improvements and thus retains much of the character of a turnpike road, with frequent bends and changes of gradient between hedges that are close to the carriageway.

The limits of the trust's road

The turnpike started from the north end of Middle Bridge in Newport Pagnell and ended at Cotton End in Northampton, immediately south of the bridge over the River Nene.

Its length and maintenance districts

After 1723 the Newport Pagnell turnpike road was 14 miles long, of which 6½ miles were in Buckinghamshire and the rest in Northamptonshire.

For ease of maintenance the road was divided into two roughly equal halves from an unknown date before 1775. The dividing point was at Three Bridges *(at grid reference SP 815 524)*, which is now an almost-invisible underbridge in the dip between Eakley Lanes in Buckinghamshire and Horton in Northamptonshire. The surveyor for each division lived on the appropriate part of the road.

In 1782 the trustees, after experiencing problems with the maintenance of the northern division *(see 'Control of the trust – surveyors' below)*, amalgamated the divisions under the one surveyor who they could rely upon. The maintenance of the trust's road thereafter remained in one pair of hands apart from 1817-19 when its administration briefly reverted to two divisions.

Initial Act of Parliament	**8 Anne c.9 (1709)** turnpiked the road from Northampton to Stoke Goldington.
Continuation Acts	**9 Geo.I, c.13 (1723)** extended the trust's control southwards from Stoke Goldington to Newport Pagnell. This was because the 'ruinous' state of that part of the road was deterring traffic from using the turnpiked section of the route to the north of it, with the result that the trust was spending more on road repairs than it was collecting in tolls.[96] The trust's powers were extended further by **15 Geo.II c.6 (1741-42), 33 Geo.II c. 43 (1759-60), 37 Geo.III c. 177 (1797), 58 Geo.III c.40 (1818),** and **2 Vic. c.13 (1839).**
Control of the Trust: TRUSTEES	In 1782 Sir Robert Gunning bought Horton Hall, which was situated in Northamptonshire, close to the trust's road. At that time the Hall with its outbuildings constituted most of the hamlet of Horton. From 1790 until the late 1830s Sir Robert and his sons dominated the chairing of the trust's meetings. It is noticeable that Horton was the scene of the only major road realignment carried out by this trust. The Hall was demolished in 1936. Few turnpike trusts could boast of a satisfactory level of attendance at trust meetings. However this one hit a particularly bad patch between 1814 and 1818 when the only meetings which had enough attendees to do business were those at the height of summer, which may say something about travelling conditions on their own road.
CLERKS	This was a trust with long-serving clerks. Charles Morgan had been clerk for at least eighteen years when he died in post in 1788. He was succeeded by Robert Abbey of Northampton, who served until 1823 and was followed by his son George, from the same firm of solicitors, who was clerk until the late 1840s. Then Thomas Mercer of Northampton took over. Although the trustees in most trusts dined together after their meetings, clerk Robert Abbey was unusual in mentioning the dinners in his newspaper adverts of trust meetings, possibly to encourage better attendance. "Dinner on table at 2.30" looked odd at the end of the legal jargon used to summon trustees.
SURVEYORS	Thomas Roe, surveyor of the northern division, died in post in 1780 and was replaced by his son, also called Thomas Roe, from Preston Deanery in Northamptonshire. It quickly became apparent that either the state of the road in the northern division had been quietly declining for years under Roe senior, or that Roe junior had little knowledge of how to maintain a road.

The upshot was that after two years of heavy hints from the trustees on how to maintain the road, Thomas Roe junior resigned in 1782.[97]

The road's two divisions were thereupon united as one under William Hayward of Stoke Goldington, who had been until then surveyor of the southern division and whose salary was doubled to £40 a year. A further £400 was then borrowed from a Newport Pagnell innkeeper to fund the repair of the former northern division and several £10 gratuities were paid to Hayward "as a reward for his extraordinary care and trouble" in getting the northern division back into a suitable condition.

Hayward remained the sole surveyor until 1817, when after a short hiatus Thomas Adams of Wavendon took over until 1840.

MEETINGS OF THE TRUSTEES

For most of the trust's life its sole meeting place was the hostelry situated in the Northamptonshire hamlet of Horton, a little north of the turnpike road's midway point. This was called the 'Coach and Horses' until 1757 and the 'Horton Inn' from 1758 onwards, a change of name possibly connected with its rebuilding at that time. In the 1840s it was renamed 'The Gunning Arms' as a nod to the owner of the adjoining Horton Hall, but today it is called 'The French Partridge'.

From 1793 for a short time the trustees sought variety by holding some meetings less than a mile to the north-west at the 'New Inn' at Hackleton. However they usually dined together after their meetings, and the patience of the landlords at Hackleton and Horton may have been tried when a high proportion of scheduled trust meetings in 1814-18 were cancelled because insufficient trustees had turned up. In 1814, under pressure from the clerk, the trustees agreed to pay each landlord five shillings ("for use of room and fire") each time they failed to dine. However this may not have been enough to appease the landlord of the 'New Inn' because they ceased to book a room there from 1815 after four consecutive cancellations.

Maintenance of the road

Beyond the unhappy affair of Thomas Roe junior (see 'Surveyors' above) the trust's maintenance seems to have continued unobtrusively without serious complaints. However, keeping maintenance going at the turn of the nineteenth century involved a major effort in persuading labourers to work on the road. Their daily wages were raised to fourteen pence in 1793, sixteen pence in 1795, and eighteen pence during the winter of 1800, but a particular problem was keeping them at work during harvest. In 1795 those who worked during the peak harvest week were given rewards, and in 1812 they received a bonus of two shillings "and steek".[98]

Improvements to the road

The Newport Pagnell Trust did not go in for major road-building, confining itself instead to several road-widening works of limited extent, some bridge-widening and rebuilding, and the raising of causeways leading up to bridges to keep traffic out of floodwaters.

AT NEWPORT PAGNELL

On the north side of Newport Pagnell the road to Northampton crossed three arms of the River Ouse on bridges confusingly known, from south to north, as North, Middle, and Lathbury Bridges. The North and Middle Bridges were controlled by the town's bridge trustees rather than by the turnpike trust, and were rebuilt in 1810 following the partial collapse of North Bridge in 1809.

In the financial year 1802-03 the turnpike trust raised their road on to a 70-yard causeway linking Middle and Lathbury Bridges to reduce the risk of the road being flooded. The work had been suggested by a trustee who lived in Lathbury and who had offered to pay half the cost, though he reduced his offer to a quarter on learning that the work had cost twice as much as he had estimated.

Following the rebuilding of North Bridge by the bridge trustees the turnpike trust widened their 1802-03 causeway on the west side to produce the largely flood-free route that we use now.[99] Today this causeway is still obvious above the adjoining field on the west side, but it is obscured on its east side because the adjoining land was raised to build a petrol filling station – which has since been demolished.

Until the 1830s Lathbury Bridge consisted of a ford for coaches beside a stone-built pedestrian bridge. In 1837 the trust felt that bridge and ford were in poor condition and, after eighteen months of argument, persuaded the magistrates that it was a county responsibility to carry out the repairs.

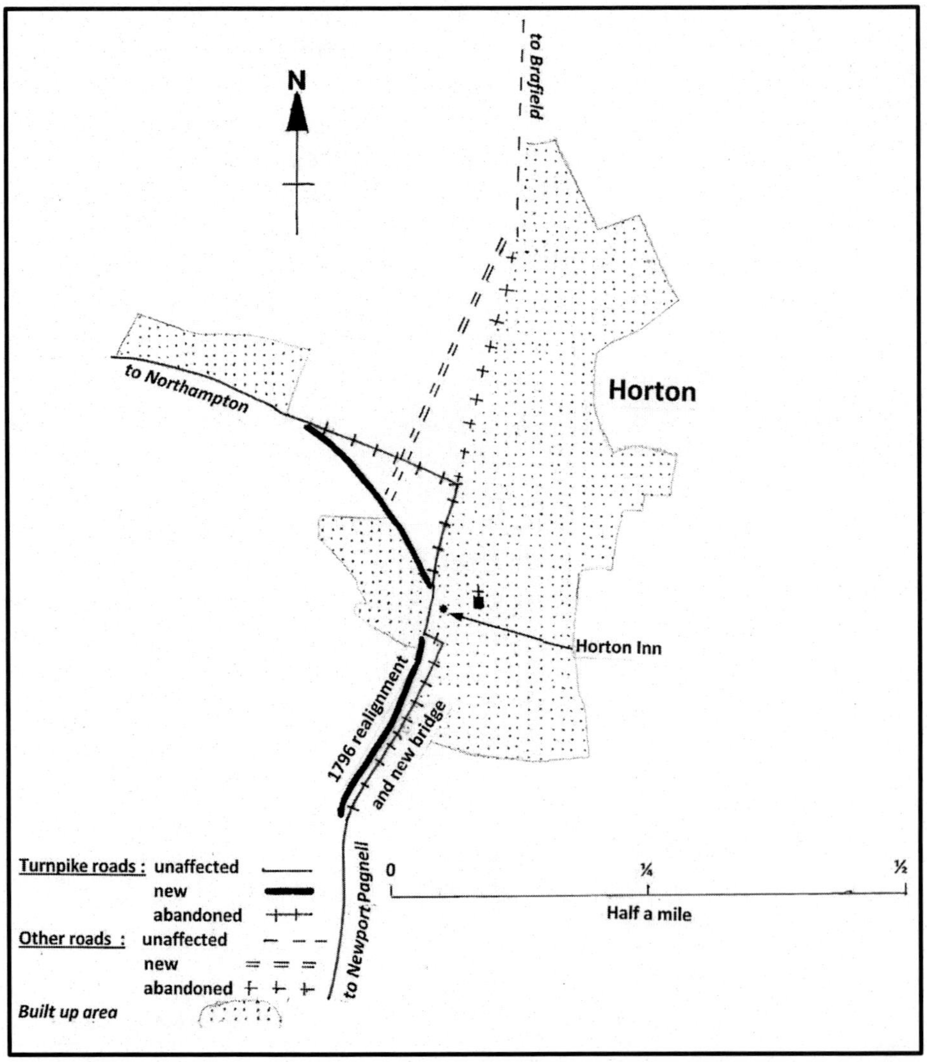

FIGURE 19:
The 1796 realignment of the turnpike road and new bridge at Horton, and the second realignment of 1830, prioritising the main route to Northampton.

By 1840 the magistrates had widened the bridge on its west side to enable wagons and coaches to cross it, and it was widened on its east side by Buckinghamshire County Council in the twentieth century. Today water is only beneath Lathbury Bridge in times of flood.

BETWEEN STOKE GOLDINGTON AND EAKLEY LANES	About a mile north of Stoke Goldington village *(at grid reference SP 828 505)*, a sharp bend was cut out by the trust in 1835, leaving to this day a wide verge on the east side where the road once ran. In 1777 a bridge was built near Eakley Grange Farm, apparently to replace a ford.
HORTON, NORTHAMPTONSHIRE	The only significant realignments of the turnpike road were at Horton. In 1796 the bridge over the stream just south of 'Horton Inn' (now 'The French Partridge') was in need of repair. It was demolished and replaced by a new, wider bridge and a new and straighter 100-yard approach road was built on the west side of the old road between the bridge and the 'Horton Inn'.

(Figure 19 shows both the 1796 and 1830 realignmets.).

The rebuilding had been suggested by Sir Robert Gunning of Horton Hall, who was a trustee, but could only proceed after Sir Robert loaned the trust enough to fund this work and pay off an existing debt.

Until the 1820s the road beyond the 'Horton Inn' headed directly north as Brafield Road, towards Brafield and Great Billing. The road to Northampton began at a T-junction about 200 yards north of the inn.

Around 1830 the trust changed its road priorities, making the road to Northampton into the main route by building a new road on a 260-yard left-hand curve, starting close to the 'Horton Inn'. At the same time the Brafield Road was realigned to the west to produce a T-junction with the realigned road to Northampton.

This 1830 realignment can be still seen today, but the earlier geography has been obliterated. The site of the pre-1830 junction is now in the back gardens of modern houses in Denton Road and The Drive, about 100 yards behind and to the east of the pair of neo-classical late Victorian lodges which front Brafield Road and once flanked the entrance to Horton Hall.[100]

HACKLETON PARISH, NORTHAMPTONSHIRE	In 1775 the trust built a bridge over the brook in Preston Lane, just west of New Hackleton, apparently to replace a ford. It was demolished and replaced by a wider structure in 1812. Three times between 1782 and 1806 short sections of road at the east end of Hackleton village were widened.
Toll gates and tollhouses	The trust had two main gates throughout its life; the southernmost of them had a change of site in the 1760s. Four side bars were added in 1797, 1829, 1839 and about 1841.
NORTH BRIDGE, NEWPORT PAGNELL	This bridge still has a most attractive toll house dating from 1810, but both bridge and toll house were owned by the Newport bridge trustees and not the turnpike trust; *(see also under Road 2: Hockliffe and Woburn Turnpike – Toll gates – Tickford Bridge')*.

LATHBURY GATE
1760s to 1871

No returns of toll income around 1836 have been found for this gate on its own. However, Lathbury and Preston Lane Gates, plus the side bars at Eakley Lanes and Filling Highway – in other words all the gates and bars in use in that year – were let together for £2,335 in the financial year 1836/37.

Lathbury Gate was situated on the bend in the road at the south end of the village *(at grid reference SP 877 452).* Its toll house was on the east side of the road on what is now part of the front garden of an eighteenth century farmhouse now called Tollgate House.

There was obviously no gate here until the trust's 1723 Act had extended trust control of the road from Stoke Goldington southwards to Newport Pagnell, and until the expiry of the same Act's ban on the erection of toll gates between those places before 1744. A meeting of the trust on 11 July 1760 discussed the erection of new toll gates on unspecified sites and sought new inward investment for this, [101] so Lathbury Gate probably started collecting tolls between 1744 and 1768, when Jefferys' map of Buckinghamshire showed it in use.

The toll house was rebuilt in 1835 at a cost of £153, and though it was still standing in 1924, long after the trust was wound up, it was demolished shortly afterwards.

GAYHURST (OR BUNSTY) SIDE BAR
PROBABLY 1839-1871

No returns of toll income have been found for this side bar on its own.

Situated just north of the village of Gayhurst, this side bar stood at the turning to Hanslope *(at grid reference SP 847 469).* It was erected late in the trust's life. In September 1830 the trust considered whether to erect a side bar here and was quickly challenged by Hanslope parish, which queried the following month whether its residents had to pay toll at the new side bar. [102] This seems to have put the project into abeyance for some years because there was no mention of it in newspaper adverts for the letting of toll gates during the 1830s.

However in 1839 the trust agreed to place a table of tolls at the side bar, which suggests that it was fairly new in that year. After that there were intermittent records of lettings of 'Bunsty Side Bar', suggesting the name had been changed to reflect Bunsty House and Wood on the road to Hanslope.

EAKLEY LANES GATES
1709-1760s
AND SIDE BAR
1829 to about 1833

No returns of toll income have been found for this gate on its own around 1836 (but see the composite rent under Lathbury Gate above).

The oddly-named Eakley Lanes is a scattered hamlet at the north end of Stoke Goldington parish. The gate across the turnpike road at this point *(at grid reference SP 817 511),* was at the junction with the side road through Salcey Forest to the Northamptonshire villages of Quinton and Wootton. The gate presumably came into use in 1709, when the trust obtained its initial Act covering the road from Northampton to Stoke Goldington. The nearby field called Toll House Close could suggest that the toll house stood on the south-east side of Bullshead Farm, which itself stands on the south-east corner of the junction.

At some time in the 1760s, long after turnpike powers had been extended south from Stoke Goldington to Newport in 1723, the gate at Eakley Lanes was discontinued and moved to Lathbury. Its tollhouse was sold for use as a private house, but in 1798 the trustees repurchased and demolished it in order to widen the road,[103] which suggests that the tollhouse had been built on the highway verge.

In the 1820s and 1830s the trust became concerned by the fall in tolls at its Preston Lane Gate in Northamptonshire, which was apparently due to traffic diverting on to a string of minor roads between Eakley Lanes and Wootton, south of Northampton, in order to avoid the gate. This loss of tolls was apparently impacting on the trust's ability to maintain its road.

In 1829, in a first attempt to deter toll evasion, a side bar was erected here across the turning at the southern end of the diversion. This remained in use until at least 1855, and probably until the trust was wound up in 1871.

The Stoke Goldington tithe map of 1847 clearly shows the bar across the side road at Eakley Lanes but does not indicate a toll house. On the tithe map Bullshead Farm on the south-east corner of the junction had become the 'Bull's Head' public house, facing a block of stables on the north-west corner which are no longer standing today. Neither of these look likely accommodation for the toll collector, so he probably sheltered in a kiosk.

FILLING HIGHWAY SIDE BAR, NORTHAMPTONSHIRE 1797-1871

No returns of toll income have been found for this gate on its own because it was always included in returns for Lathbury Gate.

This side bar stood in the hamlet of Horton across the turning to Brafield and Great Billing *(at grid reference SP 819 545)*. One reason for placing the bar here in 1797 may have been that travellers with time to spare for an indirect route were avoiding the trust's Preston Lane gate *(see below)* by leaving Northampton on what is today the A428, turning right at Brafield-on-the-Green, and joining the Newport road at Horton. (This ploy would not have worked after 1827 when the future A428 was turnpiked.)

Due partly to alterations to the road layout at Horton *(see 'Improvements' above)* this side bar was twice moved very short distances, but was always only across Brafield Road. In its final position it was served by a tollhouse of cruciform plan which stood on the east side of Brafield Road with only its porch on the highway verge. After 1871 this house became a private dwelling but was doubtless removed soon afterwards to make way for one of the imposing pair of neo-classical but late nineteenth-century lodges which flanked the drive to Horton Hall, and still stand today.

Filling Highway Side Bar's name is a mystery. Brafield Road led ultimately to the Billings, a pair of villages east of Northampton, and the writer is not aware of a place called Filling in the vicinity. However, from the outset the trust's records consistently refer to the gate as being on Filling Highway and this seems to have become self-perpetuating for, by 1866, a diversion order unconnected with the trust named Brafield Road as Filling Highway.

PRESTON LANE GATE.
NORTHAMPTONSHIRE
1709-1871

No returns of toll income around 1836 have been found for this gate on its own (again see the Lathbury Gate above for the composite rent that year).

This was the only gate to be in use on the same site throughout the trust's life. It stood on the summit of a low hill *(at grid reference SP 797 557)* ¼ mile north-west of the village of New Hackleton. Unusually, the toll gate here was stolen in 1818, and again in 1822.

The toll house stood on the south-west side of the road and long outlived the trust, probably not being demolished to make way for road-widening until the 1950s or 1960s. Today its site is part of a wide highway verge.

In the 1820s and 1830s trustees became concerned that toll income was being lost here due to some traffic leaving the turnpike road at Eakley Lanes *(see above)* and continuing on minor roads for six miles through Salcey Forest and Quinton to Wootton. Although this diversion was roughly the same length as the journey on the turnpike road, its less-well-maintained surface would only have appealed to travellers who were not in a hurry!

The trust addressed this by putting a side bar across the southern end of the diversion at Eakley Lanes in 1829, and across the northern end at Water Lane in 1841, by which time the trust's income was also being eroded by the opening of the London and Birmingham Railway.

WATER LANE OR
HARDINGSTONE
'CHAIN',
NORTHAMPTONSHIRE
1840s

This 'side gate' did not exist in 1836. It was introduced late in the turnpike era to stem the loss in the trust's income mentioned under the entries for Eakley Lanes and Preston Lane Gates *(see above)*. It stood in what are now the suburbs of Northampton, across the turning to Wooton village, still called Water Lane today, and at the northern end of the toll avoiders' diversion to and from Eakley Lanes.

The new 'side gate' was authorised by the trustees in 1841 and the first record of its takings which has been found is for 1843, when it was called Hardingstone.[104] By 1849 it was called the 'Water Lane Chain', the word 'chain' implying that the revenue did not justify building a proper toll gate.

Since takings here in 1843 ranged between five and nine shillings per week the caution was justified! The gate is very thinly documented, and there is no trace of its site today.

Weighing engine

Preston Lane Gate was provided with a weighing engine in or shortly before 1775, in the early days of such machinery when wagons had to be lifted bodily off the ground in order to weigh them. The trust suffered from being a pioneer, and recorded in 1781 that its machine was "uncertain and out of repair and almost useless." [105]

This led to the building of a replacement at a cost of £50, to a specification which sounds as if it was for the sort of weighbridge we are familiar with today. The new machine was in place by 1782, and it or a replacement lasted until 1832, when complaints about its accuracy and dangerous condition led it to be dismantled. Its replacement lasted until at least 1841.

Milestones and mileposts

The trust's continuation Act of 1741-42 implied that there were no milestones in place and encouraged the measurement of the road and the installation of milestones or mileposts. This had been done by 1766, when Jefferys mapped milemarkers running from 'London 51' just north of the Newport Pagnell bridges, to 'London 64' near Queen Eleanor's Cross south of Northampton.

The effect of trusts further south shortening the road from London led the Newport Trust to move its milestones in 1817 and 1830, the cumulative effect being to resite them nearly half a mile northwards. Interestingly the trust immediately to the south, the Hockliffe and Woburn Turnpike Trust, repositioned its milestones in 1830, but only by a quarter of a mile!

The milemarkers installed by 1766 were probably stones with incised lettering. The resiting of 1830 appears to have been taken as the opportunity to replace these stones with cast-iron mileposts by Grundy and Company of Northampton. No mileposts have survived on the section of road in Northamptonshire, but in Buckinghamshire a badly-damaged 'London 53' still stands on the west side of the road in Gayhurst village and a 'London 54' survives on the west side to the south of Stoke Goldington.

1870: The Trust wound up

The trust's total annual toll income rose steadily from around £1,100 in the early 1790s to £2,060 in 1803-04 before falling to £1,820 between 1807 and 1817. It then started to rise again, to peak at £2,464 in 1832-33 before a slight drop to £2,335 in 1836-37, which might reflect traffic moving to the Holyhead Road after its improvement by Thomas Telford.

But this was nothing compared to the fall to £1,507 a year in 1838-39, immediately after the opening of the roughly-parallel London and Birmingham Railway, and the dive to £600 a year in 1845-46 following the 1845 opening of the branch railway from Blisworth to Northampton.

The trust reduced tolls in 1846 but this did not attract traffic back and income had fallen to £382 by 1849-50. With such problems, it is surprising that the trust managed to struggle on until its winding up, authorised by **32/33 Vic. c.90 (1869)** came on 30 June 1870.

Road 4:
Beaconsfield and Stokenchurch Turnpike Road 1719

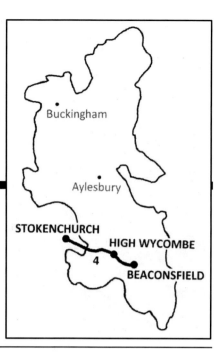

Identifying the road's route

Today this is the section of the A40 London to Oxford road between Beaconsfield and Stokenchurch, except in three places where the original turnpike road has now been bypassed: the centre of High Wycombe, at Piddington, and on Dashwood Hill.

Historic background

The trust's road was part of the important medieval highway from London to Oxford, then Worcester and mid-Wales, although until the sixteenth century most bulky goods going between London and High Wycombe or beyond went on the River Thames to the wharves at Spade Oak or Hedsor, near Bourne End. From there they took the Old Windsor Road to Wycombe. By the seventeenth century most of this traffic had moved to the road route via Uxbridge and Beaconsfield.

Due to the difficulties in crossing the high Chilterns, alternative routes had developed between West Wycombe and Stokenchurch by the end of the Middle Ages. Packhorses followed the valley bottom along what might be the original route – known as Chorley Road or Bottom Road – through Radnage (Bennett End) and up Collier's Lane, which is today a bridleway.

Meanwhile wheeled traffic, becoming more significant in the seventeenth century, adopted the higher-level route which is taken by the A40 today through Piddington and what is now Studley Green.

Ogilby's 1675 strip map of the Oxford Road[106] suggested an alternative route for coaches between West Wycombe and Studley Green which would have involved some heroic and unnecessary hill climbing between valleys – and which was therefore probably a mistake.

The limits of the trust's road

From the west end of Beaconsfield Old Town to the west end of Stokenchurch village.

Its length and maintenance districts

The trust's road was 12¼ miles long and is wholly in Buckinghamshire today. However during the turnpike era 2½ miles of this in Stokenchurch parish were in Oxfordshire. The trust's road was administered as a single unit in all years for which records have been found.

Initial Act of Parliament	5 Geo.I, c.1 (1719).
Continuation Acts	The trust's powers were subsequently renewed by **9 Geo.II, c.11 (1736), 33 Geo.II, c.37 (1760), 15 Geo.III, c.105 (1775), 34 Geo.III, c.142 (1794),** and **4 Geo.IV, c.108 (1823).**
Control of the Trust: TRUSTEES	The trust's initial 1719 Act listed 78 trustees, including Sir Francis Dashwood of West Wycombe House. In the nineteenth century chairmen included such notables as John Dashwood King of West Wycombe House and James du Pré of Wilton Park, Beaconsfield, but nobody held the post for sufficient years to make their mark on policy.
CLERKS	All those who have been identified were solicitors based in High Wycombe. James Fastnedge was clerk in the 1780s. By 1811 Robert Nash was sole clerk but from at least 1822 until 1830 he had been joined as joint clerk to the trust by John Rumsey of Crendon Lane. After them John Nash of High Street was sole clerk from 1832 until 1857; while Thomas Reynolds took over for the last few years.
SURVEYORS	In 1811, in spite of poor record-keeping by the trust's officers, trustees became aware that annual expenditure was worryingly close to annual income. This prompted an investigation of the trust's working practices, which revealed a can of worms.[107] The surveyor was apparently not putting the necessary hours into his job so that the regular deliveries of stone needed for road repairs were frequently not checked; and as a result suppliers were paid by the full cart load regardless of whether the cart had been full, or whether it had delivered at all. Furthermore, the surveyor had not kept an attendance record of the road men and did not attend the Saturday payment of wages by the treasurer, with the result that the latter paid a full week's wages to each man regardless of how many hours had actually been worked. Meanwhile the treasurer was pocketing "compliments" of one or two shillings from contractors when paying bills of £20 or £30. The inevitable outcome was the resignation of the surveyor, William Chalk. A few years later, due to the heavy traffic on this road, the Beaconsfield and Stokenchurch Trust became one of a handful in Buckinghamshire which for a time engaged a national figure to oversee the road, with a local man as 'Superintending Surveyor' to carry the work out. In this case in the 1830s Sir James McAdam, of Charing Cross, was the national figure guiding this trust and the neighbouring Red Hill Trust *(Road number 9).*
MEETINGS OF THE TRUSTEES	High Wycombe stood near the mid-point of the trust's road, so it made sense that almost all the trust's meetings were held there. Some in the eighteenth century were in the Town Hall, but in the nineteenth century the 'Red Lion'

in High Street was almost the only trustees' meeting place. This inn was replaced by shops and offices in the 1960s but the site is still recognisable by the preserved statue of a red lion on top of the supermarket's porch.

Maintenance of the road	Like the neighbouring Red Hill Trust (*Road number 9*), this was one of the few trusts in Buckinghamshire to make an effort to minimise summertime dust arising from the crushing of loose roadstone by the wheels of passing vehicles. As early as 1736 it obtained powers to extract water from the River Wye in order to sprinkle the road surface in summer months, but it is not clear when this work actually started. The trust's records mention watering the road from 1827 until 1862 at an annual cost which varied widely between about £20 and £70, presumably in response to the amount of summer rainfall. *(See the Colnbrook Trust (road number 6) for an illustration of how road watering was carried out).*

Improvements to the road: AT WYCOMBE END, BEACONSFIELD	The ¼-mile long hill dropping westwards from Wycombe End was improved by the trust in the early 1780s. Its former winding course was straightened, and its gradient made easier by excavating the road into a shallow cutting at its upper end. From the foot of the main hill to the west end of today's garden centre a further ¼ mile was straightened at the same time by slewing the road 20-30 yards to the north. Today York House and a petrol station stand on the site of the old road, whose shallow grassy holloway can still be seen under the trees on the south side of the modern road between the petrol station and the west end of the garden centre. The trust had sold off the land under the abandoned sections of old road in 1784.[108]

WHITE HILL, HOLTSPUR	White Hill, which drops more than 150ft to the west between Holtspur and Wooburn Moor, was a major obstacle to the growth of wheeled traffic. In the eighteenth century two parallel sinuous routes descended the hill, using bends to minimise the severe gradient.
	In 1827-29 the trust built nearly ¾ mile of completely new road, now part of the modern A40, between the two older routes.[109] Dropping in a straight line for 660 yards from its upper end, largely through a cutting up to 45ft. deep, this created an easier gradient of mainly 1 in 25. At the foot of the cutting the new road curved slightly to jump a narrow valley on a 380-yard embankment with a maximum height of 80ft, which was formed with the spoil brought down from the cutting above, before it briefly entering a shallower cutting for 100 yards.
	Although covered in trees today, the embankment still makes an impressive sight in winter when viewed from Watery Lane. The embankment and cutting are monuments to what civil engineering could achieve with picks, shovels, wheelbarrows, and horse-drawn carts.

WEST WYCOMBE ROAD	The road between High and West Wycombe was spectacularly improved in the late eighteenth century, though this was not carried out by the trust but as part of 'improvements' by Sir Francis Dashwood of West Wycombe

House. Until then the West Wycombe Road had followed a winding course in the valley bottom beside the River Wye.[110] As a result it was miry in wet winters.

A small improvement was made in 1748-52 by Sir Francis when, to alleviate hardship among his tenants after several bad harvests, he paid a number of them to dig a ¼-mile long line of tunnel-linked caves under West Wycombe Hill. He used the extracted chalk and flints to build half a mile of almost-straight new main road from just east of the future Chapel Lane to the junction of the Oxford and Risborough roads at West Wycombe. This new piece of road lay uphill to the north of the original route of the turnpike road by between five and 30 yards, but below the level of the present road.[111]

This also enabled Sir Francis to extend his park marginally northwards to the new road. The obelisk which stands beside the Pedestal roundabout was erected by Dashwood in 1752 to mark completion of this half mile of road.

The 1750s and 1760s saw Sir Francis laying out his landscaped park around West Wycombe House. In 1763-65 he built a family mausoleum on a prominent site in front of the parish church on West Wycombe Hill. At the same time he raised the church tower so that it could be seen above the mausoleum.

Then between 1778 and 1783, he improved on his first road-building enterprise by bypassing it on its north side with a completely new, dead straight, main road, nearly 1¾ miles long. This is the present West Wycombe Road from just east of Desborough Avenue in High Wycombe to the junction of the A40 and A4010 at the Pedestal obelisk of 1752. The new road, cut into a shelf in the valley side, lay uphill from and between 70 and 130 yards north of the old turnpike road. Travellers were thus raised clear of the valley bottom mud.

The new road was perfectly aligned on Dashwood's hilltop mausoleum and heightened church tower, so that westbound travellers emerging from High Wycombe could enjoy a splendid long view of the structures straight ahead on West Wycombe Hill, and be reminded of the Dashwoods who had built them. The view remains uninterrupted today.

In 1783 Dashwood handed the new road to the turnpike trust[112] in exchange for the site of the old road – including the half mile at the west end that he had had built in 1752 and which was now abandoned. Most of the old road was stopped up, and the half-mile 1752 road was used to plant a shelter belt of trees to screen his extended park. Today that line of trees separates the Park from modern housing.

Confusingly the new (1752) road commemorated by the Pedestal obelisk has vanished beneath this belt of trees, leaving the obelisk, which carries a 1752 date, apparently commemorating the building of West Wycombe Road in 1778-83!

The digging of West Wycombe caves in 1748-52, ostensibly to provide employment and to find road-building materials, had a third purpose. It was possibly just as important to Dashwood in creating the spectacularly carved cave chambers for meetings of his Hell Fire Club. We will probably never know.

FIGURE 20:
The realignment of West Wycombe Road between 1778 and 1783.

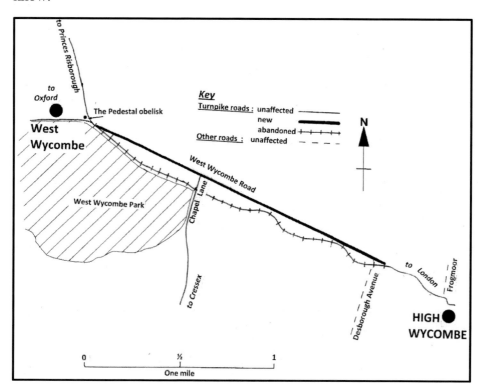

DASHWOOD HILL — Between Piddington and Studley Green the road climbs just over 200ft heading westwards. The medieval route was curving and narrow, with its width restricted for some distance by the deep hollow way which had been worn by generations of animals' hooves. It was an obstacle to the growth of wheeled traffic.

FIGURE 21:
The original Dashwood Hill, between Piddington and Studley Green, once the main road to Oxford, now a public footpath.

PHOTOGRAPH BY PETER GULLAND

At some time between maps dated 1766 and 1812, and probably after the passing of the trust's 1794 Act, the trust bypassed the old road on its south side with a completely new and largely straight ¾-mile hill on an easier gradient. This in turn would later be bypassed on *its* south side in the 1920s by an even more easily graded road, the present A40, built by Buckinghamshire County Council.

The original Dashwood Hill survives today as a public footpath while the Dashwood Hill built by the trust has become a minor road whose formal name, 'Old Dashwood Hill', ignores the survival of the far older hill on its north side.

The half-mile bypass on the north side of the original road at Piddington at the foot of the Dashwood Hills is a post-turnpike creation, probably built in the 1920s.

Toll gates and tollhouses

For such a busy trunk route and one which also carried a lot of local traffic to High Wycombe and Beaconsfield, it may seem surprising that the trust had only one toll gate until the early nineteenth century. However the trust's 1794 Act prohibited the placing of a toll gate across the Oxford road between High Wycombe and Stokenchurch – nearly half of the trust's road – in order to protect Wycombe's market trade, stating that there had never been a gate on this section of road.

After the 1794 Act had expired in 1815 a second gate was added by the trust, but like the first this too was east of High Wycombe.

HOLTSPUR GATE
about 1813-22 to 1867

Toll income at this gate was always included with that of Wycombe Gate (see below).

Holtspur Gate stood ¼ mile east of the top of White Hill, Holtspur, at the junction of the Oxford road with Broad Lane *(at grid reference SU 925 897)*. The toll collector sheltered in a kiosk in the middle of the road junction. The kiosk would have been removed as soon as the trust was wound up.

HIGH WYCOMBE GATE
1719-1867

Sample annual toll income from Wycombe and Holtspur Gates together was £3,045 in 1836.

This gate stood initially from 1719 at the east end of the town centre on a site now just east of the junction of Abbey Way and Easton Street. In 1826 it was moved 600 yards east to a site *(at grid reference SU 877 925)* which is now between the Bowerdean Road roundabout and Bassetbury Lane.

At this second location the toll house was built in a battlemented Strawberry Hill Gothick style, possibly to acknowledge nearby Wycombe Abbey. It stood on the south side of the road, with most of the building on what is now a playing field. After the trust was wound up in 1867 the tollhouse was used as a private dwelling, then as a cricket ground store, and finally as an air raid warden's post before being dismantled in 1978 and splendidly rebuilt in the Chilterns Open Air Museum in 1983-84.

WEST WYCOMBE	The legal ban on placing a gate here *(see general section on 'Toll gates and tollhouses' above)* meant that if there ever was a gate on this trust's road at West Wycombe it could only have been installed legally after the 1794 Act's provisions had expired in 1815, but no reference has been found in the Beaconsfield and Stokenchurch Trust's records to such a gate being in existence in any subsequent year.

Several writers have suggested otherwise, but this may be the result of mistaken memories. From 1795 until 1871 the Risborough Road Trust *(see Road number 19)* had *its* West Wycombe toll gate across the start of *its* road at what is now The Pedestal roundabout. At that point the West Wycombe High Street, part of the Beaconsfield and Stokenchurch Trust's road towards Oxford, forked left, while the Risborough Road Trust's Bradenham Road forked to the right, passing through their toll gate.

This misunderstanding could explain how Bryant came to depict gates across both roads at that junction on his 1825 map.[113]

Weighing engine

There was a weighing engine at High Wycombe gate. The first reference to it that has been found was in 1826, but £145 was spent on a replacement engine in 1827, which suggests that the original had been in place for some years before 1826. An engine remained in use there until 1867.

Milestones and mileposts

Milestones were put up along the road in 1744 – and some still carry this date. In 1766-68, Jeffereys' map[114] recorded thirteen stones reading from 'London 24' just west of Beaconsfield Old Town to 'London 36' at the junction with Marlow Road in Stokenchurch. Nine of these stones survive today, with incised lettering in a mix of upper and lower case styles. Seven are located on the south side of the road, with 'London 33' and 'London 36' on the north side.

These stones originally stood at an angle to the road with mileages in Roman numerals on their two front faces. At an unknown date after 1744 the legibility of Roman numerals from moving vehicles must have been questioned, because all stones were then turned around and new mileage inscriptions using Arabic numerals were cut into what had become the two new front faces.

However some stones must have been mixed up during this reworking because a small number have different mileages in Arabic and Roman on the same stone, while others have had the Roman inscription chiselled off. To add to the confusion, when they were put back on the roadside, apparently after storage during World War II, some were placed square to the road, some diagonally, and one was put back with its Roman numerals on its front face!

The 'London 29' milestone, which should have stood in the centre of High Wycombe in Cornmarket or Church Street, may have been missing for a long time because, very close to its probable site, the attractive Little Market House (built in 1761) carries the inscriptions 'TO OXFORD 25 MILES' and 'TO LONDON 29 MILES' on its string course.

(While a quick glance might suggest that the stone standing diagonally opposite the Little Market House is the missing milestone, more detailed examination will show that it is simply a large block placed to protect a particularly vulnerable arch in the arcade beneath the Guildhall).

Inscriptions on the obelisk called The Pedestal at the West Wycombe divergence of the modern A40 and A4010 also indicate mileages. Its cylindrical column is topped by a square slab on which sits a stone ball. Three sides of the slab are inscribed with Roman numeral mileages to 'The City', 'The County Town', and 'The University'. The fourth side, facing High Wycombe, is inscribed 'Lord Dashwood the Christian MDCCLII'.

The obelisk was erected in 1752 by Sir Francis Dashwood of West Wycombe Park to mark the completion of his realignment of a half-mile section of the road to High Wycombe *(see above under 'Improvements to the road')*.

1867: The Trust wound up

The opening of the Great Western Railway from London to Oxford in 1844, and to High Wycombe in 1854, precipitated major falls in traffic on the Oxford road. As a result the trust's annual toll income plummeted from £3,430 in 1837, a probable peak, to £805 in 1866.[115] In response the Beaconsfield and Stokenchurch Trust and the adjoining Red Hill Trust *(see Road number 9)* were among the first in Buckinghamshire to apply to abandon their responsibilities.

The Beaconsfield and Stokenchurch Trust ended its work on 1 November 1867 under **30/31 Vic. c.121 (1867)**, the same Act that authorised the winding up of the Red Hill Trust.

Road 5:
The Wendover and Buckingham Turnpike Road 1721

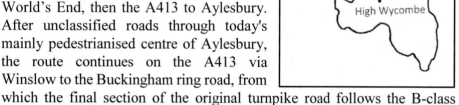

Identifying the road's route

This follows the B4009 from Wendover to World's End, then the A413 to Aylesbury. After unclassified roads through today's mainly pedestrianised centre of Aylesbury, the route continues on the A413 via Winslow to the Buckingham ring road, from which the final section of the original turnpike road follows the B-class London Road into Buckingham town centre.

Historic background

This was part of a major historic route from London to the West Midlands via Uxbridge, Aylesbury, Buckingham, Banbury, and Stratford-upon-Avon. It is therefore not surprising that the section between Aylesbury and Buckingham had been the subject of a Bill before Parliament[116] as early as 1712. Although this had been unsuccessful, the route was adopted as part of the Wendover and Buckingham Turnpike Trust only a few years later in 1721.

The trustees' energies were initially occupied in persuading traffic to accept a major move of the route to avoid a low-lying, miry, section north of Aylesbury. Once this had settled down, another issue deterring traffic growth, and therefore toll income, was the poor condition of the unturnpiked southward continuation of their road between Wendover and Uxbridge – mainly over the route of today's A413.

To address this the Wendover and Buckingham Trust promoted two Bills to Parliament in 1751 to set up the Wendover and Oak Lane and Red Hill and Beaconsfield Trusts, in order to upgrade the road to Uxbridge *(see Roads 8 and 9 below)*. Although those trusts therefore started life under the Wendover and Buckingham's umbrella, the accounts and administration of all three were kept separate from the outset.

The limits of the trust's road

From the junction of Aylesbury Road with Wharf Road in Wendover to Bridge Street, just north of London Road Bridge, in Buckingham.

Its length and maintenance districts

The trust's road was 21 miles long, and wholly in Buckinghamshire.

In the eighteenth century the road was divided for maintenance into six divisions, of which three – Creslow, Hoggeston and Swanbourne – consisted of just one parish. The others were Wendover to Holman's Bridge (north of Aylesbury), Holman's Bridge to Whitchurch, and Winslow to Buckingham.

Each length was superintended by its own surveyor, some of whom in the eighteenth century were trustees. By the 1830s the number of divisions had been reduced to two as an economy measure: Wendover to Winslow and Winslow to Buckingham.

Initial Act of Parliament	**7 Geo.I, c.24 (1721).**

Continuation Act	**15 Geo.II, c.5, (1742)** simply renewed the trust's powers. **24 Geo.II, c.32 (1751)** extended the trust's control southwards from Wendover to the Oxford Road (now the A40) at Tatling End, and along the Oxford Road from Beaconsfield to the River Colne on the edge of Uxbridge. *(See under the Wendover and Oak Lane Trust (Road number 8 below) and the Red Hill and Beaconsfield Trust (Road number 9 below) for the subsequent history of these extensions).*

6 Geo.III, c.71 (1766) renewed the Wendover and Buckingham Trust's powers. **17 Geo.III, c.82 (1776)** made the Wendover and Oak Lane Trust independent of the parent trust, and **19 Geo.III, c.83 (1779)** did the same for the Red Hill Trust.

50 Geo.III, c.99 (1810), 11 Geo.IV, c.81 (1830), 1 and 2 Will.IV, c.39 (1831), and 25 and 26 Vic., c.56 (1862) all renewed the Wendover and Buckingham Trust's powers.

The 1831 Act followed the 1830 Act so closely because the latter was quickly found to be defective because it banned the use of toll gates on this trust within Aylesbury parish – yet the trust had two gates there – and because it omitted the previous exemption from toll payable by residents within their own parish.[117]

Control of the Trust: TRUSTEES	The trust's initial (1721) Act listed 52 trustees. Over the years subsequent lists included many well-known Buckinghamshire names such as Thomas Fremantle, Thomas Lake, William Lowndes, Henry Purefoy, William Rickford and Brown Willis. However, few trustees appear to have chaired trust meetings more than two or three times, so there was no evident 'guiding hand'.

CLERKS	In contrast to its chairmen, this was another trust with long-serving clerks. Samuel Yeates was in post in the 1760s and 1770s, followed by 1783 by James Burnham of Winslow who died in post in 1803. Lancelot Wyatt of Winslow served from 1803 until 1822, when Thomas Tindall of Aylesbury took over until his death in 1850. He was replaced by his son Acton Tindall, in partnership with Edward Baynes, who remained joint clerks until the trust was wound up.

Tindall father and son were also clerks to the Aylesbury and Hockliffe Trust. It was noticeable that when both trusts were meeting in Aylesbury, they tended to meet at the same inn on the same day, either one hour apart in the late morning or one before and one after lunch. This must have put considerable pressure on the first meeting to be businesslike.

On 21 February 1855 parallel working went further when both trusts discussed the same subject – whether to put road maintenance out to contract – on the same day at the same inn.

MEETINGS OF THE TRUSTEES

No record of meetings before 1772 has been found but for the rest of the eighteenth century they were almost exclusively held at the 'Bell Inn' in Winslow. In the nineteenth century they roughly alternated between Aylesbury and Winslow, with 'The Bell' still the only meeting place in Winslow. The Aylesbury meetings were initially solely at the 'White Hart Inn', but after about 1844 this alternated with The George Inn.

Maintenance of the road

In the eighteenth century the trust worked to a norm of spending no more than £18 per year per mile on road maintenance. A possible indicator of increasing traffic levels in the 1780s and 1790s was that the surveyors were routinely spending above the norm on maintenance. In recognition of this the trust increased the norm to £20 per year per mile in 1792, but for some years after the surveyors' claims were above even that.

Improvements to the road: MAJOR RE-ROUTING

Unusually among turnpike roads in Buckinghamshire, the great majority of this trust's road (14½ out of 21 miles) only became the accepted route for travellers shortly before the trust was inaugurated.

The main medieval route from London to the West Midlands had left Aylesbury on the road towards Bicester, formerly the Roman Akeman Street, and had headed north after turning right at Quarrendon. It then passed through East Claydon before joining the present A413 route between Padbury and Buckingham (at grid reference SP 707 321 – see figure 6). A 3-mile section of this old road followed the low-lying, often deeply muddy, course of a former Roman road along the boundaries of Quainton, Pitchcott, North Marston, Hogshaw and Granborough parishes.

The mud was not a serious problem as long as most traffic was on horseback, but the slowly growing numbers of carriages and wagons in the seventeenth century would have found this section impassable in winter. This presumably led wheeled traffic to try to avoid the problem by taking to secondary roads on higher and drier ground through Whitchurch and Winslow, roughly two miles to the east of the old road, even though this was ¾ mile longer than the established route.

There is debate about when this change of route was formalised because the trust's initial Act of 1721 did not specify the route between Aylesbury and Buckingham. However its continuation Act of 1742 stated indirectly that the new route via Whitchurch and Winslow had been maintained by the trust under its 1721 Act.

Furthermore, in 1742 the trust built the present Padbury Bridge on the 'new' route about ¾ mile north-west of Padbury village. It is most unlikely that they would have built this bridge unless they were already maintaining the road which went over it. So it seems most likely that the trust adopted the alternative route via Winslow when it obtained its first Act in 1721 and then, by ceasing to maintain the old route, encouraged traffic to move to the new.

HARDWICK BRIDGE	In 1836-40 the trustees were much exercised by the need to ease the sharp bends and steep gradients on either side of the bridge at Hardwick. Four different schemes were considered for new lengths of bypass road, including one which passed around the east side of Hardwick village and another which kept to the existing line of road and eased the gradient of the hill up from the bridge. In the end they restricted themselves to rebuilding the bridge itself, and providing a new ford beside it, probably in 1845.[118]
WHITCHURCH	In the eighteenth century a terrace of cottages called Rotten Row, standing in the middle of the turnpike road at the north end of Whitchurch High Street, reduced the carriageway to a narrow alley on either side of the buildings. In 1786 the trustees purchased the cottages, demolished them, and added their site to the road.[119]
	The turnpike road climbed northwards out of the village of Whitchurch in the narrow holloway, now a footpath, between Market Hill and Mount Pleasant. The trust planned, in 1801[120] to widen the road on the hill, but nothing was done so they discussed the matter again in 1822 and as a result a short section between Market Hill and Oving Road was widened.[121] It took another 143 years, until 1965, before Buckinghamshire County Council bypassed the rest of the narrow hill, leaving the holloway as a useful reminder of the tight dimensions of some sections of turnpike road.
SWANBOURNE PARISH BETWEEN BUCKSLOW AND OAKHAM FARMS	In the south-west corner of Swanbourne parish the road formerly took an indirect route over a switchback of short hills *(at grid reference SP 787 254)* to the west of its modern alignment near Oakham Farm *(see figure 22)*. In 1826 a new, more direct length of road, just over one mile long, was built at a higher level with easier gradients. This is the route taken by the A413 today, with the old road now part public bridleway and part abandoned in fields.
SHIPTON BRIDGE	Today the A413 crosses the Claydon Brook, at the foot of the hill up to Shipton, on a bridge set in a gently curving alignment and built by the county council in 1937. The original Shipton Bridge, on the west side of the modern A413, is narrow and approached from both directions on a sharply curved road which originally suffered from flooding. In 1792 the trust addressed this by raising the approaches on to a causeway (now used as a lay-by) up to ten feet above ground level. Today the causeway is still clearly visible for about 70 yards south of the bridge, but has largely been masked by picnic site landscaping north of it.
SHIPTON, EAST OF WINSLOW	In pre-turnpike days the principal route from Aylesbury went straight ahead at Shipton, immediately east of Winslow, heading for Swanbourne, with a turning for Winslow to the left at a T-junction *(at grid reference SP 777 273)*. The prominent pair of timber-framed cottages at this point today are beside the route's original alignment. Between 1822 and 1825 the trust built a 170-yard, sharply curving road to bypass the T-junction to improve the main Aylesbury to Buckingham traffic flow.

FIGURE 22:
The rerouting of the Wendover and Buckingham road at Swanbourne in 1826

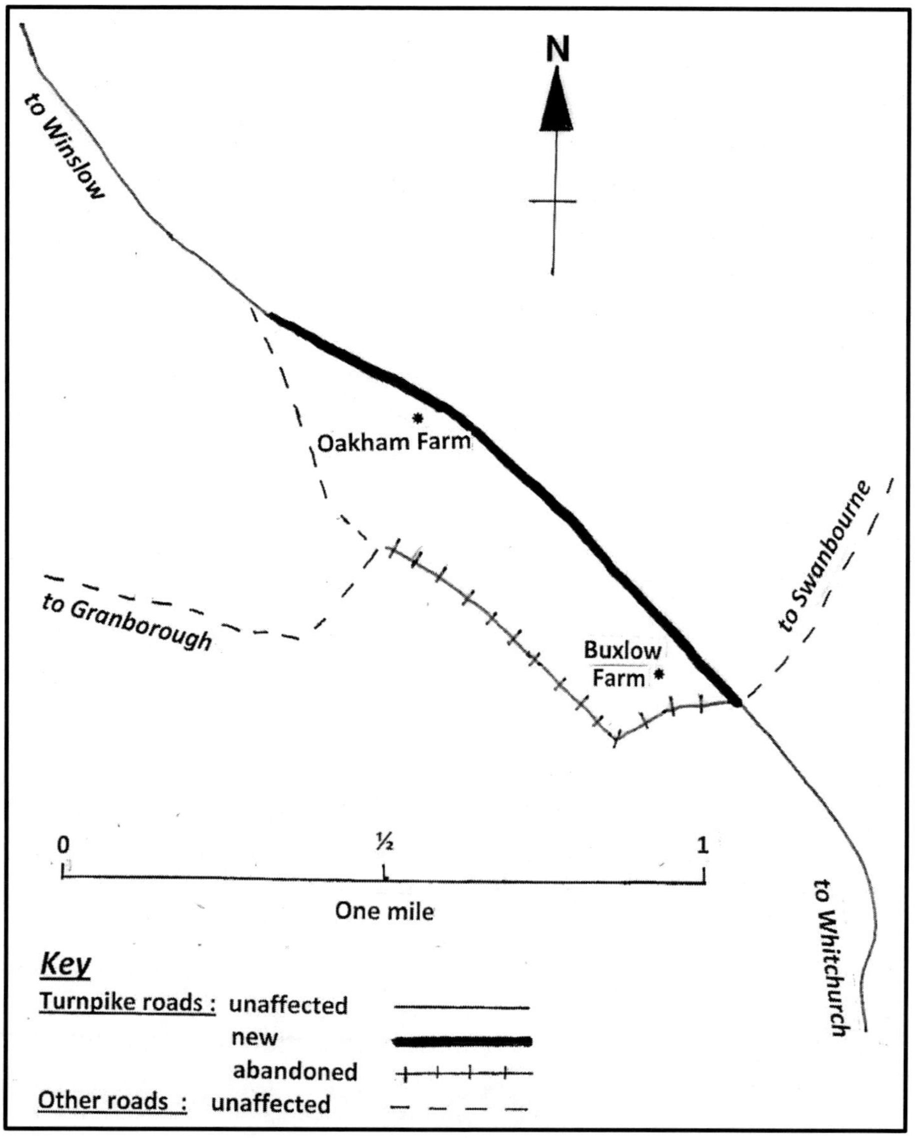

WINJSLOW

In 1835 trustees considered three alternative schemes to shorten the road between Shipton Bridge south of Winslow and the north end of the town.[122] One of the rejected routes actually bypassed the whole town centre at a time when very little property demolition would have been needed to do this.

The favoured route, running directly uphill from the bridge to join the south end of Winslow's High Street, would have been on an embankment at its lower end and in cutting as it approached the High Street in order to ease the gradient. It would have cut 300 yards off the journey, but would have caused the demolition of one of Winslow's best-known buildings – the 'Bell Inn' – whose principal rooms stood on the proposed line of road.

However in 1835 the trust was becoming financially committed to improvements at Hardwick Bridge *(see above)* and by 1840 the dawn of the Railway Age turned many road improvement schemes into pipe dreams as investment in roads dried up. This scheme was one of the casualties.

BETWEEN ADDINGTON AND ADSTOCK

The turnpike road crossed a main stream on the parish boundary between Addington and Adstock and a tributary near its junction with Adstock village street. In 1795 the trust built a bridge over the stream on the parish boundary, probably to replace a ford, and at the junction with Adstock village street a small bridge was built at an unknown date beside a ford. For ease of construction the trust placed this bridge at a right angle to the stream, causing the road to make a sharp 'S' bend to cross it, even today.

By 1799, the road between these bridges had been raised above flood level by making a low causeway which is hardly noticeable today. By 1843 the bridge on the parish boundary was out of repair, partly because too much timber had been used in its construction, and at 14ft 9in wide it was too narrow, but whether anything was done about this by the trust was not recorded.

PADBURY VILLAGE

Until 1797 the main road across the north-east end of Padbury village performed a short but steep and curving descent along Lower Way to meet the village's Main Street, then rose equally sharply to resume its previous course. In that year a useful cut-off was built on high ground across the top of the village. Although only 200 yards long, this improvement will have been a boon to the coach and wagon trades.

The significantly-named 'New Inn' stands beside the new road but its frontage is not parallel to the road, which suggests that the inn was already standing when the road was built through its front garden.

PADBURY BRIDGE

Today's northbound traffic on the A413 descends the hill from Padbury village, curves sharply to the right, and continues on a ¾-mile long straight section of road across the flood plain of the Padbury Brook.

Until 1828 this road only went ¼ mile from the bend before turning sharp left immediately to cross the brook on a two-arched bridge built by the trust in 1742 on the site of a medieval structure. The road then headed west to join the road from Aylesbury via East Claydon at its junction (beside Laurel House) with the road from Gawcott. It then headed north to rejoin the future A413 *(see figure 23)*.

As the eighteenth century progressed the crossing of the Padbury Brook on its narrow 1742 bridge and accompanying ford became a hindrance to the growing number of carriages and wagons. This traffic therefore began to leave the turnpike road to go down Padbury's Main Street in order to join the old route from Aylesbury *(see 'Major re-routing' above)* so that it could cross the Padbury Brook on Oxlane Bridge.

So in 1827-28 the trust abandoned the section of road from the 1742 bridge to Laurel House and built just over half a mile of new, straight road on a causeway above the flood waters *(see figure 23)*. This new road[123] crossed the Padbury Brook 170 yards north-west of the previous bridge and therefore required the construction of a new bridge of three stone arches over the brook.

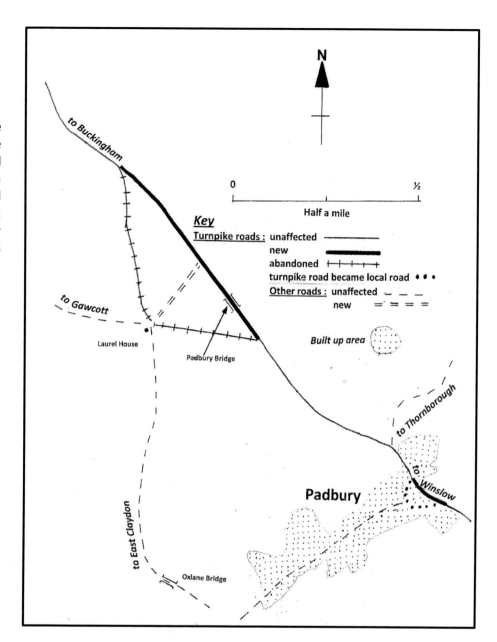

FIGURE 23: **The shortening of the Wendover and Buckingham turnpike road** at Padbury village in 1797 and at Padbury Bridge in 1827-28

This structure is still under the A413 today, albeit heavily disguised by having been widened in concrete on both sides in the twentieth century. The underside of the trust's stone arches can still be seen from the public footpath beside the brook. The former 1742 bridge thus ceased to have a road going over it, so was dismantled in 1832.

LONDON ROAD BRIDGE, BUCKINGHAM

When the trust was established in 1721 its road entered Buckingham along Ford Street and over Sherriff's Bridge, a six-arch stone-built bridge across the River Great Ouse. By the early 1800s this bridge was in poor condition. It was replaced in 1805 by the present London Road Bridge some 80 yards to the north-east with lengths of new approach road, now Bridge Street, adding 130 yards at each end. The new bridge was paid for by the Grenvilles of Stowe, and their coat of arms is displayed on the outside of the east parapet. The old bridge has been replaced by a footbridge beside a ford.

Toll gates and tollhouses

Initially the Wendover and Buckingham Trust had only two gates, at Walton south of Aylesbury and Padbury. A third had been added at Holman's Bridge north of Aylesbury by 1783 and a fourth at Hoggeston in 1865, only 13 years before the trust was wound up.

In the nineteenth century part of the resentment against turnpikes in Aylesbury grew because this trust issued tickets at gates both south and north of the town, at Walton and Holman's Bridge respectively, which did not exempt cross-town travellers from having to pay toll at both gates.

WALTON GATE,
AYLESBURY
1721-1878

Sample annual toll income: £636 in the financial year 1835/36.

This gate initially stood a short distance south of central Aylesbury, on a site just north of the junction of Walton Street with Walton Road *(at grid reference SP 824 131)*. We know nothing of the toll house except that the original was replaced by a new one 'built in a plain and economic fashion' in 1797 at a cost of £197, which also included a new gate and weighing engine.

Due, possibly, to a clerical error, the trust's 1830 Continuation Act banned the use of toll gates on this road within Aylesbury parish.[124] This instantly removed the legal basis for demanding tolls at the trust's two gates in Aylesbury, and the trust reacted at the Walton Gate by suspending the collection of tolls there for a year until an amending Act to legalise it could be 'rushed' through Parliament in 1831.

In 1829 a side bar was placed across Stoke Road at its junction with Wendover Road, about 100 yards south-east of the main gate. This would have needed an extra gatekeeper so it is not surprising that, while waiting for the collection of tolls to be resumed here in 1831, the main gate was moved south-eastwards to join the side bar at the junction of Wendover Road with Stoke Road. The 1797 toll house was demolished in 1832 after the re-siting of the gate.

In 1856 a chain, presumably across Walton Road, had recently been added to the gate's equipment.

The last toll house at Walton, a two-storied building of octagonal ground plan,[125] was designed by William Green of Aylesbury and built in 1831 on what is now a grassed area on the southern side of the junction of Wendover and Stoke Roads. It resembled Green's 1828 design for the trust's toll house at Padbury, and was demolished in 1878.

There is a strong local tradition that the terraced cottage at number 2 Stoke Road was the toll house. This theory ignores the octagonal toll house which was well-documented on the opposite corner of Stoke Road from 1831 to 1878. Furthermore a gatekeeper in the cottage number 2 would have been unable to see approaching traffic in either direction on the Wendover Road. This tradition may have grown from the cottage having been the home of a relief gatekeeper.

The toll takings at Walton Gate grew over the years in line with most gates in the area, and peaked at £1,100 a year in 1821-22 before beginning a slight fall which then plummeted to £580 in 1826-27. The cause of this was the opening of a new route into Aylesbury – the present High Street and part of Tring Road – by the Sparrows Herne Trust *(see Road number 12)*. Before this, traffic on the Sparrows Herne turnpike road, now the A41, had joined Wendover Road just south-east of Walton Gate, so had paid a toll at that gate. After 1827 that traffic bypassed Walton.

HOLMAN'S (OR WOMAN'S) BRIDGE GATE
from between 1766 and 1782 until 1878

Sample annual toll income: £668 in financial year 1835/36.

This gate stood in open country north of Aylesbury at the junction of Buckingham Road with Dunsham Lane *(at grid reference SP 817 144)*. The single-storey toll cottage stood on the highway verge on the east side of Buckingham Road, immediately north of the junction. In 1825 the trustees considered adding an extra floor to the cottage and building a self-contained extension to it "for protection of the toll house". There was no explanation in the trust's minutes as to why this protection was needed, but it may have been to house a relief gatekeeper; there is also no indication that either extension was built.

Due possibly to clerical error, the trust's 1830 Act banned the use of toll gates on its road within Aylesbury parish. The trust reacted by suspending toll collection at its Walton Gate but could not afford to do this at both gates in the parish. Instead, it hastily moved the Holman's Bridge gate over the parish boundary into Weedon parish and erected a 'sentry box' beside it to shelter the gatekeeper, who presumably continued to live in the Holman's Bridge toll house.

The 1830 Act was repealed on 2 August 1831 and, with their gates now legalised, the trustees agreed on 15 August 1831[126] to move Holman's Bridge Gate back to its original position, making the temporary gate possibly the shortest-lived toll gate in Buckinghamshire

In 1836 trustees discussed discontinuing this gate and replacing it with a new one in Hardwick parish, but nothing came of it.

HOGGESTON GATE
1865-1878

No details were found for toll income at this gate on its own.

In 1864 the trustees noted that a significant amount of traffic was using the road between Hoggeston Turn and Shipton Bridge, for which read Whitchurch and Winslow, without paying a toll. A traffic census suggested that the trust was losing about £170 a year in tolls because of this.

A gate was therefore erected at the Swanbourne turn *(at grid reference. SP 796 250)*, just inside Hoggeston parish, and the toll house was designed by William Green of Aylesbury, builder of the final toll houses at Walton and Padbury. This presumably stood on the west side of today's A413 on a triangle of highway land which had become surplus after the road was rerouted in 1826 *(see 'Improvements' above)*. The gate and toll house together cost £83 to build[127] which suggests that the house was single-storey.

The gate came into use in January 1865. This was rather late in the trust's life to focus on an area of toll avoidance that must have been a problem since its inauguration, but this presumably reflects declining revenue from the other gates making it more difficult for the trust to pay its way. The toll house was demolished in 1878 after a very short life.

PADBURY (OR BUCKINGHAM) GATE 1721-1878

Sample annual toll income: £426 in financial year 1835/36.

The two names for this gate were used interchangeably for the same location, which was just within Buckingham parish but nearer to Padbury village. The gate was initially placed immediately north of Laurel House *(at grid reference SP 708 314)*, on a section of road that would later be abandoned by the trust as a highway in 1828 *(see figure 23)*. Its toll house was demolished in 1832.

The replacement gate opened in 1828 and stood 300 yards to the north-east at the T-junction of the realigned turnpike road with the newly-extended road to Gawcott *(at grid reference SP 711 317)*. A side bar, presumably across the turning to Gawcott, had been added by 1824 at the first site and was moved to the new site in 1828, to remain in use there until at least 1859.

The toll house for the 1828 gate *(see figure 11)* stood on the north-west corner of the junction. It was designed by William Green of Aylesbury, had two storeys on an octagonal ground plan, and generally resembled the toll house that he would design for Walton Gate in 1831. It was demolished in 1878 and its site sold for £45 in the following year.

In the darkness of a January evening in 1825 three robbers tied the gatekeeper to his gate and stole the day's takings from the toll house.

Weighing engine

In 1792 trustees agreed that they needed a weighing engine to check for overloaded wagons, and fixed on a site in Winslow at the junction of Sheep Street with the road to Little Horwood at which to erect both the engine and a house for its operator.[125]

Every other weighing engine in Buckinghamshire was built beside a toll gate so that one employee could supervise both. It is therefore no surprise that, without explanation in the trust's minutes, the Winslow site was dropped and an engine erected beside the Walton toll gate in time to be advertised to let in June 1794. After the introduction of the engine the amount for which Walton Gate was let to toll contractors immediately rose by 30 per cent.

Complaints about the accuracy of the engine started quickly, resulting in its replacement by a completely new engine in 1797. This was in use at Walton until 1831, when the year's enforced suspension of toll collecting there gave time for the toll gate to be re-sited within Walton and the weighing equipment moved to Holman's Bridge Gate. The engine continued in use at Holman's Bridge until 1862.

Milestones and mileposts

The setting up of milestones was initiated by the trust's Act of 1742. Jefferys' 1766 map of Buckinghamshire shows a complete sequence of 21 milestones in place from 'London 36' in Aylesbury Road, Wendover, to 'London 56', which is near today's Tesco supermarket in London Road,

Buckingham. Jefferys also recorded a 'London 57' near the junction of London and Bourton Roads in Buckingham. This was in place until 1835 but then vanished, probably because a general re-siting of stones in that year moved the 57th mile northwards into Buckingham town centre, just beyond the end of the trust's control.

Today each of the fifteen surviving milestones stands at an average of 300 yards north of where it was located in 1766. This re-siting was carried out in 1835 to reflect the slight shortening of the route from London through road straightening carried out by trusts further south.

Bearing in mind that consistency in the siting of milestones helped travellers to spot them, it is noticeable that nowadays this trust's stones are not all on the same side of the road. Two-thirds of them are on the western verge but the five on the east are randomly scattered, which may indicate that they were taken away during World War 2 and put back in the wrong places after 1945.

The milestones are square in cross-section, with incised capital lettering. They were set at an angle to the road so that the two lettered faces were visible to approaching travellers. Most have a pyramidal top, and a triangular wedge cut off their back corner. Many trusts carried out wholesale replacement of their mile-markers from time to time, but thWendover and Buckingham made piecemeal replacements when needed, and this has left several non-standard stones.

1878: The Trust wound up

The trust entered the 1820s with a manageable amount of debt, at £900, but then embarked on major road improvements at Swanbourne, Shipton, and Padbury Bridge which increased its borrowing to £5,700 by 1828. Debt remained at this level until 1847, after which the trust began to pay it off at a rate of £100 or £200 each year. This suggests that the trustees expected turnpike trusts to last rather longer than they did!

This road's long-distance traffic was reduced by the opening of the London and Birmingham Railway in 1838, but the new rail line's route had little impact on local road traffic between Wendover and Buckingham. Total toll revenue therefore only fell initially from £1,735 in 1836 to £1,500 in 1843.

Concern about debt levels really seemed to surface only in 1847, but deepened when direct rail competition started in 1850 with the opening of the line from Winslow to Buckingham, after which annual toll income worsened to £1,010 in 1855. Even then tolls rallied to hover in the £1,040 to £1,216 range before peaking at £1,264 in 1865 after the toll gate at Hoggeston had been opened.

Probably the final straw was the 1868 opening of the railway from Aylesbury to Verney Junction near Winslow, which created a through route from Aylesbury to Buckingham, although a change of train was always needed at Verney Junction. The trust applied to be wound up in 1875, but was obliged by Parliament to carry on until 1 November 1878, when closure was allowed under **39/40 Vic. c.39, (1876)**.

Road 6:
The Colnbrook Turnpike Road
1727

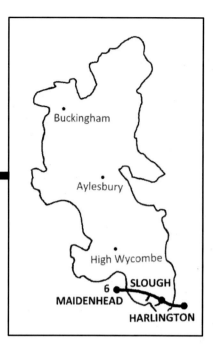

Identifying the road's route

The Colnbrook trust's main route was part of the Bath Road, today the A4, between Harlington in Middlesex and Maidenhead Bridge in Berkshire, except for sections through Slough town centre and the villages of Colnbrook and Longford, which have been bypassed. These bypassed sections of the former turnpike road are now partly C-class and partly unclassified.

The trust also controlled two short branch roads on the south side of its main turnpike road. One left the main road just west of today's M4 junction 5 and went to Datchet. In turnpike days it consisted of Ditton Road and London Road but the building of the M4 in 1962-65 obliterated nearly half of its route and Major's Farm Road, the B470, was built in the 1960s as a replacement. The other branch was from Slough to Eton along what is now the A332 and B3022.

Historic background

The road from London to the port of Bristol has figured in national history for centuries, though its exact route has varied. In the Middle Ages after reaching Maidenhead it forked into several alternative routes to the west. Until the eighteenth century Bath was only reached via turnings off the Bristol road, but with its growth into one of Georgian England's leading health and leisure resorts, the main route to Bristol switched to go through Bath – and became known as the Bath Road.

With the growth of the coaching trade in the eighteenth and nineteenth centuries the Bath Road went on to achieve legendary status. In turnpike days it was one of the most heavily trafficked roads in Buckinghamshire.

The trust's two short branches to Datchet and Eton were used as alternative routes between London and Windsor, although the choice between them ended in 1851 with the demolition of Datchet Bridge over the Thames.[128] In historic times the Datchet route had left the Bath Road at Colnbrook and continued via Horton to Datchet. It was only when the route was turnpiked that the trust upgraded Ditton Road and London Road to form the main route into Datchet.

The limits of the trust's road

The full length of the road from London to Bath was divided between and controlled by thirteen turnpike trusts. The Colnbrook Trust's part of it ran from Cranford Bridge at Harlington in Middlesex, now just east of Heathrow

Airport, to the east end of Maidenhead Bridge. Its Datchet branch, starting as Ditton Road, left the meain road (now A4) just west of the future M4 motorwat junction 5 and ended at the Thames where Datchet High Street met the north end of Datchet Bridge. The Eton branch left the main road in Slough and the trust's control ended at Eton Town End which, curiously, was only half way along Eton High Street and well within the built-up area. An inscribed stone set in a wall next to number 117 High Street, just south of the church, still marks this limit.

In 1841 the trust responded to the opening of the Great Western Railway through Slough by taking control of a short length of minor road, now William Street, between Slough High Street and the GWR station.

Its length and maintenance districts	The trust's portion of the Bath Road was 13½ miles long, of which 10 miles were in pre-1973 Buckinghamshire and 3½ miles in Middlesex. Following the transfer of Slough to Berkshire in the 1973 local government reorganisation only two miles of the trust's main road – at Colnbrook and Taplow – remain in Buckinghamshire. The Datchet and Eton branches were each 1¾ miles long, and both were originally wholly in Buckinghamshire, but now, since 1973, not at all.
	While roads of this length were usually managed as one or two units, the wear and tear by the great volume of traffic on the Bath Road was probably the reason that the trust divided its roads into several districts for the letting of maintenance contracts. Initially there were seven districts, later eight, of which the two branches formed one district each. In the nineteenth century there were several changes in boundaries between the districts.
	To add to the potential confusion the contracts awarded for road maintenance were for districts with different boundaries to those awarded for watering the road. Unlike the other multi-district trust in Buckinghamshire, the Reading and Hatfield, the Colnbrook Trust had only one surveyor to supervise the contractors in all districts, after having had two in 1727, its first year.
Initial Act of Parliament	**13 Geo.I, c.31 (1727)** turnpiked the Colnbrook Trust's section of the Bath Road.
Continuation Acts	**17 Geo.II, c.19 (1743)** continued the trust's powers and **7 Geo.III, c.61 (1767)** brought the branch roads to Datchet and Eton under the trust's control. **36 Geo.III, c.140 (1796)** and **49 Geo.III, c.57 (1809)** continued and enlarged the trust's powers. Then **7 Geo.IV, c.132 (1826)** repealed all the above Acts and replaced them. **4 Vic., c.33 (1841)** added a very short branch road, now William Street in Slough, running from the Bath Road, now High Street, to the new railway station.
Control of the Trust: TRUSTEES	Ninety-four trustees were listed in the trust's first Act of Parliament in 1727, and with well over sixty gentlemen acting as chairman during the trust's life no particular directions of policy emerged from individuals. It is of passing interest that several trustees were on the staff of Eton College, with some trust meetings being held on the school's premises in the nineteenth century.

CLERKS   The trust had eleven clerks during its 153 years of operation. In the latter years William and George Long of Windsor performed the role of Clerk one after the other from at least 1827 until 1872; and for a few years in the 1850s the two shared the job.

SURVEYORS   The trust started work with two surveyors, one for the road in Buckinghamshire and one for Middlesex. However Robert Mitchell, the surveyor for Buckinghamshire, quickly fell into disfavour by employing too many men on the road, some of whom may not have done any work.[129] He was dismissed in 1728 and Matthew Goodwin, the Middlesex surveyor, took over the whole road with an increase in salary from £20 to £25 a year.

The trust continued with one surveyor, but more problems surfaced fifty years later. William Grover was appointed Surveyor in 1773 but had aroused trustees' suspicions by 1779 when it was found that the bills of three contractors had been paid twice, and that some road repair materials delivered to the roadside by contractors had been taken by third parties for their own use. Grover was barred from commissioning any work on the road worth more than forty shillings without the authority of the trust.[130].

Suspicion of Grover rose again in 1782 when it appeared to the trustees "...that the expenses for some time past have exceeded the normal amount to an alarming degree." [131] He was ordered to buy an account book and to produce it at subsequent meetings, but the minute books for these meetings have not survived, so we do not know the outcome.

TREASURERS   One treasurer who inadvertently caused problems for the trust was Steve or 'Stiff' Leadbetter, a builder and architect of Eton. Better known for his work as an architect on Shardeloes House, Amersham, and Langley Park, Wexham, he died in post in 1766 with £772 of the trust's money in his estate. His successor as treasurer, Joseph Benwell of Eton, worked long and hard to recover the money belonging to the trust, only to become one of the victims of the poisoning at Salt Hill in 1773 (see 'Meetings of the Trustees' below).

MEETINGS OF THE TRUSTEES   Some turnpike trusts in Buckinghamshire, such as the Sparrows Herne, only met in one or two inns throughout more than 100 years of operation. In contrast the Colnbrook Trust met in at least thirteen different establishments.

In the 1720s to 1740s the trustees varied their meetings between seven inns in Colnbrook, though more than half were at the 'George Inn'. Then for more than eighty years from the 1750s they met at Salt Hill, at the crossroads of the Bath and Farnham Roads nearly one mile west of Slough. There they used two major coaching inns, the 'Castle Inn' and, between the 1750s and 1800s, the 'Windmill Inn'. The latter, one of the grandest on the Bath Road, was burned down in 1882 but its name survives on the Windmill Care Home, next door to the site of the inn.

'The Castle Inn' achieved notoriety in 1773 when ten turnpike trustees were taken seriously ill after drinking contaminated soup taken during a lunch before their meeting. Five of them died. Curiously, although both the

Treasurer and the Surveyor were among the dead, the minutes of the next trust meeting[132] did not spell out why two new officers were needed – and the trustees continued to meet and dine at 'The Castle' for many more years.

'The Castle Inn' became a private house in about 1840 after coaching traffic had been decimated by the opening of the London to Bristol railway. The house was replaced in the 1930s by a parade of shops opposite the 'Three Tuns' public house.

After the closure of the 'Castle Inn', meetings moved to Eton, first to the 'Christopher Inn' – now the 'Christopher Hotel' – in the High Street in the 1840s, then to the Petty Sessions House in Eton in the 1850s with occasional meetings in Eton College itself, reflecting the fact that several trustees were college masters.

Presumably because the Bath Road was well-established, fairly level, and lacking in sharp bends, the trust undertook few of the major road improvements which required investment decisions. So with a mostly well-managed maintenance regime and steady toll income there were periods in which trustees appeared to take little interest in its running. Attendance at most meetings varied between five and ten trustees, and peaked occasionally at 20-30 when officers or gatekeepers were to be appointed or when the accounts were challenged.

At other times from the 1750s to 1790s meetings were regularly cancelled because insufficient trustees were present. Doubtless because of this the trust's 1796 Act contained a clause banning trustees from voting at the election of officers unless they had attended a trust meeting during the preceding year.

Maintenance of the road

The trust's main preoccupation was with the wear and tear of its roads caused by the sheer weight of traffic. This doubtless explains why reference to its annual maintenance routine was such a noticeable feature in the Colnbrook Trust's minutes, when many other trusts must have had similar routines without dutifully recording them.

The digging, sieving, and delivery of gravel to each of the trust's districts was done by contractors, but the trust had its own team of labourers who used the deposited gravel in routine maintenance and carried out other tasks. Occasionally the labourers were summoned to trust meetings so that trustees could assess their continued suitability.

But equally a few entries in the minute books indicate an interest by the trustees in their workers' welfare. In 1758 Joseph Parfect, a labourer with wife and children, was allowed seven shillings a week until the trustees' next meeting after he was disabled by a fall of gravel, and James Thatcher, labourer, was paid eleven shillings per week in 1782 while he remained ill and unfit to work, 'or until the next meeting'.

WATERING THE ROAD

From probably 1763 the trust hired contractors each year from April to September to sprinkle water from the trust's water carts on to the road and thereby suppress the clouds of dust which rose on dry days as coach and wagon wheels pulverised stones on the road's surface.

At first this was just done in Colnbrook village, but the service soon extended to the whole of the trust's road. For many years water carts were laboriously filled by bucket from streams near the road, even though, at some time between 1767 and 1798, the adjoining trust to the east, the Brentford Trust, began to sink wells and erect roadside pumps.

However it was not until 1827-28 that the Colnbrook Trust's minutes recorded spending £1,357 on sinking wells and purchasing fourteen massive cast-iron water pumps to draw water up above the level of the carts. The pumps were to be spaced at one-mile intervals and the trust owned about twelve water carts.

The contractors who did the watering were required to provide "one strong horse and two able men" per cart to "...keep the said Roads damp so as effectually to prevent all inconvenience from dust to the entire satisfaction of the Surveyor." [133] While the cost of watering varied from month to month according to amounts of rainfall, expenditure on it averaged £88 per month in 1836 and seven labourers were involved in that year.

Remarkably, two pumps survive on the Colnbrook Trust's road at Poyle and Longford. The one at Poyle *(at grid reference TQ 0345 767)*, bears two plaques, the higher of which claims that it was erected in 1754 "by command of " Beau Nash of Bath. Nash, of course, never had any authority over the thirteen trusts which controlled the London to Bath road, and by 1754 his wealth and power in Bath had declined to the point at which it is unlikely that he could even have "persuaded" the trusts along the Bath Road into major expenditure. In contrast, the plaque at the foot of the pump, giving an 1827 date, accords with the entries in the trust's minutes.

Suffering loss of road traffic after the opening of the Great Western main line, the trust decided in 1849 that it could no longer afford to water the Bath Road. However watering continued on the Datchet and Eton branches until at least 1854, possibly because they, or the Eton branch at least, saw an increase in local traffic due to the opening of Slough GWR station.

Improvements to the road:

Because its route along the Thames valley was nearly level and fairly direct in its course, the trust had no hills to ease and only carried out one significant realignment of its main road. The trust's main improvement work was therefore confined to a number of localised road widenings and the rebuilding of bridges.

The A4's most famous new section, the Colnbrook Bypass, was not built until 1929.

REALIGNMENT

In the 1840s at Salt Hill, just west of the village of Slough, a 330-yard length of the Bath Road between Montem Lane and Stoke Poges Lane was moved about 30 yards to the south, apparently to eliminate a sharp bend. The former course of the road now lies just inside the southern edge of Salt Hill Park, but park landscaping has removed all trace of it.

ROAD WIDENING

Beginning in the 1760s the trust widened several short sections of narrow road which were hindering traffic flow. These were at Salt Hill in 1764 and 1822, Longford in 1779-81 and on London Road in Datchet in 1768, 1782, and 1784.

In 1781 a detailed survey of the trust's main road and branches to identify lengths which were still less than the desirable 30 ft wide found ten short sections which were only between 23 and 26ft. wide. This led to the immediate widening of some 150 yards of the Bath Road from Langley Broom towards Slough. It also added another 100 yards to the widening already in progress at Longford.

In 1841, following the opening of the Great Western Railway, the trust demolished buildings on the west side of William Street between the turnpike road at Slough High Street and the railway station to increase road width from 20 ft to 70 feet.

BRIDGE REBUILDING

Because the Bath Road crosses five streams in the course of 4½ miles at Colnbrook, Longford, and Cranford in the low-lying Colne Valley, the trust was heavily engaged during the eighteenth century in making the bridges on this section fit for the rising levels of traffic, usually after trying to get action from those who were actually responsible for carrying out the work. The bridges are listed below from west to east.

Furthest west was *Colnbrook Bridge*, on the Buckinghamshire and Middlesex boundary and within the Colnbrook village. This bridge was rebuilt in 1732 by the trust after a three-year battle to persuade others to do it. In spite of this it was so out of repair only 40 years later that the trust had to demolish and rebuild it again, with greater width and at a cost of £150 in 1777-78.[134]

Next came *Mad Bridge*, over the Wraysbury River west of Longford, where the trust built a new brick bridge in 1764 to the design of architect and builder Stiff Leadbetter, who was the trust's treasurer at the time. The new bridge was on the south side of the old bridge, which was beyond repair.

Moor Bridge, also known as *High Bridge,* crosses the River Colne between Poyle and Longford. Its repair was the responsibility of the owner of Sipson Farm at Harmondsworth in Middlesex, but the farm's lessee refused to do anything. He was indicted in 1777, and in gaol for his refusal in 1778. The matter reached the Court of King's Bench in 1779 but it was another four years before the trust gave in and itself rebuilt Moor Bridge with a £70 contribution from the Sipson Farm lessee.[135]

King's Bridge, over the Duke of Northumberland's River at the east end of Longford village, was maintained at the duke's expense because an ancestor had dug this waterway to carry water to Sion House. The original wooden bridge had been built before the turnpike trust's time, but when the duke replaced this with a stone bridge in 1767 the trust contributed £20 towards the £60 cost in order to widen it to 22 ft.[136] The present attractive cast-iron bridge, dated 1834, looks narrow and is a useful reminder of the width of bridge which was considered adequate at that time.

Furthest east, **Cranford Bridge** over the River Crane was at the junction between the Colnbrook and Brentford Turnpike Trusts. It had formerly been maintained by the Countess of Berkley and the Colnbrook Trust tried in 1764 to persuade her to repair it, but failed. Finally the Brentford Trust rebuilt it in 1776-77, with a modest financial contribution of £29 12s 0d from the Colnbrook Trust.[137] This bridge was rebuilt and widened in 1915.

| PAVING AND LIGHTING THE ROAD | In the eighteenth century the trustees spent what might seem a disproportionate amount of time considering improvements in Colnbrook village until one realises that in turnpike days this was the biggest settlement on their section of the Bath Road. |

In the 1730s they 'paved' the road with cobbles within the village, and this was extensively repaired in 1756 and 1776. In 1770 they put up lamps at 30-yard intervals on both sides of the road in Colnbrook, from end to end of the village. In 1771 "some evil disposed persons" had broken five of these lamps, but that did not deter the trust from adding eight more in 1774.[138]

Toll gates and tollhouses

Interestingly for Buckinghamshire's highest toll earner, the Colnbrook Trust almost certainly had only one tollgate on the Bath Road during its first 122 years, and no side bars for almost its first century. This was in spite of concerns voiced by trustees as early as 1756 about traffic taking to the lanes in summer to avoid the gate.[139]

A second gate on the main road was added at Harlington in 1849 and there <u>may</u> have been a third gate at Salt Hill near Slough for a short time early in the nineteenth century. At the west end of the trust's road its 1727 Act banned the placing of any tollgate across the road within two miles of Maidenhead Bridge.

Although the Datchet and Eton branch roads were turnpiked in 1767 they do not appear to have had gates across them in their first sixty years. Maintenance of the branches was thus paid for by traffic on the Bath Road. The Eton road got a tollgate in 1831 while the inauguration date of the gate on the Datchet branch is uncertain.

COLNBROOK GATE
1727-1871

Sample annual toll income from the trust's three gates at Colnbrook, Datchet and Slough Road together produced £4,028 in 1836. No separate returns for Datchet or Slough Road were recorded until 1842.

This gate was situated just outside Buckinghamshire, east of Colnbrook village at the junction of Bath Road with Poyle Road. The two-storey toll house stood on the north side of the road, on a fenced-off strip of highway verge,[140] facing the 'Bird in Hand' public house. The toll house was eventually demolished in 1962 but the 'Bird in Hand' still stands, now named 'The Punch Bowl'.

Doubtless due to heavy traffic Colnbrook Gate was already open 24 hours a day, and therefore double-manned, by 1764, when the trustees appointed an assistant gatekeeper to work the gate when neither of the principal keepers was available. Night duty was doubtless not popular; in 1771 one gatekeeper was sacked for leaving the turnpike gate open on several nights so that carriages passed through toll-free, and in 1781 another was murdered while on night duty.

References to Colnbrook's gates in the plural in gate-letting adverts between the 1820s and 1860s suggest that a side bar had been added across Poyle Road, presumably with a kiosk to shelter the gatekeeper. While this was clearly in place by 1827, there are hints of its presence as early as 1806.

Harlington Gate, from its opening in 1849, was always let with Colnbrook Gate as one lot. The main effect of the new gate was to halve the toll receipts at Colnbrook.

SALT HILL GATE
possibly 1823-1840
if it existed at all

No records of gate-letting or tolls taken at Salt Hill, just west of Slough, have been found.

This gate was not mentioned in the surviving minutes of the trust, though these end in 1784. However, a plan of part of the 1840s realignment of the Bath Road shows the 'old turnpike road' with a very small building standing in the carriageway on its south side, a few yards east of the junction with Montem Lane. While the building was not identified on the plan, the accompanying schedule described it as a "...messuage ... erected by trustees on south side of old turnpike road." [141]

If this was erected by the trust it is likely to have been a kiosk for a toll gate keeper, but the absence of a written record could mean that it had a very short life or that the plan was never put into operation.

HARLINGTON
CORNER GATE
(MIDDLESEX)
1849-1871

Sample annual toll income: £276 in 1850.

The trust suffered a serious drop in toll revenue after the opening of the Great Western Railway, running parallel to the Bath Road. In an 1849 attempt to revive income the trust placed an additional gate across the road near the eastern extremity of its control, at the junction between the Bath Road and Harlington High Street, with a side bar across the High Street itself.

From the start this gate was let with Colnbrook Gate as one contract, which was just as well because, standing only 3¼ miles from the older gate, the Harlington gate's main effect was to halve the tolls taken at Colnbrook while increasing the cost of toll collection. It is therefore puzzling that this gate remained in use until the trust was wound up.

DATCHET GATE
about 1822-1863

Sample toll income of this gate alone was £210 in 1842. Datchet's income was usually combined with that of Colnbrook Gate.

The Datchet Gate was located near the southern end of the short Datchet branch road. The gate was outside 'The Stag' public house in Datchet village, with a tiny toll house on the village green where the pub sign for 'The Stag' now stands. The "toll house" was little bigger than a kiosk, but was apparently home for many years to the last toll collector, a Mr Green, who had fought at Corunna and Waterloo and was later buried nearby in Datchet churchyard.

This gate might have been erected when the branch road was turnpiked in 1767 but toll income records for it have not been found until 1822. Since the Eton branch was also turnpiked in 1767 and definitely did not have a toll gate until 1831, it would be understandable if the Datchet branch did not have one until 1822.

In 1851 Datchet Bridge over the Thames was demolished and the public road that led from the bridge across Home Park into Windsor was closed. This made the Datchet branch road into a cul-de-sac and, with the loss of its through traffic to Windsor and the opening of the railway to Datchet in 1849, annual toll income was drastically reduced to £92 in 1857. The gate was accordingly removed in 1863.

SLOUGH ROAD GATE
1831-1871

Sample annual toll income of this gate alone was £780 in 1842. Slough Road's income was usually combined with that of Colnbrook Gate.

The Slough Road Gate, also called Eton Gate, stood south of Slough on the Windsor Road, with its toll house on the west side. The site is now totally lost between the M4 bridge and the roundabout for the slip road to the A355.

The opening of this gate in 1831 may have been prompted by a growth of traffic on the road following the Borough of Windsor's rebuilding and enlargement of Windsor Bridge over the Thames in 1824.

The opening of the Great Western Railway between London and Bristol in stages between 1838 and 1841 decimated traffic on the Bath Road. However, as Slough became the railhead for Windsor, the traffic on the Eton branch road increased significantly until two branch railways opened to Windsor in 1849. Toll income then more than halved during the 1850s but the gate was retained until the trust was wound up. The toll house was demolished in 1898.

Weighing engine

There was a weighing engine at Colnbrook Gate from an unknown date after 1740. It was repaired in 1765 and 1773. It seems to have suffered from the unreliability that other trusts recorded with their engines, but this trust persevered in spite of concerns about accuracy recorded in at least 1774 and 1794. The engine survived to be sold for £26 10s 0d when the trust was wound up in 1871.[142]

Milestones and mileposts
ON THE BATH ROAD

Thirteen milestones with a square cross-section and pyramidal top were produced by Thomas Windsor, stonemason of Windsor, for £2 8s 0d each and installed in 1741, with incised lower-case letters and Roman numerals. These showed mileages to Hyde Park Corner rising from 13 at Harlington Corner in Middlesex to 25 at the 'Dumb Bell Inn', nearly half a mile east of Maidenhead Bridge. The stones were originally set square to the road with inscriptions on their front face only.

In 1768, following comments about the stones' legibility, they were lifted, altered and then put back standing at an angle to the road so that mileages were visible to approaching travellers from both sides. During the alterations the stones were turned around and the two new front faces were inscribed with local destinations in capital letters and mileages in Arabic numerals. At the same time a flat recess was cut out of the upper part of the front of the stone to carry the mileage to London – in place of the previous Hyde Park Corner destination.

The original inscription, now on one of the rear faces, was erased on most stones but inexplicably left on four of them. Twelve out of the original thirteen on the Bath Road are still in place, and several have had the lettering on their front faces recut in a 1930s style. They can be seen today on the south side of the A4, except where moved by later road works

ON THE DATCHET AND ETON BRANCH ROADS

The two branch roads had two milestones each, and the one milestone which survives on the Datchet branch at Datchet village green resembles those on the main road.

In contrast, the solitary surviving milestone on the Eton branch road is of simple shape, square in cross-section with a pyramidal top, and "XXII miles from Hyde Park Corner 1817" in lower-case lettering on its front face only. These details suggest that this could be an original Colnbrook Trust milestone which escaped the remodelling undergone by all the others in 1768 when Roman numerals and lower-case lettering were abandoned.

It is set in a low wall bounding Eton College's frontage to the High Street and, if we measure from the nearest milestone on the main road, this stone now stands almost ¼ mile north of its correct place. The 1817 date *may* indicate when it was moved from its original position further south in Eton High Street, but that was at a time when road mileages still mattered and when moving it away from its correct place was unlikely.

Financial matters

Unusually for a turnpike trust, the Colnbrook's mortgage debt was only held by one creditor at a time from 1728 to 1824. The first was Jonathon Rogers, who invested £2,500 in 1728. This debt was down to £2,000 by 1761 and £1,500 in 1771, and was paid off in 1824. The fact that the Colnbrook Trust became debt-free at a time when other trusts were still seeking investment is a further indication that on this road capital works were less important than routine maintenance.

1872: The Trust wound up

The opening of one of Britain's earliest and most successful main-line railways in stages between 1838 and 1841, on a route which shadowed the Bath Road, was disastrous for the trusts maintaining that road. As the coaching age grew to its peak, annual total toll income on the Colnbrook Trust rose from £1,500 in 1804-05 to £2,913 in 1822-23 and £4,028 in 1836, before slumping to £2,562 by 1844. All that saved this from being worse was the spectacular growth of road traffic between Slough station and Windsor, which lasted until Windsor got its own branch railways in 1849.

After that, with total toll revenue down to £793 by 1859, the trust did well to hang on until it was formally wound up in June 1872 under **33/34 Vic. c.73 (1870)**, although it appears to have stopped work in September 1871.

Road 7:
The Buckingham and Hanwell Turnpike Road
1744

Identifying the road's route	Head out of Buckingham on Nelson Street and Tingewick Road to reach the bypass. Then follow the A421 from the end of Buckingham bypass to the Barley Mow roundabout south of Brackley (except for the B-class road through Tingewick village). The turnpike road is then the B4031 onward to Aynho, the B4100 to Adderbury, the A4260 and A361 to the centre of Banbury, and finally Warwick Road and the B4100 thence to Hanwell.
Historic background	The Buckingham to Banbury section of this trust's road was on one of the major historic routes between London and the West Midlands, going via Uxbridge, Aylesbury, Buckingham, Banbury and Stratford-upon-Avon. In contrast, the section north of Banbury, now the B4100, was a minor route to Warwick until taken in hand and upgraded by turnpike trusts.
The limits of the trust's road	The trust's southern end was always at the north corner of Buckingham Town Hall. Its northern end was initially in 1744 at Warmington in Warwickshire, but in 1769 this was moved 2½ miles south to the northern boundary of Hanwell parish, which is on the county boundary of Oxfordshire and Warwickshire. Relinquishing control of the short section of road that was in Warwickshire seems to have been purely for administrative convenience as it reduced the number of county justices that the trust had to deal with from four to three.
Its length and maintenance districts	The trust controlled 20½ miles of road after its road was shortened in 1769, of which 3½ miles from Buckingham to Finmere were in Buckinghamshire, with the rest in Oxfordshire and Northamptonshire.

This was the third longest of the turnpike roads which had a presence in Buckinghamshire; it was only bettered by the Reading and Hatfield and the Sparrows Herne trusts. To deal with this length the road was divided throughout its operating life into an Upper Division, from Buckingham to Aynho, and a Lower Division from Aynho to Hanwell. The two operated almost as independent trusts. |

In 1832 the length of road in the two divisions was made more equal by moving the boundary between them 1½ miles eastward from the 'Red Lion Inn' in Aynho (later the 'Cartwright Arms') to the eastern boundary of Aynho parish. The Lower Division was often called the Weeping Cross Road, after an ancient crossroads of that name at Bodicote, between Adderbury and Banbury.

Initial Act of Parliament	**17 Geo.II, c.43 (1744)** turnpiked the road from Buckingham to Warmington in Warwickshire, some six miles north-west of Banbury.
Continuation Acts	**9 Geo.III, c.52 (1769)** shortened the trust's road by some 2½ miles by withdrawing its northern end southwards from Warmington to the Hanwell parish boundary. Subsequent Acts which continued the trust were **32 Geo.III, c.134 (1792), 51 Geo.III, c.2 (1811), 2 Will.IV, c.34 (1831/32), 31/32 Vic., c.99 (1867/68)**.
Control of the Trust: TRUSTEES	No details have been found for chairmen of either division of the trust in the eighteenth century, or of its Upper Division in the nineteenth. Reverend Charles F Wyatt of Broughton, near Banbury, dominated the chairing of the Lower Division from 1836 until the trust was wound up in 1871.
CLERKS	The Upper Division was administered by Buckingham solicitors, with Robert Miller in post from at least 1782 until about 1818, followed by Thomas Hearn until the 1840s, then George Nelson.
	For more than eighty years from at least 1771 the clerkship for the Lower Division was dominated by the solicitor Richard Bignell and his son – and possibly grandson – of the same name. Benjamin Aplin, a Banbury solicitor, joined Bignell junior in 1842 and became the Lower Division's sole clerk from 1856 until the trust was wound up. Rather unusually for turnpike trust clerks the Bignells' addresses were seldom on the trust's road and moved several times, starting in Banbury and continuing to Middleton Stoney, Bicester, Thame, Hayes in Middlesex, and finally back to Banbury.
MEETINGS OF THE TRUSTEES	The trustees of the Upper Division met mainly at the 'Cobham Arms' at Buckingham, with well-spaced meetings in the 'White Hart' in the same town. The Lower Division met in the 'Red Lion' or 'Three Tuns' in Banbury until the 1790s, after which they usually met in Banbury Town Hall.
Improvements to the road	East of Aynho the trust's road was relatively level and direct, so there was little need for major improvement in its Upper Division. In contrast the Lower Division included the crossing of the Cherwell valley and it was here that the trust's only significant road improvements were concentrated.
AT CROUGHTON VILLAGE, NORTHAMPTONSHIRE	When the trust took over the road in 1744 the main route through Croughton village appears to have been immediately south of the church on what is now Church Lane, although it is not clear how the road linked with the present alignment west of the church. At an unknown date before the Ordnance

Survey mapped the village in 1833 the turnpike road was re-routed to pass north of the church along the present High Street.

Aynho was at the junction of the turnpike road to Banbury, which crossed the village in Hollow Way, and the route to Deddington and Chipping Norton which had been turnpiked in 1770 and which descended Roundtown to leave on what is now Station Road.

In around 1827 the Buckingham and Hanwell Trust upgraded a 100-yard link between Roundtown and the bottom of Hollow Way, changing this from a peripheral village lane to become the main turnpike road. This enabled Banbury traffic to abandon the unsuitably narrow Hollow Way and skirt the village on Roundtown instead.

In 1825-27 the trust spent £32 13s 6d[143] on easing the gradient at the top of the hill on Banbury Road down from the village into the Cherwell valley. Today this shows as a 3ft deep 'hollow way' at the upper end of the long, smooth, twentieth-century embankment down towards the crossing of the M40 motorway.

FIGURE 24:
Changes in road layout
at East Adderbury in 1744
and 1766-68.

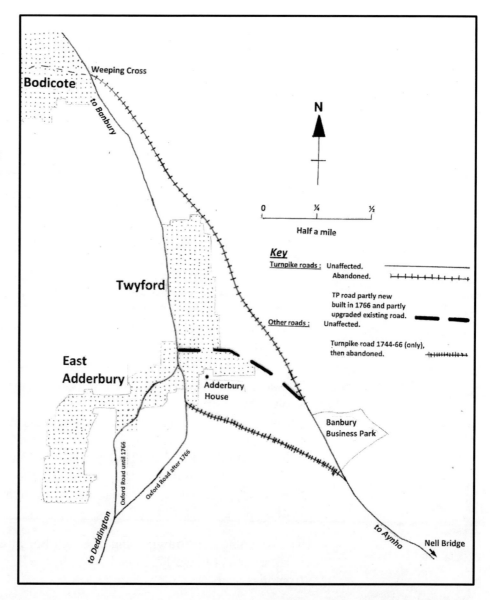

FROM AYNHO TO WEEPING CROSS (OXFORDSHIRE)

In the Middle Ages this route ran from Aynho to Banbury via Kings Sutton and crossed Twyford Bridge over the Cherwell before joining the road from Oxford at Weeping Cross, on the eastern edge of Bodicote village.[144]

During the sixteenth and seventeenth centuries traffic gradually moved its crossing of the Cherwell southwards from Twyford Bridge to Nell Bridge, north-west of Aynho. From there the newly-preferred road struck north-westwards, bypassing East Adderbury and Twyford and slowly converging on the road from Oxford, which it joined at Weeping Cross *(at grid reference SP 466 377).*[145]

When the turnpike trust was formed in 1744 it ignored this 'Adderbury bypass' and adopted a minor turning off it, starting from what is now the south end of the Banbury Business Park. From there the turnpike road headed west, passing south of Adderbury House, to join the Oxford road immediately south of East Adderbury village.

The open fields of Adderbury were enclosed in 1766-68. At such times the normal procedure was for the enclosure commissioners to avoid making alterations to any turnpike road which crossed the parish because that road was already managed under an Act of Parliament. Unusually, however, the Adderbury Enclosure Act[146] empowered the enclosure and turnpike commissioners to work together to stop up ¾ mile of the turnpike road between the modern B4100 at what is now the south end of Banbury Business Park and its junction with the road from Oxford, 200 yards south of the village green.

This abandoned road, which has left no trace, was replaced by one mile of what is now the B4100 skirting the north side of East Adderbury to join the Oxford road at today's traffic lights at a point that was then the north end of the village. This mile was partly new road and partly an existing minor one which was straightened and widened to 60ft. Although this diversion was carried out under an agricultural enclosure Act, it appears to have been done mainly to clear the way for the southward expansion of the parkland of Adderbury House!

With the turnpike road now fixed on its new course, the enclosure commissioners took the opportunity in 1768 to stop up the old main road which had bypassed East Adderbury heading for Weeping Cross. Today its route is not even a footpath.

OXFORD ROAD, BANBURY

The northbound descent into central Banbury, now called Oxford Road but known as Easington Hill in turnpike days, steepened as it approached Banbury Cross. In 1831-40 the gradient on this steeper section was eased by the trust in several stages by lowering 170 yards of the carriageway (now between Old Parr Road and Bloxham Road). This left its single pavement at the original level of the road, up to six feet above the present carriageway. On the opposite side of the road the work created a somewhat irregular cutting side up to 20 ft deep.

The widening and straightening of South Bar Street, at the foot of the hill, was carried out in the 1820s and 1830s by the Banbury Paving and Lighting Commissioners.

WARWICK ROAD, BANBURY	Also in the 1830s – probably 1832-33 – the trust smoothed the gradient of the climb north-westwards out of central Banbury in Neithrop Lane, which is now called Warwick Road. This was done by lowering a 400-yard length of road between Neithrop Avenue and Ruscote Avenue so that today front gardens on this section are up to six feet above the carriageway on the north side and three feet on the south.
Toll gates and tollhouses	The trust started work with one toll gate in each division – at Dropshort in the Upper Division and Weeping Cross in the Lower. The Upper Division gained one more gate by 1775 but saw no fewer than three re-sitings of its two gates between 1803 and about 1822. The Lower Division saw Weeping Cross Gate replaced by Adderbury Gate and Twyford Lane Side Bar between 1794 and 1821, and gained an extra gate at Neithrop early in the nineteenth century.
DROPSHORT GATE 1744 to about 1803	*No toll income has been found for this gate on its own; £361 was taken at Dropshort and Finmere Warren Gates together in 1792.* Dropshort Gate (sometimes called Radclive Gate) was located on a hilltop one mile west of Buckingham at what is now a roundabout with side roads from Gawcott and Radclive. The gate was probably put here because, while the trust would have wanted a site as close as possible to the town, its 1744 Act placated townspeople by prohibiting the placing of any toll gates between Buckingham and Dropshort. The gate's unusual name came from Dropshort Close or Ground, which was the field on the south-east corner of the junction. Dropshort Gate was re-sited just over one mile further west to Tingewick in about 1803, possibly because traffic from London to the West Midlands had been avoiding the original gate by taking a short cut between Padbury and Tingewick via Gawcott. Today there is no trace of the site of the toll house.
TINGEWICK GATE from about 1803 to 1871	*Sample annual toll income of this gate alone: £320 in 1836. Tingewick and Astwick Gates together made £502 in financial year 1821/22, while Tingewick and Croughton Gates together made £525 in financial year 1824/25.* This gate stood at the east end of Tingewick village at the turnpike road's junction with the minor road to Gawcott. Its toll cottage and garden stood on the highway verge on the south side of the turnpike road, immediately west of the Gawcott turning. Although the cottage was on highway land it appears to have continued in use as a private house for several years after the trust was wound up, and was probably demolished early in the twentieth century.
FINMERE GATE (OXFORDSHIRE) from around 1775 to between 1794 and 1804	Finmere, Astwick and Croughton Gates represent three successive sites for the same gate as it was moved westwards in search of the most remunerative location. *No toll income was found for Finmere gate on its own. In 1792 Finmere and Dropshort together produced till income of £361.*

This gate was first placed less than ¼ mile west of Warren Farm and a mile west of Finmere village – hence its usual title of Finmere Warren Gate. No details of the toll house have been found, and the single-storey Mixbury Lodge at the crossroads *(at grid reference SP 612 331)* half a mile west of Warren Farm was probably a lodge to Shelswell Park and definitely not the toll cottage.

ASTWICK GATE, NORTHAMPTONSHIRE from between 1794 and 1804 to about 1823	*No toll income has been found for this gate on its own. However Astwick and Tingewick Gates together recived toll income of £502 in 1821/22.* Astwick Gate stood about one mile east of Croughton *(at grid reference SP 564 334)* on the S-bend which is now on the north side of RAF Croughton. A substantial late-Victorian dwelling now stands behind the cleared site of the toll house.
CROUGHTON GATE, NORTHAMPTONSHIRE from about 1823 until 1871	*Sample annual toll income: £170 in 1836.* The final move for this wandering gate brought it to the west end of Croughton village, at the junction with the lane to Charlton. In this third location it was confusingly sometimes called Aynho Gate. One's eye is caught by 'Tollgate House' at number 5 Blenheim nearby, but this stands about 50 yards east of the gate site shown on contemporary maps and ignores the record that this toll house was demolished and its materials sold in 1871.[147]
ADDERBURY GATE (OXFORDSHIRE) from between 1795 and 1818 until 1871	*Sample annual toll income for Adderbury Gate and Twyford Lane Side Bar together was £817 in 1829/30.* Adderbury Gate stood at what is now the middle of the village, at the junction of the roads that are today the B4100 and A4260, with gates across both roads. Adderbury Gate replaced the Weeping Cross gate *(see below)* and had been in existence long enough by 1829 for its toll house to need replacement. The new building cost £122 16s 7d and was demolished when the trust was wound up in 1871.
TWYFORD LANE SIDE BAR (OXFORDSHIRE) from between 1795 and 1818 until 1871	*Records of toll income were merged with those from Adderbury Gate.* This side bar was located half a mile north of Adderbury Gate, at the junction with Twyford Lane, now Twyford Road. Its toll cottage stood on the north-east corner of the junction. The so-called Twyford Lane Gate was too close to Adderbury Gate to have any function on the main road so, although not described by the trust as a side bar, it must be assumed to have been only across Twyford Lane, to catch traffic from Kings Sutton which would bypass Adderbury Gate. This side bar was always let with Adderbury Gate, so the surviving records of the two are merged. Although no opening date has been found, it presumably came into use at the same time as or shortly after Adderbury Gate, with the pair forming a joint replacement for Weeping Cross Gate. The toll house and bar were auctioned in 1871.

WEEPING CROSS GATE (OXFORDSHIRE) from 1744 until between 1795 and 1818	*Sample annual toll income: £380 in 1792/93. This was initially the trust's only gate on its Lower Division.* The trust's 1744 Act prohibited the erecting of any toll gate between Banbury and Weeping Cross, so this was erected on the east side of Bodicote village *(at grid reference SP 467 377).* Weeping Cross Gate was in use until replaced by gates further south at Twyford Lane and Adderbury. Weeping Cross was once the intersection of the Oxford to the West Midlands road with a major east-west track. Today it is reduced to a minor junction. There is no trace of the site of the toll cottage, but the name Weeping Cross is perpetuated in the name of the minor road from there to Bodicote church.
NEITHROP GATE (OXFORDSHIRE) from before 1819 until 1871	*Sample annual toll income: £190 in 1829/30.* Neithrop Gate stood on Warwick Road between the present Neithrop Avenue and Orchard Way, in what are now the north-western suburbs of Banbury. Details of some of its lettings after 1819 have survived but it would be surprising if this gate did not come into operation earlier, because it would have been tapping local traffic to and from Banbury which would not pass through any other of the trust's gates.
Weighing engine	No evidence has been found that this trust ever used a weighing engine.
Milestones and mileposts	As befits part of a route from London to the West Midlands the mileages on this road continued the sequence on the Wendover and Buckingham Trust's road. The first originally showed 58 miles from London on a milestone just west of Buckingham, and this rose to 78 from London at Hanwell. In 1791 another trust turnpiked a route between Bicester and Aynho which was more than four miles less than the Buckingham and Hanwell trust's route using Aylesbury to Aynho via Buckingham. To reflect this change the milestones west of the junction between the two routes at Aynho were replaced by new ones showing the reduced mileage via Bicester. North-west bound travellers who continued to go via Buckingham would thus pass a 'London 68' milestone as they approached Aynho and a 'London 63' as they left it! None of the trust's milestones have survived in Northamptonshire, but three each in Buckinghmshire and Oxfordshire are still in place between Buckingham and Mixbury. These have a rectangular cross section and flat top with bevelled edges. They stand square to the road, with incised capital lettering and Arabic numerals on the front face only.
Financial matters	In 1791 the turnpiking of the direct road between Bicester and Aynho by another trust introduced a shorter mileage from Aynho to London and the resulting loss of traffic to this shorter route led to a reduction in toll income between Buckingham and Aynho. The need to tighten up toll collection and reduce expenditure on that section of road may have been behind the three re-sitings of toll gates on its Upper Division between about 1803 and 1822.

1871: The Trust wound up

With the eastern half of its road bypassed by a later and shorter turnpike road the Buckingham and Hanwell Trust was not in good condition to withstand the start of the railway era. Toll income peaked in 1837, then fell slightly until 1845, after which it slumped to less than half of the 1837 total by 1850.

That was the year in which two railways from London, one via Oxford and the other via Bletchley and Buckingham, were opened as far as Banbury. In spite of this the Lower Division was out of debt by 1845 but it took until 1870 before the Upper Division was debt free. After that the trust was quickly wound up on 1 November 1871 under **34/35 Vic. c.115 (1871).** Four toll gates and the materials of three demolished toll houses were auctioned in October of that year.

Road 8:
The Wendover and Oak Lane
Turnpike Road 1751

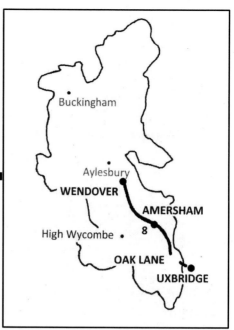

Identifying the road's route

Until the 1960s the route of most of the Wendover and Oak Lane turnpike road was simply the southern part of today's A413, from the north end of eighteenth-century Wendover south to the A40 Oxford Road at Tatling End near Denham. Since then the new bypasses around Wendover, Great Missenden, Amersham, Chalfont St Peter and Tatling End mean that the route of the historic road now weaves on and off the modern A413 as it passes through these settlements.

In addition, for a century the trust had responsibility for the first half mile of the Oxford Road, now the A40, west of the River Colne bridge at Uxbridge, although this was detached from the rest of the trust's road.

Historic background

This was part of a major historic route from London to the West Midlands via Uxbridge, Aylesbury, Buckingham, Banbury and Stratford-upon-Avon. *(See the Background section to Road nnumber 5 above for the relationship between this trust and Wendover and Buckingham Trust.*

The limits of the trust's road

From the junction of Aylesbury Road and Wharf Road in Wendover southwards to a junction with the Oxford Road at the south end of Oak Lane, Tatling End *(see 'Road Improvements – Tatling End' below for more detail of this junction)*.

In addition, Parliament in 1751 had made this trust responsible for the maintenance of the first half mile of the Oxford Road – now the A4020 – westwards from the bridge over the River Colne at Uxbridge. This half mile was across the boggy floor of the Colne Valley and was therefore expensive to maintain. The Parliament of 1751 had thought the Wendover and Oak Lane Trust would be most able to undertake the maintenance needed, even though this piece of road was 2½ miles from the nearest part of the trust's main route.

A hundred years later in 1852 Parliament finally handed the detached half mile to the Red Hill and Beaconsfield Trust, whose road abutted it. A stone boundary marker reading 'Half mile from the River Colne' still stands beside the 'London 16' milestone outside number 82 Oxford Road, Denham, to show where responsibility for maintenance changed from one trust to the other until 1852.

Its length and maintenance districts	From 1751 the trust controlled 17½ miles of road, all of it in Bucks., but this was reduced to 17 miles when it lost control of its half mile of the Oxford Road near Uxbridge in 1852. The trust did not divide its road into separate maintenance districts.
Initial Act of Parliament	**24 Geo.II, c.32 (1751)** turnpiked the road from Wendover to the Oxford Road at Tatling End, and the Oxford Road from Beaconsfield to the River Colne at Uxbridge. The two trusts thus created – the Wendover and Oak Lane, and the Red Hill and Beaconsfield – were to be subsidiaries of the Wendover and Buckingham Trust, but the finances of the three roads were to be kept separate.

Almost as an afterthought towards the end of the 1751 Act, the half mile of the Oxford Road nearest to the bridge over the River Colne at Uxbridge was placed under the control of the Wendover and Oak Lane Trust *(see 'Initial Act of Parliament' in Road number 9 below).* |
| **Continuation Acts** | **17 Geo.III, c.82 (1776)** was the first of the trust's Acts to deal with the road from Wendover to Tatling End plus the first half mile of the Oxford Road west of the River Colne as one independent entity, separate from the Wendover and Buckingham Trust. **52 Geo.III, c.30 (1812)**, and **3 Will.IV, c.12 (1833)** continued and expanded the terms of the 1776 Act.

Then in 1852 **15-16 Vic., c.97 (1852)** transferred the half mile of the Oxford Road immediately west of the River Colne from the Wendover and Oak Lane Trust to the Red Hill and Beaconsfield Trust. |
Control of the Trust: TRUSTEES	In the nineteenth century the chairing of trust meetings was mainly in the hands of various members of the Tyrwhitt Drake family, whose estate was Shardeloes in Amersham parish. However after 1851 William Lowndes of The Bury, Chesham, occasionally took the chair.
CLERKS	In the nineteenth century Thomas Marshall of Amersham was clerk on a salary of £31 10s 0d a year from the 1820s until 1843. Henry Heath of Amersham then held the post for two years before Frederick Charsley, also of Amersham, took over on a reduced salary of £25 a year until 1862. From 1863 George Isaacson, a partner with Charsley in an Amersham law firm, was clerk until 1867, when the trust was wound up.
MEETINGS OF THE TRUSTEES	The trustees met almost exclusively in Old Amersham, dividing their time between the 'Crown' and the 'Griffin Inn'.
Maintenance of the road	Various oblique references suggest that the state of the road went through a bad patch in the 1820s and then recovered. More interesting is the statement in the 'Bucks, Beds & Herts Chronicle' in 1823 that the road was not being watered enough to keep the dust down. This is the only reference that the author has found to this trust doing any road watering at all – unlike the neighbouring Red Hill Trust – and may simply be a reference to a local arrangement that did not affect much of the road's length.

Improvements to the road: GREAT MISSENDEN	The gradient of Aylesbury Road, Great Missenden was eased by the digging of a cutting varying between 5ft and 15ft in depth for about 140 yards immediately north of the junction with Rignall Road. No documentary evidence has been found to date this work, but the retaining wall of rough stone blocks in the lower part of the cutting's west side has the appearance of turnpike work rather than a later county council contract.
LITTLE MISSENDEN BYPASS	This is the third oldest bypass of a town or village to be built in Buckinghamshire, the oldest being the Reading and Hatfield Trust's bypass of Chenies.
	In 1824 the trustees agreed to build a new road to the north of Little Missenden on slightly higher ground to keep above the River Misbourne's occasional floods. The new alignment also avoided the inconvenient corner in the middle of the village. The new road, nearly one mile long, cut 220 yards from the journey between Amersham and Great Missenden. It was built in 1828-29 at a cost of £1,438.[148]
BETWEEN LITTLE MISSENDEN AND OLD AMERSHAM	The medieval road between Little Missenden and Amersham had been diverted 31 years before the Wendover and Oak Lane Trust was formed. Before 1720 the medieval main road ran along the bottom of the valley beside the River Misbourne. In that year nearly 1½ miles of the route was moved roughly 200 yards uphill out of the valley and eastwards to the present line of the modern A413 on the hillside.
	This diversion was made by Montague Garrard Drake so that he could dam the Misbourne, flooding the old road in the valley to create an ornamental lake in front of his house at Shardeloes.
OLD AMERSHAM	The town of Amersham is located on the floor of the Misbourne valley and the turnpike road dropped down into it via a short hill at each end. The gradient of one of these hills was eased at a cost of £241 3s 0d[149] in 1835-36 The record is not clear on which hill was lowered, but the age of the excavated cutting on the north side of the road for 170 yards east of 'The Chequers' public house in London Road West suggests that it was this hill.
CHALFONT ST PETER	Chalfont House – today Chalfont Park – stands just south-east of the village of Chalfont St Peter. The previous house on the site, which stood less than 100 yards from the newly-turnpiked main road,[150] was bought in 1755 by Charles Churchill. He immediately began to build a new house, the present Chalfont Park, close to the north side of the old one and employed 'Capability' Brown to improve and extend the park. Brown made room for the park's expansion by obtaining consent to move nearly ¾ mile of the turnpike road up to 300 yards westward to form the present Lower Road and Amersham Road between Claydon Lane and Marsham Lane.
	The county map by Jefferys, surveyed in 1766, shows the new road complete and the old road still visible within what had become the park, suggesting that the diversion had been carried out very recently. Only the southernmost extremity of the former turnpike road in the park was retained in the new drive to the house. The rest of the old road simply lay under grass in the park

for two centuries – until much of its route was overlaid by that of the dual-carriageway Chalfont St. Peter bypass in 1968.

TATLING END

The junction between the south-eastern end of the Wendover and Oak Lane turnpike road (known here as Oak Lane) and the Oxford Road was at Tatling End. In 1751 when the trust obtained its first Act, this junction was probably in the hamlet of Tatling End, opposite the present Pinstone Way. By 1766[151] a 230-yard length of dead straight new road – the present Old Amersham Road – had been built at the southern extremity of the turnpike road. This moved the junction about 130 yards eastward along the A40, leaving the original route of Oak Lane as a public bridleway in a shallow cutting.

No record has been found of the trust carrying out this work, but since map evidence shows that it had been completed by 1766 the implication must be that this was an early improvement by the trust because such major work is unlikely to have been done by the parish surveyor before the road was turnpiked.

The road layout of 1766 remained until the short pre-1766 bypass was itself bypassed in 1970 by another length of new road, this time a dual carriageway, which moved the junction a further 400 yards to the east.

Toll gates and tollhouses

For most of its life the Wendover and Oak Lane Trust had only two toll gates at any one time. Both were re-sited in 1828 when a solitary side bar was added. However with toll income decreasing during the 1840s and 1860s, three short-lived additional gates were installed at Wendover and Chalfont St Peter in an attempt to boost the trust's revenue. Finally a gate was added at Denham in 1848, only for the section of road on which it stood to be transferred to the Red Hill Trust in 1852.

THE FIRST GREAT MISSENDEN GATE from at least 1766 to 1828

Sample annual toll income: £344 in the financial year 1827/28.

One of the trust's two original gates stood across Aylesbury Road about one mile north-west of Great Missenden village *(at grid reference SP 884 031)*. The toll cottage stood on the west side of the road, probably on the highway verge, nearly opposite the future site of the lodge to Woodlands Park. The gate was replaced in 1828 by a new gate in the village.

THE SECOND GREAT MISSENDEN GATE with HAMPDEN LANE SIDE BAR 1828-1866

No toll income has been found for this gate on its own, but one year's total for this gate and Oak End Gate together was £957 in 1836.

The Great Missenden Gate was re-sited in 1828 to the junction of the present Aylesbury and Rignall Roads at the north end of the village. This was probably prompted by the need to collect tolls from traffic which had been avoiding the original Missenden gate by using the Rignall Road, then called Hampden Lane.

William Lacey was paid £76 18s 6d for erecting the toll cottage, a gate across Aylesbury Road, and a side bar across Hampden Lane in 1827/8.[152] As the two roads leave their junction the present Rignall Road rises while

Aylesbury Road falls in level. The toll cottage was built between the diverging roads on a small off-road site excavated down to the level of the Aylesbury Road, making it between 8ft and 9ft below the level of Rignall Road. This presumably meant that the toll collector had to climb the steep flight of stone steps beside the cottage every time that he was required to open the side bar on the Rignall Road.

At the winding-up of the trust the toll cottage and its garden were sold in 1866 for £75. Today the cottage is one of only two undisputed examples of toll cottages surviving on their original sites in Buckinghamshire; a third has been moved to the Chilterns Open Air Museum.

CHALFONT GATE from at least 1786 to 1828	*Sample annual toll income: approximately £496 in 1827/28.*

Chalfont was the other of the trust's two original gates. It stood nearly half a mile north of the village of Chalfont St Peter at the junction of Gravel Hill with Copthall Lane, with the toll house apparently on the highway verge just south of the junction and its garden on private land behind.

For reasons that are not now obvious the gate was closed in 1828 and replaced by a new one at Oak End in open country south of the village. The gate's last keeper, Oliver Hopkinson, who was earning £4 4s 0d per month, took £41 3s 6d in tolls in the old gate's last month, then moved to take up residence at the new gate on 5 April 1828.[154] Later that year the Reverend William Jones paid £70 to purchase the side garden "late belonging to the now-removed Chalfont Toll House", whereupon the trustees demolished the toll cottage and sold the resulting building materials for £30.[155].

OAK END GATE 1828-1866	*No toll income has been found for this gate on its own, but the year's total for this gate and Great Missenden together was £957 in 1836.*

This gate and toll cottage were built in 1828 at a cost of £102 14s 0d to replace the Chalfont Gate *(see above)*. Indeed the actual toll gate was moved from one site to the other at a cost of £2 in April of that year. The first month's toll takings of £41 1s 6d here were predictably similar to the last takings at the old gate.

The new gate was located about 1¾ miles south of the centre of Chalfont St Peter village, where its site is now beneath the railway viaduct which crosses the Misbourne valley. The Ordnance Survey 25-inch scale map of 1876 shows the toll house still standing on the road's eastern verge with a second garden opposite on the western verge.

Cottage and garden were sold for £68 when the trust was wound up in 1866, and the cottage must have been demolished at the latest by 1904-05 when work to build the viaduct began.

DENHAM GATE 1848-1866	*Sample annual toll income: £361 in 1849.*

The trust's 1751 Act stipulated that no toll gates could be erected between the Tatling End junction of the roads from Beaconsfield and Wendover and the River Colne at New Denham, presumably because this stretch was shared by traffic from both roads. Denham Gate was on this 'forbidden' section, but was authorised by the Wendover and Oak Lane Trust's 1833 Act to raise revenue on the expensive-to-maintain half mile of low-lying road west of the River Colne. But the gate did not start operating until 1848, and the toll house was not erected until 1849 – only three years before this troublesome half mile of road was transferred to the Red Hill Trust *(see Road number 9 below)*.

THREE SHORT-LIVED GATES	Further Gates at **Chalfont St Peter** did not appear until toll income began to fall in 1839 and have left little record.

In 1842 the trustees were considering putting a gate on a site which appears to have been at the north end of the village, possibly at the junction of Gravel Hill and Joiners Lane.[155] It was not mentioned when the trust's other gates were let in 1842, but suddenly appears in the records as one of four gates leased to Thomas Bolton in 1843. In August 1844 the trustees resolved to move 'the toll gate at present standing in the village of Chalfont St Peter' to another unspecified location in the village. The re-sited gate was offered to let in 1845 and 1846, but not mentioned again.

Twenty years later the landlord of the 'Greyhound Inn' in the village centre was unsuccessfully summonsed by the turnpike trustees for allowing travellers to avoid the latest Chalfont St Peter gate, which was at the time located beside the inn. The case before the Beaconsfield Petty Sessions in 1865 suggested that this gate may have been installed in 1863, since when the landlord had been allowing some travellers to go through the inn yard in order to avoid the toll gate.[156] The arch through the building has long since been filled in, but its position parallel to the road is still discernable.

The trustees' problems in collecting tolls in Chalfont St Peter may have been a contributory factor in their decision to wind up the trust in 1866.

The **Wendover Gate** was even more shadowy. It was proposed in 1842 for a site near some old gravel pits ¾ mile south of Wendover village, near the southern end of today's bypass. Wendover Gate was one of four gates leased to Thomas Bolton in 1843, and its first – and possibly only – toll collector presumably had a kiosk for protection because in May 1843 the trustees discussed building a permanent toll house at the new gate. Nothing seems to have resulted from the discussion although this gate was one of four leased to John Temple in January 1845. It was leased again in 1846 – after which there was no mention of it. Perhaps its income did not justify its existence.

Weighing engine	Only one reference to weighing engines has been found in the Wendover and Oak Lane Trust's papers. This is in an 1814 lease of toll gates, but does not give a location. However, the Aylesbury and Hockliffe Trust's papers[157] contain a claim in 1812 by a builder of weighing engines that he had built an engine at 'Mifsonden'. If this was indeed at the Missenden Gate, it presumably did not last for long.

Milestones and mileposts	Milestones ran from 'London 19' south of Oak End at Chalfont St Peter to 'London 35' in South Street, Wendover. Unusually, consecutive stones were placed on alternate sides of the road, and it is possible that the stones were

installed from the two ends towards the middle because two consecutive stones in Amersham are on the same side of the road!

The milestones are square in plan with a pyramidal top. On most there was an inscription on only one face, and this was placed parallel with the road. The incised capital letters give the distance to London on all stones, with the distance to Missenden added to stones north of that village, and with the local parish name recorded on stones south of Great Missenden.

In 1831 the trustees spent £17 17s 0d on re-engraving all seventeen milestones, so the lettering that we see today probably dates from that time. Only the 'London 19' and 'London 22' stones have two engraved faces, the face at the back being dated 1751, which is probably the date on which the stones were first installed. This suggests that the other stones had their original inscription obliterated in 1831. Eleven remain in place today.

1867: The Trust wound up

The Wendover and Oak Lane Trust's traffic levels were unusual because they began to decline before the start of the Railway Age. Total annual toll income peaked at £1,010 in 1829-31 and then dropped to £950 in 1832-35, £877 in 1836, £774 in 1839, and £645 in 1849, followed by a steady fall to £418 in 1860.

Clearly the opening of the London & Birmingham Railway in 1837-38 was too late to be a factor here, and the 1892 arrival of the railway which follows the A413 from Wendover to Amersham came long after the trust had been wound up. The line through Gerrards Cross and Denham was built even later, in 1906.

A more likely explanation lies with the Sparrows Herne Turnpike Trust, which controlled part of the rival route between Aylesbury and London. Its road via Watford – the A41 today – was already two miles shorter than the Wendover and Oak Lane route. Then the Sparrows Herne Trust started a major series of road improvements which were largely completed by 1827 *(see Road number 12)*. As its road became even shorter and easier to use its toll income rose – due, possibly, to a transfer of traffic from the Wendover and Oak Lane route from 1828 onwards.

The trust managed to pay off its last creditors in 1853, and the introduction of short-lived new toll gates between 1843 and 1863 may have caught local traffic which was previously moving toll-free because there was a revival of toll income to £563 a year. in 1863. Nevertheless the trust was no longer in a financial position to maintain a principal trunk road and it became the first in Buckinghamshire to be wound up. This was enacted on 24 December 1866 under **28/29 Vic, c.107 (1865)**. The gates and toll houses were sold in 1866, and the trust's final meeting was held on 22 July1867.

Road 9:
The Red Hill and Beaconsfield Turnpike Road 1751

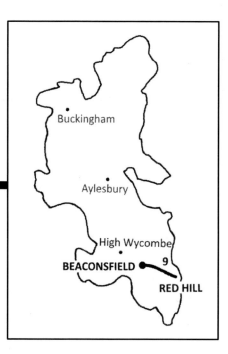

Identifying the road's route

The route of the Red Hill and Beaconsfield turnpike starts on today's A4020 from the edge of Uxbridge to the Denham Roundabout, then follows the A40 London to Oxford road to Beaconsfield. The name Red Hill survives today on a service road, which was originally part of the turnpike road, on the north side of the dual carriageway east of the junction between the A40 and the A413.

Historic background

Although this road is part of the historic highway between London, Oxford and Worcester, most bulky goods going from London to High Wycombe and Oxford until the sixteenth century went on the Thames and were unloaded at various transhipment points – such as Spade Oak or Hedsor near Bourne End for High Wycombe, and Henley for Oxford. During the sixteenth century this trade began to move to the overland route via Uxbridge, Beaconsfield and High Wycombe. The Red Hill and Beaconsfield Trust was formed to improve part of that road.

The limits of the trust's road

The west end of the trust's responsibilities was always in Wycombe End, Beaconsfield old town, at the top of the hill down towards Holtspur.

The road's eastern end was in Oxford Road, New Denham, at a point half a mile west of the River Colne bridge. A reused milestone reading 'Half a mile from the River Colne' still stands beside the 'London 16' milestone outside number 82 Oxford Road, New Denham, to mark the point where the trust's maintenance responsibilities ended.

But during the trust's final years of existence between 1852 and 1867 this eastern end of the trust's responsibility was extended to the bridge over the River Colne on the edge of Uxbridge.

Its length and maintenance districts

The trust's road was 7½ miles long, excluding the above ½ mile from the River Colne. The whole road was in Buckinghamshire.

Throughout its life this trust managed its road as a single operational unit.

Initial Act of Parliament	**24 Geo.II, c.32 (1751)** turnpiked both the Oxford road from the River Colne at Uxbridge to Beaconsfield and the Buckingham road, the future A413, from its junction with the Oxford road at Tatling End to Wendover. These two roads were placed under two separate trusts which started as subsidiaries of the long-established Wendover and Buckingham Trust, but the 1751 Act stipulated that the finances of the three trusts should be kept separate.

The point at which the two roads diverged changed over the years *(see 'Road improvements – Tatling End' in Road number 8 above for the changing location of this junction).*

The 2½ miles heading westward from the River Colne to the fork of the Oxford and Buckingham roads at Tatling End carried heavy traffic and suffered because its first half mile was across the river's flood plain. Drainage ditches 12ft deep had to be expensively maintained to keep the road surface passably dry.

Although not actually stated in the 1751 Act, Parliament presumably decided then that the Wendover and Oak Lane Trust *(Road number 8 above)* would be in a better financial position to maintain this difficult half mile than the Red Hill Trust, and therefore allocated it to the Oak Lane Trust. This decision meant that the Wendover and Oak Lane Trust had a half mile of road separated from its main turnpike road by two miles of the Red Hill Trust turnpike road. This cumbersome arrangement was to last until 1852.

Continuation Acts	**19 Geo.III, c.83 (1779)** ended the Wendover and Buckingham Trust's nominal control of its subsidiary and established the Red Hill and Beaconsfield Trust as an independent body to manage this road. The Red Hill trust was continued without alteration by **46 Geo.III, c.102 (1806)** and **9 Geo.IV, c.6 (1828)**. However **15 Vic., c.97 (1852)** transferred the half mile of road west of the River Colne from the Wendover and Oak Lane Trust to the Red Hill Trust, thereby ending an inconvenient arrangement on a section of road used by both trusts' traffic.

Control of the Trust: TRUSTEES	Chairing of the trust's meetings was shared widely, and the only particularly dominant figure to appear from among the trustees in the nineteenth century was Reverend John Gould, Rector of Beaconsfield, who chaired often between 1845 and 1862.

CLERKS	Henry Allnut of Great Marlow was clerk in the 1790s and 1800s and was a rare example of a clerk whose address was not on the road that he served.

In the trust's latter days the Charsley firm of solicitors from London End, Beaconsfield, held the clerk's post from at least 1820 to 1867.

SURVEYORS	The Red Hill Trust was like the adjoining Beaconsfield and Stokenchurch Trust *(see Road number 4 above)* in engaging a national figure to oversee the maintenance of the road – presumably due to the heavy traffic on the Oxford road. In the 1820s to 1850s the General Surveyor, on a salary of £100 a year, was Sir James McAdam of London, who appointed a local man, John

Miller of Gerrards Cross, as Superintending Surveyor to supervise day-to-day work for £60 a year – which was paid by McAdam.

As traffic levels decreased after the 1840s the trust dispensed with McAdam's services and appointed Thomas Robinson of High Wycombe in 1852 to take sole control as General and Superintending Surveyor until the trust was wound up in 1867.

MEETINGS OF THE TRUSTEES	Almost all of the trust's meetings were held in the 'Saracen's Head Inn' at Beaconsfield or the 'Bull Inn' at Gerrards Cross. The isolated occasions when they met elsewhere were probably when considering major local expenditure – as in 1821 when they met at the 'Hare and Hounds' at Red Hill in Denham while viewing a proposed realignment of the road nearby.

Poor attendance by trustees in later years led to their meetings being reduced to two per year in the early 1850s, in spite of the quorum needed to conduct business being reduced to only three trustees. The situation was summed up in plaintive evidence to a parliamentary committee in 1852 by John Charsley, the clerk: "I have sometimes, at my own expense, taken a horse and gig and gone six or seven miles to fetch a trustee, and have gone in another direction to get a trustee, and have been unsuccessful." [158]

Maintenance of the road

The Red Hill Trust, like the neighbouring Beaconsfield and Stokenchurch, was notable as one of the few in Buckinghamshire which watered their road in summer to keep the dust down. It built a water tank and pump on the edge of Bulstrode Park in Hedgerley parish – and there were presumably others – and employed water carts to sprinkle the road from perhaps the late 1820s until the trust was wound up in 1867.

The range of costs which were recorded for watering by the trust in the 1840s, between £19 and £38 per season, presumably reflected the variability of the weather. On the winding up of the trust the site of the Bulstrode Park water tank was sold back to the Duke of Somerset for £16 10s 0d in 1877.

Improvements to the road

The trust only carried out one major realignment of the road, and this probably dates from 1821 when trustees were considering altering the road at Red Hill in Denham parish *(at grid reference TQ 033 868)*. At the top of Red Hill 200 yards of road – the present eastbound carriageway of the A40 – was lowered into a cutting to ease the gradient up from Denham. The visible effect of this work by the trust has been largely swallowed up by twentieth-century widening. Further down the hill 250 yards of smooth curve replaced a sharp bend on the north side of the road, where the original alignment can still be seen as a holloway in the tree belt uphill from the pylon line.

A local author asserts that the Oxford road was diverted in 1805 to allow the southward extension of Wilton Park, but this is a misreading of the diversion order,[160] which shows that the stopping up of the Beaconsfield to Wilton's Green road enabled the park to be extended across that road to a new boundary *fronting* the undiverted Oxford Road.

Toll gates and tollhouses

The 1751 Act stipulated that no toll gates could be erected between the Tatling End junction of the roads from Beaconsfield and from Wendover and the River Colne at New Denham, presumably because this stretch was shared by traffic from both roads. So for many years, the Red Hill trust's only gate was the Red Hill Gate at Tatling End, immediately on the Beaconsfield side of the junction.

RED HILL GATE 1751-1867

Sample annual toll income : £1,347 in 1836.

This toll gate was in use throughout the trust's life. It was situated at Tatling End, ¾ mile west of the hamlet of Red Hill, with the gate across Oxford Road on the east side of its junction with Fulmer Lane, now called Pinstone Way *(at grid reference TQ 019 872).*

While tolls appear to have been collected initially from a kiosk in the middle of the road,[159] in later years the gatekeeper lived and worked in a brick-built, slate-roofed, single-storied toll house, with side windows in the bay which projected on to the highway verge. This stood on the north side of Oxford Road on the corner of Oak Lane, which was then the turnpike road from Wendover but is today downgraded to a bridleway.

The toll house was sold for private residential use in 1867 and demolished for road widening in 1929. Its site today is partly beneath the pavement and partly in the front garden of a house called Twin Oaks.

DENHAM GATE 1848-1867

Sample annual toll income: £365 in 1850.

Denham Gate was on the first half mile of road west of the River Colne, a section of road controlled from 1779 to 1852 by the Wendover and Oak Lane Trust, and on which the erection of a toll gate had been forbidden by Parliament since 1751. Installation of the gate was authorised by the Oak Lane Trust's 1833 Act, but it was 1848 before that trust installed it, and 1849-50 before it spent £222 2s 4d on building a rather expensive toll house and shed, although the price included the gate which had already been erected.

The Oak Lane Trust got little income from the gate before toll house and gate were transferred to the Red Hill Trust in 1852 at the time when the half mile of road was handed over.

Although this was late in the turnpike era to be adding a new gate, this half mile of road was disproportionately expensive to maintain *(see 'Initial Act of Parliament' above)*, and this was probably a last attempt to increase toll revenue to pay for its maintenance.

The gate was sited in New Denham, immediately south of the Oxford road's junction with Knighton Way Lane *(at grid reference TQ 047 851)*. The toll house and its narrow garden and shed were on the highway verge. Both were sold for £25 for private residential use in 1867 and, strangely, were described as 'freehold toll house' when auctioned in 1919. Both were removed to make way for road-widening in 1931 and today their site is beneath the lay-by in front of numbers 83-93 Oxford Road.

Weighing engine	No record has been found to show that this trust ever had a weighing engine.
Milestones and mileposts	Milestones were in place by 1763 and ran from 'London 16' in Oxford Road, New Denham, to 'London 23' in London Road, Beaconsfield, just east of the town centre. They were placed on the north side of the road – though one at Denham has subsequently moved to the south side – and were square in cross-section, with a pyramidal top rising to a small flat summit. They were set with one face parallel to the road and had incised lower-case lettering on two or three faces which gave distances to London, Uxbridge, Beaconsfield, Wycombe and Oxford. All but one of the eight still survive.
	The stone marking 'Half a mile from the River Colne' *(see 'Limits of Road' above)* is a reused milestone with part of its barely legible former inscription on the upper half of its reverse side. It stands close to the 'London 16' milestone outside number 82 Oxford Road, New Denham.
1867: The Trust wound up	The opening of the Great Western Railway precipitated a major fall in traffic, and therefore tolls, on the Oxford road. The start of rail services from London to Maidenhead in 1838, and on towards Swindon in 1840, prompted many stage coaches to switch from working the Oxford road to acting as feeder services to the new rail stations. As a result the Red Hill Trust's toll income fell from £1,361 a year in 1838 to £889 in 1841.
	The opening of rail branches to Oxford in 1844 and High Wycombe in 1854 hit directly at what traffic was left on the Oxford road and further reduced toll income to £771 a year in 1845 and £535 a year in 1857.
	The Red Hill Trust had been debt-free since the early 1840s so had a little padding with which to weather the beginning of the storm. It even contemplated reducing tolls in 1852 and 1856. However once it became obvious that road travel was not going to recover in the foreseeable future, the Red Hill trust, along with the adjoining Beaconsfield and Stokenchurch, was among the first in Buckinghamshire to apply to abandon its responsibilities.
	The Red Hill Trust ended its work on 1 November 1867 under **30/31 Vic. c.121 (1867)**, the same Act that authorised the winding up of the Beaconsfield and Stokenchurch Trust.

Road 10:
The Bedford and Newport Pagnell Turnpike Road 1754

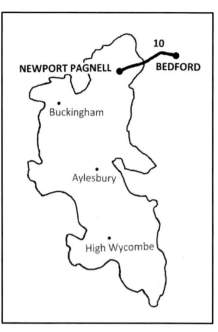

Identifying the road's route

The turnpike route follows today's A428 from central Bedford to Biddenham, then a C class road through Bromham, before taking the A422 from the west end of Bromham bypass to the roundabout on top of Chicheley Hill – but ignoring the Stagsden and Astwood bypasses. Finally the route follows a C class road, Chicheley Hill, until it ends at the junction with the road from Olney 300 yards east of Sherington Bridge.

Historic background

As a continuation of the Buckingham and Newport Pagnell Trust's road from Buckingham *(see Road number 22)*, this was part of a cross-country route between Oxford and Cambridge which was already well-known in the seventeenth century. Indeed its two crossings of the River Great Ouse at Bromham, near Bedford, and Sherington, near Newport Pagnell were important enough to have had bridges approached by causeways by the thirteenth century.

However with the growth of wheeled traffic in the seventeenth and eighteenth centuries, a miry 1½ miles between Hardmead and Chicheley, where the road closely follows the Chicheley Brook, had become notoriously difficult to use in winter. This appears to have led long-distance traffic to desert this route during the turnpike era in favour of the easier parallel route to the south via Aylesbury and Leighton Buzzard *(see Road number 21)*.

The history of this route in the turnpike era was thus of a continuous effort by two successive trusts to improve the road and win back traffic lost to the southern route. Under its 1754 Act the first trust made a promising start but by the 1760s had run out of money with its worst section, the floodable 1½ miles between Hardmead and Chicheley, still impassable in wet weather. Consequently traffic – and therefore toll income to pay for the improvements – did not increase. The outcome was that the trust quietly stopped work in or soon after 1773.[161]

The limits of the trust's road

Initially in 1754 this stretched from St Loyes Street in the centre of Bedford to the junction with the Newport Pagnell to Kettering road south of Sherington village and 300 yards east of Sherington Bridge, with a branch from Bromham to Lavendon. By the time that the trust was re-established in 1814 *(see 'Continuation Act' below)* the Bromham to Lavendon branch had been taken over by a separate turnpike trust *(see Road number 16)*, so the new trust only covered the route from Bedford to Sherington.

Its length and maintenance districts	After 1814 the trust controlled 11¼ miles of road, of which the western five miles were in Buckinghamshire and the remainder in Bedfordshire.
	The road appears to have been maintained as a single unit throughout the first and second trusts.
Initial Act of Parliament	**27 Geo.II, c.34 (1754)** turnpiked a pair of roads under one trust. The principal route linked Bedford with Sherington Bridge, for Newport Pagnell via Bromham and Stagsden in Bedfordshire, while a branch on its north side *(see Road number 16)* went from Bromham via Turvey in Bedfordshire to Lavendon, where it connected with the road to Northampton.
	This Bedford and Newport Pagnell trust's road met that of the Kettering and Newport Pagnell Trust some 300 yards east of Sherington Bridge over the Great Ouse. All traffic from the Bedford direction thus had to join the Kettering road and cross the bridge to reach Newport. In view of this the Bedford Trust's 1754 Act required it to contribute half the cost, up to £250, of repairing, rebuilding, or widening the bridge even though it was not on the trust's road.
	Early efforts exhausted the first trust financially in about 1773 and the initial Act was not renewed. Maintenance of the road thereafter reverted to the parishes which had allowed it to get into its poor state in the first place.
Continuation Act	A completely new trust, which was only for the road from Bedford through Stagsden to just short of Sherington Bridge, was formed in 1814 under **54 Geo.III, c.124 (1814)**. There do not appear to have been any subsequent Acts which were specific to this trust.
Control of the Trust: TRUSTEES	The trust's 1754 Act listed 216 initial trustees, including 50 clergymen, and the 1814 Act listed 128, including 23 clergymen. Although there had been a 41-year hiatus since the demise of the previous trust, eleven of the initial trustees listed in the 1814 Act had the same surnames as twelve trustees listed in the 1754 Act, suggesting continuing local family support for the project.
	At least 24 men took turns chairing the second, post-1814 trust's meetings, but only George Peter Livius, sometime Mayor of Bedford, provided any continuity. He chaired at least one meeting each year from 1839 to 1853.
CLERKS	R Finch was clerk of the 1754 trust from 1754 until at least 1757.
	The second, post-1814 trust had a long association with the well-established firm of Pearse, solicitors, in Bedford. Theed Pearse was clerk from 1814 until his death in post in 1847, when he was replaced by his son, another Theed Pearse, and grandson Theed William Pearse, who were joint clerks

until 1857. In that year Theed Pearse junior resigned, leaving Theed William Pearse as sole clerk until 1870.

From at least the 1830s to the 1850s the Pearses were also clerks to the Bedford and Luton, Bedford and Woburn, and Bedford and Great Barford Trusts. This led to a tendency for more than one trust to meet at a particular inn on the same day, with one unfortunate consequence *(for which see 'Surveyors' below)*.

SURVEYORS

An unremarkable history of surveyors to the trust ended in discord with the election of Charles Berril of Bedford as surveyor on 5 February 1856. The four trusts for which the Pearses were clerk were meeting in the same inn on the same day and, although it is not explained in this trust's minutes, two members of another trust managed to vote for Berril as surveyor to the Bedford and Newport Pagnell when not entitled to do so. One of the other candidates complained but the trust refused to revisit the result, and Berril remained surveyor until 1870.

MEETINGS OF THE TRUSTEES

Meetings of the first, 1754 trust varied between the 'Saracen's Head' and 'Swan Inn' at Newport Pagnell, and 'Swan Inn' at Bedford. The second, 1814 trust, with its officers based overwhelmingly in Bedford, met almost exclusively in the 'Swan Inn' in Bedford.

Maintenance of the road

Intermittently through its cash-strapped life the trust tried to reduce its maintenance budget. Although Sherington Bridge was just beyond the western end of the trust's road, most of the trust's traffic continued over it and the 1754 Act required the trust to contribute to the cost of the bridge's maintenance, which was mainly the responsibility of the Kettering and Newport Pagnell Trust.

After the new Bedford and Newport trust had been established in 1814 it therefore joined the Kettering trustees in 1815 to successfully persuade the county to take over responsibility for this bridge. In 1844 the trust convinced the county that it should also repair a decayed bridge over a brook between Bromham and Stagsden, and in 1850 the surveyor was instructed not to repair a road within Bedford town in the hope that the borough would deal with it.

The major exception to this pattern of reducing the trust's liabilities was the extensive rebuilding of the long medieval bridge over the Great Ouse and its flood meadows at Bromham in 1814-15. This produced the 26-arched structure and dead straight eastern approach causeway that we see today.

After the trust was wound up, Bromham Bridge was widened to its present 18ft width in 1902-03, but this, plus the absence of a pavement, became a major postwar constriction on the A422-A428 route and a prime reason for the bypassing of the village *(see below)*.

Improvements to the road

With £2200 invested, half of this by the Duke of Bedford, the first trust made a good start during the 1750s in levelling and improving the surface of its road. By 1765 the main Bedford to Sherington section had been upgraded except for three lengths, totalling two miles, between Bromham Bridge and Stagsden which needed to be widened, and the notoriously wet Chicheley Washes, 1½ miles between Hardmead and Chicheley with the worst half mile of road at Swans River. The latter was impassable at times of flood because the road lay in a shallow trench beside the Chicheley Brook, which had to be forded twice.

By 1766 the money invested in the trust had run out and low toll takings – for example £173 a year in 1764-65 – were not enough to complete the improvements.

In 1766 fresh financial support came from the Duke of Bedford and several Bedford residents, but either the promised money was not fully subscribed, or the scale of the task had been underestimated. Although work continued until at least 1769, the worst sections do not seem to have been tackled and the trust appears to have gone quietly out of business in or soon after 1773.

Reawakening came in 1813 and the plans submitted with the second trust's application for an Act of Parliament showed a renewed intention to deal with the road's deficiencies. This time the work was done, with a 220-yard straightening of the road at the east end of Bromham Bridge and the construction of short sections of new road, on higher ground close to the old, in the short distance between Astwood and Hardmead.

A little further west, Hardmead and Chicheley Bridges were built to replace fords through the Chicheley Brook and some 500 yards of new road was built on slightly higher ground close on the north side of the old road at Brandon's Wood, where the invisible route of the old road is now under a narrow belt of trees.

Since the start of development in Milton Keynes in the 1970s, the A422 has become a major traffic artery. To cope with this bypasses have been built for Newport Pagnell, Astwood, Stagsden, and Bromham and several sharp bends have been cut out. This work has left the western ¾ mile of the trust's road with its turnpike-road character but east of the Newport bypass roundabout the unimproved historic route of the turnpike road is difficult to appreciate today as it survives only as a series of disconnected sections through villages and as lay-bys on the stretches in between.

Toll gates and tollhouses

The 1754 trust probably had three toll gates, only one of which may have been continued by the 1814 trust. This had two main gates throughout its life and added three side bars between 1823 and 1854 as pressure for income grew.

BROMHAM GATE (BEDFORDSHIRE) 1754-1770s

Sample annual toll income: £103 in 1764/65.

Authorised by the trust's 1754 Act, this gate stood at the corner of Swan Green just north of the 'Swan Inn' in Bromham village. It was placed across Stagsden Road at its junction with Box End Road, and was presumably in use until the first trust failed in the early 1770s.

The start of the Bromham and Olney Trust in 1790 *(see Road number 16)* revived the need for a gate in the same general location so it seems likely that the Bromham and Olney's 1790 gate was on the site that had been used by the 1754 trust. It may even have used the same toll cottage on the north side of the road.

When the revived Bedford and Newport Trust obtained its Act in 1814, both trusts were barred by Parliament from having toll gates between Bedford and 20 yards west of Peacock's Lane in Bromham, which is now Northampton Road. To comply with this the Bromham and Olney Trust moved its gate from Swan Green to a new location at Bromham Grange, north-east of the village. Today there is no trace of the toll cottage at Swan Green.

WEBB'S LANE, BROMHAM, SIDE BAR 1823-1870

Annual toll income always recorded with that of Stagsden Gate (see below).

The removal of the Bromham and Olney Trust's gate from Swan Green in 1814 *(see above)* seems to have had the unintended consequence of attracting cattle drovers on the Bedford to Rushden turnpike road, the later A6, to avoid tolls at its Clapham Gate by making a lengthy detour via Bromham village. A side bar across the drovers' route was therefore erected in Bromham village in 1823, near Swan Green, to control the south end of Webb's Lane – now Village Road – and deter the drovers.

For many years the trust allowed Bromham villagers to pass through the gate toll-free, but in 1858, with toll income dwindling, the trust ended the residents' exemption.[162] There was a predictably outraged response from the villagers!

STAGSDEN GATE (BEDFORDSHIRE) 1814-1870

Sample annual toll income including Webbs Lane side bar (see above): £190 in 1836/37, and with the addition of Stagsden side bar (see below): £155 in 1851/52.

This toll gate stood just south-west of Bromham village but was confusingly called Stagsden Gate because it was across the Stagsden Road.

The trust's 1814 Act prevented it from erecting toll gates between Bedford and a point 20 yards west of the divergence of the Newport Pagnell and Olney roads at Peacock's Lane, now Northampton Road, in Bromham. The Bedford and Newport Trust's gate at Bromham was thus erected about 170 yards west of the junction of Stagsden Road and Northampton Road. Its single-storey toll cottage was built on the north side of the road and still stands today, doubled in size, as Tollgate Cottage, number 110 Stagsden Road, near Tollgate Close.

KEMPSON GATE (BEDFORDSHIRE) possibly 1764-1770s

Kempson Gate was not mentioned in the trust's 1754 Act and only the sketchiest of references have been found to a gate with this name. It was probably located in Stagsden village, near the church, and was placed across Spring Lane, which came from Kempston, on a site which was later to be used by the second (1814) trust for a side bar from 1849 onwards *(see 'Stagsden Side Bar' below)*. The only toll income found for it was 8s 3½d. in 1764/65,[163] which was so small that it must have been for part of the year – because the toll collector at Kempson Gate was paid £3 18s 0d in that year!

If this gate did stand across Spring Lane it would actually have been a side bar. The few references to it all call it a gate, but 1765 was an early date for side bars so the terminology may not have developed by then.

| STAGSDEN SIDE BAR 1846-1870 | *Annual toll income for this side bar was always recorded together with that of Stagsden Gate and Webbs Lane Side Bar (see above).* |

In 1846 trustees became concerned about an aspect of toll avoidance which was not explained in their minutes but which seems to have been by Bedford to Newport Pagnell traffic diverting via Kempston to avoid the trust's tollgate in Bromham. The solution was to erect a side bar in Stagsden village across Spring Lane at its junction with Bedford Road. Spring Lane once led to Kempston, but today it is cut off by the bypass.

This may have been on the site of the shadowy Kempson Gate *(see above)*. Significantly, in spite of this side bar's formal name as Stagsden Side Bar**,** its gate keeper gave his address as 'Kempston Gate' in 1855 when applying to rent Great Staughton and Riseley Gates on the Great Staughton and Lavendon Trust.[164]

The side bar was probably installed in September 1846, by which time a "covered box or stand" had been provided to protect the toll collector. The spartan nature of the toll collector's accommodation probably explains why the "covered box" was not mentioned in an 1870 valuation of the gate.[165] The inhabitants of Stagsden and Kempston were allowed to pass toll-free through this side gate in return for an annual payment of £2 and £3 per parish respectively. Today the only trace of this site is that, nearby, number 1 High Street is called 'Gate House'.

| ASTWOOD SIDE BAR 1854-1870 | *Toll income for this side bar was always recorded as part of Sherington Gate's income.* |

This side bar was erected in 1854 at the west end of Astwood village across the minor turning of Turvey Road to Astwood Bury – now Dove House – Newton Blossomville and Turvey. Although the trust planned to erect a toll house, the low cost of construction, at £9 19s 1d, and the fact that the first toll collector (William Dunkley) lived in the village, imply that only a shelter was erected. Today the site of the shelter is beneath the western end of the Astwood bypass.

From the start Astwood Side Bar was let as one lot with Sherington Gate *(see below)* and, since the latter's income rose slowly albeit unsteadily after 1854, this suggests that the installation of this bar was worthwhile.

| SHERINGTON GATE at the top of CHICHELEY HILL 1814-1870 | *Sample annual toll income: £100 in 1836-37 for the main gate alone, and £86 in 1855/56 with tolls from Astwood Side Bar included.* |

The new trust formed to run the Bedford and Newport in 1814 installed their Sherington gate on top of Chicheley Hill *(at grid reference*

SP 895 456), where Bedford Road, Sherington, meets Chicheley Hill more than half a mile east of the junction with the Kettering road.

The toll cottage, which stood mainly on private land but with its porch on the highway verge, was in the north-east angle of the junction. It was sold to the adjoining landowner for £38 in 1870 and was still standing in 1882, but its site – now beside an artificial hilltop mound covering a small reservoir – was obliterated by highway works in the 1970s when Bedford Road was widened at the junction.

SHERINGTON GATE at the foot of CHICHELEY HILL 1754-1770s

Sample annual toll income: £69 in 1764-65.

The turnpike roads from Bedford and Kettering to Newport Pagnell converged 300 yards north-east of Sherington Bridge, just over a mile north-east of Newport. In obtaining their initial Acts of Parliament during the same Parliamentary session in 1754 the trusts for these two roads were required to site their toll gates one furlong east and north respectively of the junction of their roads.

The Bedford trust's first Sherington Gate was therefore sited at the foot of Chicheley Hill, some 330 yards east of the junction *(at grid reference SP 889 455)*, but then abandoned when the trust failed in the 1770s.

Weighing engine

For a time the trust operated a weighing machine to identify overweight wagons at its Sherington gate but it is not clear when it was installed. However the minutes do reveal that in 1837 "the weighing machine at Sherington Gate had been put up for sale by auction but was in such a decayed state that there was no bidder."

Milestones and mileposts

The first (1754) trust installed mileposts or stones showing mileage rising from zero just west of Bedford to eleven just east of the junction with the Kettering road near Sherington Bridge. By 1825 the whole sequence had been moved 600 yards west from their original positions, presumably because of a change of the measuring base in Bedford. This is unlikely to have happened in the cash-strapped final years of the 1754 trust, so was probably one of the first acts of the 1814 trust.

While four mileposts survive today on the road's northern verge in Buckinghamshire, there are none in Bedfordshire. The four survivors are of plain steel to the 'Bucks Pressing' standard design that postdates turnpike trusts. Interestingly, two mileposts in the Astwood area were recorded on the Ordnance Survey's 1881 map without any inscriptions and with the note 'Defaced MP'.

Financial matters

With the vicious circle of an inferior road surface and resulting low traffic levels the Bedford and Newport Pagnell trust was one of the poorest toll-earners in Buckinghamshire. The first (1754) trust exhausted its financial reserves and faded away by 1773 without having completed its improvement of its road. Its successor, the 1814 trust, raised only £2,400 in loans out of the £4,000 that it said was needed to bring the road up to an acceptable standard.

In spite of this the 1814 trust succeeded in removing most of the hindrances to travel on its road, but in doing so brought itself into debt by 1815. With a low level of toll income the trust's debt grew to £3,260 by 1843 in addition to £4,401 of unpaid interest. No interest had been paid to investors since 1833.[166]

By 1853 the trust's debt had fallen to £2,600 but with income barely covering running expenses there was no hope of paying interest or of paying off the debt. Accordingly, in that year the creditors for £2,250 agreed to abandon their loans and, in 1857, justices for Bedfordshire and Buckinghamshiire made an order requiring parishes along the road to contribute a total of £95 16s 7d towards the cost of maintaining the road in that year. By 1866 the trust could record itself as debt-free.

1870: The Trust wound up

This was one of the few turnpike trusts in Buckinghamshire that was not directly threatened by a new railway, although the opening of the Oxford to Cambridge line in stages between 1846 and 1862 must have taken away some of its long-distance traffic. However the trust's continually weak position made it unsurprising that this became only the fifth trust in Buckinghamshire to be wound up, which happened on 30 June1870 under **32/33 Vic. c.90 (1869)**.

Road 11:
The Kettering and Newport Pagnell Turnpike Road 1754

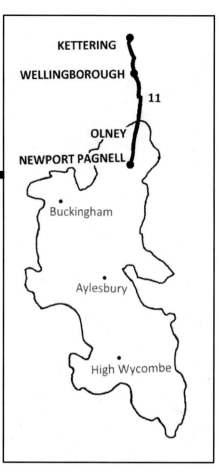

Identifying the road's route

Between Kettering and Olney the old turnpike road is basically the A509, except where it becomes the A5193 through Wellingborough. Heading south from Olney the former turnpike road starts as the A509 but then diverges to pass through Sherington as a C-class road to its junction with the B526 just north of Newport Pagnell.

In detail, however, more than a third of the historic turnpike route was bypassed in the late twentieth century *(see 'Improvements to the Road', below)*, leaving isolated sections of the former turnpike road as local roads through villages and laybys.

Historic background

The Kettering road developed during the eighteenth century as a northward continuation of the Hockliffe and Woburn Trust's road, which ends at Newport Pagnell *(see Road number 2)*, one of a pair of additional routes linking London and the East Midlands *(Road number 3 was the other)*. As traffic grew, these secondary routes became main roads filling the gap between the future A5 and A6.

The limits of the trust's road

The trust's northern end was about ¾ mile south of Kettering's town centre, at the point where, as Pytchley Road, it diverged from what was to become the A6 and is now the A6003 Barton Road. Its southern limit was at the junction with the Newport Pagnell to Northampton road, now the B526, just north of Newport's bridges over the Great Ouse.

Three major bridges on the route were not always the trust's responsibility: Olney Bridge, Sherington Bridge which became a County Bridge in 1815, and Long Bridge, just south of Wellingborough, which was certainly a County Bridge by 1837 but it is not clear when it acquired this status.

Its length and maintenance districts

The trust managed 22½ miles of road, making it the fourth longest road controlled by a trust with mileage in Buckinghamshire. The southern eight miles of its road were in Buckinghamshire and the remainder in Northamptonshire.

The road was administered separately in each county until the 1820s, after which it was administered in between one and three units at different times *(see 'Control of the trust – treasurers and surveyors' below).*

Initial Act of Parliament	**27 Geo.II, c.31 (1754)** turnpiked the road from Kettering through Wellingborough and Olney to just north of Newport Pagnell. This Act gave the trust powers to repair, widen or rebuild Sherington Bridge, while the accompanying 1754 Act for the Bedford and Newport Pagnell Trust, whose road joined the Kettering road just east of Sherington Bridge, required that trust to contribute to the maintenance of the bridge.
Continuation Acts	**13 Geo.III, c.87, (1773), 21 Geo.III, c.103 (1781), 42 Geo.III, c.37 (1802), 4 Geo.IV, c.67 (1823),** and **19/20 Vic., c.37 (1856).**
Control of the Trust: TRUSTEES	The trust started work with 210 trustees, but no eighteenth-century chairmen have been identified. In the nineteenth century the Higgins family of Turvey in Bedfordshire chaired the trust intermittently through three generations; John 1804-17, Thomas 1833-62, and William 1861. This family was also active on the Bromham and Olney Trust, whose road passed through Turvey and connected with the Kettering and Newport Pagnell at Olney. From further north Charles Hill of Wellingborough was a frequent chairman between 1814 and 1845.
CLERKS	The trust's first clerk was J Nicholls, who served from 1754 until the 1760s, after which William Bryan of Wellingborough was clerk until 1780. Bryan was followed by a lengthy stint from the Hodson firm of Wellingborough solicitors, starting with John Hodson, who served for 34 years from 1780 to 1814. He was followed until the 1820s by Charles Hodson before Henry Hodson and George Burnham of Wellingborough became joint clerks from 1829 at the latest until at least 1862. By the 1870s George Hodson Burnham of Wellingborough was sole clerk.
TREASURERS	Due to the length of the trust's road it was initially felt advisable to split the responsibilities of the treasurer and surveyor between the section in Buckinghamshire and the section in Northamptonshire. This was not an equal split by mileage but for a long time there were two surveyors for the road in Northamptonshire to make up for this.

In the 1820s growing concern about expenditure led to several attempts to make do with one treasurer and one surveyor. After the first sole treasurer, James Woolley of Wellingborough, died in office in 1834 he was found to owe the trust £747 8s 6½d. To set this in context, the trust's total toll income in that year was £1,139. Woolley's executors found that they were only able to pay back one-third of the amount owed and the trust had no option but to accept. |
| **SURVEYORS** | In the nineteenth century the trust spent a lot of time organising and reorganising its management of the road, starting in the 1820s by replacing its three surveyors – two for Northamptonshire and one for |

Buckinghamshire – with one man. The first sole surveyor, Alexander Rintoul of Wellingborough, was dismissed for incompetence in 1836 and his successor as superintending surveyor was put in charge of three 'working surveyors', each of whom controlled a section of the road. One of the latter soon had to be replaced due to financial irregularities but his replacement was accused of "extravagant expenses" before being discharged as an "inefficient surveyor [who] does not duly attend to the interests of the road." [167]

After a short experiment with contracting out the surveying and road maintenance of the southern end of the road in the 1840s, the trust reversed policy and appointed John Mash, of Pytchley in Northamptonshire as sole surveyor in 1853. A final reversal of policy followed in 1861 when it was agreed that the road was too long for one surveyor. Mash was then restricted to the northern end while John Simco of Sherington was appointed to look after the southern end.

MEETINGS OF THE TRUSTEES

Due doubtless to the 22½-mile length of the trust's road, its first Act stipulated that there should be an annual minimum of one meeting of trustees in Buckinghamshire and two in Northamptonshire. Early Buckinghamshire venues were in Newport Pagnell but presumably to minimise travelling for trustees they were soon moved north to Olney where 'The Bull Inn' became the trust's invariable meeting place.

All meetings in Northamptonshire were held in Wellingborough, using 'The Swan' for much of the eighteenth century, 'The Hind Inn' from the 1790s to 1820s, and the Town Hall thereafter.

Attendance of trustees at these meetings was patchy, with between four and nine trustees making a typical gathering. Several meetings before 1818 were abandoned for lack of a quorum. In the early nineteenth century this level of attendance meant that sometimes gaps of up to two years occurred between meetings.

An exception to this apathy came on 13 October 1857 when, for one meeting, a highly controversial proposal to move some existing tollgates and put up others brought 31 trustees to what sounds like a heated meeting *(see below 'Tollgates – Isham Side Bars, Wellingborough Bridge Gate, and Emberton Side Bar')*. Apart from this isolated event the lack of interest may partially explain why the trust made so few improvements to the alignment of its road.

Maintenance of the road

Overall the trust's maintenance of its road seems to have been low-key but adequate, punctuated by local problems with bridges and difficulties with its surveyors. In 1809 trustees, concerned by the cost of maintenance, sought to contract this work out at a fixed sum per mile – but the bids received would have cost more than the trust was already spending, so the subject was dropped.

A revived concern in 1818 about value for money in maintaining the road again came to nothing. In 1841 the trust did actually contract out the whole surveying and maintenance operation for the road between Newport Pagnell and Olney to John Dudley of North Crawley for £30 per mile per year. In 1846 the contract passed to a farmer, John Leete of Emberton, after which it appears to have been quietly ended.

WELLINGBOROUGH LONG BRIDGE AND LONDON ROAD	Long Bridge, the major structure which carried London Road over the River Nene south of Wellingborough, may have been a county responsibility throughout the turnpike era, and was certainly so by 1837. Nevertheless the trust appears to have been paid to maintain it on the county's behalf.

In 1845, after the opening of Wellingborough's first railway station, at a level crossing over the turnpike road immediately south of Long Bridge, the increase of traffic on London Road quickly led to deterioration in the bridge's condition and increased wear on the trust's road on both sides of the station. For the railway's contributions to road maintenance costs and the trust's attempts to move the toll gate to a location at which it could collect more tolls, *see 'Toll Gates – Wellingborough Bridge Gate' below.*

OLNEY BRIDGE South of the town of Olney stands the 420-yard long bridge and approach causeway across the Great Ouse, its floodplain and Lord Dartmouth's millstream. In 1767 the jury at Aylesbury Quarter Sessions decided that the structure was in great decay and, since responsibility for repairs was uncertain, the county should repair it. After this had been done the bridge was maintained by Olney parish, responsible for 22 arches, Emberton parish, responsible for the southernmost arch, and Lord Dartmouth, responsible for the bridge at the north end over the millstream. So the turnpike trust clearly had no responsibility for the bridge.

Sixty years later an 1828-30 survey[168] found most arches to be decayed and complaints were made that the bridge was dangerous. This time, perhaps because of the scale of the problem, the magistrates appear to have taken it back as a County Bridge in 1830, and in 1831-33 to have replaced the small medieval arches over the river and its flood meadows with the three 40ft arches that we see today, with a 20ft arch on each side. The roadway was widened over the new arches and along the existing causeway. A temporary bridge had to be built alongside while the main bridge was under repair, and this may be the reason why the contractor lost between £1,700 and £2,000 on the job.

Olney Bridge was widened again and refurbished by Buckinghamshire County Council in 1975.

SHERINGTON BRIDGE AND LATHBURY LANE CAUSEWAY This bridge and the causeway leading south-westwards from it cross the River Great Ouse and its flood plain. The bridge stands one mile north of Newport *(at grid reference SP 884 453)*, and has a ¾-mile link called Lathbury Lane to the Newport to Northampton road, today the B526. The north-eastern 350 yards of Lathbury Lane are on a causeway built up to about eight feet above the Great Ouse flood meadows.

Although the bridge and causeway were vested in the Kettering and Newport Trust, the Bedford and Newport Trust, whose road joined the Kettering road a short distance east of the bridge, was obliged by its initial Turnpike Act to contribute to the upkeep of Sherington Bridge. In practice this did not mean much because the Bedford trust was dormant between about 1773 and 1814.

One of the Kettering trust's first actions in 1754-56 was to rebuild Sherington Bridge. Repairs were then carried out in 1774 and the trust obtained further powers in 1802 to repair and widen the bridge. In spite of this, parts of the bridge were again in a ruinous condition by 1814. In 1815 the Kettering and Bedford trusts managed to persuade the county to adopt the bridge, and in 1818 the council rebuilt it.

In 1972 its deck was widened and provided with new parapets in 1972 but the historic structure beneath was retained.

Lathbury Lane causeway was repaired in 1754-55 while the bridge was being rebuilt. The causeway was back in the news again in 1797-98 when several travellers drowned after straying off it during floods. The trust's solution was to erect a post and rail fence on one side of the causeway, but as late as 1864 another man drowned after stepping off it into a flood.

Improvements to the road

There were few major alterations to the route of the road by this turnpike trust.

A quarter-mile long bypass was built between 1827 and 1835 on the west side of **Great Harrowden** village in Northamptonshire. This new road ran south from the crossroads beside the church to the top of Red Hill near the Wellingborough boundary, avoiding an awkward 'dog leg' around the east side of the church and past Wentworth Farm.

In **Wellingborough** the turnpike road forded Swans Pool Brook in the centre of town until the trust spent nearly £400 building a two-arched brick bridge over the water in 1802-03. Today the trust's arches are still visible when viewed from water level but the bridge deck and parapets were replaced in the twentieth century.

The trust replaced the old indirect route of the turnpike road which entered **Wollaston** village in Northamptonshire from the north via Cobb's Lane and left it via High Street. The new road, built possibly in 1812, was a 700- yard bypass called London Road around the south-western side of the village. This was itself bypassed by the modern A509 in the 1970s.

In 1802 the trust attempted to eliminate the half mile of severe bends at **Warrington**, north of Olney, but was frustrated by the opposition of Lord Dartmouth to the purchase of the necessary land. The bends therefore remained until bypassed in the 1970s as part of the improvement of access to the new city of Milton Keynes.

Beyond these works the trust confined itself to bridge rebuildings, short local road widenings, and some lowering of hills. Most noticeable were the easing of gradients on two hills between Great Harrowden and Wellingborough. One can be seen today south of **Great Harrowden,** on what is now the bypassed Wellingborough Road, where 500 yards of the southbound descent from Red Hill was lowered into a cutting by up to 15 ft north and south of the modern turning to Grange Road.

A mile further south is the steep-sided 230-yard cutting on Harrowden Road in **Wellingborough**'s northern suburbs. Here the trust lowered the carriageway by up to 10ft between today's turnings to Roche Way and Sandy Close in order to ease the southbound climb into the town.

The road's fortunes changed completely in the second half of the twentieth century. Emberton was bypassed in the 1960s. Then, with the development of Milton Keynes from the early 1970s, this route underwent major upgrading with bypasses built around Wollaston, Bozeate, Warrington, Sherington and Newport Pagnell, plus lesser realignments at Prospect Place, Emberton, and in Northamptonshiree between Kettering and Wellingborough. As a result some 8 miles of the original 22½-mile historic turnpike route are now disconnected fragments of local road or layby and much of the rest of the road has been widened and gently realigned so that it is now difficult to imagine the character of this road in turnpike days.

Toll gates and tollhouses

The trust had three main toll gates throughout its life, and a fourth which was in place by the 1760s. Two of its main gates were re-sited and five side bars were added, four in the nineteeenth century but one unusually early in 1792, but never more than three were in use at any one time.

The Kettering Gate itself did not belong to the Kettering and Newport Trust, but to a trust responsible for a section of the future A6 road.

PROPOSED SIDE BARS AT ISHAM, NORTHAMPTONSHIRE

The 1857 opening of the Leicester to Bedford railway, which ran parallel to the trust's road between Kettering and Wellingborough, quickly altered traffic flows in the area as each station became a railhead. On 13 October 1857 at a meeting in which a number of changes to toll gate locations was considered,[169] trustees discussed putting side bars across the turnings north and south of Isham to the new stations at Burton Latimer and Finedon. This was because some of the traffic to these stations had begun to use the turnpike road without passing through a toll gate. But the meeting decisively rejected the idea.

GREAT HARROWDEN LANE GATE, NORTHAMPTONSHIRE 1754-1878

Sample annual toll income: £160 in 1835/36.

The village of Great Harrowden lies about two miles north of Wellingborough. This toll gate was originally located south of the village at the top of Red Hill, on what is now a by-passed one-way side road.

In 1834 the trust demolished the original toll house and moved the gate about 200 yards northwards towards the village. The move had little impact on toll income. A new toll house, specified to be similar to the one built by the trust at Sherington in about 1830,[170] incorporated materials recovered from the toll house demolished at the earlier site. It was sold for £10 10s 0d in 1878 when the trust was wound up. Today there is no trace of either site.

WELLINGBOROUGH SIDE BAR
from at least 1792 to 1838

Toll income was always grouped with that from Wellingborough Bridge Gate (see below).

While it is clear from the evidence of advertisements offering to let the tolls at a side bar in Wellingborough that one existed for many years, the author has found only contradictory evidence as to where it stood. The most likely site is one mile north of the town centre where Harrowden Road dips down to Kettering Road Bridge to cross a stream. At the north end of the bridge – where a modern bungalow is intriguingly named Turnpike Cottage – the side bar may have stood across the long-lost turning to a water mill, known for a time as Kilborn's Mill.

Uncertainty is increased by the trust's minute book where a decision on 20 September 1836 referred to the side bar at the <u>south</u> end of Wellingborough. However a fruitless search for a realistic location south of the town suggests that 'south' may have been a clerical error for 'north'.

In 1806 John Sharp, who held the lease of the Wellingborough Bridge gate and side bar, complained that he was losing tolls at the side bar because there was no shelter for the toll collector. The trust thereupon contributed four guineas towards the construction of a shed or building but, without explanation in its minutes, ordered the demolition of the building only three years later in 1809 and recompensed Sharp for his cost in building it.

Again without explanation the trustees' meeting on 20 September 1836 ordered that the side bar be abandoned.[171] Although two years passed before this was actually done, this abandonment had no noticeable impact on tolls collected in Wellingborough.

WELLINGBOROUGH BRIDGE GATE
1754-1878

Sample annual toll income, including that from Wellingborough Side Bar: £580 in 1836/37.

Situated about a mile south of the town centre, this gate stood between the junction of the Newport and Higham Ferrers roads – now A509 and A45 respectively – and Wellingborough or Long Bridge over the River Nene.

In 1845 the London and Birmingham Railway opened its branch through Northampton to Peterborough. It had a level crossing over London Road, south of Wellingborough, and a station nearby. This was also close beside the toll gate, which must have caused complications.

By 1846 the trust's road was experiencing greatly increased wear and tear as travellers and goods headed for the station. At the same time it saw a fall of one-third in its toll income at Wellingborough Bridge Gate because traditional turnpike traffic was reduced, while much of the new traffic going to and from the station from the north was somehow avoiding the toll gate – though the trust's minutes are silent on how this was done.

In 1847, after a threat from the trust to move the toll gate to the north of Wellingborough Bridge in order to catch toll-evaders, the railway company started to pay £20 per year towards the upkeep of London Road, on condition that the toll gate was not moved. On 30 August 1853 the trust held a special meeting to claim that £20 a year was insufficient, after it had had to use 400 tons of Hartshill stone to repair London Road between the station and town. It proposed moving the existing toll gate towards town and introducing a new gate south of the station in order to raise toll revenue.

At what sounds like a difficult meeting townspeople prevailed upon the trust to do nothing, at least until the proposed Leicester and Hitchin Railway had opened so that its impact on traffic flows could be assessed.

Once the new railway was open and the London and Birmingham Railway's contribution to road repair had been reduced to £10 a year, the trust called another special meeting to reconsider the changes to toll gate locations which had been rejected in 1853. On 13 October 1857 an unprecedented attendance of 31 trustees roundly rejected the idea again and the trust was left to soldier on with income from its existing gate not meeting the cost of maintenance.

The toll house was sold in 1879 for £85. The cleared site of the gate and tollhouse is now beneath the A45 flyover.

BOZEAT WOLD AND WARRINGTON GATES 1760s-1878

Sample annual toll income at Warrington Gate: £131 in 1835/36.

Although not one of the trust's three original gates, Bozeat Wold was installed before 1766 to plug the 13-mile gap between Wellingborough Bridge Gate and Sherington Gate. It was located precisely on the Buckinghamshire-Northamptonshire county boundary, just north of Northway House – today Northey Farm *(at grid reference SP 901 562)*. The toll house stood on the east side of the road.

In 1807 the trust moved the gate to Warrington Crossroads, ¾ mile to the south. The Bozeat toll house was immediately demolished and the building materials and toll gate sold for £15 to William Chapman, the last gate keeper there. Chapman moved to become the Warrington gate keeper, and the toll gate posts were moved with him to the new site.

In its new location from 1807 the gate was on the northern exit from the crossroads, with its toll house on the highway verge opposite the site now occupied by a petrol filling station. From the start the new gate was provided with side bars at the crossroads across the turnings towards Bedford and Northampton – and an immediate increase in toll takings of nearly 30 per cent at this gate proved the wisdom of the move. It is assumed that the side bars were removed when the east-west road was turnpiked by the Northampton and Cold Brayfield Trust in 1827.

Curiously, long after the turnpike era had ended the Ordnance Survey briefly labelled the crossroads with the name 'Warrington Toll Bar', and today the council perpetuates this with 'Warrington Toll Bar Roundabout' nameplates.

LORD DARTMOUTH'S OLNEY BRIDGE TOLL GATE

At the south end of the town of Olney the turnpike road crossed a millstream, the River Great Ouse and its flood plain on a substantial structure consisting of bridges and a causeway. While the maintenance of the majority of this structure lay with parishes until the county took it over in about 1830, maintenance of the bridge over the millstream at the northern end of the structure fell to the mill's owner who, in the 1830s, was Lord Dartmouth.

A map[172] indicates a toll gate on the bridge over the millstream in 1829, and labels it 'Lord Dartmouth's Bridge Toll House'. This author has not found any other source to show how long Lord Dartmouth was recouping the cost of bridge maintenance in this way, but he may have removed his gate in 1830 when the turnpike trust moved its Sherington Gate to the top of Sherington Hill, barely two miles south of his lordship's gate.

EMBERTON SIDE BAR
1859-1878

Always let with Sherington Gate: in 1861/62 they together produced toll income of £410.

The trust's Sherington Gate had a nomadic existence *(see 'Sherington Gate' below)* and was moved to its third site on the hill between Sherington and Emberton villages in 1830. But the trustees clearly became unhappy with its financial performance and discussed moving or removing it in 1841, 1857, and 1858. During this time they installed a side bar at Filgrave Lane, between Sherington Gate and Emberton in 1844 *(see 'Filgrave Lane' below)*.

In 1858 they finally agreed to erect a gate across the main road at the south end of Emberton village *(at grid reference SP 888 494)*, and beside it a side bar across the turning to Clifton, Petsoe, and Hardmead. Although nothing was minuted in 1858 about removing the gate on Sherington Hill, this must have been the intention because it stood only a mile from the proposed gate at Emberton. However by November 1858 the trust was letting a new side bar at Emberton <u>with</u> the existing main gate at Sherington. At the last minute they had reprieved the gate on Sherington Hill and did not install one across the turnpike road at Emberton.

Emberton's side bar was continuously let as one contract with the main gate on Sherington Hill and clearly caught traffic which had so far eluded the toll keeper at Sherington: tolls for the two were briefly around £50 a year up on what had been collected before. But this effect did not last beyond the 1860s. Emberton toll house was sold for £18 in 1878.

FILGRAVE LANE
SIDE BAR
1844-1859

Always let with Sherington Gate: in 1849/50 they together produced £330 in toll income.

The turning to Filgrave and Tyringham lies between Emberton and Sherington villages *(at grid reference SP 888 483)*. The hamlets on this lane would have been unlikely to generate enough traffic to justify the employment of a gate keeper and the trust's minutes do not indicate why an extra gate was needed. This side bar, which was let as a package with Sherington Gate, was only in use for fifteen years. It boosted takings by nearly £20 in its first year but its impact quickly waned. It closed in the year that the Emberton side bar opened, possibly with the gatekeeper transferring from one to the other.

If that was the case the move would have been to better accommodation because Filgrave Lane only had a "box or shed" to protect the toll keeper whereas at Emberton a proper toll house was built, possibly in the short period when the trust was planning to move its main gate from Sherington Hill to Emberton.

**SHERINGTON GATE
1754-1878**

Sample annual toll income, including that from the weighing engine: £293 in 1836/37.

The trusts for the two roads from Newport Pagnell to Bedford and Kettering, when obtaining their initial Acts of Parliament in 1754, both wanted a toll gate near Newport. In order to separate them their Acts required their toll gates to be sited at least one furlong (220 yards) east and north respectively of the junction of their roads near Sherington Bridge. The Kettering and Newport trust's Sherington Gate was therefore initially sited in 1754 *(at grid reference SP 886 457)*, about 240 yards north of the junction. There is no trace of this site today.

In those early days the Bedford road trust contributed to the cost of maintaining the substantial bridge at Sherington, although it stood just beyond the end of their road. During the 1770s, however, the Bedford trust failed *(see Road number 10)*. As a result, the Kettering and Newport Trust found themselves maintaining the bridge single-handed without collecting the necessary tolls from travellers from Bedford, who continued to use it.

In addition, travellers on the road from Kettering began to avoid that trust's Sherington gate by leaving the main road, skirting to the east of Sherington village to join the Bedford road, and passing through the abandoned site of the Bedford trust's gate. So when theKettering Turnpike Trust Act came up for renewal in 1781, the trustees obtained authority to move their gate south-westwards to the north end of Sherington bridge *(at grid reference SP 884 454)*, in order to increase toll revenue by catching the Bedford traffic and toll evaders.

While at this location the gate was known as 'Sherington Bridge Gate' and it had toll houses on both sides of the road, one of which may survive as the two-storey Bridge Leys Cottage which stands immediately north of Bridge House.

In 1814, however, a new trust was formed to run the Bedford road. Its trustees reactivated a gate on their road near Sherington Bridge, although this time they installed it ¾ mile east of the bridge, on top of Chicheley Hill. Because the Kettering Trust's gate was still at Sherington Bridge, travellers from Bedford thus began to pay toll twice to enter Newporrt, once at each trust's gate. In 1823 they petitioned Parliament with their grievance when the Kettering Trust's Act came up for renewal.

The 1823 continuation Act authorised the Kettering trustees to move their gate for a second time, but they did not do this until 1830. The new turnpike gate, known simply as 'Sherington', was placed north of the village on top of the hill between Sherington and Emberton on the boundary between the two parishes *(at grid reference SP 890 478)*.

The 1830 toll house – or more likely its demolished building materials – was sold for £5 in 1879 and today its site is lost beneath the junction between the road from Sherington to its bypass.

Weighing engine

In 1809 a weighing engine capable of checking wagons up to a weight of ten tons was erected at Sherington Bridge Gate. It was in use until the gate was moved to Sherington Hill in 1830. It is unclear whether the original machine was moved to the new site, or whether a new one was built there, but a weighing engine continued in use on Sherington Hill until 1866.

After 1846 references to the engine in the trust's accounts become sporadic but there is no indication whether this was due to intermittent mechanical failure or just indifferent record-keeping.

Milestones and mileposts

Milestones were placed along the Kettering and Newport Pagnell road at an unknown date between 1766 and 1775. Each of them was then re-sited about 300 yards northwards between 1775 and 1814 to reflect remeasuring and a shortening of the route from London by trusts further south.

Some of these stones must have been removed or defaced by 1837 when a Great Harrowden resident requested that 'milestones be placed down upon the turnpike road'. Whatever the reason behind the request, a set of cast-iron mileposts with raised lettering was put in place during 1838, followed in 1839 by the offer of a reward of £3 for information leading to the conviction of anyone "wantonly breaking, defacing, or damaging the new mile directors on the road". The installation of the cast-iron mileposts may have been the occasion for the second re-siting, this time by ¼ mile northwards.

By the time the trust was wound up in 1878, the mileage recorded ran from 'London 50' just north of Newport Pagnell to 'London 74' just south of Kettering toll gate. Interestingly the northernmost milepost on the Hockliffe and Woburn Trust's road, which stands one mile away just south of Newport Pagnell, is also 'London 50'!

Only six mileposts survive today, all of them in Buckinghamshire. Four have had their cast-iron posts of 1838 with raised lettering replaced by pressed-steel posts of the 1890s or later with inscriptions painted on to smooth surfaces. The other two are of cast-iron by Barwell Foundry of Northampton and are 'London 54' near the entrance to Emberton Country Park, and 'London 56' just south of the Warrington-Olney parish boundary.

Financial matters

The trust had a bad start in 1754, with initial running costs seeming to outstrip toll income. This led to serious cuts in 1754-55 during which the gatekeepers' wages were slashed from nine shillings to three shillings a week. The fees of the clerk were cut from £20 to £10 a year and those of the surveyor from £50 to £40 a year. At the same time interest paid to creditors was cut from 4½ per cent to 4 per cent.

After this shaky start matters improved steadily. The £3,700 loaned to the trust in 1754 rose to £7,600 from at least 1830 to 1856, after which the treasurer had sufficient money in hand to start to pay off the trust's debts.

These were down to £883 in 1877 in preparation for the winding up of the trust.

1879: The Trust wound up	In the early years of the Railway Age the Kettering and Newport Pagnell Turnpike Trust's toll income held up unusually well, in fact it increased slightly between 1839 and 1845, doubtless because its road was not closely paralleled by a rail line until the Midland Railway opened its Bedford to Leicester section in 1857. Even then direct road against rail competition was only between Kettering and Wellingborough, so total annual toll income only declined gently from £1,168 in 1838 as the railway era dawned, to £956 in 1877, the year before the trust stopped work.

The trust was formally wound up on 1 November 1878 under **41/42 Vic. c.62 (1878)**, with the trustees' final meeting to dispose of their assets held on 25 February 1879.

Road 12:
Sparrows Herne Turnpike
Road 1762

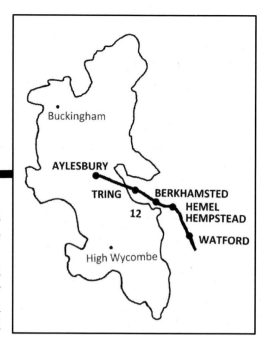

Identifying the road's route

Most of the historic route of this road has been bypassed by the modern dual-carriageway A41 since the 1970s. To follow the old road take the A41 from Aylesbury to the start of the Aston Clinton bypass, then a C-class road through Aston Clinton, and the B4635 through Tring.

South-east of Tring the route follows the A4251 through Berkhamsted, past Hemel Hempstead and through Kings Langley to rejoin the A41 at Junction 20 of the M25 motorway. A short section of the modern A41 takes the old turnpike road to the edge of Watford, where minor roads lead through pedestrianised central Watford to the A411 to Bushey.

Historic background

In turnpike days this was on one of the three main routes from London to the west Midlands, in this case via Aylesbury and Banbury. However it was less important in the late Middle Ages and some seventeenth and eighteenth century mapmakers ignored it.

Use of the route seems to have increased with the growth of trade in the mid-eighteenth century and by the time of the turnpike heyday in the 1830s it was a trunk route. The trust takes its curious name from the short length of road in Bushey at the southernmost extremity of its control, which to this day is called Sparrows Herne.

The limits of the trust's road

The trust's northern end was initially at a junction with the Wendover Road at Walton, just south of Aylesbury, but in 1826 the construction of a length of new road – Aylesbury High Street and the western end of Tring Road – moved this end to the top of Aylesbury High Street, adjoining Market Square. The turnpike road's southern limit was always just south-east of Watford at the junction of today's A411 Elstree Road and the A4140 High Road in Bushey.

Its length and maintenance districts

The trust was responsible for 25½ miles of road, of which the northern 5½ miles were in Buckinghamshire and the rest in Hertfordshire. This was the third longest for a trust working in Buckinghamshire.

Between 1762 and 1806 the trust's road was initially divided for surveying purposes into three districts which met at the northern boundaries of Wigginton and Abbott's Langley parishes; each with its own surveyor. The three districts were amalgamated into a single entity in 1806. Confusingly, when trustees decided to put toll collection out to contract in 1802 the road was split into two sections, north and south of Bourne End Mill, for awarding these contracts.

Initial Act of Parliament	**2 Geo.III, c.63 (1762).**
Continuation Acts	**23 Geo.III, c.93 (1782-83), 43 Geo.III, c.39 (1803),** and **4 Geo.IV, c.64 (1823)**. The 1823 Act authorised the construction of one mile of new road from Aylesbury Market Place to what is now called Oakfield Road, creating the present High Street and the western end of Tring Road, and half a mile of new road – part of the present Hempstead Road – at Nascott Farm, north of Watford town centre. **8 Vic., c.9 (1844)** was the trust's last continuation Act.
Control of the Trust: TRUSTEES	There were three periods in which chairing of trust meetings was in the hands of a small group of men who oversaw the important phases in the trust's life. From 1803 to 1825 the Earl of Bridgwater, from nearby Ashridge House, the banker Thomas Dorrien, and the Reverend George Nugent, both of Berkhamsted, directed the trust's great period of road building and hill easing. Then Granville D Ryder MP, of Bourne End, dominated chairing of the trustees from 1833 to 1843 through the peak of the trust's fortunes, after which Frank Moore, a magistrate from Northchurch, was almost the only chairman from 1844 to 1874 as he balanced the trust's responsibilities against falling toll income. In other years more than sixty men took turns at chairing this trust. This number could have given the trust a lack of direction if it were not for the guiding hand of the long-serving clerk William Hayton.
CLERKS	This is another trust with remarkable records of service by its clerks. William Hayton of Ivinghoe was its clerk and treasurer from the trust's inception in 1762 until his retirement in 1806, and carried out his duties without remuneration. Trustees marked their appreciation in 1806 by presenting him with a piece of plate worth 100 guineas. He was replaced by Harry Grover, a Hemel Hempstead solicitor, as clerk and treasurer on a salary of £50 a year until the General Turnpike Act of 1822 ended the practice of one person holding both posts. Thereafter Grover continued as clerk only, still on a salary of £50, until 1826. His replacements as joint clerks were two partners from his Hemel Hempstead law firm, William Smith and Charles Ehret Grover, who worked

together until 1855, after which Charles Grover carried on alone until the trust was wound up in 1873.

SURVEYORS

From 1762 until 1806 the trust divided its road between three surveyors who were paid £24 a year each *(see 'Length of the trust's road' above)*. During those years at least four post-holders were in trouble with the trust for neglect of duties or accounting irregularities or both. In 1806 the three were replaced by John Crayford, who supervised the whole road for £150 a year until 1821.

With traffic levels rising, the trust then appointed James McAdam as General Surveyor to direct policy and methods of working to a Superintending Surveyor. McAdam continued until 1853 when, with road use declining, his services were terminated and the Superintending Surveyor was left in charge.

MEETINGS OF THE TRUSTEES

Throughout the trust's 111 years its trustees met almost exclusively in 'The King's Arms' on Berkhamsted High Street, which was near the mid-point of their road. The main exception to this occurred in 1825-26,[173] when the trust was building its new road into Aylesbury and encountered so many problems that an Aylesbury Committee was set up. This met in the 'George Inn' and 'White Hart Inn' in Aylesbury until the issues were resolved.

Attendance was usually between four and nine trustees, but from the 1770s numerous meetings were abandoned for want of a quorum. This led to the quorum being reduced from nine to five by the trust's 1803 Act. In 1826 absenteeism was still a problem and it was decided that trustees who had not attended for twelve months would not be notified of future meetings.[174]

Maintenance of the road

In 1827 the trust started to use water carts to sprinkle the road on dry summer days to lay the dust, but restricted this work to the parishes of Bushey and Watford. This service was stopped in 1838 due to its cost, but quickly resumed in 1840.[175]

An unusual problem arose in 1813-16 at Hunton Bridge, between Kings Langley and Watford, when the miller there progressively raised the level of his head of water, leading to flooding and damage to the turnpike road.

Improvements to the road

This was one of the most active trusts when it came to improving the alignment of the road and the gradients of its hills. Between 1810 and 1827 the trust built 3½ miles of completely new road, including the substantial easing of gradient on 1¼ miles of its steeper hills. Thus by 1827 nearly 14 per cent of its route was newly constructed.

HIGH STREET AND TRING ROAD, AYLESBURY

Until 1827 traffic leaving Aylesbury for Tring had used Walton Street, travelling as far as what is now the Walton gyratory system then branching left off Wendover Road on to a now-lost road which met the Tring Road at Oakfield Road. In 1825-26 the trust built a one-mile-long new road, the present High Street and Tring Road, from Market Square to Oakfield Road, cutting more than ¼ mile off the journey from Aylesbury to Tring.

The route originally planned in 1823 would have been dead straight from the curve at the top of High Street to Oakfield Road. However the price being asked for some of the land was considered to be so exorbitant that a special meeting of trustees was called in 1825.[176] This was unusually well-attended, with twenty trustees present in place of the usual between four and eight, and the decision was taken to re-route the road around the contentious sites on to the course we know today, with two straight sections joined by a bend at the Park Street junction.

The new road was opened on 1 January 1827 and the old road was immediately stopped up, its surface broken up, and stone from it was taken away for use elsewhere by the trust. Within a month the General Post Office complained that the condition of the new road was unsuitable for mail coaches, but the nature of the problem was not specified and the complaint was not repeated.

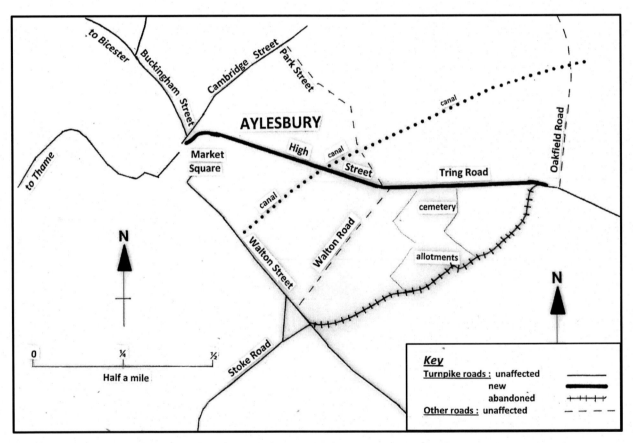

FIGURE 25: **The Sparrows Herne Trust's new approach to Aylesbury**, opened in 1827. For clarity almost all non-turnpike roads have been omitted.

TRING HILL   This was a steep, winding half-mile climb from Aston Clinton up on to the lowest part of the Chiltern Hills. During 1824-25 Bull and Morris, contractors of Tring and Aston Clinton respectively, straightened the road and excavated the upper ¼ mile of the hill until the road was in a cutting 36ft below the level of the adjoining land. They moved the resulting spoil downhill to lengthen the hill and thereby reduce its gradient by forming a ¼-mile long embankment ending just west of the canal bridge.

The result *(see the photograph at figure 5)* was a typical product of turnpike trust 'hill easing', with a straight alignment and constant gradient which can still be appreciated even though the cutting was widened by Buckinghamshire County Council in 1975.

TRING TOWN

Tring has had its traffic arrangements drastically altered twice in the past 300 years. Originally the road between Aylesbury and Watford followed a straight course along the south side of the town. Today Park Road and Park Street are surviving parts of that main road.

But in 1711 the owner of Tring Park obtained consent to stop up the road where it crossed his park and to divert traffic on to an indirect chain of existing minor roads outside the park. One of those roads is the present Tring High Street. In the 1720s the High Street was also lowered where it crossed the northern avenue from Tring Park mansion in order to remove the travelling public from the view from the house.

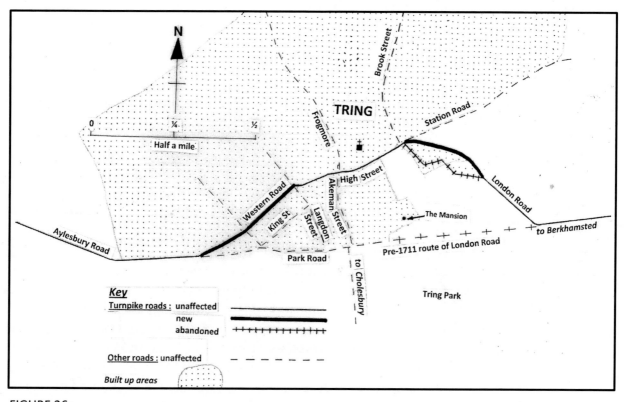

FIGURE 26:
The changing route of the main road through Tring.

For clarity only side roads mentioned in the text are shown.

The 1711 diversion through Tring, with five sharp turns in its course, was entirely unsuitable for the growing volume of traffic. Once the trust had been formed it set about two separate improvements.

In 1823 the trust built the 600 yards of Western Road through fields from Park Road to Langdon Street. This replaced the indirect entry to the town from the west, which since 1711 had been via Park Road, King Street and Langdon Street to reach the High Street. Two or three years later the trust built the smooth curving 300 yards of London Road between Brook Street and today's Tesco supermarket to replace the route which, through three right-angled bends, had followed the eastern edge of the park since 1711.

These improvements helped traffic but left the bottleneck of High Street itself between the two new sections of road. This was resolved only by the opening of Tring bypass in 1975.

NASH MILLS (HERTFORDSHIRE)	Half way between Apsley and Kings Langley the former turnpike road today passes the 'Red Lion' public house and goes beneath a railway bridge. From the 'Red Lion' the road originally followed a short loop to the east, beside the line later taken by the railway, to go around the foot of a steep-sided spur of high ground. Between 1813 and the early 1820s the trust excavated through this spur to produce a straight 260-yard section of new road with a high bank on its western side, between the 'Red Lion' and the 'Eagle' public house, which is today a cafe.
KINGS LANGLEY (HERTFORDSHIRE)	In pre-turnpike days the main road approached the village of Kings Langley from the north along what is now Rectory Lane, then turned right up a short, steep hill called The Nap before resuming its current route along High Street. In 1819-21 the trust built a new, 220-yard road – Hempstead Road – to bypass Rectory Lane and The Nap with a gentler climb into High Street.
HUNTON BRIDGE (HERTFORDSHIRE)	Until the 1820s the main road went through the village of Hunton Bridge on Bridge Street and Old Mill Road. Initially the trust made several minor improvements to the route through the village to reduce the impact of sharp corners, but after a stagecoach overturned on one in 1818 the trust's thoughts moved towards a bypass. In 1824-26, after lengthy negotiations with local landowners accompanied by problems about how the Grand Junction Canal was to be crossed,[177] a half-mile bypass was built around the west side of the village to form what is today the A4251.
HEMPSTEAD ROAD, WATFORD (HERTFORDSHIRE)	From today's M25 spur road roundabout, nearly two miles north of Watford town centre, Hempstead Road climbs southward at an easy and constant gradient for more than half a mile to the turning at Courtlands Drive. The road is on a ledge cut into the eastern side of the Gade Valley, incised between 5ft and 10 ft. on its eastern, uphill side and built up by a similar amount on its downhill side. The smoothness of the gradient and the obvious engineering of the 'ledge' make this <u>look</u> like the work of a turnpike trust, but no documentation has been found to prove this. Further south Hempstead Road originally descended gently along the eastern boundary of Cassiobury Park towards the centre of Watford. Just north of today's town centre, between the present Langley Way and Hyde Road, the pre-turnpike road made a ¾-mile loop to the west, cutting a bite out of the park. In 1823-24 the trust straightened the route on to its present alignment by building a little over half a mile of new road on the east side of the old road through the fields of Nascott Farm. This realignment led to a small eastward expansion of Cassiobury Park across the site of the old road, which was

initially retained within the park as a private drive called Green Drive. Since the 1920s this part of the park has vanished beneath housing.

CHALK HILL, WATFORD, AND LONDON ROAD, BUSHEY (HERTFORDSHIRE)

Chalk Hill and London Road still today make a stiff ¾-mile climb eastwards out of Watford. In their pre-turnpike form they must have presented as much of a challenge to horses as did Tring Hill, fifteen miles to the west.

In 1810 the trust dug four lengths of cutting on the hill to even out its steepest parts into a steadier climb, and further easing was carried out in 1815 and 1820. Today the steep-sided cuttings which resulted from this work are visible at several places on the climb, especially on the lowest section between the railway viaduct and Aldenham Road, where the retaining wall is faced with flints dotted with an intriguing collection of reused building stones.

Toll gates and tollhouses

Throughout its life the Sparrows Herne Trust had four toll gates across its road at any one time. This was probably insufficient for such a long road, and probably the reason for this trust's recurring concerns about toll evasion.

The original four gates were grouped in two pairs controlling the entrance and exit to Tring and to Watford, leaving 12½ toll-free miles between the New Ground and Ridge Lane Gates. This meant that inhabitants of the areas around Berkhamsted and Hemel Hempstead could use the turnpike road to visit these towns without payment. Meanwhile those around Tring and Watford paid for every visit to their local markets, an inconvenience which was strongly resented.

In 1823 Mr. Rickford, MP for Aylesbury, sought to persuade the trust to remedy this by moving the New Ground Gate from just east of Tring to a site between Berkhamsted and Bourne End and by reducing tolls at the other three gates. This would have spread the imposition of tolls more fairly, but the trust stuck to its long-established practice.

In addition to the four main gates the trust had six side bars at one time or another, but never more than four of them at the same time.

The trust ceased to employ toll collectors directly in 1804-05, putting toll collection out to contract from the following year. Toll income promptly rose by 20 per cent.

VATCHES FARM GATE 1762-1810

No independent toll income has been found for this gate, but £500 was taken by Vatches Farm and New Ground Gates together in 1809/10.

This was one of the trust's original four gates and was also knwn as Veeches Farm Gate. Its toll house cost £23 10s 0d to build, which was the same amount as at New Ground Gate. It stood half a mile west of Aston Clinton *(at approximately grid reference SP 866 124).*

There were apparently serious doubts about the honesty or diligence of the gate's first toll collector. In 1764 trustees ordered the gate keepers here and at New Ground, east of Tring, to make a daily record of the categories of traffic which presented toll tickets showing toll had been paid *at the other* of these two gates, in order to compare the survey results with the takings. After a lengthy pause during which Thomas Boughton, the original Vatches gate keeper, remained in post – and presumably under observation – toll collection at Vatches Farm Gate was suspended from 1 July 1767. When the gate came back into use on 31 October 1768 it had a new gatekeeper.

The trust's minutes do not elaborate on the matter, but the leisurely response to the problem by trustees suggests that, as a new trust, they had not gained experience in dealing with suspected fraud and were making up the rules as they went along.

Vatches Farm Gate was replaced by Weston Gate in 1810, after which its toll house was let as a private dwelling until it was demolished in 1824. The ill-fated Edward Needle started work as a gatekeeper at Vatches Farm Gate in 1803 before moving to Weston Gate in 1810 *(see below)*.

WESTON GATE AND SIDE BAR 1810-26

Sample annual toll income: £352 7s 10½d in 1824-25.

Weston Gate was erected at a cost of £102 10s 0d just east of Aylesbury at the junction of Aston Clinton Road with Broughton Lane. Its toll house stood in the angle between the two roads. This must have been a substantial building because its construction cost more than four times the £23 10s 0d paid for the Vatches Farm and New Ground toll houses.

In 1822 Weston Gate was the scene of the brutal murder of the gate keeper Edward Needle and his wife during night-time robbery by James Croker and Thomas Randall. The assailants were hanged in Aylesbury Market Square in March 1823.

Weston Gate was given a side bar across Broughton Lane, possibly in 1810 and certainly by 1815.[178] The main gate was replaced by Aylesbury Gate on 1 January 1827, when the new road into the town was opened *(see 'Improvements' above)*. It is assumed that the side bar was closed at the same time because the Weston toll house had been demolished by 19 March 1827. With toll evasion on their minds the trustees discussed whether to put the side bar back across Broughton Lane in 1835 and again in 1841.[179] But they did nothing.

AYLESBURY GATE AND SIDE BAR 1827-1873

Sample annual toll income: £457 16s 3¼d in 1824-25.

When the new road into Aylesbury was opened in 1827 *(see 'Improvements' above)* a gate was placed across it between the Park Street and Walton Road side turnings, at what later became known as Hazells' Corner. A side bar was erected at the same time across Park Street. The toll house, main gate and side bar cost £136 10s 0d to build, a price which suggests that the toll house was quite an impressive building. Its site is now within a roundabout. Trustee discussions in 1857 and 1860 about moving the gate back to the junction with Broughton Lane came to nothing.

DRAYTON BEAUCHAMP GATE - probably not erected	In 1860, when the use of main roads was in decline, the trust resolved to erect a gate across the main road at the top of Tring Hill, with a side bar across the Upper Icknield Way, today the B488. This was presumably an attempt to increase revenue from what little traffic still flowed by catching east-west travellers on the Upper Icknield Way between Bulbourne and Wendover as they briefly used the trust's road between the top and bottom of Tring Hill. However the author has not found any evidence that this gate or its side bar were actually put in place.
NEW GROUND GATE AND SIDE BARS (HERTFORDSHIRE) 1762-1873	*Sample annual toll income: £594 12s 8¾d in 1829/30.* This group of gate and side bars was situated just over 1½ miles east of Tring at the crossroads with turnings to Aldbury and Wigginton. It had side bars across both side roads and a single-storey toll house which cost £23 10s 0d to build and stood on the southern corner of the crossroads. Throughout the gate's existence there were intermittent problems with toll avoidance here but the trust's minutes are not clear on the route taken by toll evaders. An inspection of the toll house by trustees in August 1816 found it in deplorable condition,[180] with its back room extremely dirty and used to house chickens and a hen. When the trust was wound up in 1873 the toll house and garden were sold to Baron S N de Rothschild for £40. Today their site is part of the grounds of a pumping station.
RIDGE LANE GATE, WATFORD (HERTFORDSHIRE) 1762-1873	*Sample annual toll income: £1,000 17s 4¼d in 1824/25.* This gate was initially sited north of central Watford near the present Kenilworth Court *(at grid reference TQ 099 976)*. The cost of building its toll house was cut to £21 by using old bricks. The gate was on a half-mile curving section of road on the approach to Watford from the north, between Kenilworth Court to a little north of Hyde Road. This section was closed in 1823 and replaced by the straight route followed by Hempstead Road today *(see 'Improvements' above)*. The closure moved the road away from the gate, so the toll house was demolished and its gate carried just over ½ mile north to the side turning called Ridge Lane, where it was re-erected on the north side of the junction. The new toll house was built on the west side of Hempstead Road at a cost of £129, implying a substantial, probably two-storey building. Its site is now beneath the widened carriageway of Hempstead Road. Because the new 1823 gate was on the north side of the junction with Ridge Lane it was felt necessary to place a side bar across Ridge Lane itself to catch traffic filtering on to the turnpike road without having paid.
CHALK HILL GATE, WATFORD (HERTFORDSHIRE) 1762-1873	*Sample annual toll income: £1,443 6s 11d in 1824/25.* This gate was located at the south end of Watford town centre where Lower High Street meets Chalk Hill, Pinner Road and Eastbury Road. The gate stood between the River Colne and the site of today's railway viaduct, and

its site is indicated today by a preserved boundary marker *(see 'Milestones' below)*. The original single-storey toll cottage was built for £25 in 1762 and stood on the south side of the road on a site which is probably now under the slip road.

An inspection in 1818 found the toll cottage to be in a ruinous condition, partly due to the raising of the road's surface by the trust, because this put its floor below ground level. It was immediately rebuilt on the same site as a square-plan, single-storey cottage with pyramidal roof and central chimney which cost £102. This in turn was replaced after 1840 by a two-storey house, but that had been demolished for road widening by 1896.

In 1763 the trustees agreed that a side bar should be erected, presumably across Pinner and Eastbury Roads. This is a little odd because most traffic through the side bar would also pass through the nearby main gate. The trust's minutes in 1779[181] record a problem with the side bar but after this date documentary evidence for its existence is thin. It would almost certainly have been in the way of building the railway viaduct in the 1830s and would probably have been re-sited then. The last reference found for it was in 1837.

As early as 1763 trustees agreed that Chalk Hill and Ridge Lane Gates would be open all night and introduced a rota by which three gatekeepers would attend the two gates. This arrangement was still in force in 1821.

In 1846 trustees complained of an unusual form of toll evasion at Chalk Hill Gate whereby people were parking their carriages near the gate and walking through toll-free into Watford to conduct their business!

Weighing engine

Trustees began to consider the principle of building a weighing engine in April 1800,[182] but it was 1815 before they purchased a 10ft by 50ft piece of ground opposite the Chalk Hill toll cottage in Watford for £10. They then contracted Mr Ringrove of Naseby in Northamptonshire to build a weighing engine on it for £72, excluding brickwork. The engine was in use from 1816 and had what sounds like a complete rebuild in 1826. In 1847 it was removed due to trouble in maintaining its accuracy.

Investigations in 1823 into the benefits of erecting a second weighing engine at New Ground Gate came to nothing.

Milestones and mileposts

Mileposts made from 'heart of oak' were erected in 1764. They were 12 inches square and 5ft 6 inches high, of which 3ft stood above ground, and had Roman numerals. A typical post was lettered '[XVI] miles from LONDON'.[183] Their mileages rose from 'London 13' at the north end of Sparrows Herne to 'London 37' on Tring Road in Aylesbury, just east of the future King Edward Avenue. Originally the 'London 38' milepost stood near Walton, and when that section of road was abandoned and replaced in 1826-27 by the extension of Tring Road and the building of Aylesbury High Street it should have been moved to its new position near the top of the High Street. Whether or not this happened at the time, it is not there now.

The trust's survey of the condition of its 25 mileposts and milestones in 1803 found that twenty were oak posts and two were of stone.[184] Three were not mentioned. Perhaps they were missing. It was decided to replace six decayed posts with new ones "of sound heart of oak, properly painted and lettered".

The Sparrows Herne Trust did not replace its wooden posts with cast-iron ones until 1826, making it one of the few trusts to continue with wood into the nineteenth century. In that year R Barrett made and installed a set of cast-iron posts for two guineas each. Interestingly trustees ordered Barrett to model his mileposts on those in use on the Bath Road. As these were made of stone, in Buckinghamshire at least, it is not surprising that there is little resemblance between the two trusts' milemarkers!

Today only two of the trust's mileposts survive, at 31 and 37 miles to London on the south side of the road in Tring and Aylesbury respectively. Both are cast-iron replacements with raised lettering, which presumably date from 1826.

BOUNDARY MARKERS

The trust is unusual in the survival of three boundary markers, possibly dating from 1826, which indicated the edge of highway land at that time – although one is now apparently well inside private property! These markers, which were originally made of cast-iron with the words 'Sparrows Herne Trust' in raised letters, are to be found in:

- *Tring*, against the wall of the Memorial Gardens on the south side of the road at the junction of High Street with London Road. This is a 1992 replica after the original was lost in drainage works;
- *Berkhamsted*, on the north side of High Street, just west of the junction with Park Street, in front of National Tyres' premises;
- *Watford*, on the north-east side of Lower High Street, at the site of Watford Toll Gate.

Financial matters

The trust got off to a vigorous start, raising £9,000 in loans at 4½ per cent interest in its first three years. Its finances continued on a sound footing until 1823-27, when the trust carried out major improvements in seven locations. However such was public confidence in its management that it was able to raise £10,000 in loans in 1825, followed by a further £2,500 in 1826.

1873: The Trust wound up

In the last pre-railway years toll income for the whole trust was in the range of £3,250 to £3,755 per year. The London and Birmingham Railway, whose line closely followed the Sparrows Herne Trust road from Tring to Watford and which competed for the trust's longer-distance traffic, was opened in stages between London and Bletchley in 1837-38. The trust's toll income promptly dropped sharply and stood at £2,064 a year in 1846. After this income settled at a new level of between £1,700 to £1,900 a year, probably because the trust's road was acting as a feeder to the nearby railway stations. The trust was able to reduce its debt from £6,700 in 1844 to £700 in 1869 and became debt-free in 1873, whereupon it was wound up on 1 November 1873 under **36/37 Vic. c.90 (1873).**

Road 13:
The Reading and Hatfield Turnpike Road 1767

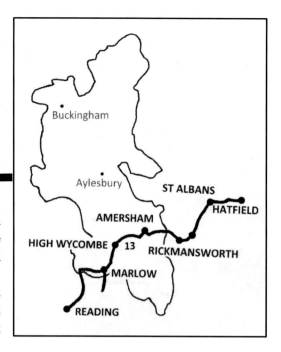

Identifying the road's route

This route orbiting north and west London once had a single identity as a turnpike road linking Reading with Hatfield. Today it is lost in the numerous road numbers of modern routes heading for different destinations.

The old turnpike road now forms the A4155 from Reading to Marlow, then a string of C-class roads to the top of Marlow Hill above High Wycombe. From there the A404 leads to Rickmansworth – except in central High Wycombe and Old Amersham where the turnpike route is now bypassed. At Rickmansworth the route again continues as C-class roads through the town centre, followed by the A412 to Garston Park, the A405 from there to the M1 flyover, and the unclassified Old Watford Road on to Oakwood Road in Brickett Wood.

From there the old turnpike route is the A405 again to the south end of Chiswell Green, the B4630 and A5183 into and through the centre of St Albans, and the A1057 to the Comet Way roundabout on the edge of Hatfield. Within Hatfield disconnected unclassified sections of the original road carry the names St. Albans Road West and East but are now largely bypassed by the modern B6246.

The branch road from Marlow to Knowl Hill on the A4 west of Maidenhead is a C-class road to Bisham, the A404 to Burchett's Green, and C-class again to rejoin the A404 north of Knowl Hill.

Historic background

For one turnpike road to have disintegrated into so many modern identities confirms that it no longer forms a popular travel corridor, if, indeed, it ever did. This road obviously links nine Home County market towns, but the outer ones have so little in common that we need a stronger reason why this 50-mile-long route was developed as a turnpike road in the eighteenth century.

Its improvement is popularly rumoured to have been initiated by Lord Cecil, the Earl of Salisbury, who lived at Hatfield House in the pre-turnpike days of the early 1700s. It is known that, as a gout sufferer, he travelled intermittently to Bath to benefit from the mineral waters there and, en route, suffered considerable pain as he was shaken about in his private coach on the 130-mile journey via London. What is more difficult to verify is the theory that, in order to reduce the length of his suffering, he identified a short cut from Hatfield to the Bath Road at Knowl Hill west of Maidenhead, and initiated some improvements to smooth its surface. At that time the road was still maintained by the parishes, but he might have paid for some uprgrading.

His most direct route would have been via Hemel Hempstead and Amersham, but fellow sufferer the Earl of Essex, at Cassiobury Park near Watford, wanted to share in any improvements – so the 'short cut' was extended to take in Watford and Rickmansworth. Even with this detour Lord Cecil's new route would cut some 20 miles off the journey from Hatfield to Bath via London.

The tradition of Cecil involvement is maintained by all the turnpike trust's mileposts, which carried the distance to Hatfield at the top of the posts with a prominence and consistency that is normally reserved for London on other trusts' mileposts. Furthermore in 1767 Sir Thomas Salisbury was one of the first Reading and Hatfield trustees, although he was outnumbered by four members of the Drake family of Amersham, who would have had more local reasons for road improvements.

The Cecil connection is also highlghted by several local histories which imply that the route was known in the eighteenth century as The Gout Track, although the present author has noticed that this name does not appear in print until the mid-twentieth century!

On the other hand, the inaugural meeting called to discuss forming this turnpike trust was held in High Wycombe, not Hatfield, and the first scheme proposed by the trust was to improve the road from St Albans, not Hatfield, to Reading.

How much improvement work Lord Cecil actually paid for is obscure. An article in the 'Luton Times' in 1903 said, without any supporting evidence,

FIGURE 27:
Towns linked by the Reading and Hatfield turnpike road
under the trust of 1767.

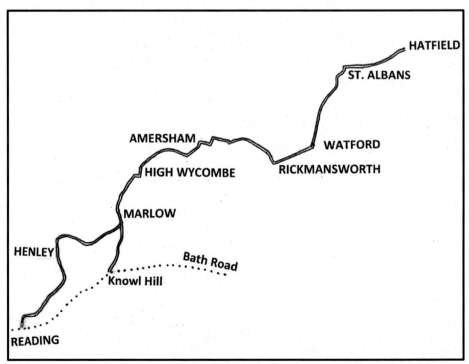

that Lord Salisbury and the Earl of Essex "acquired land and constructed the thoroughfare". If even partly true this could explain two stretches of obviously engineered road between High Wycombe and Amersham which appear, on map evidence, to have been straightened and realigned immediately *before* the trust started work in 1767 *(see 'Improvements to the road' below)*.

However nothing has been found in the Cecil papers to support this. In 1881 the trust's general clerk stated that the road had been put together in the 1730s by the then "Marquis of Salisbury" who "converted several driftways into a good turnpike road".[185]

It thus seems possible that, having identified his preferred way through a tortuous network of minor lanes, possibly by erecting a distinctive set of milestones along it *(see 'Milestones and mileposts' below)*, Cecil paid for one or two major improvements and hoped that others, perhaps the parishes, would work on the rest of it.

Whatever the truth of the matter, Cecil created enough interest in the route for a group to form a turnpike trust and take it over in 1767. From the outset, the Reading and Hatfield trust made the southern end of Lord Cecil's suggested route – from Marlow to Knowl Hill on the Bath road – a branch road off what became their main route from Marlow through Henley to Caversham Bridge in Reading.

The limits of the trust's road

The trust's southern extremities were at the north end of Caversham Bridge, Reading, for its main route, and on the Bath Road (today's A4) just north-east of Knowl Hill, for its branch from Marlow.

The road's north-eastern limit was initially at its crossing of the Great North Road at the north end of Hatfield town, but at some time between 1787 and 1829 it was pulled back nearly a mile to Hatfield's western parish boundary.

The trust's control did not extend to parts of the route in the towns of Henley, Marlow, High Wycombe, Amersham, Rickmansworth, St Albans, and Hatfield where either the urban authorities or other turnpike trusts were already responsible for maintenance.

Its length and maintenance districts

With a distance of 50 miles from Reading to Hatfield, plus the 4½ miles from the south end of Marlow Bridge to Knowl Hill, this was by far the longest length of road under the control of any one Buckinghamshire trust. Of the trust's road 22½ miles were actually in Buckinghamshire, four in Berkshire and the rest in Hertfordshire.

The trust's road was so long that it was always divided, for operational purposes, into three districts. Over the years there were minor boundary moves but the general arrangement of districts was: (1) north end of Caversham Bridge, Reading, to Marlow, (2) Marlow to the border between Buckinghamshire and Hertfordshire near Chorleywood, (3) from the county border to Hatfield.

Initial Act of Parliament	8 Geo.III, c.50 (1767) turnpiked the road from Reading to Hatfield, together with a branch from Marlow via Bisham to Knowl Hill on the Bath Road (now A4).

Continuation Acts	**27 Geo.III, c.81 (1787), 49 Geo.III, c.97 (1809), 10 Geo.IV, c.133 (1829)** and **22/23 Vic. c.11 (1859).**
	Due possibly to Parliamentary misdrafting, the 1829 Act introduced the paying of one toll per day for travel over the *whole length* of the trust's road. This was belatedly corrected by the trust's 1859 Act to paying one toll per day for travel in each *District*.

Control of the Trust: TRUSTEES	With such a long road to administer through so many communities the trust started work with 505 trustees, but they became fewer over the years until there was a more manageable 125 by 1859. However in spite of the number of trustees on the books, so few turned up for some General Meetings that they had to be abandoned for lack of a quorum.
	As mentioned above, the trust's road was always divided into three districts, each of which had its own clerk, surveyor, and chairman. Upon appointment each trustee was allocated to a specific district – they often lived within it or nearby – and thereafter met within that district. There they supervised work on their part of the road, under the overall control of the General Meetings which could, theoretically, be attended by all trustees.
	No eighteenth-century chairmen of General Meetings have been identified. In the nineteenth century Thomas R Barker of Hambleden, just off the trust's road between Henley and Marlow, was a dominant figure in the trust between 1829 and 1864. For part of that time he also chaired the Great Marlow and Stokenchurch Trust.

CLERKS	The General Meeting of all trustees was served by a General Clerk who was not one of the divisional officers.
	A Marlow solicitor, Henry Allnut, was the trust's first General Clerk. Between 1775 and 1782 he handed the reins to James Payn of Maidenhead, who held the post until at least 1821, after which Wards, solicitors of Maidenhead, took over until the trust was wound up in 1881. W J Ward was first, from at least 1827 until he died in post in 1851, and his son R A Ward continued until 1881.

MEETINGS OF THE TRUSTEES	Representatives of the three districts attended the trust's General Meetings which in theory were held a minimum of four times per year, twice a year in Great Marlow and once each in Rickmansworth and St Albans. In practice, although Rickmansworth was nearer to the mid-point of the road, most General Meetings were held at Marlow in the inn at the top of High Street known at different times as the 'Upper Crown Inn', 'Crown Inn', and 'Crown Hotel'. When at Rickmansworth the trustees met at the 'Swan Inn', and when at St Albans in the town hall.

Improvements to the road	New road built along this route during the eighteenth and nineteenth centuries amounted to 7¼ miles, all but ¾ mile of it west of Croxley Green in Hertfordshire. The trust definitely built 3¼ miles, and the Earl of Shelburne, of Wycombe Abbey, built a further half mile. It is unclear whether the trust was responsible for building the remaining 3½ miles *(see 'Background' above)*.
FAWLEY (OXFORDSHIRE)	One mile of road between Northfield End, Henley, and the northern entrance to Fawley Court was rerouted by the trust between 1797 and 1809 under powers originally granted in 1767. This was seemingly more to improve the amenities of the Freeman family at Fawley Court than to help road users, because it took the road further from the house and allowed the enlargement of their park between the old and new lines of road.

Lodges were built in 1814 at the points where the house's north and south drives left the new road. Most of the new road from the northern edge of Henley to Fawley Court's North Lodge can be recognised today as three straight sections joined by two sharp bends. Nearly ¼ mile of the Court's northern access drive is on the site of the old turnpike road and is still on a low causeway. |
| **DANESFIELD (OXFORDSHIRE)** | In 1844 the trust moved their road further from the Thames-side mansion of Danesfield by building a ¾-mile length of new road about 40 yards west of the old one, as shown on a map in the Centre for Buckinghamshire Studies.[186] In doing this they eased the gradient of a steep hill. With its west end on the sharp bend at the corner of Milbank Wood *(at grid reference SU 812 843)*, the new road climbs steadily eastward on a ledge cut into the hillside, with a sharp drop on its north-west side until it enters a short, steep-sided cutting beneath a lattice iron bridge near the summit.

Old and new routes met just east of today's roundabout access to the Thames Reach estate. The western end of the old road became an estate drive for Danesfield after 1844 and is flanked by a lodge house where it leaves the A4155, although a modern garage stands across it just beyond the lodge. Behind the garage the course of the old road, although now disused, can be seen continuing as a low causeway amongst the trees.

Ironically although this diversion made the main road invisible from Danesfield, a later owner demolished the house in 1899-1901 and built a new mansion twice as far from the road. This is now a hotel. |
| **MARLOW** | The trust's branch road from Marlow to the Bath Road at Knowl Hill originally crossed the Thames on a wooden bridge with medieval origins at the foot of St Peter's Street, Marlow. This bridge was maintained by bridge wardens using various charity monies. In 1829 a private Act authorised the construction of a replacement bridge, the present suspension bridge, at the foot of High Street and this required a 150-yard extension of High Street to link it with the new bridge. The turnpike trust contributed £600 towards the construction of this link road, which was opened in 1832. |

The main parts of the conspicuously straight Marlow Hill and Amersham Hill into and out of the valley-bottom town of High Wycombe had been constructed shortly before the turnpike trust was inaugurated.

Until about 1760 **Marlow Hill** followed a gently curving dry valley about 160 yards east of the modern road. In about that year the Earl of Shelburne, of Wycombe Abbey, built the present half-mile-long straight hill, extended his park out to it, and incorporated the old road into the park. The top and bottom sections of the hill remained on winding alignments (Marlow Hill and Road at the top and the original alignment of St Mary Street and Crown Lane at the bottom) until the twentieth century.

The mile-long straightness of **Amersham Hill** replaced a more sinuous medieval route which started from Castle Street and climbed in a holloway 30-40 yards to the west of the modern road to a point just above the present Maybrook Gardens, where it crossed the line of today's A404 and swung up

FIGURE 28:
The straightening of Amersham Hill and Marlow Hill
in High Wycombe in the eighteenth century.

The diagram does not show all side roads.

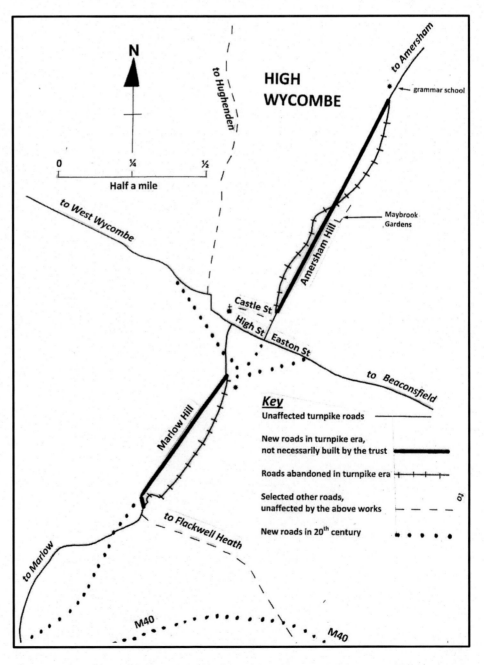

to 100 yards to the east of Amersham Road before converging on it at today's Grammar School site. The only readily-traceable reminders of the old climb are shallow dips in Priory Avenue and Priory Road where they cross the former holloway.

The Earl of Shelburne's estate map dated 1762 did not show the modern Amersham Hill because it was surveyed before work on the new road had started,[187] but Jefferys' county map, surveyed in 1766-68, shows it completed. Since the turnpike trust did not start work until 1767 it is difficult to credit them with building this major length of new road unless the Jefferys map is actually showing a planned road rather than what was on the ground. The other possibility is that this steeply-sloping road was indeed engineered by Lord Salisbury and the Earl of Essex in the 1760s *(see 'Background' above)*.

| FROM HAZLEMERE TO AMERSHAM | Today the 2½ miles across the former Wycombe Heath from Inkerman Farm, Hazlemere, to below Woodrow Farm, Amersham, is formed of long straight sections and long, smooth curves which suggest a planned road rather than one which has developed over the centuries. Its predecessor was a much less direct route which swung from side to side of the present A404, particularly in the vicinity of Mop End and Penn Street. |

Roque's map of 1752 entitled 'An actual survey of Berks, Oxford, and Bucks' appears to show the old road still in place while Jefferys' map of Bucks. in 1766-68 shows the present road. If the modern A404 was laid out between 1752 and 1766 the work was just too early for turnpike trust involvement and much too early for it to be a result of the enclosing of Wycombe Heath in 1815 and 1855. The identity of the road builder thus remains a mystery but as at Amersham Hill, the combined resources of Lord Salisbury and the Earl of Essex are possible providers.

| AMERSHAM AND LITTLE CHALFONT | Until the end of the eighteenth century White Lion Road followed a long, gentle curve near the southern edge of Amersham Common, largely on the north side of its present dead straight route between Blackhorse Bridge and Bell Lane. Logically the straightening should have been carried out by Amersham's enclosure commissioners when they parcelled up Amersham Common in 1816. However the Ordnance Survey's draft two-inch scale map, surveyed in 1812, shows the modern half-mile-long straight road already in place and no sign of its curving predecessor, so the work was presumably carried out by the turnpike trust. |

The section of Amersham Road which bypasses the original turnpike route via Church Grove at the east end of Little Chalfont was built in the twentieth century and thus post-dates the trust. Note that the 'Hatfield 21' milepost has been moved from the old to the new alignment.

| CHENIES | In the early years of the turnpike trust the main road turned off its modern alignment to go into Chenies village and across the top of the village green. The building of a 500-yard bypass, today's A404, on the south side of the village enabled traffic to avoid the awkward detour through it. This bypass |

was built by the trust before the Ordnance Survey mapped it in 1812. It was one of the first village bypasses to be built in Buckinghamshire.

CHORLEYWOOD (HERTFORDSHIRE)	The 250-yard cut-off of Chenies Road at the end of North Hill, Chorleywood, immediately on the Hertfordshire side of the county boundary, post-dates the turnpike trust.
RICKMANSWORTH (HERTFORDSHIRE)	In turnpike days Reading and Hatfield traffic dropped down to pass through the town centre along High Street. The short bypass north of the railway in Park Road was not built until the 1930s.
CROXLEY GREEN (HERTFORDSHIRE)	Just north-east of Rickmansworth the steepness of the 350-yard climb up Scots Hill to Croxley Green at a gradient of 1 in 8 caused a lot of turnpike road traffic to deviate well to the south along Tolpits Lane. The trust proposed a half mile-long diversion, running 100-200 yards from the old road around the south side of the hill. Plans for the diversion were drawn up in 1828, and powers to build it were obtained in 1829, but it was not built. The gradient of the existing hill was later eased by the trust by excavating a 150 yard cutting. Finally in 1973 the county council created a short section of dual carriageway by building a separate carriageway for uphill traffic on the north side of the old turnpike road.
ST ALBANS (HERTFORDSHIRE)	Probably shortly after 1837 the trust rebuilt the bridge over the River Ver in St Albans at the foot of Holywell Hill, and built new approach roads at each end of the bridge, resulting in some ¾ mile of new and virtually straight road. This work included bypassing the loop now called Grove Road, which had formerly been the turnpike road and had been fronted on its east side by Holywell House. Following the demolition of the house in 1837 the trust built the present straight road through its gardens. South of this new piece of road the route climbs St Stephens Hill on a gradient which has clearly been smoothed by lowering the road into a cutting up to 6ft deep. However the author has not found any evidence to date this work, so cannot positively credit it to the trust.

Toll gates and tollhouses

Whatever input Lord Cecil made to the Reading and Hatfield Turnpike Road, it had one of the lowest toll incomes per mile among turnpike trusts with roads in Buckinghamshire, in spite of having ten or eleven main gates throughout its life and two side bars initially, rising to seven after the 1820s. This lack of income speaks volumes about its lack of importance in the turnpike road network.

From 1829 to 1859 low income was also partly due to the trust taking only one toll per day from each traveller, regardless of how many gates he or she passed through, an oddity which was later blamed on bad drafting of the trust's 1829 renewal Act.

Of particular note is the extraordinary growth of toll collection points between St Albans and Hatfield from the 1820s. After having just one toll gate on this five-mile section from 1767 until the early 1820s, the trust added four side bars in thinly-populated countryside in the 1820s and 1830s, and put a second toll gate across the main road at Hatfield in the 1830s.

The likely toll takings at the four side bars and the extra income from the second main gate were so low that it is difficult to see the commercial case for them. Perhaps it indicates a harder, almost obsessive line on toll evasion taken by the trustees of the eastern district compared to that of their colleagues further west.

The siting of the original ten toll gates is another relic of the complications surrounding the early days of this road. In 1881 the Clerk of the trust, when making a declaration,[188] gave the opinion that doubts about the legal status of the sites of toll houses went back to 1767 when adjoining landowners reputedly gave small parcels of land on which toll houses could be built without formal conveyance. The actual siting of these gates thus apparently depended more on landowner willingness to give land for toll houses than on the ideal locations for collecting revenue.

SHIPLAKE GATE (OXFORDSHIRE) 1859-1881

No information has been found on toll income for this gate on its own.

Some writers state that Henley Gate *(see below)* was moved in 1859 to a new location in Shiplake parish about a mile south of its old position. Such a move would bring us to the single-storey Victorian lodge at the turning off the A4155 to Lower Bolney Farm *(at grid reference SU 768 804)*. This stands too far back from the main road to have acted as a turnpike toll house, and has its projecting gate keeper's portion fronting the farm track, not the main road. It is more likely that this was one of the lodges to nearby Bolney Court, particularly since the 1878 edition of the Ordnance Survey, surveyed when the trust was still operational, labelled it a lodge, and did not show a toll gate in the vicinity.

However contemporary sources[189] recorded that the Henley toll gate was removed in 1859 and replaced by a new gate on the Reading side of 'The Plough' public house – now 'The Plowden Arms' – at the southern end of Shiplake *(at grid reference SU 763 782)*. The stated reason for the move was to make the gate more equidistant between Henley and Reading, but the popular effect of it was to give toll-free travel into Henley for a wider area of country dwellers south of the town.

HENLEY GATE 1767-1859

Sample annual toll income: £272 in 1832/33.

This gate was sited on the south side of the town centre, at what is now Reading Road's junction with Upton Close. In the eighteenth century this was in the fields, but it was later built over *(see Shiplake Gate above for the demise of Henley Gate)*. The toll house stood on the east side of the road. Its site was obliterated by the twentieth-century construction of Upton Close.

The two square, stuccoed lodge houses which flank Marlow Road at the north end of Henley town – one of which now carries the name 'Toll House' – were associated with nearby Phyllis Court and Fawley Court, not with the turnpike trust.

GREENLANDS GATE
1767-1881

Sample annual toll income: £235 in 1832/33.

Greenlands Gate was siituated two miles north-east of Henley at what is now Greenlands College *(at grid reference SU 774 855)*. This gate stood on the east side of what is now the junction between the A4155 and the access road to the college's sports halls and car parks. The site of the toll house is now in the small hedged car park.

'DANESFIELD',
IN MEDMENHAM
PARISH

A local curiosity is that the Ordnance Survey's first edition one-inch scale map of 1822 does not show Greenlands Gate – but does show a turnpike gate 2½ miles to the east of it at the west end of the Danesfield estate *(at grid reference SU 812 843)*. The author has found no other reference to a gate in this position and notes that toll takings were recorded at Greenlands before and after 1822 while none were recorded at Danesfield at any time. Either the Ordnance Survey caught a very temporary re-siting of Greenland Gate in 1822, or there was a surveying error.

BISHAM GATE
1767-1881

Sample annual toll income: £362 in 1832/33.

This was the only gate on the trust's branch road from Marlow to the Bath Road near Knowl Hill. It was situated on a sharp bend at the north-east end of the village of Bisham. The single-storey, brick-built toll house still stands, much extended, but its porch, which projected on to the highway, has understandably been demolished.

GREAT MARLOW OR
CHAPEL STREET GATE
1767-1832

Sample annual toll income: £146 13s 4d in 1831/32.

Chapel Street Gate stood about 130 yards west of the junction between Little Marlow Road and Wycombe Road in Great Marlow. It was quickly a victim of toll evasion but the provision of a side gate to catch avoiders *(see below)* seems to have reduced the trust's losses.

Local residents had petitioned unsuccessfully for removal of the Chapel Street Gate in 1787 but after an 1830 court case on toll evasion at this gate, trustees bowed to strong local feelings against paying tolls at the Bisham and Great Marlow gates, which were only a mile apart, and then again at Wycombe Hill Gate only three miles further on. So the trustees voted in 1831 to remove Chapel Street Gate, and did so in 1832.

In 1835 the trust sold a property that included a building in Chapel Street for five shillings. The low value suggests that if this property was indeed at the toll gate, the toll collector had been provided only with a kiosk for shelter.

The years1829-32 had been a period of reappraisal of the effectiveness of the trust's toll gates, with one gate moved from Hazlemere to Terriers and a new one introduced near Amersham, so the removal of Marlow's gates in 1829 *(see below)* and 1832 should be seen in that context.

'AGGLETON GREEN' SIDE BAR
from at least 1774 to 1829

Estimated annual toll income: £90 in 1827/28.

Until 1829 Great Marlow Gate had the unusual feature of a side bar which was nowhere near the turnpike road. This was known in Marlow as the Lower Turnpike, and by the trust as 'Aggleton Green Side Bar', involving a persistent but incorrect spelling of the name of nearby Addlestrop Green.

The side bar stood 400 yards to the south of Chapel Street in the parallel road now called Station Road, about 30 yards west of the Mill Road junction. Its function was to catch toll evaders to and from the north and east, who were using what are now called Newtown and Station Roads to enter Marlow while avoiding the Chapel Street Gate.

While the main gate may only have had a kiosk to shelter the toll collector, another oddity here is that this side bar was served by a two-storey house. The removal of the side bar in 1829 led to a predictably serious drop in toll takings in Marlow, which was followed by the abandoning of toll collection in the town altogether in 1832. The toll house was demolished in the 1990s.

WYCOMBE HILL GATE 1767-1881

Sample annual toll income: £226 in 1832/33.

The steep 1 in 10 gradient of Marlow Hill has its descent broken by two short 'platforms' of easier gradient. Wycombe Hill Gate was sited on the upper 'platform', just down from Daws Hill Lane. Its toll house was on the east side of the road, standing partly on the highway verge and partly in the grounds of Daws Hill House. When the trust was wound up, this toll house was sold together with Terriers toll house for £120 on 1 December 1881.

CRENDON LANE SIDE BAR 1767-1829 renamed TERRIERS GATE AND SIDE BARS 1829-1881

Until 1829 the gate at the Terriers road junction *(at grid reference SU 879 947)*, appears to have been called Crendon Lane Gate and to have consisted only of a side bar across Totteridge Lane. No information has been found about its accommodation for a gatekeeper. During this period the gate across the main road was located nearly a mile to the north-east at Hazlemere *(see below)*, and the two gates were let together as 'Hazlemere and Crendon Lane Gates'.

The situation was reversed in 1829 when the main gate was moved to the Terriers road junction. The side bar across Totteridge Lane was continued and joined by a side bar across Kingshill Road. After these changes the toll gate on the Amersham Road and the side bars beside it continued to be let together but from then on were known as 'Terriers and Hazlemere Gates'.

At Terriers a toll house was built after 1829 on the south side of the junction. This was a two-storey brick-built building with its bowed front projecting on to the highway verge of Amersham Road. When the trust was wound up in 1881 Terriers toll house was sold together with the Wycombe Hill toll house for £120. In 1970 it was replaced by two shops.

HAZLEMERE GATE
1767-1829
HAZELMERE SIDE BAR
1829-1850s

Sample annual toll income for Hazlemere main gate and Crendon Lane side bar: £115 11s 8d in 1823/24.

This gate was initially across the main Wycombe to Amersham road at Hazlemere crossroads. It gained a side bar across Green Street – an ancient but less direct route from High Wycombe – at a date before 1829 which has not been found. The Hazlemere toll house seems to have been on the north corner of the junction of Amersham Road and Green Street on a site now occupied by shops.

In 1829 the gate across the main road was moved to Terriers *(see above)*, leaving Hazlemere's toll house simply controlling the side bar across Green Street. The toll house was used as a private residence for several years after the side bar had been discontinued in the 1850s. It was sold in 1868.

WHIELDEN LANE
GATE, AMERSHAM
1829-1881

Sample annual toll income: £46 13s 4d in 1832/3.

Whielden Lane Gate, which was not brought into use until the trust's toll gate reorganisation of 1829-32, stood at the junction of the Amersham to Wycombe road with the side turning to Winchmore Hill *(at grid reference SP 940 957)*. The single-storey, brick-built toll cottage stood wholly on the highway verge almost opposite the 'Queen's Head' public house, which is now a private house called Whielden Gate House.

The toll cottage was not demolished when the trust was wound up in 1881, but was swept away in a 1929 road-widening which preceded post-war realignment to ease the former sharp bend here. The cottage's site is buried beneath the landscaped spoil from the road works, which left this piece of the former turnpike road as a cul-de-sac significantly called Whielden Gate.

WHITE LION ROAD,
LITTLE CHALFONT
possibly 1767-1773

No records of toll income at this gate have been found.

Jefferys' map of Buckinghamshire, surveyed in 1766-68, showed a turnpike gate just east of the junction of White Lion Road and Bell Lane, in what is now Little Chalfont. It would have been very close to the site occupied today by the attractive two-storey lodge to Beel House.

Faden's map of the country 25 miles around London, dated 1800 but probably based on much earlier mapping, showed a turnpike at the same place and no turnpike at Chorleywood. Finally Julian Hunt has published a 1930s photograph[189] of the Beel House lodge with what looks like a small, single-storey toll house in its garden, behind a fence. The lodge still stands, but the possible toll house has gone.

Unfortunately no records of a toll gate or of toll takings at White Lion Road have been found, and even the name of the gate has not survived. One possibility is that a gate was erected here in 1767 but quickly found to be poorly-sited for toll collection, then replaced by a gate at Chorleywood, four miles to the east before the first toll collection was recorded there in 1773.

**CHORLEYWOOD GATE
(HERTFORDSHIRE)
early 1770s to 1881**

Sample annual toll income: £283 in 1832/33.

Cartographic evidence suggests that this gate started life in White Lion Road, Little Chalfont, *(see above)* but was quickly re-sited to Chorleywood before the first toll receipts were recorded there in 1773.

Once the gate was erected at Chorleywood several maps show it standing just east of Chorleywood Common, nearly 200 yards east of the Rickmansworth Road-Solesbridge Lane crossroads. The toll house stood on the south-west side of the road. However at an unknown but probably late eighteenth-century date, the gate was moved again, this time to the crossroads. A new toll house was built on the south corner, where 'Tollgate House', built in 1887 after the trust had been wound up, now stands.

'The Gate' public house just west of the crossroads was built in 1773 in sight of the second toll gate location. It used to have a hanging sign which compared the services of the inn to those of the toll gate in the words "This gate hangs well and hinders none; refresh and pay, and travel on."

**HAGDEN LANE GATE
(HERTFORDSHIRE)
1767-1881**

Sample annual toll income: £532 in 1832/33.

This originally stood in open country on a site which is now in west Watford, at the junction of Rickmansworth Road, now the A412, with Hagden Lane. The gate was on the east side of the junction with its toll house on the north side of Rickmansworth Road, but the spread of later development has obliterated any trace of it.

**SIDE BAR AT MOUNT
PLEASANT LANE,
BRICKET WOOD
(HERTFORDSHIRE)
from at least 1822
to 1881**

No details of toll income found, with takings probably included with Black Boy Gate.

This side bar *(at grid reference TL 119 021)* was across Mount Pleasant Lane at its junction with the turnpike road, now the A405 north of Watford. Little has been found about it – not even its name, although it *may* have been called the Black Boy Side Bar.

The 1871 Ordnance Survey map showed that it was operated from a kiosk in the middle of the lane, as would befit a side bar. It is assumed that it was leased and worked in conjunction with the Black Boy Gate which stood half a mile further north. Today its site is about 30 yards north of the M1 motorway overbridge, and has been completely obliterated by the revised road layout at the junction of the M1 and the A405.

**BLACK BOY GATE,
BRICKET WOOD
(HERTFORDSHIRE)
1767-1881**

Sample annual toll income: £114 in 1832/33, which may include income from the side bar at Mount Pleasant Lane.

Situated north of Watford at Bricket Wood, this gate was across the Old Watford Road which is the former route of the turnpike road but is now a service road on the east side of the A405 North Orbital Road between its crossings of the M1 and M25 motorways. The toll house was on the east side of the road on the north corner of the junction with what is now called Short Lane, about 340 yards north of the 'Black Boy' public house. There is no trace of the toll house's site today.

| CAMP ROAD SIDE BAR, ST ALBANS (HERTFORDSHIRE) 1820s-1881 | *No details found of toll income for this bar on its own. Its income was probably included with Horseshoe Gate.* |

No details found of toll income for this bar on its own. Its income was probably included with Horseshoe Gate.

A once-rural side bar whose site *(at grid reference TL 158 071)* is now in the eastern suburbs of St Albans, at the junction of Hatfield Road, the A1057, with Camp Road. The 1871 Ordnance Survey map shows that the side bar was across Camp Road with its tiny toll house, probably just a kiosk, on the highway verge on the south-west side of Camp Road.

It is highly possible that the toll barrier was simply a chain hung across the road because the 1840 Tithe Map recorded that an earlier name for nearby Clarence Park was Chainbar Meadow. Chains tended to be used where toll income was expected to be minimal. Little information has been found about this side bar, which was across a track serving only a handful of cottages at Camp Hill. There has to be doubt as to whether the tolls collected at it ever covered the cost of collection.

SUTTON ROAD SIDE BAR, ST ALBANS (HERTFORDSHIRE) probably 1830s-1881

No details found of toll income for this bar on its own, as its income was probably included with Horseshoe Gate.

Sutton Road did not exist until 1826, and then only as a track serving a few cottages south of the turnpike road,[191] so the placing of a side bar – possibly only a chain – across it seems to have been overkill. However the 25-inch scale Ordnance Survey map dated 1898, and therefore made seventeen years after the trust was wound up, shows a cruciform-plan building on the south side of Hatfield Road at what is now its junction with Sutton Road *(at grid reference TL 167 072)*. The building's garden encroached on to the highway verges of the main road and Sutton Road in a manner which strongly suggests an earlier use as a turnpike toll house. However no documentary record of it has been found and the site has long since been redeveloped as the 'Rat's Castle' public house.

COLNEY HEATH LANE SIDE BAR, ST ALBANS (HERTFORDSHIRE) from at least 1822 to 1881

No details found of toll income for this bar on its own, so its income was probably included with Horseshoe Gate.

The side turning *(at grid reference TL 179 072)* to Colney Heath and Welham Green was a more substantial road than the tracks guarded by the nearest two side bars to the west. The only evidence found for the existence of this side bar is on the Ordnance Survey's 1822 and 1879 maps and in an 1882 painting of the toll house.

While detail on the 1822 edition is minimal, the 1879 sheet clearly shows, at 25-inch scale, a side bar a few feet into Colney Heath Lane and a kiosk for the toll collector beside it in the carriageway. The painting by John Westall, possibly prompted by the winding up of the turnpike trust in the previous year, shows that the 'kiosk' was actually a tiny one or two-roomed hut. The absence of a gate from the picture implies that here too the side bar was a chain. The picture is a very rare depiction of the small structures which sheltered toll collectors at side bars.[192]

| HORSESHOE GATE AND SIDE BAR, SMALLFORD (HERTFORDSHIRE) 1767-1881 | *Sample annual toll income: £102 10s 0d in 1832/33, which probably includes income from side bars on either side.* |

HORSESHOE GATE AND SIDE BAR, SMALLFORD (HERTFORDSHIRE) 1767-1881

Sample annual toll income: £102 10s 0d in 1832/33, which probably includes income from side bars on either side.

Initially called the 'Three Horshoes Gate' after the nearby inn, this was situated in Smallford at the crossroads of Hatfield Road, now the A1057, with Station Road and Oaklands Lane. It stood almost half way between St Albans and Hatfield and was the only toll gate across Hatfield Road between these towns for much of the trust's existence. It had a side bar across what became Station Road.

In the niineteeth century the toll house was a substantial two-storey brick-built house with garden which stood wholly on the highway verge on the north-east corner of the cross roads, with an open-sided porch opening directly on to the junction. The whole site has since disappeared beneath road widening.

No records of the individual toll incomes of the four nearby side bars, three to the west, one to the east, or of the Horseshoe Fiddle Gate *(see below)* have been found. The trust's advertisements for contractors to lease them imply that their takings had been included in the income of nearby gates on the main road. If this was the case, and if Horseshoe Gate's 1832-33 income of £102 10s 0d was indeed the total from one main gate and four side bars, this emphasises how little the side bars at the eastern end of the trust's road were contributing to its income.

NAST HYDE SIDE BAR, WILKINS GREEN (HERTFORDSHIRE) 1828-1881

No details have been found for toll income for this bar on its own, so it was probably included with Horseshoe Gate.

The Nast Hyde side bar stood one-third of a mile east of Horseshoe Gate *(at grid reference TL 201 079)* on the south side of the road to catch traffic coming up a lane from the hamlets of Wilkins Green and Nast Hyde. Once again on the St Albans to Hatfield section we are left wondering at the economics of having a side bar to toll such a potentially small flow of traffic.

THE FIDDLE or HORSESHOE FIDDLE GATE AND SIDE BARS, HATFIELD (HERTFORDSHIRE) from early 1830s to 1881

No details of toll income found for this gate on its own – it was probably included with Horseshoe Gate.

The road layout in the west Hatfield suburbs has been heavily altered in the twentieth century, making it difficult to follow the route of the Reading and Hatfield turnpike road on its final section through Hatfield. Today the surviving sections of road are in St Albans Road West and East.

Probably in the early 1830s a side bar was placed across the end of Fiddlebridge Lane at its crossroads with St Albans Road West and Roe Green Lane *(at grid reference TL 219 085)*. A hut was provided for the toll collector beside The Fiddle public hoouse – which has since been replaced with a small block of flats.

By 1833 trustees were considering removing this side bar and putting a gate across the then main road in its place. This was obviously done because in 1847 the trust discussed retaining the main gate here and putting back the side bar. By 1849 a chain had been put across both side turnings but although the main gate continued in use until the trust was wound up, little more has been found about the two chains.

The name 'Horseshoe Fiddle Gate' suggests that it was linked to the Horseshoe Gate, which stood barely 1½ miles to the west, and was let to the same contractor. Both gates were in continuous action after the 1830s, which makes little economic sense in view of their proximity and the fact that tickets issued at one of them would probably have given free passage through the other.

| **Weighing engine** | Although the trust's 1829 Act made provision for it to erect weighing engines, there is no indication that it did so. |

| **Milestones and mileposts** | The original milestones were a set of thin stones with a domed top, roughly curved front and three flat faces behind. Two of them, with lower-case lettering, survive as gateposts in Flackwell Heath, east of High Wycombe, and two as driveway ornaments in Terriers. A fifth, which originally stood in Little Chalfont, is now in the Chilterns Open Air Museum. |

The rather primitive appearance of these stones suggests that they may pre-date the trust and may have been provided by Lord Cecil early in the eighteenth century to identify the route *(see 'Background' above)*. A 1770 advertisement for the supply of 50 milestones with capital lettering presumably led to the replacement of the original stones.

The new stones were themselves replaced by a set of 50 cast-iron mileposts which had a triangular cross-section, triangular top and raised lettering. On all of these the distance to Hatfield is at the top of the post. They were made by Wilder and Sons of Reading and judging by their design they date from the early nineteenth century. At Marlow Bottom one of the Wilder cast-iron posts was replaced by a steel milepost in 'Bucks Pressing' style in the post-turnpike era.

There are long sections of road on which no mileposts survive today, but there are still three cast-iron posts in Berkshire, three in Buckinghamshire and six in Hertfordshire, in addition to the pressed-steel milepost at Marlow Bottom. The greatest concentration of mileposts is the run of five between St Albans and Hatfield.

A tall stone obelisk was also erected by the trust in 1822 at the top of Marlow's High Street, where the branch road to Knowl Hill leaves the main Reading to Hatfield road. The four faces on its plinth record distances to predictable places on the trust's road, plus Abingdon, Aylesbury, Bath, Maidenhead and Oxford, which are well off its road. The inclusion of Bath, 80 miles away, is another reminder of the origins of this route.

| **1881: The Trust wound up** | The road's popular modern name, the 'Gout Track', has given it a fame well above its actual value for travel. In reality the Reading and Hatfield's orbital route around north and west London was not a big toll earner and did not tempt railway builders to follow it. |

As the Railway Age developed the trust's road came to be crossed by seven main lines, and to carry traffic to and from stations on those lines. As a result, and in contrast to most turnpike trusts, its total toll revenue rose at the start of the Railway Age from £2,256 a year in 1832 to £2,930 a year in 1840. It then fell gently through £2,500 a year in 1854 and £1,885 a year in 1866 to £1,635 in 1877.

The trustees were therefore in no hurry to end their work and this became the last road in Buckinghamshire to be dis-turnpiked, an event which happened on 7 November 1881 under **43 Vic. c.12 (1880)**.

Road 14:
The Aylesbury, Thame and Shillingford Turnpike Road 1770

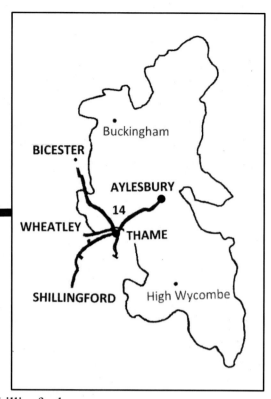

Identifying the road's route today
MAIN ROUTE

The turnpike route follows today's A418 from Aylesbury to the east end of the Thame bypass, takes the B4445 Aylesbury Road and North Street and C-class High Street and Oxford Road through Thame, then the A329 from the west end of Thame bypass to Shillingford.

BRANCH ROADS

The turnpike road also had three branches from Thame:

(1) following the B4012 to Postcombe, (2) following the B4011 to Blackthorn, south of Bicester, but with sections immediately north and south of the crossing of Thame bypass which are now unclassified, and (3) following the A418 from the west end of the Thame bypass to the A40 east of Wheatley, except the westernmost 260 yards before the A40 junction where the turnpike route is now abandoned and bypassed.

Historic background

Most turnpike trusts in Buckinghamshire looked after just one road. Exceptions were the Reading and Hatfield Trust and the Risborough Road Trust, which had one branch road each, and the Colnbrook Trust, which had two. The Aylesbury and Shillingford Trust, however, started with a single road in 1770, then between 1785 and 1838 added branches from Thame to Postcombe – for Wycombe and London, to Blackthorn – for Bicester, and to Wheatley – for Oxford.

As a result the trust's name became progressively longer and more complicated until a popular title of Thame United Trust was adopted in 1838.

MAIN ROUTE

In the late Middle Ages a pair of parallel routes linked Oxford with Bedford, where they joined and continued as one to Cambridge. Today's A418 route, passing through Thame, Aylesbury, and Leighton Buzzard, was part of the southern arm of that pair. It seems to have become so subordinate to the northern route via Bicester, Buckingham and Newport Pagnell that by the late seventeenth century it was not recognised by map makers as a cross-country route.

However during the turnpike era the importance of the southern route grew, possibly because worsening road conditions between Newport Pagnell and Bedford deflected traffic to it from the northern arm.

When the Aylesbury and Shillingford turnpike trust was formed in 1770, the southern route was still so much less important than the northern that west of Thame the trustees saw the Thames at Wallingford, approached via Shillingford, as a more significant source of traffic than Oxford.

The main pre-turnpike route west of Thame had been through Moreton and over Horsenden Hill to Tetsworth, crossing the London to Oxford road, to continue via Stoke Talmage and Brightwell Baldwin to the Thames at Wallingford. This went out of use after the trust decided to turnpike the parallel route, today's A329, via Rycote Lane and Stadhampton to Shillingford in 1770. A major incentive was probably the 1767 opening of a bridge to replace the ferry across the Thames at Shillingford, thereby shortening journeys to Wallingford from the north and east.

BRANCH
ROADS
While Aylesbury to Shillingford was turnpiked to improve an existing traffic corridor, two of the three branch roads radiating from Thame appear to have been taken over by the trust in order to improve communications from the town rather than because they carried significant existing traffic.

The road to Postcombe had been long-established as a popular short cut from Thame to head south on the Oxford to London road, although its original alignment was partly within Thame Park. It was turnpiked in 1785.

However the branches to Wheatley and Blackthorn were simply chains of thinly-trafficked indirect local lanes until the trust took them over. Sixty years were to pass before the trust turnpiked the direct route from Thame to Wheatley in 1838. This was for Oxford-bound traffic, shortening the previous route to Oxford along Rycote Lane, today's A329, to join the London to Oxford Road at Milton Common. This new Wheatley branch has gone from strength to strength since turnpiking.

But thin toll income on the Blackthorn branch, turnpiked by the trust in 1833 as a new link between Thame and Bicester, demonstrated that there was little demand to travel this route.

The limits of the trust's road
The main turnpike route started in Aylesbury, at what is now the roundabout at the junction of Friarage, Gatehouse, and Oxford Roads, and terminated in the village of Shillingford at the junction of Warborough, Henley, and Wharf Roads.

The Postcombe branch left the main route in the middle of Thame at the junction of North Street with Upper High Street, and terminated at its junction with the Oxford to London road, now the A40, just north of the village of Postcombe.

The Blackthorn branch left the main route in Thame at the junction of Lower High Street with Priestend, and terminated on Blackthorn Hill, north of Ambrosden village, at its junction with the Aylesbury to Bicester road, now the A41.

The Wheatley branch left the main route just west of Thame at the junction of Oxford Road with Rycote Lane, and terminated at its junction with the Oxford road, now the A40, east of Wheatley. The last 260 yards of the turnpike route were abandoned when a new alignment to the A40 was opened in the 1960s, but a pair of hedges still mark its course.

Its length and maintenance districts

The Thame United turnpike trust was second only to the Reading and Hatfield for total road length of a trust operating in Buckinghamshire, with 42¾ miles. The next longest road, with 22½ miles, was the Kettering and Newport Pagnell.

The Thame United trust's main route was 21¾ miles long, of which 8½ were in Buckinghamshire and the rest in Oxfordshire. The four miles of the Postcombe branch were all in Oxfordshire. The Blackthorn branch was 12 miles, of which 8 miles were in Buckinghamshire and the rest in Oxfordshire. The Wheatley branch was 5 miles, all in Oxfordshire.

This gave the trust a total 42¾ miles to oversee, of which 16½ were in Buckinghamshire.

To simplify the administration of this steadily expanding trust, its 1833 Act divided its roads into three districts: Aylesbury to Shillingford, Thame to Postcombe, and Thame to Bicester. Tolls collected in each district were ring-fenced to the maintenance of the road in that district. When the 1838 Act added the Wheatley branch this was attached to the Aylesbury to Shillingford District, which became grandiosely renamed the Aylesbury, Thame, Oxford and Shillingford District.

Initial Act of Parliament

10 Geo.III, c.58 (1770) turnpiked the main route from Aylesbury through Thame and Stadhampton to Shillingford.

Continuation Acts

25 Geo.III, c.127 (1785) extended trust control to the Postcombe branch. **31 Geo.III, c.136 (1791)** merged the provisions of the two earlier Acts and separated the accounts of the trust's two roads. **3 Will.IV, c.86 (1833)** superseded the previous three Acts, extended trust control to the Blackthorn branch, and split the trust's roads into three districts. Finally **1 Vict. c.46, (1838)** superseded the 1833 Act, added the Wheatley branch to the trust's responsibilities, and ended the requirement to keep the accounts of the main road and Postcombe branch separate from those of the other branches.

Control of the Trust:
CLERKS

Giles Prickett, an Oxford solicitor, was the trust's clerk from 1770 to 1791, after which John Hollier and his son (also called John), solicitors of Thame, held the clerk's post continuously until 1855. From 1793 to 1854 the two Holliers were also joint clerks to the Wheatley and Stokenchurch Trust, part of the Oxford to London Road and future A40, which crossed the Aylesbury and Shillingford trust's road at Milton Common. In 1855 R Holloway of Thame took over as clerk of the Thame United until the trust was wound up in 1880.

No particularly dominant chairmen have been identified on this trust.

MEETINGS OF THE TRUSTEES	With Thame at the hub of the trust's roads and with the clerks' professional offices in that town from 1791, it is unsurprising that all meetings of trustees were held in Thame apart from some meetings in the 1780s at 'The Bell' in Shillingford, and from 1772 to 1791 at the 'George Inn' and 'White Hart Inn' at Aylesbury.
	Four inns were used at Thame, starting with the 'Red Lion' at numbers 1-2 High Street – now partly McColls newsagents – from 1770 until about 1819, followed until 1837 by the 'Crown Inn' at 99 High Street – its site now occupied by a pair of 1960s shops on the north-east side of the market place, and finally the 'Spread Eagle' at numbers 16-17 Cornmarket from 1837 to at least 1864, apart from a short period at 'The Greyhound' at number 105 High Street in 1844-45.
Maintenance of the road	The trust's paperwork has not been found and no major issues over maintenance have been recorded in other sources such as newspapers.
Improvements to the road	With its road mainly in the low-lying Vale of Aylesbury and Thames Valley this trust did not have any serious hills to surmount, so no major earthworks. Some 2¼ miles of completely new road were built, spread through five locations.
CHANGES BEFORE THE TURNPIKE ROAD	Speculation without documentary evidence is dangerous but there are a number of cartographic clues to show that six miles of the current A418 route between Hartwell, west of Aylesbury, and Grove End, at the top of Scotsgrove Hill *(at grid reference SP 715 076),* lie up to half a mile north of the road's pre-turnpike alignment – which possibly went through Upton, Dinton, Westlington and Haddenham. However the analysis of evidence is too detailed for the scope of this book and traffic had almost certainly moved to the A418's present route before the turnpike trust was formed.
A PROPOSAL AT HADDENHAM	In 1832 the trust proposed to upgrade some six miles of a minor road, today a C-class road from Hartweell to Grove End via Haddenham village, which ran up to a mile to the south of the turnpike road, now the A418, and to dis-turnpike the corresponding section of the existing route. This move was probably prompted by the enclosure of the open fields of Haddenham parish in 1830-33, in which the minor road in question had been drastically rebuilt, straightened and shortened by the enclosure commissioners. But no more was heard of this scheme, which would have brought trunk road traffic through the middle of Haddenham.
STONE	In the village of Stone just west of Aylesbury the trust eliminated an awkward dog-leg immediately north and east of the church, by building in about 1820 a gently curving 300-yard cut-off to the north of the old road, and abandoning the redundant section.
ON THE RIVER THAME FLOODPLAIN	On its approach to the north side of Thame the pre-turnpike road descended Scotsgrove Hill as now but then bore right, across the foot of the hill, before making a sharp turn south to cross the floodplain of the Scotsgrove Brook. Around 1800 the trust built a 660-yard causeway straight across the flood

plain from the foot of Scotsgrove Hill. Today this carries the A418 to the northern edge of the Thame bypass roundabout. In 1836 the section of causeway in Buckinghamshire was widened to 48ft. As well as marginally shortening the route, the new causeway's height placed it above the seasonal floods which had afflicted the old route.

Where the new causeway crossed the county boundary, the bridge over the Scotsgrove Brook was built with a sharp bend at each end. This was an economy measure, to enable the bridge to cross the brook at a right angle instead of crossing it obliquely. In 1851, after years of complaints from the travelling public, the trust built a new bridge obliquely over the brook and slightly realigned the causeway to eliminate the bends.

| RYCOTE LANE AT NORTH WESTON (OXFORDSHIRE) | Rycote Lane has a 500-yard straight section running nearly north-south between two sharp bends south of Manor Farm, North Weston *(at grid reference SP 682 048)*. This straight section was built sometime before the 1790s, cutting out two sides of a triangle and shortening the road by 250 yards. On the west side of the triangle the old turnpike road remains a public bridleway today. The lack of trust records prevents any dating of this work beyond the observation that maps show it completed by the 1790s. |

| GREAT MILTON VILLAGE (OXFORDSHIRE) | Great Milton village was on the through road in the seventeenth century but had been bypassed by the time of Davis' map of Oxfordshire in 1797 - and this bypass remains the A329 today. In the absence of trust documentation it has proved difficult to say whether the one mile-long bypass was built before or after the trust took over in 1770. |

Jefferys' 1766 map of Oxfordshire shows the main road going <u>through</u> the village as well as the new route bypassing to the south, suggesting that the bypass was planned in the 1760s and built immediately after the route was taken over by the turnpike trust. Support for this interpretation comes from the fact that this was not a main road until adopted by the turnpike trust, so it is unlikely that any other agency had an incentive to build the bypass.

| STADHAMPTON (OXFORDSHIRE) | Davis' 1797 map of Oxfordshire appears to show the main road through the village, running south of the green some 120 yards to the east of the present route, passing the water mill and the 'Bear and Ragged Staff' public house, with the present road shown as a minor road. Today the old route is a public footpath at its northern end and a minor road at its southern end, with just a water meadow in between. |

By 1811 the draft Ordnance Survey map showed the present layout in place and the Davis route not even a through road. This leaves us with the options that either Davis made an error, or that the turnpike trust rerouted traffic to the present main route between 1797 and 1811. In the absence of the trust's minutes this must remain speculation.

| FROM STADHAMPTON TO SHILLINGFORD (OXFORDSHIRE) | Between Stadhampton and Shillingford the modern A329 has the appearance of a string of indirect country lanes stitched together by the trust to form a through route. Jefferys' 1766 map of Oxfordshire shows no road at all over Grange Common at Warborough although Davis' Oxfordshire |

map of 1797 showed the modern road in place, forming a half-mile curve around the edge of the former common. The common was not enclosed until 1853, so the map evidence points to the trust having built the present road around it.

POSTCOMBE BRANCH (OXFORDSHIRE)	There appear to have been no improvements in alignment carried out by the trust on this branch road.

BLACKTHORN BRANCH	When the Blackthorn branch was taken over by the trust in 1833 it consisted of a string of wandering lanes leading to various destinations. In the years between 1833 and 1880 the trust upgraded the lanes into a through road by widening the carriageway, realigning two T-junctions and constructing two lengths of new road to shorten the distance.

The longest new section was the 600-yard straight at Addingrove Farm *(at grid reference SP 664 112)*, between Long Crendon and Oakley. This cut out a triangular detour to the south-west. Addingrove Farm's previous buildings were half a mile north of their present site, and were moved to stand beside the new road.

In Oakley a 160-yard new road, now called Bicester Road, was cut across the north end of the village, bypassing the angular junction formerly made by Manor Road and the appropriately-named 'The Turnpike'.

The 550-yard bypass around the south-western side of Blackthorn village was not built until the 1970s.

WHEATLEY BRANCH	Like the Blackthorn branch, the Wheatley road was a string of minor lanes when the trust obtained powers to turnpike it in 1838. Such Thame to Oxford traffic as there was went via Rycote Lane, now the A329, to join the Oxford road at Milton Common.

The Wheatley branch was turnpiked at the dawn of the railway age and the beginning of turnpike decline. Although in 1838 the trust had submitted to Parliament a map of how it intended to shorten the route by cutting out three bends in the road, it did not carry any of them out.

Indeed as late as 1906 there were complaints that the carriageway was still only 12ft wide between North Weston and the junction with the Oxford road east of Wheatley. Later in the 1930s Oxfordshire County Council implemented one of the trust's 1838 schemes by cutting through the wide-curving S-bend immediately west of North Weston *(at grid reference SP 676 058)* with a gently curving, ¼-mile new section of road.

Toll gates and tollhouses	The Thame United trust's 21¾-mile main route between Aylesbury and Shillingford had four gates across it until about 1840, then five, of which two were re-sited during the trust's life. It also had two side bars, but not at the same time.

After the Postcombe and Blackthorn branch roads had been taken into the trust's control three more main gates were added, plus one short-lived side bar and one even shorter-lived main gate. The eastern end of the branch road to Wheatley started near the Priest End toll gate at Thame, so that branch was never provided with a separate gate.

AYLESBURY GATE
1770-1880

Sample annual toll income: £492 in 1836.

The Aylesbury Gate stood in Oxford Road beside the site now occupied by the Sir Henry Floyd Grammar School. The toll cottage and its garden stood on the southern verge of the highway, and remained there until demolished in 1881 after the winding up of the trust.

An altercation about the Aylesbury Gate's opening hours saw its gatekeeper brought before the justices of the peace in 1805, when he was found guilty of a 'misdemeanour'.[193] His offence had been to lock his gate for the night at 11pm instead of the advertised time of midnight – and then tell a traveller arriving at 11.20pm that he could stay there all night for all that the gate keeper cared.

THAME MILL GATE
1770-1880

Sample annual toll income: £200 in 1836.

The Thame Mill Gate's first site is now beneath the roundabout at the north end of Thame. In about 1800, when the trust shortened the road slightly by making a straight new causeway across the flood meadows *(see 'Improvements' above)*, the first Thame Mill toll house was in the way and had to be demolished.

The toll gate was immediately replaced by a new one on the causeway, 300 yards north-east of today's roundabout. The new toll house had two floors and stood on the south-east side of the road, with its porch on the highway verge but the rest of the building in a garden forming a triangle cut out of the adjoining field. The porch was probably removed when the trust was wound up in 1880, but the tollhouse continued in use as a private dwelling until demolished in the 1950s to allow the verge to be widened, and ultimately to provide a site for the present layby.

PRIEST END GATE
AND SIDE BAR,
THAME
1770-1880

Sample annual toll income: £386 in 1832, including takings at Priest End side bar, and £291 in 1836 after the side bar had been removed.

The first Priest End Gate was erected at the T-junction at the north-west end of Lower High Street in Thame. The main gate here was across Oxford Road, with a side bar across Priestend, which was then the road to Blackthorn and Bicester. The tiny toll kiosk appears to have stood in the road at the west end of the house called Stribblehills.

When the road to Blackthorn was itself turnpiked in 1833 it was decided to separate toll collection for the new branch from that of the existing main road. Accordingly, in 1834, the side bar was removed and a new gate for the Blackthorn branch was built in Long Crendon parish *(see 'Long Crendon Gate' below)*. The gate on the main Oxford Road was also moved nearly half a mile west to the top of the hill – now just above Lord Williams' Grammar School. A toll collector's house was built on the northern highway verge, and a length of verge was fenced off as its garden. Although no longer at Priest End the new gate retained its previous name until the trust was wound up, whereupon the tollhouse was demolished.

MORETON SIDE BAR, NEAR THAME
from between 1838 and 1851 to 1880

No separate toll records have been found for this side bar, which was operated as one with the Priest End Gate.

Moreton side bar was situated about one mile west of Thame, with its bar across the turning off Rycote Lane to the hamlet of Moreton. The small tollhouse, which would have been swept away at the winding up of the trust, stood on the southern verge of Rycote Lane on the west side of the junction.

As with a number of side bars in this book, the traffic to and from the hamlet of Moreton itself would not appear to have justified the provision of a permanently-manned gate and a fully-fledged toll house, especially as anyone going from Moreton to Thame would pass through Priest End Gate.

The toll board from this side bar has survived and is displayed in Thame Museum. The trust had repainted it several times and its legibility has been complicated by the weathering away of some of those layers. Nevertheless it is a rare survival and a tangible link with this turnpike trust.

BROCKHAMPTON OR BROOKHAMPTON GATE (OXFORDSHIRE)
1770-1880

Sample annual toll income: £200 in 1836.

This toll gate was situated at the junction of today's A329 and B480 towards the southern end of the combined villages of Stadhampton and Brookhampton. For most of its life the gate stood only across the road to Thame, but a second gate was added across Newington Road, now the A329, possibly in 1840. Technically this second gate was not a side bar because it was across the continuation of the turnpike road itself.

The second gate may have been a response to a sudden increase in traffic heading from the Oxford area to Didcot after the railway station was opened there in 1840. The impressive two-storey, bow-fronted toll house remains today as a private dwelling.

POSTCOMBE BRANCH GATES

For a 4-mile branch road the road from Thame to Postcombe had a remarkably complicated history of toll gates, though for most of its life it had only one at a time. This included the White Hound Pond Gate, the Brick Kiln Gate, and the Attington Gate.

WHITE HOUND POND GATE, THAME
1785-1792 and for some years 1824-32

Toll income from this gate appears always to have been recorded with Thame Brick Kiln Gate.

White Hound Pond Gate stood in the vicinity of the modern war memorial at the south-east end of Thame's Upper High Street. It was erected when the Thame to Postcombe branch road was first turnpiked. Because it was located just within the built-up area of Thame there may have been friction with residents living 'outside' the gate as they went into town.

Whatever the reason, in 1792, after only seven years, the gate was re-sited ¼ mile south-east to the Brick Kiln site *(see below)* on the edge of town at the junction of Chinnor Road and Thame Park Road.[194] This early move probably indicates that the 'toll house' was actually only a small kiosk without the usual living facilities, and thus easily dismantled.

In 1824 the White Hound Pond Gate was reinstated, almost certainly as a ploy to deter the building of a new turnpike road from Princes Risborough which would end in Thame as East Street *(see Road number 19 below)*. The Aylesbury and Shillingford Trust became caught up in Thame's opposition to the new road and resurrected their gate between East Street and the market place, a siting which meant that travellers from Risborough would have to pass through it and pay toll for a minimal distance on the Aylesbury and Shillingford Trust's Postcombe branch road.

This second gate on the White Hound Pond site was probably only a temporary affair in use intermittently during the 1824-30 campaign against the new road, and for a couple of years afterwards. We know about it because the Thame and Risborough Road Act of 1825 required the re-siting of an unnamed turnpike gate which "had been erected" between the point where the new road would enter town and the market place. This gate was not in use during 1826 and possibly 1827, when the campaign was in low key.

During 1824-32 the Brick Kiln gate remained in use, and a ticket bought at one gate would have given free passage through the other, thus bringing no financial benefit to the trust. Once the Risborough to Thame road was complete and further obstruction was pointless, the White Hound Pond Gate was removed for a second time, although it took two years to do it.

BRICK KILN GATE AND SIDE BAR, THAME 1792-1839

Sample annual toll income (including from its side bar): £210 in 1834.

This gate replaced White Hound Pond Gate in 1792 *(see above)* and was located just outside the town limits at the point where Park Street splits into Chinnor Road and Thame Park Road. The toll house was built in the angle between the two roads. Map evidence suggests that the gate was initially only across Thame Park Road but that a side bar was placed across Chinnor Road between 1813 and 1823.

In 1839, for reasons which have not been found, trustees moved the gate for a second time, this time right out of town to Attington *(see below)*. The triangle of land on which the Brick Kiln tollhouse stood was sold in 1853 to become the site of Thame's new police station, which was built in 1854. The police station was carefully sited behind the former tollhouse, which suggests that the latter may have been used as a private dwelling – or as a police station until the new building was ready.

ATTINGTON GATE, NEAR TETSWORTH (OXFORDSHIRE) 1839-1880

Sample annual toll income : £132 in 1840.

The third and last gate site on the Postcombe branch road collected its first full year of tolls in 1840. It occupied a lonely location nearly three miles south of Brick Kiln Gate and just south-east of Tetsworth village *(at grid reference SP 699 011)*. The gate was provided with a hexagonal two-storey toll house designed in a vaguely historical style, presumably in deference to

Thame Park's castellated lodge houses which had been built in 1830 on the same road. The 'working' part of the house stood on the highway verge while its rear portion, plus its garden, stood on private land. The building remains in use as a private house today, but its single-storey side wings have been extended since turnpike days.

BLACKTHORN BRANCH GATES	The branch turnpike road from Thame to Blackthorn had two toll gates, at Long Crendon in the south and Piddington further north.

LONG CRENDON GATE
1834-1880

Sample annual toll income: £233 in 1836.

Until 1834 traffic on the unturnpiked route from Bicester via Blackthorn or Brill had entered Thame through the side bar of Priest End Gate. Once the Bicester road had been turnpiked, however, the trust wanted to separate the new branch's income from the main route's takings. To do this a gate was placed across the causeway on the northern approach to Thame Bridge, about 100 yards north of the river and just inside Long Crendon parish.

The toll house was situated on the west side of the road, at causeway level, presumably with a 'basement' beside the causeway. It had been demolished by 1930 at the latest but in 2016 the long, narrow outline of its garden on the floodplain, parallel with and well below the road, was still marked by a ragged line of hawthorn trees which once presumably formed its hedge.

PIDDINGTON GATE
(OXFORDSHIRE)
1835-1880

Sample annual toll income: £60 in 1836.

The Piddington Gate was presumably intended to catch traffic between Brill and Bicester, which otherwise would have travelled nearly four miles on the new Blackthorn road without passing a tollgate. When this road was turnpiked in 1833 the trust proposed to put the gate at the oblique crossroads with turnings to Brill and Piddington *(at grid reference SP 634 158)*.

Delays ensued in 1834 when an alternative site was suggested nearly a mile southwards at the turning from Brill via Touchbridge *(at grid reference SP 632 144)*. This, however, was objected to on the grounds that its siting would inconvenience cross-country traffic from Oxford to the newly-opened spa at Dorton so, in 1835, the trustees went back to the crossroads site which had been proposed originally.

There the tollhouse and its garden were built on the highway verge on the west side of the crossroads and the two toll gates were placed across the two arms of the turnpike road leading out of the junction. Technically this constituted a gate and side bar but, since both gates were across the turnpike road, it must (pedantically) be regarded as one main gate in two parts.

Since the toll house stood on highway land, it was probably demolished immediately after the trust was wound up in 1880. A guided-walk leaflet issued in the 1990s by Cherwell District Council stated that number 75 Thame Road in Piddington village, almost opposite the church "used to be the toll house adjacent to Piddington crossroads". External inspection shows that this cottage has three walls of brick, as do many neighbouring properties, but has a rear wall of Northamptonshire ironstone, which is not a common local building material. It is possible that the rear wall of number 75 is formed of the recycled remains of Piddington toll cottage.

WHEATLEY BRANCH	Unusually the Wheatley branch road never had a toll gate. In the absence of the trust's minutes we must assume that the Priest End toll gate at Thame, which stood on the trust's main road only ¼ mile from the eastern end of the branch road, was expected to collect tolls from traffic to and from Wheatley until that traffic had grown sufficiently to make a gate on the branch road itself viable. However growth didn't happen until long after the turnpike era, so the gate was not needed.
Weighing engine	An engine was installed at Aylesbury Gate some time between 1800 and 1819 and remained in use there until at least 1857. While this location, at the eastern extremity of the trust's roads, might seem a little remote, Aylesbury had by far the busiest of the trust's gates and thus could make most impact on deterring or surcharging over-weight wagons.
Milestones and mileposts	The Aylesbury, Thame and Shillingford trust was dilatory in erecting milemarkers. When its initial 1770 Act expired, the renewal Act of 1791 noted that no milestones had been erected and required this to be remedied.
	This had been done on its core section between Aylesbury and Thame by 1813, when the Ordnance Survey's draft two-inch scale map recorded eight milestones in place between these towns, but there is no evidence of milestones between Thame and Shillingford at that time. On the eight milestones in place by 1813 the mileage to London started at 39 outside Aylesbury, as a continuation of the Sparrows Herne turnpike road's mileage via Watford.
	At an unknown date between 1824 and 1836 the trust replaced its milestones between Aylesbury and Thame with cast-iron mileposts with raised lettering, made by Seymour of Aylesbury. The distances they displayed had a new mileage base, measured from central Aylesbury instead of central London as previously, which meant that the new cast-iron posts had to be sited roughly half way between the previous milestones – which were removed. It is assumed that the identical cast-iron mileposts between Thame and Shillingford were installed at the same time.
	Today three of these mileposts survive in Buckinghamshire on the south side of the road between Aylesbury and Thame, and a fourth has been preserved in the garden of the County Museum at Aylesbury. However only one survives in Oxfordshire, near the entrance to the Oxfordshire Golf Club two miles west of Thame, and this is assumed to have been missed in 1940 when mileposts were removed as a wartime security measure.
POSTCOMBE BRANCH	The author has not found any evidence that the short Postcombe branch road ever had any milemarkers.
BLACKTHORN BRANCH	No evidence has been found for any milemarkers on the Blackthorn branch road during the turnpike era. However it subsequently had a set of twelve

mileposts standing on its west side. These were steel pressings with a triangular ground plan and round top which gives them a superficial resemblance to the cast-iron posts on the main Aylesbury to Shillingford section, but the posts on the branch road have mileages painted on to a flat surface. These, named as 'Bucks Pressings' by the Milestone Society, were almost certainly installed after the turnpike era by the new highway authorities, probably in the 1890s or 1900s.

There is cartographic evidence that all twelve 'Bucks Pressing' mileposts were in place between Thame and Blackthorn Hill until the 1939-45 war, but the five in Oxfordshire – from Piddington to the A41 – do not appear to have been replaced after the general removal of milemarkers for security reasons during that war. Those in Buckinghamshire were either not removed during the war – perhaps their mileages were overpainted – or were put back after the war, because all seven were in place in the 1970s. Since then their numbers have been depleted by theft or traffic accidents, and one of the four survivors is being eaten away by rust.

WHEATLEY BRANCH

Five milestones or mileposts were placed along the south side of the Wheatley branch road by the trust but none are there now. Cartographic evidence suggests that they were all in place until 'temporary' removal at the outbreak of the 1939-45 war and, as with the Oxfordshire section of the Blackthorn branch, it seems that the county council did not replace them in 1945, for there has been no record of them since.

1881: The Trust wound up

The Thame United Turnpike Trust had no directly competing railways until 1864, when the Great Western Railway's Thame to Oxford branch line was built closely parallel to the trust's Thame to Wheatley branch road. It is worth noting that the Princes Risborough to Bicester railway was not opened until 26 years after the trust had been wound up.

However, right at the start of the Railway Era a branch of the London and Birmingham Railway arrived in Aylesbury in 1839. The Thame United Trust's turnpike route from Thame to Aylesbury quickly came to act as a feeder to the railway line from places further west.

As a result this was one of the few Buckinghamshire turnpike trusts whose toll income went up at the start of the Railway Age, and reasonable toll takings over the next few years meant that it was 1874 before the trustees felt the need to petition for closure. That first application to Parliament was unsuccessful, but a second application in the following year led to **38/39 Vict., c.194 (1875),** which required the trust to continue work until 1 November 1880, on which day it ceased work, although the final meetings of trustees to wind up their affairs were held in 1881.

Road 15:
The Bicester and Aylesbury Turnpike Road 1770

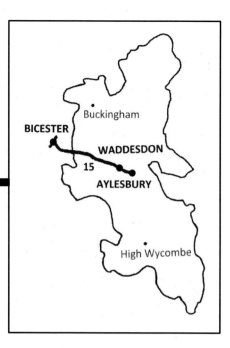

Identifying the road's route

The route of the turnpike road follows the B4100 London Road from Bicester town centre to the Bicester ring road, then the A41 to the Aylesbury ring road, and finally a C-class road, Bicester Road, from the ring road to central Aylesbury.

Historic background

The Bicester and Aylesbury Turnpike Trust's road generally followed the route of its Roman predecessor, Akeman Street, from the outskirts of eighteenth century Aylesbury to Blackthorn Hill, about two miles short of Bicester. West of the hill the Roman road continued westwards towards the short-lived Roman town at Alcester, which was superseded on a fresh site by Bicester. By the late eighteenth century, however, a probably minor road branched off Akeman Street west of Blackthorn Hill and curved north-west into Bicester. This was the route adopted by the trust.

However, while the course of most of the Roman road survived physically through the Middle Ages, it does not seem to have been the natural choice for travellers by the eighteenth century. This was probably because west of Waddesdon between Sharp's Hill at Kingswood and Blackthorn Hill, the route crosses a low-lying vale of Jurassic Clay, which could be flooded or seriously muddy in winter.

In 1586 an estate map of Doddershall, near Quainton, showed Akeman Street to the west of Waddesdon duplicated on its north side by an alternative route which went through Grendon Underwood. The map labelled this route 'the Road to London' while the Roman road was simply called 'Ackman Street'.[195] Tradition has it that at about the same time William Shakespeare worked on two of his plays during stays at the 'Ship Inn' at Grendon Underwood. While this was less than a mile from Akeman Street, it was right beside the alternative route, which Shakespeare could have used while travelling between Stratford and London.

In 1675 Ogilby's atlas of English main roads did not depict Akeman Street at all between Aylesbury and Bicester, leaving Bicester-bound travellers to go round via Buckingham. In 1701 Robert Morden's Buckinghamshire map showed an Aylesbury to Bicester route on the line of Akeman Street between Aylesbury and Waddesdon, but west of Waddesdon this left the Roman route and swung to the north along what is now a public footpath past Binwell Lane Farm *(at grid reference SP 712 191)*. Morden's route then went through Grendon Underwood and Marsh Gibbon to join Ogilby's Buckingham to Bicester route at Stratton Audley. This confirms the main road route shown on the 1586 Doddershall map but is confused by Morden mistakenly labelling it 'Ackman Street Waye'.

Although this diversion via Marsh Gibbon added 2½ miles to the Aylesbury to Bicester journey, it was nearly ten feet above the level of Akeman Street when crossing the clay lowlands, so was probably passable in all weathers. Yet in spite of this, by 1768 Jefferys' map of Buckinghamshire showed the modern A41 route along Akeman Street as the only main road between Aylesbury and Bicester and did not show the section between Waddesdon and Grendon Underwood at all

In order to address the seasonal problems of Akeman Street a Parliamentary Bill[196] had been introduced in 1711 to turnpike the road from Aylesbury to Bicester. This was opposed by the town of Buckingham on the grounds that Aylesbury–Buckingham–Banbury was on the established route from London to the west Midlands and upgrading a route via Bicester would damage the existing trade in Buckingham.[197]

So it was only in the eighteenth century that Akeman Street was again recognised as a main road, and this Bicester and Aylesbury turnpike trust started the work which would ultimately revive its fortunes as a route from London to the west Midlands.

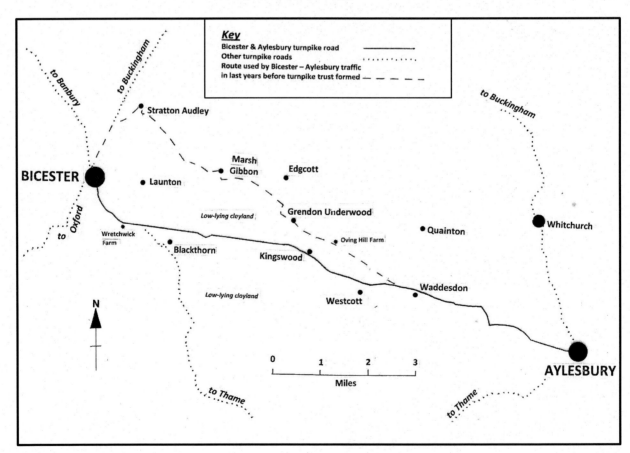

FIGURE 29: **The route of the Bicester and Aylesbury turnpike road**, and the alternative which was in use before the trust was formed.

The limits of the trust's road	The trust's responsibilities within Bicester started in the Market Place. At Aylesbury its control ended where its road met that of the Wendover and Buckingham Turnpike Trust at the junction of the Bicester and Buckingham roads, where the Royal Bucks Hospital stands today.[198] The Wendover and Buckingham trust had controlled Buckingham Street in Aylesbury since 1721.
Its length and maintenance districts	The Bicester to Aylesbury turnpike road was 16 miles long, of which 12 were in Buckinghamshire and four in Oxfordshire. Throughout its life the trust appears to have managed the road as a single entity.
Initial Act of Parliament	**10 Geo.III, c.72 (1770).**
Continuation Acts	**31 Geo.III, c.101 (1791)** was a short Act dominated by the issue of re-siting the Launton side bar. Subsequent Acts were: **53 Geo.III, c.194 (1813), 3 Will.IV, (1834), 27/28 Vic., c.75 (1863/64),** and **28/29 Vic., c.107 (1865).**
Control of the Trust: TRUSTEES	The trust's 1770 Act listed 153 trustees. This was one of the trusts in which many members took turns in the chair so that few were driving forces on the trust's work. Notable among the few was William Rickford, the Aylesbury MP, who was the power behind turning around the trust's lamentable performance at road maintenance, first while an ordinary trustee, then as chairman in 1823-29.
CLERKS	Henry Churchill, a Bicester solicitor who was also clerk to the two other turnpike trusts in that town, was clerk from 1770 until at least 1800, after which another Bicester solicitor, Henry Walford, held the post until his death in 1825. From then on James James, an Aylesbury solicitor, and his son and grandson – both also called James James – occupied the clerk's post for fifty years between them until the trust was wound up. The clerk's salary of £25 peer year was the same throughout the James' tenure of office until it was reduced to £19 a year in 1865 as an economy measure.
MEETINGS OF THE TRUSTEES	In spite of the trust's 1770 Act specifying that meetings would alternate between Bicester and Aylesbury, the 'King's Arms' in Bicester seems to have been the sole venue until 1819. After that and until 1858, they varied between the 'King's Arms' in Bicester and the 'White Hart Inn' in Market Square, Aylesbury – demolished in 1864 to make way for the arches beside the Crown Court. A few Aylesbury meetings were held at 'The George Inn' in the 1850s-1870s but after 1858 most were at 'The Crooked Billet' – now the 'Akeman Inn' – at Kingswood, near the mid-point of the trust's road.
Maintenance of the road	Much of the trust's road lay on Jurassic Clay, a soft water-holding stratum into which wheels sank easily. Worst was its dead level crossing of the River Ray flood plain between Blackthorn Hill and Sharp's Hill, Kingswood, a

4½-mile length of road which was regularly inundated in winter and which needed an above-average rate of levelling and stoning. The surrounding expanses of clay and alluvium offered no prospect of digging locally for gravel to maintain the road, so stone had to be expensively carted many miles to where it was to be spread on the road.

This was challenging territory for the most determined trust, but the Bicester and Aylesbury seems to have suffered from lengthy periods of trustee apathy, during which the road's condition deteriorated. After raising £3,300 in the 1770s for the initial re-laying of the road's upper layers, the trust seems to have rested on its laurels, so road quality quickly relapsed. As a result, and unlike many other turnpike roads, the road improvements here were not immediately followed by the start of serious stagecoach services over the route. A Bicester–Aylesbury–London stage coach started to run twice a week in each direction in 1774 but quickly faded out.

In 1793, following an apparent burst of road repair, a second Bicester to London stage coach service was started, but with only one coach running on three days a week in each direction. It was followed in about 1814 by a Kidderminster–Bicester–London service, but further apathy by the trustees led the owners of that coach to indict the trust at Quarter Sessions in 1816 for the deplorable condition of their road.

This clearly shook the trustees, who then elected a number of new, local and more active men, including William Rickford, an Aylesbury banker and MP. He prompted such an improvement in the early 1820s that a second Kidderminster–London coach was started in about 1821, and 'The Sovereign' Warwick–Bicester–London coach service started in 1825. Matters did not relapse again, but traffic, as measured by toll income, never grew at the rate seen on some other Buckinghamshire trusts.

| **Improvements to the road:** AT BICESTER | Probably because much of the Bicester to Aylesbury road was based on a direct Roman military alignment, the trust carried out only one re-routing during its century of operation. This was at Bicester, away from the Roman road. In early turnpike days the south-eastern exit from Bicester was via Priory Road or Chapel Street or both, continuing across the line later taken by the railway before converging on the line of London Road south-east of what would become the site of the railway station *(at grid reference SP 587 217)*. In the eighteenth century what was to become London Road petered out near the future site of the railway level crossing. |

During the early 1820s trustees debated possible improvements to this rather indirect route but were constrained by the trust's poor finances. Finally in 1826 they simplified the exit from the town by constructing 300 yards of new road – now London Road – running due south from the site of the future level crossing to the first bend in the modern road, now a roundabout. The work was timely because when the Bletchley to Oxford railway was built in 1850 part of Chapel Street was obliterated by the new goods yard and a diversion via the present level crossing would have been inevitable.

BLACKTHORN HILL, SHARP'S HILL AND THE LOW GROUND IN BETWEEN

The easing of hills also did not rank high in the trust's work because, with more than half of its road's length across dead-level clay vales, its hills were limited to two isolated rises where small outcrops of limestone break through the generally flat surface. These were at Blackthorn Hill two miles out from Bicester, and Tetchwick Hill – now Sharp's Hill – just west of Kingswood.

In 1824-25 it was decided to lower both hills. Cuttings totalling barely ¼ mile in length for the two were made through the summits of both hills during 1825-26.

Both hills were further lowered around 1980 by their respective county councils. At Sharp's Hill the 1980s work included building a short length of dual carriageway.

Flooding was more of a problem for the trust, particularly on the level 4½ miles between Blackthorn Hill and Sharp's Hill. Today it is clear that this arrow-straight stretch has been raised on a causeway above the winter floodwaters of the River Ray. However, while it can be assumed that the base of this structure is probably Roman, the author has been unable to establish whether subsequent raisings to its present height are the work of the turnpike trust or the county councils which followed it.

AT WADDESDON

A curiosity of the Bicester and Aylesbury turnpike road is that it actually lost a village bypass. Jefferys' county map of 1766 clearly shows Waddesdon bypassed by a fairly straight road on the north side of the village. However, by the time the Ordnance Survey first visited Waddesdon in 1814, the bypass had vanished, although parts of its hedge lines were still on the resulting map.

June Strong notes that the original west-east road through the village was indirect and went via what is now known as Baker Street, and that in 1779 the turnpike trust built a new road, part of the present High Street, across what was then the village green.[199]

The enclosure of Waddesdon's open fields began in 1775 and this is the most likely cause of the closure of the bypass route. If this is the case then it may be that the enclosure and turnpike commissioners combined to build the replacement new main road through the village (now known as High Street).

Whatever the perceived advantages of eliminating the bypass at the time, Waddesdon has ever since straddled a trunk road between London and the west Midlands and has suffered its traffic as a result since the Motor Age began.

Toll gates and tollhouses

The trust had three toll gates across the main road throughout its life, one of which had a change of site in 1826. It also had the Launton side bar, which was moved from one site to another in the 1780s, and another side bar at Stonebridge which was probably only in existence for a few years in the 1820s.

| WRETCHWICK OR CHAPEL LANE GATE, BICESTER 1770-1826 | *Sample annual toll income: £264 in 1824/25, including the income of Launton side bar.* |

Sample annual toll income: £264 in 1824/25, including the income of Launton side bar.

When the trust came into being the exit from Bicester towards Aylesbury was via Priory Road and Chapel Street, continuing in a straight line southwards from Chapel Street across the future site of the railway goods yard. To collect tolls the trust put a gate across the road immediately south of the junction of Priory Road and Chapel Street, and this was in use until Chapel Street was bypassed by the new London Road in 1826. It appears to have been called the Wretchwick Gate because the road through it continued past the former hamlet of Wretchwick.

The author has not found any details of the gatekeeper's accommodation beyond the fact that the building stood on the west side of the road, and that it survived until at least 1969, before being demolished to make way for new housing.

SECOND WRETCHWICK GATE, BICESTER 1826-1875

Sample annual toll income: £290 in 1834, including income of Launton side bar.

The opening of the new, more direct route southwards out of Bicester in 1826 bypassed the first Wretchwick or Chapel Lane Gate. To remedy this a new gate was erected, presumably in that year, immediately south of the junction of the old and new roads *(at grid reference SP 587 217)*. It was on a site near the hamlet of Wretchwick which is now occupied by the southern side of the roundabout at the junction of Talisman Road and Mallards Way, 300 yards south of the level crossing.

The toll house, a stone-built single-storey building with a square ground plan and central chimney, stood with its garden on the western verge of the road until demolished in the 1970s.

LAUNTON SIDE BAR 1770s-1875

Toll income from Launton side bar was always included with that of Wretchwick Gate.

Soon after the trust started work in 1770 it became concerned that its toll gate at Chapel Lane in Bicester was losing income because traffic was avoiding it. For example westbound travellers were apparently leaving the trust's Akeman Street route, today's A41, at the Blackthorn crossroads *(at grid reference SP 620 202)* and continuing toll-free into Bicester via Launton, or they were avoiding Bicester altogether when heading for Banbury by going through Launton and Caversfield.

To capture this revenue the trust had installed Launton Side Bar on an unknown site by 1781. For the rest of the trust's life this side bar was let to toll contractors as one unit with the Wretchwick toll gate at Bicester.

We know that this side bar had two successive sites because it was clearly moved to Blackthorn crossroads at some time between 1781 and 1791. The change of sites *appeared* to be heralded by the trust's 1791 Act,[200] which renewed the trust's powers and specifically authorised the installation of a side bar at Blackthorn crossroads.

However the trustees' meeting on 11 July 1791 discussed collecting tolls from Blackthorn to Launton traffic crossing the turnpike road at an existing toll house![201] Either the toll house had been built very quickly after the Act was passed on 11 April 1791, or the side bar and toll house had been moved to Blackthorn crossroads during the 1780s without the authority which was granted retrospectively in 1791.

This begs the question of where the side bar had been until the 1780s. Logically its first and second sites could only have been at the two ends of the minor road from Bicester through Launton to Blackthorn crossroads which was being used to evade tolls. Although not supported by any evidence, the most likely scenario is that the side bar was first in Bicester, at the start of Launton Road, where the present number 2b Launton Road could have been the toll cottage, although the building has been heavily altered in later years.

After 1791 the side bar's history is straightforward. A single-storey cottage of stone with thatched roof stood on the highway verge at the north-west corner of the crossroads ¼ mile west of the modern railway bridge. When the trust was wound up the cottage became a private dwelling but still had its toll board attached to it when it was demolished in 1925 during road widening work.

WESTCOTT GATE from about 1781 to 1875	*Sample annual toll income: £262 in 1833.*

Sample annual toll income: £262 in 1833.

This gate stood just east of Newhouse Farm at the point where the public footpath from Upper Barn Farm met the road *(at grid reference SP 714 177)*. The toll cottage was on the north side of the road and was being considered for replacement by a new building in 1835.

STONEBRIDGE GATE 1770-1875

Sample annual toll income: £472 in 1833.

This was the trust's principal toll collection point. In the nineteenth century it often took almost as much as the Wretchwick and Westcott Gates and Launton Side Bar together. The gate was situated one mile out of Aylesbury on the summit of Haydon Hill at the junction with what is now called Rabans Lane. The gate took its name from Stone Bridge over the River Thame, half a mile along the turnpike road to the north-west.

There are contradictory references to a side bar across the north-east end of Rabans Lane in the early 1820s. There were no references to it in gate-letting advertisements before 1821, but it was clearly let with the main gate to a contractor in 1821 and 1822.[202] Also a Mr Loosly of Haydon Mill, at the west end of Rabans Lane, was prosecuted in 1823 for breaking down 'the side gate' at Stonebridge Toll Gate – though this could have been the pedestrian gate beside the main road gate. Confusingly, however, in January 1824 trustees were to discuss erecting a side bar across the lane to Hartwell Mill – presumably Haydon Mill – after which no further mention of a side bar has been found.

Weighing engine

Doubtless because of the amount of traffic passing through Stonebridge Gate, it was chosen for the installation of a weighing engine at some time between 1801 and 1818, and the engine was still there when the trust was wound up in 1875. Once the engine was in operation the fines imposed on overweight wagons ensured that Stonebridge maintained its position as the trust's principal source of revenue.

Milestones and mileposts

The trust's original milemarkers, which are assumed to have been milestones, started at 41 miles from London in Aylesbury's Bicester Road, just downhill from the future site of the Royal Bucks. Hospital. This '41' continued the distance recorded on milestones along the Wendover and Buckingham Trust's road south of the town. The mileage count rose to 57 on the final milemarker, which was in Bicester.

Between 1815 and 1818 the trust changed its London mileage base from the Wendover and Buckingham Trust's mileage, measured via Uxbridge, to that of the Sparrows Herne Trust, via Watford, which was two miles shorter between London and Aylesbury. All the Bicester and Aylesbury Trust milestones were accordingly altered to show their distance from London reduced by two miles. This was probably done by moving each of the existing stones to stand two miles further from London, adding two new stones – 39 and 40 miles from London – at the Aylesbury end, and taking away the two highest at the Bicester end.

Then in the early 1830s the trust replaced all its milestones with the present cast-iron mileposts made by R Barrett of London. During this replacement the opportunity was taken to reduce the London mileage still further to reflect the fact that the Sparrows Herne Trust had shortened its road in several places in the 1820s *(see Road number 12)*. Thus each new 1830s milepost was sited nearly 600 yards further west than the milestone it replaced between Aylesbury and Westcott and – presumably due to a surveying error – 750 yards further west between Westcott and Bicester.

Today only four of the seventeen mileposts survive in Buckinghamshire, standing on the north side of the road, and there are none in Oxfordshire. This suggests that Oxfordshire did not replace them after the general removal of milemarkers during the 1939-45 war.

Financial matters

The trust had an intermittently poor record for maintenance of its road and struggled with debt for most of its life. By 1862, when its net annual toll income was £728, it had debts of £3,300 and unpaid interest on those debts of £5,280.[203]

1875: The Trust wound up

After 1838 the Bicester and Aylesbury turnpike trust was one of a number of trusts which lost long-distance traffic as a result of the opening of the London and Birmingham Railway. In this case, however, the impact was lessened because the trust already appeared to be losing traffic to better-maintained road routes to the west Midlands on the Holyhead and Oxford roads.

The result was that the trust's total toll revenue peaked early at £1,223 per year in 1825. It then gently declined through £1,003 a year at the dawn of the Railway Age in 1836 before stabilising in the £700 to £800 range in the 1850s and 1860s. By then the trustees could see the writing on the wall and were focussing on paying off their debts rather than making any further road improvements.

The trust first applied to close in 1864, when it was still £3,300 in debt, but this was refused. It then concentrated successfully on debt reduction so that it could finally be wound up on 1 November 1875 under **38/39 Vic., c.194 (1875).**

Thereafter the road came to be paralleled by two main-line railways, one on each side, but both opened after the end of the turnpike era so had no effect on the story of the Bicester and Aylesbury Trust.

Road 16:
The Bromham and Olney
Turnpike Road 1790

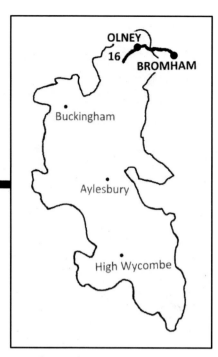

Identifying the road's route

The Bromham and Olney turnpike road starts at Bromham village in Bedfordshire in Northampton Road, a C-class road, and follows this out to the bypass. The route then follows today's A428 to Cold Brayfield and the B565 to the northern edge of Olney. In Olney, Wellingborough Road and High Street were not controlled by this trust *(see Road number 11)*, but its route continues from the south end of Olney High Street on a C-class road, initially Weston Road, through Weston Underwood to the fork in the road west of Ravenstone Mill. Finally the route takes the southern arm of that fork, still on a C-class road, to meet the B526 near the boundary between Gayhurst and Stoke Goldington parishes.

Historic background

The Bromham Road, as this trust came to be known, looked after most of the eastern end of the 20-mile link between Bedford and Northampton. The long bridges of thirteenth-century origin which carry this road over the Great Ouse at Bromham and Turvey in Bedfordshire point to the early importance of the route.

In spite of this the volume of travellers between these two towns seems to have been low by the eighteenth and nineteenth centuries. This is suggested by the fact that the route was not adopted by a single Bedford to Northampton turnpike trust which had the needs of inter-urban traffic in mind, but by two trusts which met near the tiny Buckinghamshire village of Cold Brayfield.

Furthermore, far from the demands of heavy traffic leading to the improvement of this route early in the turnpike era, the western end of this Bedford to Northampton link *(see Road number 24)* was almost the last piece of road in Buckinghamshire to be taken over by a turnpike trust.

The eastern end of the Bromham and Olney Trust's route was first turnpiked between Bromham and Lavendon in 1754 as a six-mile branch of the Bedford and Newport Trust's road *(see Road number 10)*. However, after starting work in 1754, the Bedford and Newport was soon in financial difficulties and went out of business in the 1770s. When a second trust for the Bromham Road was set up in 1790 it was a trust in its own right and not a branch of another road. It avoided Lavendon and was extended south-west to Olney and beyond.

The limits of the trust's road	When the this turnpike trust was established in 1790 its eastern extremity was at the western end of the multi-arched Bromham Bridge.

However when the second Bedford and Newport Trust *(Road number 10)* was established in 1814 it naturally took over Bromham Bridge and the road on through the village, so the Bromham and Olney Trust withdrew to the parting of the Stagsden Road and Northampton Road on the west side of Bromham.

At Olney the Bromham and Olney trust did not control the road through the town *(see Road number 11)*. Instead its road ended at its junction with the Wellingborough road, now the A509, north of Olney and resumed south of the town centre as Weston Road, a turning off High Street.

The western end of the trust's responsibilities was in open country on the Gayhurst and Stoke Goldington parish boundary, where it met the Newport Pagnell to Northampton road, now the B526, just north of the hamlet of Gayhurst.

Its length and maintenance districts

From 1790 to 1814 the turnpike road was 12 miles long, of which seven were in Buckinghamshire and the remainder in Bedfordshire. After 1814 it was 11½ miles long, still with seven miles in Buckinghamshire.

In 1790 the trust divided its road into three operational districts: Bromham to Turvey, Turvey to Olney, and west of Olney. However this seems only to have been in order to organise the initial works to get the road into better shape, because the whole road was subsequently treated as one operational entity in the trust's records.

Initial Act of Parliament

30 Geo.III, c.114 (1790).

Part of the Bromham and Olney's road had been turnpiked earlier under **27 Geo. II, c.34 (1754)** by the Bedford and Newport Pagnell turnpike trust *(see Road number 10)* which fell into financial difficulties and went out of business in the 1770s. The new trust was entirely independent of the old.

Continuation Acts

Powers for this trust were subsequently extended by **51 Geo.III, c.72 (1811), 2 Will.IV, c.18 (1832), 26/27 Vic., c.94, (1863), and 27-28 Vic., c.79 (1864).**

Control of the Trust:
TRUSTEES

Two of the three branches of the Higgins family of Turvey in Bedfordshire dominated the chairing of the trust's meetings for 48 years in the nineteenth century. Thomas Charles Higgins of Turvey House and William Bartholomew Higgins of Picts Hill House, Turvey, were driving forces, while Charles Longuet Higgins of Turvey Abbey had a lower profile as a trustee. In due course the Higgins family became supporters of the Midland Railway's Bedford to Northampton line, which was to bring about the end of the turnpike trust.

OFFICERS	The majority of clerks, treasurers, and surveyors of the trust were based in Olney. W Andrews was the first clerk of the second trust but by 1800 he had given way to John Garrard of Olney. After this a John Garrard was clerk right through until 1874, which suggests that this must represent a father, son, and probably grandson combination of solicitors.

Similarly the Palmers of Olney – William, Thomas and John in succession – occupied the treasurer's post from before 1834 to 1874. A fourth Palmer of Olney – Joseph – was surveyor from at least 1835 until 1857, after which Henry Ellis of Turvey occupied the post until 1873, and John Simes of Sherington took over for the trust's last two years.

MEETINGS OF THE TRUSTEES

With the trust's officers almost exclusively based in Olney it is not surprising that virtually all meetings after 1790 were held in Olney at 'The Bull Inn', with the tiny number of exceptions held at 'The Three Fishes' in Turvey. After 1833 the trust's minute book[204] failed to record the venue of a number of trust meetings but we have no reason to doubt that these too were held at 'The Bull'.

As befits a not-very-active trust, meetings were only twice-yearly in most years after the mid-1830s, thereby greatly restricting discussion of possible improvements. Any exchange of ideas was also limited by normal attendance being between three and six trustees, for the two meetings in 1857 when 13 and 16 trustees were present, probably to consider the controversy over the new side bar in Bromham *(see Tollgates – Bromham Side Bar below)*.

Maintenance of the road

The trust's long-serving surveyor, Joseph Palmer of Olney, was congratulated on the excellent state of the road when he retired in 1857. Only a few years later, however, the building of a railway which paralleled the trust's road between Bromham and Olney led to serious damage to the road surface by railway construction traffic in 1870-71. Ironically the trust had not objected to the scheme for this railway, which was supported by members of the Higgins family who dominated the turnpike trust. In 1871 the railway company agreed to pay compensation but the trust's minutes suggest that its road did not return to its previous form.

In addition to these problems, the trust suffered a serious blow at the end of 1872 when floodwaters on the River Ouse tore down a substantial part of Turvey Bridge on the border between Bedfordshire and Buckinghamshire. A temporary timber deck was built on the old piers commendably quickly by March 1873, thereby getting traffic going – and tolls coming in, but it was estimated that a full repair was going to cost between £150 and £200.

Improvements to the road

With a route which generally followed the Ouse Valley this road enjoyed a fairly direct course and mainly gentle gradients. As a result the trust carried out few realignments or diversions and even today the route remains largely as it was in the pre-turnpike era. Although a number of improvements are listed below, they are on a very small in scale compared to the work of some other trusts in Buckinghamshire.

AT BROMHAM (BEDFORDSHIRE)	The sharp corner on the Northampton Road beside Bromham Grange Farm – now converted to housing – was said in 1838 to be narrow and dangerous. In 1842 the trust purchased a strip of the farmyard 166ft long and a maximum of 36ft wide to produce the less severe but still sharp bend that we see today.
AT TURVEY (BEDFORDSHIRE)	Due south of Picts Hill Farm at Turvey a small spinney on the south side of the road (*at grid reference SP 967 517*) is on the site of a sharp bend which was bypassed by the trust on an unknown date after 1835. Three-quarters of a mile further west the hill was eased by excavation in the 1860s at Priory Farm. The low 100-yards-long retaining wall of stone opposite the farm was hurriedly built in 1866 when the new cutting side began to subside. In Turvey village a 130-yard bypass to the original turnpike road crosses the green south-east of the church – but it was not built until after the Second World War.
AT OLNEY	At an unknown time between 1790 and 1814 the trust eased the gradient on the hill in Weston Road down from Olney to the Weston Underwood parish boundary, where a cutting marks the section of road that was altered.
Toll gates and tollhouses	From 1790 to 1874 the Bromham Road Trust had three main gates throughout its life, although one was on two successive sites. This was probably too few principal gates, because the trust seemed to have almost continuous cash flow problems. By 1864 its debts almost equalled five years' toll income. The trustees showed intermittent awareness that a significant amount of traffic was using the turnpike road quite legally without having gone through any toll gates. Finally, largely from the 1830s, six side bars were added in an attempt to improve toll collection, but this was to a certain extent offset by the granting of toll exemptions or reductions to the villages most affected by the new side bars.
SIDE BARS	The trust was unusual in having no fewer than six side bars at which to collect tolls from traffic entering and leaving the road between the main gates. Among trusts with roads in Buckinghamshire only the Sparrows Herne and Reading and Hatfield Trusts had the same number or more side bars – and both were much longer roads than the Bromham Road). Each of the Bromham and Olney's side bars was operated as one unit with the nearest main gate, and was always let to contractors with that gate. Bromham, Stevington and Stagsden side bars were let with the Bromham gate, Turvey side bar with Lavendon Mill gate, and Weston Underwood and Ravenstone side bars with Ravenstone's main gate.
THE FIRST BROMHAM GATE 1790-1814	*Sample annual toll income: £90 in 1805/06.* This was sited in Bromham village beside Swan Green, at the junction of Stagsden Road with Box End Road. It was presumably on the site of the gate

authorised by the Bedford and Newport Pagnell trust's 1754 Act *(see Road number 10)*. The toll house was on the north side of the road but there is no trace of the building or its garden today.

THE SECOND BROMHAM GATE 1814-1874	*Sample annual toll income: £173 in 1831, without any side bars, and £195 in 1860 including side bars in Bromham and at the turnings to Stagsden and Stevington.*

In anticipation of the 1814 revival of the Bedford and Newport Trust *(Road number 10)*, the Bromham and Olney Trust's 1811 Act stipulated that its gate in Bromham should be moved off the new trust's route on Stagsden Road, and this was done in 1814. The new site of this gate was beyond the edge of the village in 1814, but it is now at the west end of the modern village *(at grid reference TL 000 510)*, some 200 yards west of the junction of Northampton Road with Grange Lane.

The long-gone toll house stood on the south side of the road, on a narrow strip of land between the carriageway and a stream. Nowadays, following twentieth-century road widening, its site forms part of the strip of grass which separates pavement and carriageway.

BROMHAM SIDE BAR 1857-1874	*Toll income recorded with Bromham (main) Gate.*

In 1853 the trust suddenly started to discuss the need to erect a side bar in Bromham across the west end of Bonnell's Lane, today Grange Lane *(at grid reference TL 002 510)* to collect tolls from people joining Northampton Road from the north end of Bromham village.[205] No reason was given for this, but it may have been in preparation for the Bedford and Newport Trust's implementation of its controversial decision to toll Bromham villagers passing through its side bar at Webbs Lane – now Village Road – at the east end of the village *(see Road number 10 for background)*. The purpose of the new side bar in Bonnell's Lane would have been to catch people evading the Webbs Lane side bar.

In the event the Bonnell's Lane side bar was not put in place until 1857, but even that was ahead of the introduction of tolls for villagers at Webbs Lane in 1858. The £12 5s 0d cost of its construction was jointly paid for by the Bedford and Newport and Bedford and Luton Trusts, which demonstrated that the Bromham Road Trust had no real interest in it and was simply helping fellow trusts and collecting a few tolls while doing so.

The trust's minutes did not mention the building of a toll house so we must assume that the gate keeper was provided only with a kiosk. The facilities of the main Bromham Gate toll house were only 200 yards away.

STEVINGTON SIDE BAR 1845-1874 and STAGSDEN SIDE BAR 1832-1874	*Toll income recorded with the second Bromham Gate.*

Almost half way between the villages of Bromham and Turvey the side turnings to Stevington on the north and Stagsden on the south, both in Bedfordshire, were apparently the source of traffic, presumably going to Turvey, which was using the turnpike road toll-free. Several meetings of the trust, starting in 1828, contemplated whether a side bar across either turning would make economic sense.

Finally in 1832 a bar was erected across the turning to Stagsden. It was let for the rest of the trust's life with Bromham Gate. The jump in Bromham Gate's annual takings from £173 in 1831, which was the last year of Bromham Gate on its own, to £240 in 1834, the second year with the side bar, confirmed that the trust had been losing revenue.

In 1841, however, the trust introduced an exemption from toll at Stagsden side bar for all residents of Stagsden parish, on the grounds that they were already paying tolls at the trust's other gates and bar at Bromham, Turvey, and Lavendon – so the side bar's long-term value to the trust is doubtful.

Initially a 'wooden watchbox' was erected to shelter the toll collector at the Stagsden road junction *(at grid reference SP 977 513)*, but in 1833 this was replaced by a toll house on the west corner of the junction. That house was badly in need of repair by 1860 and in 1863 one of the trustees, W B Higgins of Picts Hill House in Turvey, on whose land the toll house stood, demolished it, built a replacement nearby, and began to charge the trust £3 a year in rent for the new house. This initiative appears to have been without any consultation with the other trustees. Today the site of the toll house is part of a large triangular sight line beside the road.

A side bar was proposed in 1835 for the turning to Stevington, 170 yards east of the Stagsden Side Bar, but it was 1844 before trustees actually agreed to erect the bar and to build a cottage 'on a small scale' beside it for the toll collector. It was 1845 before this was done.

The Stevington side bar remained in use for the rest of the trust's life, but, by 1867 at the latest, it was being manned by the toll collector at the Stagsden side bar, with the implication that the Stevington bar's cottage had been demolished or was being rented out. The minutes are silent on how one toll collector managed two gates 170 yards apart. Today there is no trace of the Stevington cottage's site.

TURVEY SIDE BAR (BEDFORDSHIRE) 1812-1857

Toll income recorded with Lavendon Mill Gate.

In 1812 the Turvey side bar was placed across the side road to Newton Blossomville – now called Newton Lane – a few paces from its junction with the main road through Turvey village. This was a first attempt to collect toll from traffic which was using the trust's road but not going through any gates. The toll cottage was built on the east side of the road on a narrow strip of land between the road and a stream.

An 1849 dispute with a local farmer as to whether he was entitled to exemption from toll at this bar appeared in 1850 to have ended with defeat for the farmer.[206] However the farmer kept the issue alive and it may be no coincidence that his surname – Higgins – was the same as that of three trustees, because in 1857 the trust gave in and ordered the removal of the side bar on 1 January 1858.

The toll cottage was demolished in 1861 and initially replaced by a village smithy. Today, however, a modern lock-up garage in the garden of a house named Winterbourne stands on the site between road and stream.

| LAVENDON MILL GATE 1790-1874 | *Sample annual toll income: £160 in 1837, including Turvey side bar, and £133 in 1860 without the side bar.* |

The Lavendon Gate was erected in a lonely location *(at grid reference SP 906 525)*, some 200 yards east of Lavendon water mill. This was where it could catch traffic from the village to the mill in addition to through traffic on the turnpike road. In 1859, in a changed travel environment, the trust exempted residents of Lavendon from toll if going to or from the mill, in return for a single payment by the parish of one shilling per year, which increased to two shillings and sixpence in 1863.

Initially the gatekeeper had to make do with what looks on the parish's 1801 enclosure map like a small kiosk in the carriageway on the south side of the road.[207] By 1814 the kiosk had gone and a proper toll cottage had been built on the northern roadside verge, with a long, narrow section of verge to the east of it fenced off for the toll collector's garden. Today the site of the cottage, which was probably demolished in 1874, is simply highway verge.

| WESTON UNDERWOOD SIDE BAR 1835-1874 | *Toll income recorded with Ravenstone Gate.* |

By 1835, although income was keeping abreast of running costs, trustees were becoming concerned that they were losing revenue from people coming on to their road between Ravenstone Gate and Olney without paying toll. In that year they therefore erected a 'wooden watch box' for the toll collector at the west end of Weston Underwood village, with a side bar across the turning to Ravenstone *(at grid reference SP 862 503)*. The watch box appears to have been the toll collector's only shelter until it was sold in 1874.

From the outset Ravenstone residents could pass through the Weston side bar without payment when going between places within Ravenstone parish, and from 1860 Weston Underwood and Ravenstone parishes were allowed to make an annual payment of one shilling each for all their parishioners to pass this side bar freely. The cost of composition was increased to two shillings and sixpence per parish in 1863. This side bar was let with Ravenstone Gate and side bar as one lot.

| RAVENSTONE SIDE BAR 1835-1874 | *Toll income recorded with Ravenstone Gate.* |

In 1835 a growing concern about possible lost toll income on the Gayhurst to Olney section of the road led the trust to erect a side bar across the road from Ravenstone village, some 200 yards east of the main Ravenstone Gate *(see below)*. Due doubtless to its proximity to the gate on the main road, this side bar was only provided with a "wooden watch box" for the toll collector, and this appears to have remained in use until the trust was wound up. There is no trace of its site today.

From the outset Ravenstone residents could pass through the side bar toll free when going from one part of Ravenstone parish to another. From 1860, the parish was allowed to make an annual payment of one shilling for all parishioners to pass the Ravenstone side bar freely on *any* journey. This was increased to two shillings and sixpence in 1863.

In spite of this arrangement, which applied to the Weston side bar as well, the two side bars noticeably increased the Ravenstone group's meagre takings, with toll income rising from £64 a year in 1833 to peak at £101 a year in 1865.

RAVENSTONE GATE 1790-1874

Sample annual toll income: £60 in 1836 and £75 in 1869, both figures including income from two side bars).

The Ravenstone Gate was set up, with its tollhouse and garden on the northern highway verge *(at grid reference SP 851 486)*, some 200 yards west of the crossroads at Ravenstone water mill. It was therefore not well-placed to catch mill-bound traffic from Ravenstone village. In 1835, in belated recognition of this, a side bar was erected *(see above)*. In 1865 William Scrivener, the miller at Ravenstone, applied to pay a flat rate per year to pass through this gate. When he was unsuccessful he responded by bidding successfully to lease the gate in 1867-70!

Today a strip of hawthorn thicket on the northern verge of the road marks the site of the toll collector's garden, with a space near the middle of it where the toll house once stood.

STOKE GOLDINGTON

Two maps, an Ordnance Survey map of 1834 and an estate map drawn some time before 1858,[208] show a gate just south of Stoke Goldington village, placed across the northern arm of the Y-shaped junction of roads at the western extremity of the Bromham and Olney turnpike road *(at grid reference SP 839 483)*. Neither map names the gate, nor shows a building for a toll collector beside it.

No record of tolls collected has been found for this site and, since the gate was less than one mile from Ravenstone Gate and on the wrong arm of the Y-shaped fork in the roads, it seems most unlikely that it was a toll gate.

Weighing engine

The trust invited tenders to erect a weighing engine in 1806 and one had been installed beside the Lavendon Mill gate by 1817. It was there until 1843, when trustees ordered its removal "it being entirely useless".[209]

Milestones and mileposts

Milestones on this road marked the distance from Bedford, so the trust's lowest numbered stone was read 'Bedford 3' in Bromham, near the eastern end of its road. Mileage rose to 'Bedford 11' just short of the junction with the Kettering road at the north end of Olney, but the detached continuation of the trust's road from the south end of Olney to the Northampton to Newport road does not appear to have ever had any milemarkers. Today no milemarkers can be seen anywhere along the trust's roads.

1874: The Trust wound up The section of the trust's road south-west of Olney had no obvious traffic sources or objective and must have been one of the most lightly-trafficked sections of turnpike road in Buckinghamshire. Financially it was probably carried by the section between Bromham and Olney.

Railway competition to the Bromham Road came late. As a result the trust's modest income held up well during the 1840s-1860s, although economies had to be made and it became increasingly difficult to find contractors to collect the tolls.

The Bedford to Northampton railway, which was to follow the Bromham Road closely between Bromham and Olney, obtained its Act of Parliament in 1865 but construction was slow to start. Once work began, traffic connected with railway construction did considerable damage to the turnpike road between Picts Hill and Turvey without passing a toll gate at which it could have contributed to repairs *(see 'Maintenance' above)*.

The railway opened in 1872 and the trust's annual toll income plummeted from £483 in 1871 to £265 in 1873. Since the trust's debt had been more than four times its income throughout the 1860s, the near-halving of income in the 1870s, combined with serious damage to Turvey Bridge in 1872, left trustees with no option but to apply for their trust to be wound up. They applied unsuccessfully in 1873 but obtained the sought-after consent in 1874, under **37-38 Vic., c.95 (1874),** which set an end date of 1 November 1874.

Road 17:
The Banbury and Brackley Turnpike Road 1791

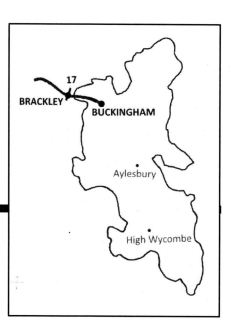

Identifying the road's route

The turnpike road followed the route of today's A422 from central Buckingham to the Brackley bypass, then along Buckingham Road through east Brackley to High Street.

The former A43 along High Street and Market Place through the middle of Brackley was not controlled by this trust until 1851. From the start of Bridge Street, however, the route continued on Banbury Road through west Brackley, then on the A422 again to the east end of the Middleton Cheney bypass.

From there into Banbury the old turnpike route is still in place but has been severed as a through route in two places and is now superseded by twentieth-century road improvements which form the modern A422. The old route was along Main Road through Middleton Cheney, then Mansion Hill, Banbury Lane – now cut by the A422 dual carriageway, Blacklocks Hill – cut by the M40 motorway, and finally Middleton Road into Banbury.

Historic background

One of the major late-medieval routes between London and the west Midlands ran via Uxbridge, Aylesbury, Buckingham, Aynho and Banbury and was turnpiked early *(see Roads 5, 7 and 8).*

Between Buckingham and Banbury the route via Aynho was more than a mile longer than a more northerly course through Brackley would have been. However through traffic was apparently deterred from going via Brackley because of the <u>perceived</u> indirectness of the route between there and Banbury. It was claimed in the preamble to the Banbury and Brackley trust's 1791 Act that there was no direct main road between the two towns.

The route of the modern A422 west of Brackley was therefore developed by the turnpike trust as an easier, less hilly route, partly to accelerate traffic between London and the west Midlands, and partly to bring coaching trade into Brackley. However, in spite of the major improvements carried out by this trust, little Buckingham to Banbury traffic seems to have been attracted to the route through Brackley.

AN ATTEMPT TO IMPROVE TRUST FINANCES

After its pro-active early years of road-building the trust seems to have lapsed into lethargy which by the 1830s was developing into mismanagement. Meanwhile the Towcester and Weston-on-the-Green

Trust, whose road crossed the Banbury and Brackley trust's road in Brackley, had come to share the same clerk and some of the same trustees with the Banbury and Brackley Trust and had descended into the same state of mismanagement.

In an attempt to deal with this the Home Office recommended that the two trusts should merge, although it was not spelled out why merging two failing trusts would improve them! Nevertheless the merger went ahead and the two trusts combined in 1851 under the title of the Brackley Consolidated Trust.

The limits of the trust's road

Initially the eastern end of trust control was at Buckingham Town Hall, but this was moved westward in 1851 to the Buckingham parish boundary. The western end was always in Banbury at the junction with the turnpike road from Daventry – now the junction of Middleton Road and Daventry Road. Excluded from this, however, were High Street and Market Place in Brackley, which had already been turnpiked by the Towcester and Weston-on-the-Green Trust.

The terminal points of the Towcester and Weston-on-the-Green Trust were its junction with the Holyhead Road – today's A5 – in Towcester at the crossroads of Brackley Road and Watling Street, and just south of Weston-on-the-Green village at what is now the junction of the B430 and the A34.

Its length and maintenance districts

Until 1851 the trust's road was 15½ miles long, of which 6½ miles were in Buckinghamshire, ½ mile in Oxfordshire, and the remainder in Northamptonshire.

The Towcester and Weston Trust, which merged with the Banbury and Brackley Trust in 1851, was 23½ miles long of which 13½ miles were in Northamptonshire, and 10 miles in Oxfordshire. As none of this mileage was in Buckinghamshire, this book gives only the barest details of this trust's activities.

The Banbury and Brackley Trust appears to have managed its road as one unit until 1851, when it became the Buckingham to Banbury division of the Consolidated Trust.

Initial Act of Parliament

31 Geo.III, c.133 (1791) included powers to bypass Westbury, reroute the road through Brackley, build 3½ miles of new road between Brackley and Farthinghoe, and make half a mile of new road from Middleton Cheney to Banbury Lane.

Continuation Acts

50 Geo.III, c.133 (1810), 1 Geo.IV, c.200 (1820), and **14-15 Vic., c.61 (1851)**. The 1851 Act amalgamated this trust with the Towcester and Weston-on-the-Green Trust to form the Brackley Consolidated Trust.

Control of the Trust: CLERKS

The trust had few clerks. George Thomas of Brackley and Robert Miller of Buckingham seemed to alternate in the post from 1790 until around 1818. The Weston family firm, of Brackley, Robert followed by Arthur, followed from at least 1818 for the remainder of the trust's life, including being clerks to the Brackley Consolidated Trust from 1851 *(see 'Background' above)*. The Westons had been clerks to the Towcester and Weston Trust for many years before the merger.

MEETINGS OF THE TRUSTEES	With Brackley near the middle of the trust's road, and with most of its clerks based in that town, it is not surprising that trustees met there almost exclusively, initially varying their meetings between the 'Crown Inn' and the 'Red Lion Inn', but concentrating on the 'Crown' after 1813. The rare meetings in Buckingham were at the 'Cobham Arms' and 'White Hart'.

Maintenance of the road

In its early years the trust concentrated on building sections of new road, but it also widened and improved the surface of the rest of the road. Its 1791 specification for improving the road was by widening it "to the breadth of 24 feet, 16ft whereof to be stoned 12 inches deep where the ground is tender and 9 inches deep where the soil is stony and firm".[210]

This author has found little detail about the quality of this trust's road maintenance beyond an observation in its 1810 Act that the road between Farthinghoe and Banbury was currently not in an acceptable condition.

Improvements to the road

A popular impression that there was no direct main road between Brackley and Banbury before this trust was established has already been mentioned. To address this and to improve the route between Westbury and Brackley, the trust started work with vigour and created the main road that was wanted by building 5¼ miles of new road in four locations, as well as widening the existing road in several places.

This means that one-third of the resulting main road between Buckingham and Banbury had been built from nothing by the trust between 1790 and 1814. The easy curves and smooth gradients of the new or improved road west of Westbury still contrast with the switchback road with numerous sharp bends to the east of that village, where the road's alignment, handed down from the Middle Ages, was not improved by the trust.

After all this early activity the trust settled down to a quiet existence, but with substantial debts and growing mismanagement. As a result its 1851 Act barred it from borrowing any more money against the security of the tolls. This meant that no further improvements could be carried out although, curiously, tenders were sought as late as 1868 for the easing of Water Stratford Hill between Buckingham and Westbury by lowering it.

THE WESTBURY BYPASS	Between 1792 and 1814 – an exact date could not be found – a ¾-mile bypass was built north of the village of Westbury, making this one of the first settlements in Buckinghamshire to be bypassed.

BRACKLEY EAST OF THE HIGH STREET	The turnpike road crossed into Northamptonshire on Bandlands Bridge, which spanned the Great Ouse close to the present bypass roundabout. The bridge had apparently been built, possibly in place of a ford, shortly before the trust took over the road in 1791. That bridge was demolished early in

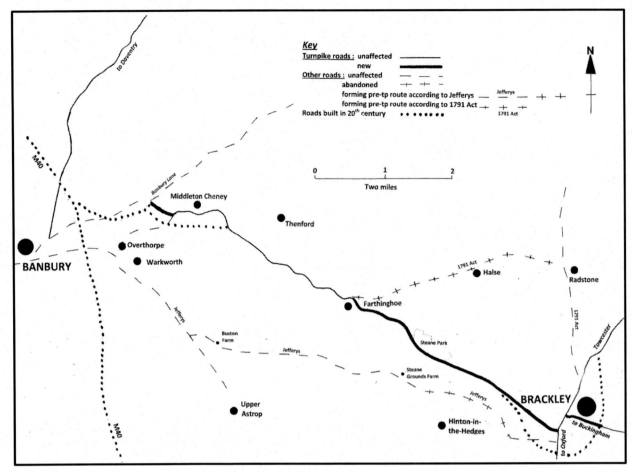

FIGURE 30:
New sections of road built by the Banbury and Brackley Trust.

the 1990s and replaced by the concrete bridge we see today. At the same time Buckingham Road was realigned to meet the new roundabout on the bypass. The alignment of the pre-1990s road from the Turweston turning down to Mill Lane, Brackley is still marked by a line of former roadside trees on the north side of the present road.

Immediately west of Bandlands Bridge the pre-turnpike route swung on to a partly-lost line to the north of the present main road to pass St. Peter's church in Old Town. From there it climbed Church Road to enter the High Street opposite Halse Road. At some time between 1792 and 1814 the trust built a new, nearly half-mile road, the present Buckingham Road, climbing from Bandlands Bridge to enter the High Street above Market Place.

BRACKLEY HIGH STREET

The trust's 1791 Act also authorised it to demolish a number of buildings standing uphill from the town hall in the middle of what is now the wide part of Market Place. This created the impressive open space that we see today. It is however difficult to see why Parliament committed this trust to carry out the demolitions, because the trust was not going to control Market Place. This was already part of the Towcester and Weston-on-the-Green Trust's route and its traffic was apparently flowing down the west side of the street beside the doomed buildings.

While this sounds like an eighteenth-century forerunner of 'planning gain' for the community, there may have been fears that if the Banbury and Brackley Trust was successful in attracting traffic from the Aynho route *(see*

'Historic Background' above), the additional traffic might have clogged the narrow lane beside the buildings which had encroached on to the road.

BETWEEN BRACKLEY AND FARTHINGHOE	From Brackley High Street the main pre-turnpike road to Banbury ran on a line between ½ to 1½ miles south of the modern A422 on a route which today has partly ceased to exist. Leaving the south end of Brackley and taking a road which is not even a footpath today to skirt north of the village of Hinton-in-the-Hedges, the old route then followed the present C class road past Steane Grounds Farm and continued on what now starts as a byway and ends as a bridleway – Green Lane, then Sandy Lane – to Buston Farm. From here it joined the road from Upper Astrop and continued along it into Banbury.

Confusingly this route is clearly mapped as the main road on Jefferys' 1775 map of Northamptonshire but the trust's initial Act of 1791 ignored it and implied that the route to be replaced left the north end of Brackley on Radstone Road before turning west at Radstone to go through the hamlet of Halse to Farthinghoe and on via Middleton Cheney and Overthorpe.

At an unknown time between 1792 and 1812 *(see 'Steane Gate', below)* the trust built a new, gently-graded 3½-mile road, the present Banbury Road, starting from Bridge Street below Brackley town hall. From there it headed for Steane Park, where it skirted the southern edge of the park before continuing on steeper gradients to Farthinghoe village. There it met the existing minor route from Brackley via Halse mentioned by the 1791 Act, a route which is partly reduced to a bridleway today.

Westwards from Farthinghoe the trust upgraded the existing road to Middleton Cheney. Initially the contrast between the gentle curves of the new road east of the village and the more sinuous alignment of the improved old road to the west is very obvious.

WEST OF MIDDLETON CHENEY, NORTHAMPTONSHIRE	The final part of the trust's creation of their new main road started on the west side of Middleton Cheney village where Mansion Hill crossed the stream in a little valley. From there an old pre-turnpike road, Warkworth Road, had approached Banbury through the village of Overthorpe where expensive property demolition would have been needed to ease the three right-angled corners among the houses.

So after 1792 the trust built a half-mile of new road westwards from Middleton to link up with the historic Banbury Lane, now the B4525, and used that to bypass Overthorpe and provide a more gently-graded descent into Banbury.

Although this short length of new road used a shallow valley to make a smooth climb out of Middleton, its whole length was cut into the valley side, necessitating a 15ft-high embankment on one section. Today Warkworth Road is cut by the Middleton Cheney bypass and the trust's link to Banbury Lane has been partly diverted to join a roundabout.

Toll gates and tollhouses	The Banbury and Brackley trust's 1791 Act banned both it and the Towcester and Weston Trust, which it crossed at Brackley, from erecting

any toll gates within Brackley and this trust from erecting any gates between Farthinghoe and Banbury *(see 'Financial Matters' below)*.

Initially the trust had three gates across its main turnpike road and one side bar. A fourth gate was added in 1812 and two more in the 1850s as the trust's financial problems grew. So by the time of its winding up the trust had six main road gates and four side bars.

BUCKINGHAM GATE **1791-1851**	*Sample annual toll income from this gate plus Radclive Side Gate and Turweston Hill Gate: £395 in 1830/31.*

The Buckingham gate, which was in use for most of the trust's life, stood across West Street, just east of its junction with Stowe Avenue. The official list of Buckingham's historic buildings claims that number 14 West Street was the toll cottage, but a modern drawing in Buckingham Gaol Museum suggests that the toll house was a smaller building immediately west of number 14 but demolished in the 1990s.

This gate became increasingly unpopular with Buckingham people because it was so close to the town centre that it was catching people on very local journeys, particularly those using Stowe Avenue, and making them pay a standard rate for what were short journeys on the turnpike road. The sensible solution was found in 1851 when this gate was removed and replaced by a new gate across the main road 1¼ miles to the west at Radclive crossroads, next to the side bar that had been there for many years.

RADCLIVE GATE AND **SIDE BARS** **1791-1873**	*No separate toll income for this site is known because records always included its takings with those from gates at Buckingham, Bandlands Bridge and Turweston.*

Only a side bar was erected in 1791 at the crossroads north of Radclive village. This stood across the turning to Radclive, presumably to prevent traffic from the Brackley direction diverting south via Radclive on to the Tingewick Road – now the A421 – to avoid paying toll at this trust's Buckingham Gate. The toll cottage stood on the northwest corner of the crossroads.

In 1851 the gate across the main road at Buckingham was discontinued and replaced by a main road gate and two side bars at the Radclive crossroads.

BUFFLER'S HOLT GATE **AND SIDE BAR** **after 1851**	*No record of toll income found.*

The toll board from Turweston Hill Gate, which is preserved in Turweston Village Hall, dates from after 1851 and refers to a gate at Buffler's Holt. Here there are two junctions, ¾ mile apart. The eastern junction leads to Chackmore, Stowe and Dadford. The 1880 edition of the Ordnance Survey map shows a side bar across this turning and a possible toll house on the north-west corner of the junction. Roseveare[211] indicates that the side bar was installed in the early 1850s, but virtually no information has been found about it by the present author.

| TURWESTON HILL AND MILL GATES from around 1821 to 1873 | *No separate record of toll income for these sites because records included their takings with those from gates at Buckingham and Radclive.* |

Between 1818 and 1825 Bandlands Bridge Toll Gate *(see below)*, on the eastern edge of Brackley at the foot of Turweston Hill, was replaced by a new gate, Turweston <u>Hill</u> Gate, 630 yards to the east at the top of the hill. The new toll house stood on the north-east corner of the turning to Turweston village. Its site is now part of the cleared sight line at the junction. The house was declared to be beyond repair in 1856 and was replaced in that year by a new toll house and gate situated near the windmill, 230 yards further east, at the turning to Evenley – now a bridleway. Unsurprisingly the new gate was called Turweston <u>Mill</u> Gate.

What appears to be the last toll board from Turweston <u>Hill</u> Gate, because details on it date it after 1851, is preserved in the village hall. It is very unusual in that its text, while perfectly normal in wording, has been carved in raised lettering on the toll board. The cost of making it in this fashion suggests that this is the work of a talented local wood carver with a private project – possibly to commemorate the end of the trust – rather than something commissioned by an impecunious turnpike trust.

| BANDLANDS BRIDGE GATE 1791 to about 1821 | *No separate toll income for this site because records always included its takings with those from gates at Buckingham and Radclive.* |

This bridge over the Great Ouse straddled the county boundary on the east side of Brackley. It is now beside a roundabout on the town's bypass. A toll gate was erected at the east end of the bridge when the trust started work in 1791. There is now no trace of the site of its toll house, which was on the north side of the road.

The gate was moved uphill to the top of Turweston Hill 630 yards to the east between 1818 and 1825. In the absence of the trust's main records we can only surmise that the reason for the move was to catch traffic leaving Turweston village and heading east.

| STEANE GATE AND SIDE BAR 1812 to at least 1854 | *No separate toll income for this site is known because records always included its takings with those from Farthinghoe Gate.* |

The Steane Gate and its side bar were located 2½ miles west of the centre of Brackley, near the south-west corner of Steane Park *(at grid reference SP 551 387)*. The main gate stood across the new road built by the trust between Brackley and Farthinghoe. An 1812 advert in the 'Northampton Mercury' described gate and side bar as 'newly erected' and this could indicate the date of the opening of the new road.

The side bar was erected across the minor road to Hinton-in-the-Hedges, and the toll house stood on the south-west corner of the junction. In the absence of the trust's main records it is difficult to see how the expense of a pair of gates here, only 1¼ miles from the gate at Farthinghoe, could be justified.

The site of the toll house is now part of a field but, confusingly, a much-extended, two-storey lodge house on the opposite side of the road beside the start of an abandoned drive to Steane Manor House, has its bow front facing the turnpike road instead of the drive. In spite of this, no evidence has been found to link this building with the turnpike trust.

FARTHINGHOE GATE **1791 to at least 1854**	*Sample toll income for Farthnghoe Gate, Steane Gate and its side bar together: £263 in 1830/31.* The siting of a gate just west of Farthinghoe village was the result of a clause in the trust's 1791 Act *(see 'Financial Matters' below)*. While no details of the toll house have been found, contemporary maps show the gate with its toll house on the north-east side of the road *(at grid reference SP 533 399)*, near the junction with New Road.
GRIMSBURY GREEN **GATE** **from about 1851** **to 1873**	*No data found for toll income at this gate.* The saga about tolls paid at Banbury Bridge Gate *(see 'Financial Matters' below)* ended with its removal after 1851 and its replacement by two gates, one for each of the two trusts converging on the east side of Banbury, just east of their junction in the suburb of Grimsbury. In the absence of the Banbury and Brackley Trust's main records almost nothing has been found about this gate.
Weighing engine	This trust appears never to have had a weighing engine, and nor did the rival Buckingham to Banbury turnpike route via Aynho.
Milestones and **mileposts**	The trust used a design of milestone that was unusual in Buckinghamshire. Instead of the familiar stones with a square cross-section, these were thin stone slabs with a bowed top, to the front of which was screwed a cast-iron plate with raised capital lettering. Mileage on them rose from 58 miles to London just west of Buckingham to 73 at Nethercote east of Banbury. Until the 1980s almost all milestones on the Buckinghamshire part of the road were in place and intact, but during that decade all of these had their plates stolen, and all but three of the stones vanished. The only known surviving stones outside Buckinghamshire are in Banbury and just west of Farthinghoe, and they too are without their plates.
Financial matters	Traffic from Brackley entered Banbury along Middleton Road and over Banbury Bridge. The bridge and the westernmost half mile of Middleton Road were both controlled by the Banbury and Lutterworth Trust, which charged tolls at its Banbury Bridge Gate. The Lutterworth Trust had started work 26 years before the Banbury and Brackley and was thus able to secure a clause in the latter's 1791 Act to prevent it from erecting any toll gates between Banbury and a point 100 yards west of the village of Farthinghoe. In recognition of this the Act required that westbound traffic which had paid toll between Brackley and Banbury could pass Banbury Bridge Gate without further payment on production of the appropriate toll ticket, and eastbound

traffic, having paid toll at Banbury Bridge, could similarly pass Farthinghoe Gate freely.

Since traffic to and from Brackley travelled only half a mile on the Lutterworth Trust's road, from the junction of Daventry and Middleton Roads, eastbound tolls paid at Banbury Bridge were passed on to the Brackley Trust after deduction of one shilling in the pound for expenses.

In return the 1791 Act required the Banbury and Brackley Trust to pay the Lutterworth Trust £10 a year to maintain that part of Middleton Road, Banbury, which lay west of the junction of the two trusts.

This arrangement was felt to be unfair to the Banbury and Brackley Trust and that trust's 1810 Act replaced it with a requirement for the Lutterworth Trust to contribute £15 a year to the Banbury and Brackley for the maintenance of their road between Banbury and Farthinghoe.

The administration and enforcement of these provisions led to low-level friction between the two trusts for years, ending with Banbury Bridge Gate being closed after 1851 and replaced by a pair of gates, one on each trust's road, near their junction. The gate on the road from Brackley was called Grimsbury Green Gate.

1873: The Trust wound up

The trust had started life in fine style by building 5¼ miles of new road and rebuilding much of the remainder west of Westbury in its early years. After this it appears to have rested on its laurels, with little of its initial debt paid off and signs of mismanagement appearing by the 1830s.

The financial situation was not helped when the Buckinghamshire Railway opened its Bletchley to Banbury line in 1850 on a course which closely paralleled the trust's road all the way from Buckingham to Banbury.

The formation of the Brackley Consolidated Trust in 1851 *(see "Background" above)* found the joint debts of the two trusts totalling £4,830 in 1853, when annual toll income in that year was £1,396. The trustees thereafter concentrated on reducing that debt and brought it down to £3,300 by 1869, helped by a small but steady growth of toll income during the 1850s and by not paying any interest to their creditors.

The combined trust had to carry on while this was happening, but it was ready to be wound up by 1872, and this duly happened on 1 November 1873 under **35-6 Vic., c.85 (1872)**.

Road 18:
Great Marlow and Stokenchurch Turnpike Road 1791

Identifying the road's route

The route of the Great Marlow and Stokenchurch turnpike road is today the B482 from Marlow to Stokenchurch.

Historic background

This trust grew out of a wish to improve communication between Marlow and Oxford. The minor road chosen for upgrading to do this made the journey four miles shorter than by the turnpike roads already existing via Henley and Dorchester, or via High Wycombe and Wheatley.

Unfortunately the promoters' expectations of traffic growth were over-optimistic. In consequence toll income per mile of road was easily the lowest of any turnpike trust in Buckinghamshire, and not far into the nineteenth century trustees became more concerned with economies than with road improvements. In the end the trust appears to have gone quietly out of business without the formality of being wound up.

With such a history it is tantalising that little contemporary information about the trust has been found. The author has not located any minute or account books for the Marlow and Stokenchurch trust and the usual fall-backs in such cases – items in the local newspapers – are few. So we know little about one of the most intriguing – even if least important – trusts in Buckinghamshire.

The limits of the trust's road

From the junction of Dean Street and Spittal Street in Marlow to the junction of Marlow Road and Wycombe Road in Stokenchurch.

Its length and maintenance districts

8 miles, of which 5½ miles were in the Buckinghamshire of 1836, when Stokenchurch parish was in Oxfordshire. Today the whole road is in Buckinghamshire.

From the little information found, it appears that throughout its life this trust maintained its road without any operational sub-divisions.

Initial Act of Parliament

31 Geo.III, c.135 (1791).

Continuation Act

53 Geo.III, c.44 (1813).

Control of the Trust:	The trust's initial Act listed 111 trustees, including thirteen with titles and six clergymen.
TRUSTEES	Reverend Henry Colbourne Ridley, vicar of Hambledon, chaired the trust intermittently between 1824 and 1831, and Thomas R Barker, also of Hambledon, continued in the role from 1833 to at least 1850. In most years between 1829 and 1864 he was also chairman of the Reading and Hatfield Trust, whose road met this one in Marlow.

OFFICERS	The trust's first clerk was Henry Goldsmith, solicitor of Marlow. Next was John Wright, another Marlow solicitor, who was clerk from at least 1821 until 1838, and was followed by W L Ward of Marlow by 1850.
	A measure of the trust's poor financial condition is that it paid its clerk only a paltry five guineas a year between 1836 and 1850 and does not appear to have employed a treasurer or surveyor for much of the nineteenth century.
	Wright was also clerk to the second district – Marlow to Rickmansworth - of the Reading and Hatfield Trust for a number of years, and Thomas Barker, who chaired the Marlow and Stokenchurch Trust during at least 17 years, also chaired the Reading and Hatfield Trust during an overlapping period of 35 years.
	These connections <u>may</u> have led the Reading and Hatfield Trust to prop up its weaker neighbour by providing basic management services to the Marlow and Stokenchurch Trust when these were needed, thus explaining the latter's apparent lack of a treasurer and surveyor. However no evidence has been found to confirm this.

MEETINGS OF THE TRUSTEES	Almost inevitably, with only one town on the trust's road, its business was mainly conducted in Marlow. Although its 1791 Act specified a minimum of four trust meetings per year, two in Marlow and two in Stokenchurch, almost all meetings after the early years seem to have been held at the inn at the top of Marlow High Street which was variously called the 'Crown Inn', the 'Upper Crown Inn', and the 'Crown Hotel'.

Maintenance of the road	Little detail has been found about the Marlow and Stokenchurch trust's day-to-day operations. The trust's 1791 Act gives a clue to a possible maintenance issue in this area with a forty-shilling penalty for anyone transporting a tree who allowed it to drag on the road.

Improvements to the road	The trust made a promising start, raising around £2,870 in loans and building two miles of new road. However, when the expected toll income did not materialise the trust was unable to repay loans and became saddled with serious interest payments. This led, from the 1820s at least, to the trust having no treasurer or surveyor, a state of affairs which guaranteed that no further road improvements would be carried out.
	Contemporary information about the Marlow and Stokenchurch is scarce. Finding the dates when changes were made to the road has therefore been

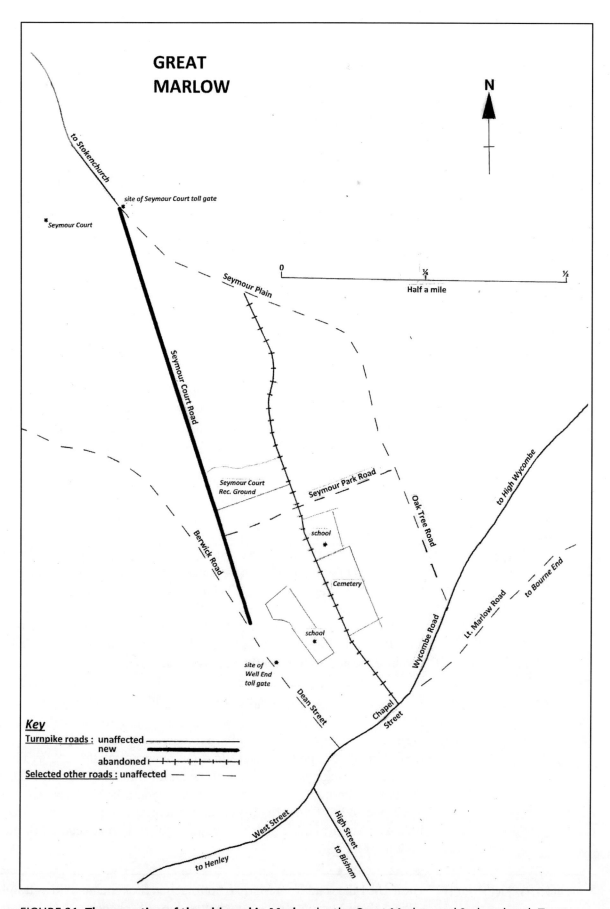

FIGURE 31: **The rerouting of the old road in Marlow** by the Great Marlow and Stokenchurch Trust.

by comparing contemporary maps. This shows that between the mid-1760s survey for Jefferys' map of Buckinghamshire and the first edition of the Ordnance Survey's one-inch scale map in 1822, new alignments built to cut out detours and sharp bends had come to form two miles, a quarter of the trust's road existing in 1822.

IN GREAT MARLOW

Until the formation of this trust the route out of Marlow towards Stokenchurch started opposite number 64 Chapel Street and ran northwards, parallel to Dean Street and what is now Seymour Court Road up to 250 yards to the east. The route joined Seymour Plain and followed it to the point where today it becomes the modern B482 opposite Seymour Court. Although now largely lost as a road except for Seymour Plain, two-thirds of the old route can be followed northwards from Chapel Street on footpaths between houses and along the western boundary of the cemetery. Where it forms the east end of Seymour Court Recreation Ground the modern footpath runs beside an overgrown, tree-lined holloway which marks the route of the pre-turnpike road.

Between 1796 and 1801 the trust took over the southern end of Dean Street, then a minor road leading to Monday Dean, and built a ¾-mile straight new road – now named Seymour Court Road – between Dean Street and the junction with Seymour Plain opposite Seymour Court. On paper this immediately replaced the old route, but it seems to have taken time for traffic to move to the new road *(see 'Toll Gates – Seymour Court Gate' below)*.

Although the turnpike road was the same length as the old route it has an easier, more consistent gradient, is wider, and starts from nearer to the town centre.

AT LANE END

One-third of a mile south-east of the centre of Lane End *(at grid reference SU 812 914)* the old road went around a sharp bend on a level break in the hill up to the village. Between 1791 and 1812 the trust built a ¼-mile section of straight road across the inside of the bend. For many years the old road remained as a loop serving Cutlers Farm – formerly Priest's Farm - on the east side of the present road, but only part of it remains today, forming the access to recently-built houses.

BETWEEN BOLTER END AND CADMORE END

In pre-turnpike days the road's course described an S-shaped route between Bolter End crossroads and the west end of Cadmore End village. Heading west from the crossroads the old road veered up to 150 yards away on the north side of the present road, on a course now totally lost, as far as the entrance to Rackleys Farm, west of which it formed the present village road through Cadmore End to the south of the modern B482. Between 1796 and 1812 one mile of new road was built, incorporating two straight sections linked by a short kink which is a section of the old road, cutting through the middle of the 'S'.

IN STOKENCHURCH

Until 1861 the road from Marlow approached Stokenchurch in a straight line – the present Marlow Road – along the edge of Stokenchurch Common until, just before meeting the Oxford Road, it veered west across the common to join what is now the A40 near Rose Corner. But by 1861 the Marlow and Stokenchurch trust has ceased to exist.

In that year during the enclosure of the common, the Stokenchurch enclosure commissioners took the opportunity to straighten and shorten Marlow Road. They moved the junction of the two roads some 300 yards south-east to the place where it is today.

Toll gates and tollhouses	The trust had two gates for most of its life, possibly three during a short period in the 1820s and 1830s. They were always let as a group to one contractor, so no records for the individual gates appear to have survived.

PENLEY HOLLIES GATE 1791 until 1850s	*Sample total annual toll income for this and the gate in Marlow: £90 13s 6d in 1836, and £63 8s 4d in 1850.*

This was the only tollgate to remain in use throughout the trust's life. It stood just over a mile south of the road's end at Stokenchurch, today's junction of the B482 with the A40. Today its site *(at grid reference SU 769 944)* is in the caravan park near Penley Farm, at the southern end of the 'S' shaped deviation up to the 1970s bridge over the M40.

The tollhouse, with an unusually large garden for its gatekeeper, stood on private land on the east side of the road, and the trust paid £6 a year ground rent for the house and garden.

SEYMOUR COURT GATE, MARLOW from 1791 to about 1801 and from about 1821 to the 1850s	*No separate data on tolls has been found for this gate, whose takings were included with Penley Hollies Gate (see above).*

Information found about this gate is sketchy. It stood on the long climb out of Marlow at what is now the junction of Seymour Court Road with Seymour Plain *(at grid reference SU 841 882)*. The gate was probably installed when the trust started work in 1791, at a time when the route from Marlow towards Stokenchurch lay up to 250 yards east of the present road until it reached Seymour Court.

After only a few years the building of Seymour Court Road *(see 'Improvements' above)* led to the placing of the Well End toll gate across Dean Street, which made the Seymour Court gate seem redundant and it was removed sometime between 1796 and 1801.

In the absence of other information it is assumed that after the building of Seymour Court Road some traffic continued to use the old route and thus avoided the new toll gate in Dean Street. Whether or not that was the reason, the toll gate at Seymour Court, which could collect tolls from both routes, was re-established shortly before 1821 and probably remained in use until the trust was wound up.

In its 1821 form it consisted of a kiosk on the grass verge between the converging roads, flanked by gates across both of them.[212] While several such kiosks, built as an economical alternative to a toll house, were used in the north of the county, they were unusual in mid and south Buckinghamshire, which is a further hint at the trust's financial difficulties.

WELL END GATE, MARLOW
about 1801-1831

No separate data for tolls has been found for this gate.

This was the second of the trust's gates in Marlow. When the trust made its new route out of Marlow between 1796 and 1801 it placed this toll gate across the new road in Dean Street, immediately south of Queen's Road, to replace the gate at Seymour Court. The enclosure map of 1855 names Dean Street as Well End, which explains the long-forgotten name of the gate.

For a toll house the trust took over an existing cottage on the east side of the road, and apparently added a porch extending across the highway verge to the gate.

Notes on the Seymour Court Gate *(see above)* suggest the reason for re-establishing that gate and removing the one in Dean Street. The evidence indicates that it took several years to decide on the removal. The Francis map of Great Marlow[213] shows this gate still in use in 1830, but the former toll house was one of several dwellings in Dean Street which were sold by auction in 1833,[214] giving a narrow window for when the gate was taken out of use. The toll house had been demolished by the time of the 1880 Ordnance Survey map.

Weighing engine

Although a weighing engine was authorised by the trust's 1791 Act, no record has been found of one being erected.

Milestones and mileposts

At some time between 1791 and 1822 the trust put up eight milestones of an unusual design with a square base rising into an upper part which has a circular cross-section, with the mileage shown on this upper part. The rounded section could indicate that these are second-hand stones from another trust, originally with a wholly square cross-section but which have been reshaped to remove their original incised wording. If this is so, it is another indication of the trust's frugal existence. Only four of these stones survive today.

The Trust stops work

The Great Marlow and Stokenchurch Turnpike Trust, having raised loans totalling around £2,870 in the 1790s to fund its ambitious road-building programme, found that poor traffic growth meant it was unable to make repayments. It was still carrying the same capital debt in 1850.

By then that debt stood at 45 times the trust's annual toll income and the trust was paying £144-a-year interest on the loans. With annual toll income averaging £107 in the years 1820 to 1839, and £72 from 1840 to 1850, the trust had clearly got into an impossible situation. Winding up its affairs was the only solution, but Parliament would not entertain this until the debts had been discharged.

By 1857, when Stokenchurch's enclosure commissioners were listing public roads to be stopped up or diverted,[215] the road to Marlow had ceased to be a turnpike road. There had not been the necessary Act of Parliament to authorise this, so we are thus left with the impression that the trustees simply stopped work and hoped that the parishes along the road would step in and replace them. What happened to the creditors can only be imagined.

Road 19:
The Princes Risborough and Thame Turnpike Road 1795

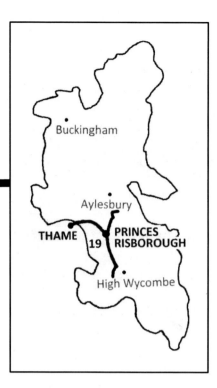

Identifying the road's route

The main route of the Princes Risborough and Thame Turnpike Trust, often known as the Risborough Road Trust, followed today's A4010 from Stoke Mandeville southwards to West Wycombe, except for the town-centre bypass in Princes Risborough where the turnpike road used High Street.

The road also had three branches:

(1) from Terrick to World's End, Wendover, which is today the B4009 Nash Lee Road at its western end but declassified at its eastern end as a result of being cut by the Wendover bypass.

(2) from Princes Risborough to Thame in Oxfordshire, following today's A4129 to the outskirts of Thame, and the B-class Kingsey Road and East Street within Thame.

(3) from West Wycombe Road to Cressex Road in High Wycombe, following the A4010 Chapel Lane and New Road to today's Cressex Road roundabout.

Historic background

This pro-active turnpike trust created what is now a strong travel corridor between Aylesbury, Princes Risborough and the Oxford road at West Wycombe. However, before the trust came on the scene there does not appear to have been enough traffic between Aylesbury and Risborough to mark out an obvious road linking these towns. Seventeenth and early eighteenth-century map makers failed to agree on a recognisable route.

Indeed the public meetings held in 1794 to form the trust started by supporting the use of part of the Lower Icknield Way and the road through Askett, bypassing what finally came to be the trust's route through Great Kimble. South of Princes Risborough map makers all agreed on one route – which has become the present A4010 – as far as the hamlet of Slough, today known as Saunderton Station, but southwards from there some showed two alternative routes to West Wycombe, either via Bradenham Road – now the A4010 – or via Slough Lane and Chorley Road.

There was also no noticeable historic traffic flow between Princes Risborough and Thame. Indeed the two 'direct' routes between these towns were so bad that in 1767 an early Thame to London stagecoach service was routed between Thame and Risborough via Chinnor. The promotion of the trust's Thame branch road was an unsuccessful attempt to link the two towns by providing a proper road between them.

The same theme of providing a new road link where none existed was behind the trust's proposal in 1822 to link West Wycombe – and therefore Aylesbury – with Marlow, but here again the travelling public was so unsupportive that the trust actually abandoned its project before it was completed.

The limits of the trust's road	The main route began at the junction of Station Road and Wendover Road in Stoke Mandeville. Its southern end was at The Pedestal roundabout on West Wycombe Road, West Wycombe.
	The three branches ran: (1) from World's End, Wendover, to join the main route at Terrick; (2) from the junction of Aylesbury Road and Longwick Road at the north end of Princes Risborough town centre to the junction of East Street with Upper High Street in Thame; and (3) from West Wycombe Road to Cressex Road in High Wycombe.
Its length and maintenance districts	The trust's road was originally 11½ miles long between World's End and West Wycombe. The extension to Stoke Mandeville increased this to 13 miles, and the Thame branch brought it up to 19¾ miles. All these roads are in Buckinghamshire except for 1¾ miles of the Thame branch in Oxfordshire. The 1½-mile extension to Cressex had ceased to be a turnpike road before the Thame branch was built.
	For most of its life the trust managed its roads as a single unit. However, during 1825-30, when it was under considerable stress while building the branch road to Thame, the roads were divided into three divisions: West Wycombe to Thame, Princes Risborough to Great Kimble, and Little Kimble to World's End and Stoke Mandeville. Each had its own surveyor. As soon as construction of the Thame branch was completed the trust cut costs by reverting to managing its roads as one unit under one surveyor.
Initial Act of Parliament	**35 Geo.III, c.149 (1795)** turnpiked the road from World's End, Wendover, to West Wycombe.
Continuation Acts	**57 Geo.III, c.17, (1817)** renewed the initial Act.
	3 Geo.IV, c.92, (1822) authorised taking over the road (today's A4010) from Terrick through Stoke Mandeville village to the Wendover Road, with an extension – which was not built – from near today's Stoke Mandeville railway station northwards to a different point on the Wendover Road. This Act also authorised the construction of a largely new road from West Wycombe to Handy Cross, south of High Wycombe, to shorten the distance from Aylesbury to Marlow, but only part of this was built.
	6 Geo.IV, c.45 (1825) authorised the addition of a branch road from Princes Risborough to Thame.

Control of the Trust: TRUSTEES	Two local notables played leading roles in the trust's affairs during the first half of the nineteenth century. John Grubb, of Horsenden House, near Princes Risborough, chaired the inaugural meetings and went on to attend 74 trust meetings between 1824 and 1841 and to chair 55 of them. Sir Scrope Bernard-Morland, a banker who lived at Nether Winchendon but was acquiring an estate in the Kimbles on the line of the road, attended 44 trust meetings between 1824 and 1829 and chaired 29 of them.
CLERKS	This trust was another which had long-serving clerks. George Fell was clerk from before 1821 until he died in post in 1829. Edward Prickett took over in 1829 and continued until he resigned in 1851, after which Joseph Parrott continued until the trust was wound up in 1871. All three were Aylesbury solicitors.
MEETINGS OF THE TRUSTEES	Almost all the leading trustees lived in the Risborough area, and its surveyors worked there, so although the known clerks were all from Aylesbury, virtually all trust meetings were held in Princes Risborough near the mid-point of the trust's roads.

Meetings there were in High Street premises and mainly at the 'Cross Keys' public house, now a medical centre, the 'George Inn', (now the 'George and Dragon'), and occasionally until 1827 at 'The Wheatsheaf', now Lloyd's Bank, and 'The White Hart', whose site has since been redeveloped. |
Maintenance of the road	It must be assumed that the problem of adjoining landowners pushing their fences out on to the highway verge was a problem for all trusts, but only a few seemed to record concern at the practice in their minute books. Therefore the numerous references to removing encroachments on to the highway which appear in this trust's minutes[216] probably reflect the prejudices of its trustees rather than indicate a particular problem on its roads.
Improvements to the road	This was a very active trust which built 5½ miles of new road to shorten the route by cutting out detours. Of this 1½ miles were on the main route between Stoke Mandeville and West Wycombe, three miles on the Thame branch and one mile on the Handy Cross extension. On the main route between Stoke Mandeville and Princes Risborough this work converted an indirect string of local lanes into a main road.
STOKE MANDEVILLE	The dead straight Station Road was built by the enclosure commissioners when they were rearranging the parish's field and road network in 1797. The turnpike trust extended its control from Terrick to the Wendover Road in Stoke Mandeville in 1822 and, in doing so, took over Station Road. At the time they had intended to build a short cut from a point near today's railway station to join the Wendover Road at what is now the Silver Birch Way roundabout. Unfortunately only £200 was subscribed towards the £662 estimated cost of building this and the project lapsed.
LITTLE KIMBLE	Two hundred yards east of today's Little Kimble railway bridge the local road that became the turnpike road detoured up to 200 yards to the north of

the present A4010, with the western end of the detour opposite Brookside Farm. Around 1805 the trust cut out this loop by building a 600-yard bypass to the south – which is still the road today. The original loop *(at grid reference SP 825 073)* is lost without trace.

In pre-turnpike days the route of the Upper Icknield Way between Ellesborough and Great Kimble churches followed an undulating course along the face of the Chiltern escarpment, between 40ft and 70ft above the level of the present C-class road.[217] This met the road that is today the A4010 just north of Great Kimble church, where a modern lodge house stands beside the track of the old way.

The trust's 1795 Act mentioned that a diversion had already been agreed to build a shorter and more level road to replace the old high-level route. The new 700-yard road was built between 1797 and 1805, leaving the turnpike road where it passes Little Kimble church and continuing to the sharp bend *(at grid reference SP 832 065)* half way to Ellesborough church where it joins the old route from north of Great Kimble church.

The new road, which was to be made by the turnpike trust even though it was not a turnpike road, was built across part of an estate in Great and Little Kimble and Marsh which had been acquired during the 1790s by Sir Scrope Bernard-Morland of Nether Winchendon as part of his plan to build a

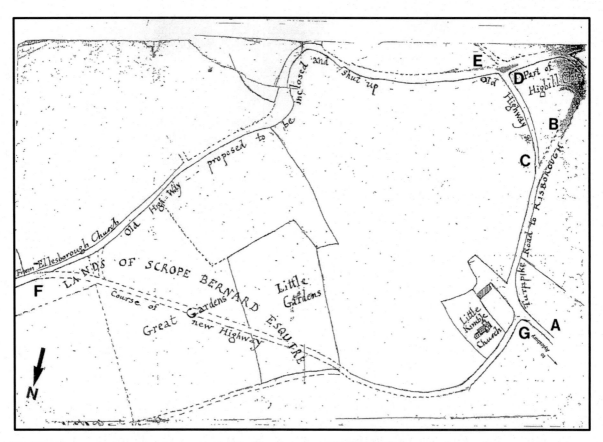

FIGURE 32: **Road alterations near Little Kimble Church 1797-1805.** The original turnpike route (A-C-D then right at the crossroads) was replaced by cutting the corner at B. At the same time part of the Upper Icknield Way (E – F) was replaced by the present Ellesborough Road (F – G), built by the turnpike trust although it was not a turnpike road.

mansion at Kimble. He had been an initial subscriber to the Risborough Road in 1795 and was to be one of its principal chairmen in the 1820s.

The 1795 Act stated the trust's intention to build this new route to improve the link between Ellesborough church and the hamlets of Marsh and Kimblewick even though none of these three was on the turnpike road. Both hamlets, however, were part of Sir Scrope's new estate and we can only surmise that the new road would have improved access within the estate and to the proposed mansion. In the event Sir Scrope's bank fell on hard times, he died in 1830s, and the mansion did not materialise.

LITTLE KIMBLE HILL	The road's present 200-yard long climb south of Little Kimble church was built to replace an even steeper climb on the east side of the present A4010. The former road, still visible as a narrow holloway between fields and as a nick in two contours on the Ordnance Survey 2½-inch map, had gone straight ahead up the slope above Church Farm to make a T-junction with the old road to Ellesborough church.

Contemporary maps suggest that the diversion was made between 1797 and 1805. The trust's minutes mention considerable work in straightening and widening the road here in 1837, but this could refer to upgrading the existing road between Little Kimble church and the foot of the new hill. |
| **ASKETT** | The tellingly straight section of road running for ¼ mile north-east of today's Askett roundabout and for 160 yards south-west of it to Letter Box Lane was built, probably in 1803-05, as a replacement for the considerably less direct old road whose course meandered only a few yards to the south-east. In particular this work eliminated the offset double T-junction by which the turnpike road had formerly crossed Cadsden Road. |
| **PRINCES RISBOROUGH** | Until 1820 the road's southern exit from Princes Risborough was via Bell Street and what are now known as Station Road and Poppy Road, with a right-angled turn between the last two. In that year the turnpike trustees persuaded the parish's enclosure commissioners to build the ¼-mile curving section of Wycombe Road *(at grid reference SP 804 028)* to cut off the corner.

It was unusual for turnpike trustees to work with enclosure commissioners *(but see Adderbury on Road number 7)* but here it made sense while the commissioners were laying out other new roads during the enclosure of the parish's open fields. The turnpike trustees, of course, paid for the new road and were so anxious for the work to go ahead quickly that their chairman, Sir Scrope Bernard-Morland, offered to make a personal contribution.

About ¼ mile further south the A4010 today crosses the Ridgeway Path and starts to climb southwards on Culverton Hill. The pre-turnpike road at this point, as well as being steep, took the form of an 'S' as it swung from side to side to lessen the gradient. In 1831-35 the Overseers of Princes Risborough parish – at the expense of the turnpike trust – rebuilt the |

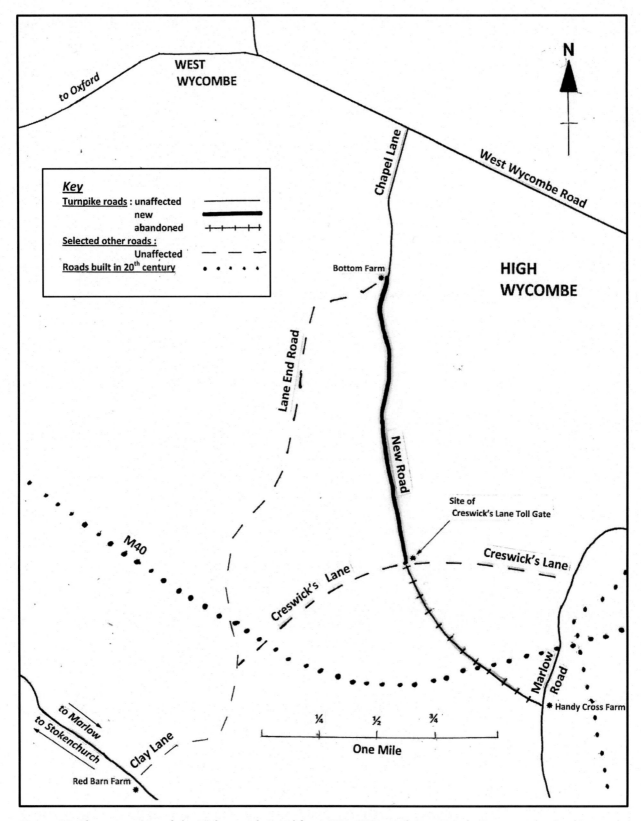

Figure 33: **The extension of the Risborough Road from West Wycombe to Handy Cross**, authorised in 1822 but only built as far as the crossroads of New Road and Cressex Road.

steepest half mile of the hill, from the Ridgeway to the Shootacre Lane junction. They drove a new, gently curving road through the middle of the former 'S' and excavated cuttings to even out the gradient. Some of the spoil from this was carried downhill to form a low embankment across a shallow valley at the bottom and thus to reduce the height to be climbed.

THE WEST WYCOMBE TO HANDY CROSS EXTENSION

During the initial discussions in 1794 about forming the trust the intention was to make a short cut from West Wycombe to Marlow. The plan was to turnpike the existing Chapel Lane, Lane End Road and Clay Lane to connect to the future B482 at Red Barn Farm, south-east of Lane End.

However the 'gentlemen of Marlow' refused financial support for the project. They had only just subscribed to the rather expensive start of the Marlow and Stokenchurch Trust *(see Road number 18)*. So the scheme was dropped.

In 1822 the trust revived the idea in a different form and obtained powers to make an extension from West Wycombe to Handy Cross, which was on the Reading and Hatfield Trust's road between High Wycombe and Great Marlow. This extension would have been across open country and would have cut more than half a mile off the journey from Aylesbury to Marlow by avoiding High Wycombe.

Starting from the West Wycombe Road *(at grid reference SU 843 942)* just over half a mile east of today's Pedestal roundabout, the plan was to take over the existing half mile of Chapel Lane down to Bottom Farm - now the Lane End Road junction – and then build a one-mile-long new road which is still, appropriately, called New Road, uphill beside Rowliff Wood and on to cross Creswick's Lane – today's Cressex Road.

Beyond that it would end at a junction with the Wycombe to Marlow road, today the A404, at Handy Cross Farm, which point is today just south of the M40 Handy Cross junction. Except for the already extant Chapel Lane the new road was to be 30ft wide, stoned with broken flints twelve inches deep on the central 16ft and six inches deep at the sides.

In a reaction familiar in modern times the Bucks, Beds and Herts Chronicle of 9 November 1822 considered the scheme to be a waste of money - because it avoided High Wycombe – and thought that the money would have been better spent on more straightening of the existing road between Aylesbury and West Wycombe.

Construction of the new road probably began in 1823 and reached Creswick's Lane crossroads in that year. However with only £839 subscribed against a predicted cost of £1,350, work then came to a standstill, leaving just over half a mile to Handy Cross not built. As traffic was able to use Creswick's Lane reach the Marlow road, albeit by an indirect route, a toll gate was installed at the junction of New Road with Creswick's Lane but, possibly because the route was so hilly, traffic was so thin that the gate was soon abandoned as uneconomic.

By 1833 Sir John Dashwood, of West Wycombe House, was pressing for payment for the land to form the last half mile to Handy Cross, which had been taken from him but not used. The trust decided not to continue. New Road thus became a white elephant which the trust was obliged to maintain – though as High Wycombe grew in the late twentieth century it became a vital part of the town's traffic circulation.

THE PRINCES RISBOROUGH TO THAME BRANCH ROAD

The towns of Princes Risborough and Thame were seven miles apart but were linked only by two indirect strings of lanes. The shorter of these went through Longwick, Ilmer and Towersey and included a wet, low-lying section between Ilmer and Towersey which could be impassable in winter. Nearly half a mile of this route *(at grid ref. SP 754 049)* survives as a green lane today. The longer, but higher and drier route was via Longwick, Kingsey and Towersey.

From the start of their preparatory meetings in 1794 the trustees of the Risborough Road trust had wanted to include a branch to Thame in their plans. They reasoned that if they could improve the route between Princes Risborough and Thame, then traffic on the London to Oxford road might be attracted to divert from that road at West Wycombe to travel via the Risborough Gap in the Chiltern escarpment and then on to Oxford through Thame and Wheatley.

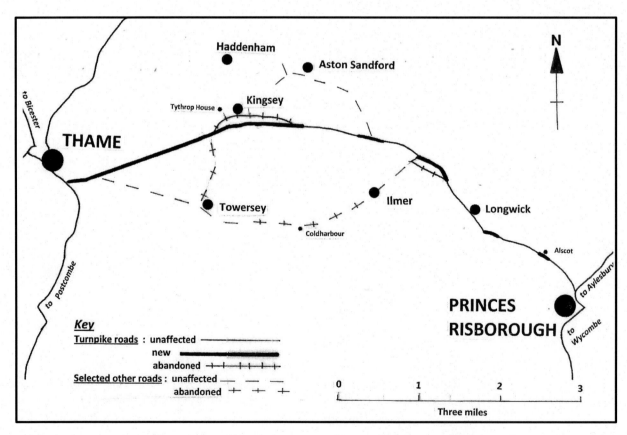

FIGURE 34: **The Risborough Road's branch road to Thame**, showing pre-turnpike routes via Kingsey and Ilmer, and the five lengths of more direct turnpike road built in 1825-30 to shorten the journey.

This was a significantly lower and less steep route than Aston Hill on the Oxford Road and the trustees hoped it might bring increased trade to Princes Risborough and more tolls to the Risborough Road Trust's West Wycombe gate.

But it was clear that the low-level route between Princes Risborough and Thame via Ilmer would have to be abandoned and a shorter version of the higher-level route created. This meant that nearly half of the road between Risborough and Thame would have to be new construction across fields.

In 1794, however, most of the proposed sections of new road were across a patchwork of long, narrow strips in communal open-field arable cultivation. The prospect of negotiating the purchase of land for the road from the owners and occupiers of hundreds of these strips was too daunting, so the Thame branch was dropped from the 1795 bill.

Between 1820 and 1826 the situation changed, when the open fields of four of the five parishes along the high level route were enclosed, and in the fifth, Aston Sandford, only three furlongs had to be crossed. The turnpike trustees now had to treat with only a handful of owners.

A new Act was obtained in 1825, authorising the construction of a 7-mile road from Princes Risborough to Thame. Starting from Risborough the old road was rebuilt, straightened and widened, with short lengths of new construction as far, roughly, as the site where the railway bridge would be built in Kingsey parish. From there three miles of new road was built across Kingsey parish and into Thame.

An early beneficiary from the new road was Philip Wykeham of Tythrop House in Kingsey. He was able to substantially enlarge his park by stopping up the old road, which lay fairly close to the south front of Tythrop House, once the new one had been built 200 yards further away. Between 1825 and 1828 Wykeham made the largest of all private loans to the Thame branch road – £800 out of £3,380 raised. He went on to be a trustee of the Risborough Road from 1828 to 1832.

Princes Risborough parish was also anxious to see the link to Thame built. Accordingly during the enclosure of its open fields in 1820-23, the parish agreed for its enclosure commissioners to bring the eastern 2¼ miles of the future turnpike road (from Princes Risborough to the Ilmer turn) up to turnpike standard, using the powers grannted by Parliament for the enclosure even though the turnpike road had yet to be authorised.

West of Ilmer the turnpike trust did the work and started briskly between Ilmer and Kingsey in October 1825, with 100 men on site. The new road was opened between Risborough and Kingsey church in May 1826. With no major earthworks to deal with, they should have continued at a similar pace into Thame, but there it all ground to a halt.

Lord Abingdon, one of the principal landowners in Thame parish, had clashed with the trust in 1824-25, when its Bill was at a preliminary stage, over the proposed route of their road across his land. His objections were met by a slight re-routing of the trust's road so that, instead of crossing

Thame parish in a straight line from the parish boundary to High Street, it would be built in two straight sections up to 100 yards south of the original alignment. These met in a fairly sharp bend – still apparent – at the crossing of Pound Street, now Wellington Street, then on the outskirts of Thame.

With this strategy certain properties belonging to Lord Abingdon were avoided, but he had set the tone for friction between his tenants and the trust as it entered Thame. By 1826 the enclosure of Thame's open fields was in full swing and the turnpike trustees were trying to build a road through a constantly changing landscape as the new hedged fields were being laid out. Every mistake by the trust's contractors – and there were several – resulted in bad feeling and delays as a result of which it was not until July 1830 that the road was complete.[218]

The trust had originally estimated the cost of making the 7-mile road at £2,837 but the final total was pushed to £5,380 by the unexpected delays and costs due to legal disputes in Thame parish. This was made up of £3,380 invested privately plus a £2,000 Exchequer loan.

After all this the trustees' intentions were not fulfilled because, although some long-distance traffic did divert off the Oxford road through Thame and Risborough, most of it did not. Local traffic between the two towns grew only slightly. Even today the A4129 is one of the more lightly trafficked A-class roads in Buckinghamshire.

Toll gates and tollhouses

The Princes Risborough and Thame Turnpike Trust was one of those that went to considerable lengths to prevent toll avoidance. On its 19¾ miles, excluding the short-lived Cressex extension, it started with three main gates and increased this to six by 1845, making an average of just over three miles between gates, which compares with a Buckinghamshire average of five miles. In spite of this it had one of the lowest toll incomes per mile in the county. Four side bars were added between 1827 and 1845.

TERRICK SIDE BAR 1827-1871 AND GATE 1838-1871

Sample annual toll income of side bar: £65 in 1833/34.

The Terrick side bar appears to have been the trust's attempt to catch toll evaders who avoided Little Kimble Gate by diverting via Butlers Cross and Ellesborough Road. It was erected 1¼ miles south of Stoke Mandeville village at the crossroads where Aylesbury Road, Chalkshire Road and Nash Lee Road meet, initially simply as a side-bar across Chalkshire Road, leading to Butlers Cross.

Although the trust's control was extended along the main road to Stoke Mandeville in 1822, it was not until 1838 that a gate across the main road was added to the side bar across the road to Butlers Cross.

There is no record of any shelter for the toll collector during the side bar's first year, but a cottage was completed late in 1828 on the north side of the cross roads at a cost of £110, which suggests a two-storey structure. However when a gate was placed across the main road ten years later the toll house was replaced by a new building which was sited on the highway verge, so as to project into Aylesbury Road and give the toll collector a better view of approaching traffic. The Ordnance Survey's 1877 edition recorded this building as still standing, but today its site is beneath the forecourt of the adjoining garage.

It is claimed locally that the two-storey building with flint-faced walls standing immediately north-west of the garage, and named Forge House, was the toll house but this cannot be so because it had not been built when the Ordnance Survey surveyed the site in 1877. It seems more likely that Forge House was built in the 1880s a few yards north of the site of the second toll house.

Terrick Gate hit the local headlines in 1850 when a burglar entered the toll house at night and terrified the elderly gate keeper, but fled empty-handed after a scuffle.

LITTLE KIMBLE GATE
1795-1871

Sample annual toll income: £65 in 1829/30.

Until 1863 there was a crossroads at the north end of Little Kimble hamlet where today the B4009 from Longwick joins the A4010 Risborough to Stoke Mandeville. In that year the building of the Princes Risborough to Aylesbury railway converted the crossroads into a pair of T-junctions separated by the railway bridge. Back in 1795 the trust had chosen what was then a crossroads as a suitable place for its tollgate, and had rented an existing house beside it for the gatekeeper.

The two-storey house named Crossways beside the railway bridge was extended on its west side in Victorian times but the original building may well have been the toll-keeper's rented house. If it was not, it must have replaced that house shortly after the gate was moved away in 1838.

By 1832 trustees were presumably concerned that traffic from Wendover via Ellesborough was coming on to the turnpike road at Little Kimble church without paying toll. Ironically they had made this route more attractive at the turn of the century by improving Ellesborough Road *(see 'Improvements' above)*. So in 1833 they agreed to erect a side bar across Ellesborough Road beside Little Kimble church.

Nothing happened immediately, but in June 1835 the trust agreed to build a new toll house on the highway verge beside the proposed side bar at Little Kimble church and to move the existing Little Kimble gate to stand across the main road nearby. The house was to cost £46 and to be of the same dimensions and materials as the fairly small single-storey toll house at Longwick.

By December 1835 it had been found that the verge was not wide enough to take the toll house and negotiations were under way to purchase a small piece of the adjoining field. The purchase was then heavily delayed and it was April 1840 before the site of the new toll house was staked out and building commenced. In the meantime the gate had been moved from its original position in 1838, presumably leaving the gatekeeper exposed to the elements!

MONKS RISBOROUGH GATE 1795-1871

Sample annual toll income: £105 in 1829/30.

In 1795 this toll gate was placed across Aylesbury Road ¼ mile south-west of the old Monks Risborough village centre at a site that is today close to the Windsor Hill side turning, with the toll house on the south side of the road. The gate's siting meant that it missed traffic from Owlswick, and potentially from Thame, which came on to the turnpike road near the village church and then turned north. However plans in 1832 and 1845 to place a side bar across the Owlswick road, Mill Lane, appear to have come to nothing.

By 1835 trustees were worried about main road traffic using the Upper Icknield Way to bypass the gate at Monks Risborough. They offered to share the costs of putting up posts on the Upper Icknield Way to prevent its use by carriages, but there is no evidence that this was done.

By 1840 the toll house was in such a dilapidated state that it was agreed to replace it with a new one and to take the opportunity to move it and the gate nearer to Monks Risborough village. This could have indicated a wish to move it to the corner of Mill Lane, where a side bar could have been installed. However no evidence has been found for this happening, so perhaps the 'very ruinous' toll house was patched up to soldier on until 1871. It had certainly been removed by 1880.

PROPOSED SIDE BAR AT SLOUGH POND

Traffic could evade paying toll at West Wycombe Gate by using Slough Lane and Chorley Road between the Risborough Road at Slough – now near Saunderton Station – and the Oxford Road at West Wycombe. A side bar to catch this traffic at Slough Pond was proposed in 1854 but not installed.

It is curious that nothing had been done earlier about this obvious gap in toll collection, but it is possible that the steep grades of Slough Lane had been a disincentive to toll evaders until parish improvements to the lane suddenly made this route more attractive.

WEST WYCOMBE GATE 1795-1871

Sample annual toll income: £283 15S 0d in 1829/30.

The West Wycombe Gate stood across the Bradenham Road near its junction with the Oxford Road, known today as the Pedestal roundabout. The toll house stood on the east side of the road immediately north of the site now occupied by the Pedestal Garage.

By 1838 the toll house was dilapidated and trustees considered replacing it with a new one beside a re-sited gate a short distance to the north, but after further consideration they kept the existing house and spent £15 on its refurbishment later in the same year.

After the trust had built a virtually new road between Risborough and Thame in 1825-30 some Oxford to London traffic must have diverted from the main Oxford road between Wheatley and West Wycombe to use the new road and the more gently-graded crossing of the Chiltern ridge via Risborough. In the late 1830s this made West Wycombe the trust's most profitable gate.

CRESWICK'S LANE GATE
1823-1824

No records of tolls found.

The saga of the short-lived extension from West Wycombe towards Handy Cross has already been told *(see 'Improvements' above)*. The extension was authorised in 1822 and although work from the West Wycombe Road end probably started quickly it is unlikely that the suitably-named New Road would have been completed to Creswick's Lane – now Cressex Road - before the end of 1823.

A gate and its toll house were erected, presumably in 1823, at the junction of New Road and Cressex Road. However traffic must have been <u>very</u> light because with almost indecent haste the trust decided in July 1824 to dispense with the services of the gatekeeper, because the tolls collected at Creswick's Lane were not enough to pay him. There was no further mention of this, possibly the shortest-lived toll gate in Buckinghamshire, although it is commemorated today in the names of Turnpike Road and Turnpike Way nearby. The toll house became a private dwelling until 1871, when it was demolished and the site of house and garden sold for £25.

LONGWICK GATE
1826-1871

Sample annual toll income: £136 in 1836 for Longwick Gate alone, and £152 in 1857 including income at Kingsey Gate.

This gate was situated within the village of Longwick at the junction of Owlswick Road, now Bar Lane, with Thame Road. It came into use in August 1826, when the new turnpike road had only been completed from Princes Risborough as far as Kingsey, hence its income of only £80 3s 4½d in 1828.

The gate was initially only across Thame Road, and was sited on the south side of the junction with Bar Lane. This enabled toll evaders to divert via Bar Lane and Owlswick and, since this was done under the nose of the gate keeper, quickly became a concern for the trustees when they were told what revenue was being lost. In 1831 they decided to place a side bar across the road to Owlswick, hence its later renaming as Bar Lane, but then hesitated while they debated whether or not to abandon Longwick gate and build a new gate and toll house at Ilmer crossroads, where evasion would be more difficult. Possibly swayed by the relative initial costs of putting up a side bar in Longwick against building a new toll house at Ilmer, they proceeded with their original plan late in 1832.

Due to complications over land acquisition there was no shelter for the Longwick gate keeper for the first five months of toll collection. In January 1827 he was provided with a 'temporary toll house' at a cost of £7. The speed of erection and low price suggest that this was a kiosk or 'watching box'. Within months the new toll cottage was complete as a single-storey building on private land on the south-east side of the crossroads, with a porch extending across the Thame Road verge to the toll gate.

After the trust was wound up in 1871 the long porch was demolished but the toll cottage remained, undergoing progressive rebuilding and extension over the years, until it was demolished in 2002 to make way for a housing development.

| KINGSEY GATE AND SIDE BAR 1845-1871 | *This was always let with Longwick Gate, and no separate income for Kingsey has been found.* |

In April 1845 the trust decided to put a toll gate across the main road at Kingsey church with a side bar across the turning to Haddenham. Tolls started to be collected there in the same year and there were miscellaneous references to the gate and its side bar over the next 25 years. No information has been found about the actual need for this gate, but a likely scenario is that Haddenham residents bound for Thame were avoiding tolls at the Thame Mill Gate of the Thame United Trust on the future A418 by cutting across to Kingsey *(see Road number 14)*. From there they would be able to use the Thame and Risborough Trust's road to get to Thame without passing through a toll gate.

Kingsey's 1848 tithe map did not record a building at the toll gate, so we must assume that a kiosk or 'watching box' was erected initially and possibly later replaced by a toll house on the corner opposite the church. If built, the shelter or house must have been demolished soon after the trust was wound up in 1871 because the semi-detached house now standing on the corner carries a builder's date of 1874.

Weighing engine

The trust never used a weighing engine.

Milestones and mileposts

The Risborough Road Trust owned the most primitive milestones of all trusts in Buckinghamshire. They were simply rectangles of stone, roughly shaped to an average of 10½ inches by 11½ inches in cross-section, and set square to the road. The stones, no two of which were the same, were painted white with town names and mileages painted in black on the one face parallel to the road.

While one or two have been repainted relatively recently, many have lost a lot of their paint, making it very difficult to read their inscriptions. Perhaps because they lack the character of other trusts' stones, nine out of thirteen have survived on the main Risborough road and five out of seven on the Thame branch.

1871: The Trust wound up

The Princes Risborough and Thame Turnpike Trust was not adversely affected by the early stages of railway development. Indeed total toll income peaked at £761 a year in 1839 and held up fairly well in the £625-£653-a-year range during 1841-44 as traffic patterns changed to focus on the new railway stations at Aylesbury and Oxford.

An unexplained slump in tolls during 1845-55 was followed by recovery as the Wycombe Railway was opened from Maidenhead to High Wycombe in 1854, then on to Princes Risborough and Thame in 1862, and on to Aylesbury in 1863. This railway closely followed the routes of the Risborough Road and its Thame branch and annual toll income recovered to average £623 in 1857-65 as the turnpike road was used to access the railway stations.

After 1866, however, tolls slumped again and the trust, having brought its debts down to £100 by 1869, reacted quickly before income fell too far.

After applying unsuccessfully to Parliament in 1870, the trust was wound up on 1 November 1871 under **34/35 Vic. c. 115**. Trustees met for the last time on 27 December 1871 to finalise the trust's affairs and learned that £108 10s 0d had been raised from the sale of toll houses, gates and surplus land.

Road 20:
Great Staughton and Lavendon Turnpike Road 1802

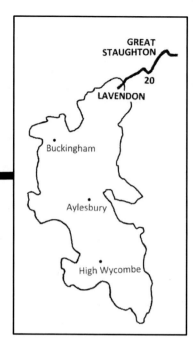

Identifying the road's route

Unusually for a trust in this book, the roads controlled by the Great Staughton and Lavendon do not include any A or B-class roads today. Instead, they form a string of C-class roads from Great Staughton in Cambridgeshire, through Pertenhall, Swineshead, Riseley, Bletsoe, Sharnbrook, Odell and Harrold in Bedfordshire, to Lavendon in Buckinghamshire. Although traffic on this route uses a short section of the A6 between Bletsoe and Sharnbrook, that part was not controlled by this turnpike trust.

Historic background

Most of the trusts in this book were established to improve travel on a route which was already well used. In complete contrast the Great Staughton and Lavendon, like the Great Marlow and Stokenchurch Trust, and the Thame and Handy Cross branches of the Risborough Road, was created to develop a new link which its promoters believed to be needed. In this case the hope was to connect north Bedfordshire, and thus north Buckinghamshire, to the Great North Road, now the A1.

The intention was to take a string of country lanes and tracks which was far from direct and not particularly obvious as a route and to upgrade them to form a through route. At the first public meeting to promote the scheme in 1801 the route put forward was from Kimbolton in Cambridgeshire, on the St. Neots to Higham Ferrers turnpike road, today's B645, through Odell to Lavendon with a branch from Harrold in Bedfordshire to Bozeat in Northamptonshire on the Kettering to Newport Pagnell road. From Lavendon, traffic would use two miles of another trust's road to reach Olney.

An attendee at that 1801 meeting came away with the impression[219] that any money loaned to the project would be lost, and he was correct to the extent that in 1855 the trust was forced to reduce the rate of interest paid to lenders and to extinguish all arrears of unpaid interest.

Doubtless to keep costs down, the branch to Bozeat was dropped from the scheme and the northern terminus moved from Kimbolton to Great Staughton before it went before Parliament.

The limits of the trust's road

The northern end of the trust's control was at the junction with what is now the B645 in Great Staughton village, and the southern end at its junction with the Bromham to Olney turnpike road *(Road number 16 above)* near

Lavendon Mill, south-west of Lavendon village. Near the mid-point of the trust's route its traffic used ¾ mile of the Luton Turnpike Road, now the A6, between the Bletsoe and Sharnbrook turnings.

Its length and maintenance districts	The trust's road was 18 miles long, of which 1½ miles were in Huntingdonshire (now part of Cambridgeshire), 14½ miles in Bedfordshire, and 2 miles in Buckinghamshire.
	The short central section on which this trust's traffic used the future A6 neatly split its road into two parts, and from 1802 until 1855 the trust divided the administration of its work into the same two parts. Riseley District covered Great Staughton to Bletsoe, and Odell District dealt with Sharnbrook to Lavendon. This split reflected the significantly different geological formations on which the two districts lay, and the resulting different problems and costs in keeping each of those parts of the road in repair. From 1802 to 1855 the finances of the districts were kept separate and each had its own list of trustees, although in practice about a quarter of them served both districts. One clerk served both districts, but each had its own treasurer and surveyor.
	In 1855, however, with finances ever more stretched, the trust decided to reduce management costs by merging the districts into one operational unit. This was done on 23 May of that year.
Initial Act of Parliament	**42 Geo.III, c.64 (1802)**. In a rare publicising of highway history, a circular 'blue plaque' in Riseley High Street commemorates the passing of this Act on 25 February 1802.
Continuation Acts	**4 Geo.IV, c.85 (1823)** and **19/20 Vic., c.12 (1856)**.
Control of the Trust: TRUSTEES	The Great Staughton and Lavendon trust does not appear to have been dominated by any trustees occupying the chair for significant periods except for Sharnbrook landowner John Gibbard, who chaired both districts intermittently in the 1820s and 1830s. However turnpike experience would have been brought to meetings by Thomas Charles Higgins of Turvey in Bedfordshire, whose family dominated the nearby Bromham and Olney Trust for decades in the nineteenth century.
CLERKS	It is possible that throughout its life this trust was served by only two clerks. William Day, a solicitor from St Neots, was in post from 1802 and continued until after 1833. Samuel Day, also of St. Neots, was clerk by 1850 and continued until the trust was wound up.
SURVEYORS	The Odell District, in recognition of its growing financial difficulties, had by 1855 taken the fairly drastic step of dispensing with the services of a surveyor, saying that 'the trustees act as surveyors'.[220] After the merging of the two districts in 1855 the trust employed two surveyors, presumably one for each of the former districts. Thomas Gell, who had been surveyor to the Riseley District before 1855, continued in post until 1870. William Rogers of Chellington, near Harrold, was his opposite number from 1855 until

replaced by Arthur Sanders of Odell before 1870. Sanders continued as sole surveyor from 1870 to 1877.

MEETINGS OF THE TRUSTEES	Until the districts were merged in 1855 trustees of the Riseley District met in the 'Five Bells'' at Riseley or the 'Falcon Inn' at Bletsoe, while those of the Odell District met mainly in the 'Wheatsheaf Inn' at Harrold and the 'Falcon Inn' at Bletsoe. There may have been other locations but for several years the trust's records did not indicate the venue of the May meeting of Odell District. After the merger the trustees of the two former districts met at the 'Falcon Inn' at Bletsoe, near the mid-point of the road.

Improvements to the road

The trust's task in 1802 was to take over a series of country tracks and lanes and to upgrade them into a main road which would attract through traffic. In this it was helped because five of the ten parishes passed through, accounting for 11 of the route's 18 miles, had had their roads straightened, widened and improved during parliamentary enclosure of their open fields between 1776 and 1802. Characteristic sections of straight road with broad verges, as so often laid out by enclosure commissioners, can still be seen for ¾ mile north-east and 300 yards south-west of Riseley village, and for nearly a mile north-east of Odell village.

With minimal gradients and only one significant river crossing (at Great Staughton) this road lacks the hill-easing and improved river crossings which characterise many turnpike roads, with one exception. Significant earthworks were needed to maintain a roughly level course along the valley side between the Buckinghamshire boundary and Harrold village.

The trust therefore concentrated on keeping acceptable surfaces on the improved roads which it had taken over, but still managed to become heavily in debt while doing only this.

FROM RISELEY TO BLETSOE	The only section of new road built by the trust was between Riseley and Bletsoe. Here the way had formerly wound through Bletsoe Park, but at some time between 1804 and 1825 the park was substantially reduced in size, leaving the present Galsey Wood as a remnant. At the same time the old winding route of the road was replaced by about a mile of straight new turnpike road built along the western edge of the wood and southwards through fields covering the site of the former park towards the hamlet of North End.
IN SHARNBROOK VILLAGE	Traffic approaching Sharnbrook from the east along Mill Road originally found that the road briefly divided, one arm going left past Ouse Manor - previously Waterside, then Riverside House – while the other bore right on Kennell Hill. The two routes met again at a crossroads at the south-east end of Sharnbrook High Street *(at grid reference SP 998 593)*. In about 1813 the arm via Ouse Manor was downgraded to a private drive and the trust confirmed the arm via Kennell Hill as the turnpike road.

FIGURE 35:
An 1866 advert by the Great Staughton & Lavendon Trust to let its toll gates. Confusingly, this trust's only gate in Buckinghamshire was known by different names on the two sides of the county boundary – as Lavendon on the Buckinghamshire side and Snelson in Bedfordshire.

BY KIND PERMISSION OF THE BEDFORDSHIRE AND LUTON ARCHIVES AND RECORDS SERVICE (their reference GA 576 315).

TOLLS TO LET.

Great Staughton and Lavendon Turnpike Road.

Notice is hereby Given,

That an adjourned Meeting of the Trustees of the Turnpike Road leading from GREAT STAUGHTON, in the County of Huntingdon, to LAVENDON, in the County of BUCKINGHAM, will be held at the FALCON INN, in BLETSOE, in the County of Bedford, on WEDNESDAY, the 16th day of May next, at One o'clock in the afternoon, when the said Trustees will choose new Trustees in the room of such as may then be dead or refuse to act, transact other business relative to the said Road; and at the same Meeting the Tolls arising and to be collected at the Gates upon the said Road at or near

GREAT STAUGHTON,
RISELY,
ODELL,
SNELSON and HARROLD,
FELMERSHAM BRIDGE, and
SHARNBROOK, (with the Side Gates)

will be Let in Lots by Auction to the best bidder for One whole year, from the hour of 12 o'clock at noon on the First day of July, 1866, in the manner directed by the General Turnpike Acts now in force, and which Tolls produced in the preceding year, clear of the Salaries of the Collectors, Six Hundred and Seventy-five Pounds, and will be put up in such Lots, and at such sums as the Trustees then present may think fit. Each person, before his name be taken as a bidder, will be required to pay the sum of Twenty Pounds into the hands of the Clerk to the Trustees, to be returned to him unless he should become the Renter, and in that case, the Twenty Pounds deposit to remain with the Treasurer to the said Trustees, in part payment of the first month's Rent in advance, or in default of signing an Agreement and Bond, with sufficient Sureties to the satisfaction of the Trustees, such deposit to be forfeited to the Trustees. The best bidder for the Tolls must at the same time pay One Month's Rent in advance, (taking Credit for the Twenty Pounds deposit,) at which such Tolls may be Let, and immediately after the Letting give Security with two Sureties aforesaid, to the satisfaction of the Trustees present at such Meeting, and previous to taking possession of the said Gates, enter into Bond for payment of the Rent monthly in advance, and for performance of the conditions and agreements to be made and entered into on letting the said Tolls.

AND NOTICE IS ALSO HEREBY GIVEN,

that at the same Meeting the said Trustees will proceed under and by virtue of the provisions of the Acts of Parliament passed in the 12th and 13th and 13th and 14th years of the Reign of Her present Majesty, for continuing certain Turnpike Acts and making further provisions respecting Turnpike Roads in England, to apply a sum of £237. 11s. 0d., set apart under the provisions of the said Acts, in or towards the discharge of any monies owing on security of the Tolls of the said Road, to the Creditor or Creditors who shall by a proposal in writing, to be transmitted to me at my Office, in Saint Neots, on or before the 14th day of May, now next, have offered to accept the lowest composition upon or in respect of such monies as may be due, and owing to such creditors respectively,

St. Neots,   *SAML. DAY,*

April 14th, 1866.   *Clerk to the Trustees.*

BETWEEN HARROLD AND LAVENDON

Before 1799 the route between Harrold and Lavendon villages was a basic track, in places in Lavendon parish little more than a public right of way across the fields. When the two villages' open fields were enclosed – Harrold in 1799 [221] and Lavendon in 1801 [222] – the enclosure commissioners for both parishes surveyed a 40ft-wide road generally following the course of the previous track, though they do not appear to have built it.

From Harrold to the county boundary the planned new road wound to keep roughly level on the 190ft contour along the side of the Ouse Valley. To do this it kept its western or uphill side generally level with the fields beside it by having its eastern side heavily built up, with a drop varying between 10ft and 30ft from the road down into the adjoining fields.

These were major earthworks for a minor road and look more like the work of a turnpike trust creating a new main road than of parish enclosure commissioners. It seems likely, therefore, that the commissioners, having set out the route, stood aside so that the road's actual construction could become one of the turnpike trust's first projects in 1802.

Toll gates and tollhouses

Records of the individual gates of this trust have been found through to 1866, but not after that year except for the depiction of Riseley toll gate on an estate map dated 1869. In the absence of later information it is assumed here that all gates remained in use until the trust was wound up in 1877.

Almost inevitably for a turnpike road promoted along a route that did not have a strong history of travel, this trust saw minimal traffic flows and tried to compensate for this with an unusually high number of toll gates in an attempt to improve income.

Although the Great Staughton and Lavendon trust's five toll gates were spaced at an average of 3½ miles apart, as against the Buckinghamshire average of 5½ miles, only two trusts with roads in the county received lower toll incomes per mile of road.

GREAT STAUGHTON GATE 1802-1877

Sample annual toll income: £150 1s 3d in 1832/33.

The Great Staughton Gate was located about half way between the junction with Green Lane, today's B645, and the parish church, at the east end of the causeway across the River Kym's flood meadows. There is now no trace of the toll house, which stood on the south side of the road.

RISELEY GATE 1802-1877 WITH SIDE BAR FROM 1850

Sample annual toll income: £54 12s 10d in 1832/33.

This gate was at the south end of Riseley village, at the point where the more direct road to Sharnbrook leaves the road to Bletsoe. The main gate was across the road to Bletsoe. A side bar, presumably across the road to Sharnbrook, appeared in the accounts for 1850 but nothing else has been found about it. The long-lost toll house stood on the south-west corner of the junction, probably on the highway verge, with a garden on private land behind it.

SHARNBROOK GATE 1802-1877	*Sample annual toll income for Sharnbrook Gate alone: £91 in 1817/18, and for Sharnbrook Gate with Felmersham Lane Side Bar: £104 3s 10d in 1831/32.*

Tolls started to be collected in Sharnbrook in 1802 at an unknown location in the village. In 1805 trustees moved the toll gate and house to what is now a sharp bend at the former crossroads of High Street with Kennel Hill and Pinch Lane *(at grid reference SP 998 593 – see 'Improvements' above)*. The toll house probably stood on the east side of this former crossroads, opposite the attractive lodge cottage dated 1840, which still stands at the start of what has been the private drive to Ouse Manor since about 1813. The toll house was probably demolished soon after the winding up of the trust because there was no sign of it on the Ordnance Survey 25-inch scale map dated 1884.

Curiously, although toll takings were recorded for Sharnbrook Gate from the commencement of the trust's work, no such gate was shown within the village on maps until 1835, when an Ordnance Survey map showed a toll gate at the 'new' 1805 location.

In the 1820s toll-letting advertisements[223] began to indicate intermittently that Sharnbrook Gate had side bars, one across Felmersham Lane *(see below)* while the other was presumably across Pinch Lane beside Sharnbrook Gate itself. From 1822 Sharnbrook Gate and Felmersham Lane Side Bar *(see below)* were advertised to toll contractors as a combined letting.

FELMERSHAM LANE SIDE BAR 1820-1877	*Always let with Sharnbrook Gate, so no separate toll takings found.*

The village of Felmersham, which lies a mile south of Sharnbrook, was only half a mile from the turnpike road, but separated from it by the River Ouse and its flood plain. This was presumably not an issue until the road gained turnpike status in 1802. Thereafter a five-arch bridge was built across the Ouse in 1818 and partly rebuilt in 1819 after two arches had fallen. The flood plain between the Ouse and the turnpike road lies in Sharnbrook parish but it was left to Felmersham parish to make a straight road across it from bridge to road in 1820.

This of course brought a new stream of traffic on to the road so the turnpike trust placed a side bar across the new road from Felmersham in 1820, and built a toll house on the south-east corner of the junction. Tolls recorded at Sharnbrook, which of course included this side bar, promptly rose by one-third.

The side bar had been renamed Felmersham Bridge Side Bar by 1850. The toll house had been demolished by the time of the Ordnance Survey 25-inch map dated 1884.

ODELL GATE AND SIDE BAR 1802-1877	*Sample annual toll income: £114 17s 11½d in 1831/32.*

The Odell Gate was in fact situated at the T-junction at the eastern end of Harrold High Street. Its misleading name presumably comes from the fact that the parish boundary runs through the junction so that the toll house, while visibly part of Harrold village, stood on the eastern side of the junction so was in fact in Odell parish. Just to confuse matters further, the trust occasionally used the name Harrold Gate instead of its official Odell Gate.

A side bar across the road to Carlton was probably in place throughout the main gate's life, but the trust's records only refer to it from time to time. There is no trace of the toll house today. For most of their lives Odell and Snelson gates were advertised to toll contractors as one letting.

SNELSON OR LAVENDON GATE 1802-1877	*Sample annual toll income: £29 6s 6d in 1831/32.*

This was the trust's only gate in Buckinghamshire, and it was only there by a whisker because the gate was placed right on the boundary of Buckinghamshire and Bedfordshire – although the toll house was wholly in Lavendon parish in Buckinghamshire *(at grid reference SP 934 546)*.

The gate was called Snelson to identify a tiny community on the Bedfordshire side of the boundary. The toll gate was on the site of a private gate across the road, put there to stop animals straying from parish to parish. The land in the parishes adjoining the county boundary had been communally worked in open fields until the enclosure of Harrold parish in 1799 and Lavendon parish in 1801.

The toll house, much extended since its turnpike days, remains in use as a dwelling with the predictable name of Tollgate House.

In most years Odell and Snelson gates were advertised to toll contractors as one letting. Confusingly Snelson Gate was also occasionally called Harrold Gate because it stood on the boundary of Harrold and Lavendon parishes, and after about 1850 it became known as Snelson and Harrold Gate.

Weighing engine	The Great Staughton and Lavendon trust never had a weighing engine.
Milestones and mileposts	There are no milemarkers beside the trust's road today, and the author has found no reference to there ever having been any.
Financial matters	In financial terms this was a route which should not have been turnpiked. It did not follow an existing travel corridor and failed to create a new one, facts emphasised when no railway line was built to compete with it.

Only two of the 24 trusts with roads in Buckinghamshire in the 1830s had a lower toll income per mile of road than this one. Although the trust's activities had been largely limited to road-surface improvement and maintenance, insufficient income meant that its debts grew until in 1855 its capital debt stood at £2,777, more than five times its annual toll income.

To address this the trust was allowed by the government in that year to extinguish all arrears of unpaid interest and to reduce the rate of interest on its future debts from 5 per cent to 3 per cent. The mortgagees were consulted about this solution and the fact that more than two-thirds of them agreed shows either local public spiritedness or resignation to the reality of the trust's situation.

1875: The Trust wound up   This action to reduce the trust's debt must have been successful because under **38/39 Vic. c.194 (1875)** the trust was given until 1 May 1877 to wind up its affairs, thus bringing to an end its relatively short life. Understandably it did not leave much of a legacy, with no route that became an A-class or even B-class road in the twentieth century.

Road 21:
The Aylesbury and Hockliffe Turnpike Road 1810

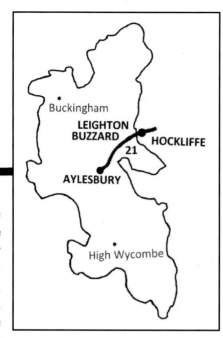

Identifying the road's route

The Aylesbury and Hockliffe turnpike road follows today's A418 from the junction of Cambridge Street and New Street in Aylesbury to the A505 roundabout south-west of Linslade, except in Bierton and Hulcott parishes where the Old Rowsham Road is the former turnpike road. The road continues through Linslade and Leighton Buzzard on Wing Road, Leighton Road, Bridge Street, High Street, Hockliffe Street and Hockliffe Road, and then follows the A4012 to it junction with the A5 at Hockliffe in Bedfordshire.

Historic background

For centuries the long cross-country route from Oxford to Bedford and on to Cambridge split into two alternative routes of roughly similar length between Oxford and Bedford. The northernmost route went from Oxford via Bicester and Buckingham to Bedford, while the southern route went via Aylesbury and Leighton Buzzard.

By the late Middle Ages the Buckingham route was so much preferred that late seventeenth-century cartographers such as Ogilby in 1675 did not mention the southern route on their maps. In the eighteenth century, however, the deteriorating condition of the eastern end of the road via Buckingham seems to have displaced traffic to the south so that, during the turnpike era, the Aylesbury to Leighton Buzzard route started a come-back – a step towards the vital traffic artery that it is today.

The limits of the trust's road

From the junction of Cambridge Street and New Street in Aylesbury to the junction of Leighton Road with the Holyhead Road, now the A5, in Hockliffe, except for Leighton Road, Bridge Street and High Street in Leighton Buzzard, which continued to be maintained by the parish.

Its length and maintenance districts

The Aylesbury and Hockliffe turnpike road was 14 miles long, of which 8½ miles were in Buckinghamshire, and the remainder in Bedfordshire.

Initially the road was divided for administrative purposes into two districts, which met at the parish boundary of Wing and Linslade. Each had its own surveyor. The expense of doing this was quickly questioned and from July 1811 one surveyor controlled the whole road.

Initial Act of Parliament	**50 Geo.III, c.94 (1810)**, which addressed the concerns of Leighton Buzzard residents by forbidding the erection of toll gates or weighing engines between the town and the Wing parish boundary to the west and Eggington village to the east.
Continuation Act	**2 Will.IV, c.63 (1831).**
Control of the Trust: TRUSTEES	The chairmanship was shared amongst many trustees, so there was no figurehead, although William Rickford, MP for Aylesbury 1818-41, chaired the trust intermittently between 1810 and 1845. In its early years, however, one trustee, John Grant of Leighton Buzzard, chaired meetings on a few occasions between 1816 and 1824 but devoted a considerable amount of time to inspecting the road and reporting back to fellow trustees.
CLERKS	Thomas Tindall of Aylesbury was clerk from the outset in 1810 and remained in this position until he died in office in 1850. He was replaced by his lawyer son, Acton Tindall, and Edward Baynes, both of Aylesbury, who remained as joint clerks until the trust was wound up in 1868.

Through most of this trust's life these same solicitors were also clerks to the adjoining Wendover and Buckingham Trust. Doubtless for their convenience the two trusts occasionally met in the 'White Hart Inn' at Aylesbury on the same day, and on one of those occasions even discussed the same policy issues on that day. |
| SURVEYORS | After starting with two surveyors the trust quickly cut this to one in 1811 as an economy measure. In 1825, with trustees claiming that their road was in excellent condition, they economised further by not having a surveyor at all. The resultant backlog of maintenance work forced a rethink in 1837, when Benjamin Simons of Aylesbury was engaged as sole surveyor, a post that he held until 1868. |
| MEETINGS OF THE TRUSTEES | Travel for trustees was minimised by the terms of the trust's 1810 Act, which stipulated that venues of trust meetings were to alternate between Aylesbury and Leighton Buzzard. At Leighton Buzzard 'The Swan Inn' in Market Square was used throughout the trust's life, while Aylesbury meetings were in Aylesbury's Market Square, at the 'White Hart Inn' in 1810-11 and occasionally in the 1840s and 1850s, otherwise at 'The George Inn' until the trust was wound up. |
| **Maintenance of the road** | The trust's Act of 1810 exempted it from maintaining the road in Leighton Buzzard between the canal bridge and the Market House. This was in compensation for the ban set by the Act on toll gates between the west end of Leighton Buzzard town and the Wing parish boundary. Its 1831 Act extended this maintenance exemption to the whole of the road in the built-up areas of Aylesbury and Leighton Buzzard.

At the start of the trust's work in 1810 its surveys showed that the surface of the road was generally sub-standard and around £2,000 needed to be spent on it. The worst road conditions were in Eggington parish in Bedfordshire. |

AYLESBURY AND HOCKLIFFE Turnpike.

THE Trustees of the said Road, do hereby give Notice, that they will meet at the WHITE HART Inn, in *Aylesbury*, on MONDAY the 9th Day of JULY next, at ELEVEN o'Clock in the Forenoon, when they will proceed to the Appointment of two *Surveyors* to superintend the Formation and Repairs of the said Road, the one to undertake the Management thereof from *Aylesbury*, to the division of the Parishes of *Wing* and *Linslade*, and the other from the last mentioned Point, to the termination of this Turnpike Road at *Hockliffe*. Any Person therefore who may be desirous of undertaking either of the said Appointments, is requested to signify his intention to the Clerk previously, and to attend at the Meeting with his Proposals.

By order of the Trustees,

THOMAS TINDAL,

Clerk.

AYLESBURY,
28th JUNE, 1810.

(J. H. Marshall, Printer, Temple-Street, Aylesbury.)

FIGURE 36: **The Aylesbury and Hockliffe Trust prepares to start work in 1810** with two operational districts and a surveyor for each.

BY KIND PERMISSION OF THE CENTRE FOR BUCKINGHAMSHIRE STUDIES (their reference T.1/10).

After the usual advertising for funds, £2,400 was loaned by 19 investors and this was used to bring the carriageway surface up to an acceptable standard.

Throughout its life this trust focussed on minimising costs in order to minimise tolls. Central to this was dispensing with its own directly employed workforce and making heavy use of the labour which parishes were obliged to provide by statute. In the trust's early years this 'statute labour' on the road was totalling around 1,000 man-days per year.

Possibly because of poor output under this highly unpopular compulsory system, the trust started in 1816 to pay the nine parishes along the road for their labours. Initially a sum varying between £20 and £50 per year was shared amongst the parishes but, by 1834, the trust was sharing £300 a year between them. This peaked at £515 a year in 1841 before falling to £314 a year in 1846.

This policy of payments may have originated from a dispute in 1812 between the trust and Eggington parish. The trust claimed that the road within that parish was in the worst condition of any length between Aylesbury and Hockliffe and asked the parish surveyor to rectify this. The parish agreed to do the work but demanded payment. The trust's initial offer was rejected; but eventually a compromise was agreed.

In the years between 1810 and 1820 the trust was involved in a long-running wrangle about Rowsham Bridge, which was three miles north-east of Aylesbury (*at grid reference SP 846 175*). This had been built between 1670 and 1700 and was now so decayed that repair was beyond the capabilities of Hulcott parish, which had maintained it so far.

The trust intermittently attempted to persuade the Buckinghamshire justices that this was a County Bridge so its rebuilding was not the responsibility of the turnpike trustees. These attempts seem to have failed, because in 1825 the trust spent £60 on rebuilding Rowsham Bridge.

Improvements to the road: HULCOTT PARISH	In turnpike days the route north-east from Bierton was via Old Rowsham Road. As early as 1815 the turnpike trust was contemplating bypassing this length of road, partly to eliminate the sharp bend in it. However with continuously tight purse strings, the trust never got to the job. So it was not until 1956 that Buckinghamshire County Council built the ½-mile section of the A418 which has bypassed it.
WING PARISH	The hill leading up from Wing Mill to the west end of Wing village had its gradient eased by the trust in classic turnpike style at an unknown date. The upper 250 yards of the hill was lowered into a cutting and the spoil resulting from this was used to create a short embankment at the downhill end of the cutting. The result was a gradient which was gentler and more uniform than that of the original hill. The cutting has been widened by the County Council in more recent years. In pre-turnpike days some traffic passed *through* Wing using High Street and Stewkley Road. While some contemporary maps imply that the main road had moved to skirt the edge of the village on Leighton Road by 1825, there is no evidence whether the turnpike trust had a hand in this, or whether the change was simply the result of travellers deciding to avoid the narrow, congested village street. Indeed as late as 1925 the Ordnance Survey was still showing the High Street and Stewkley Road route as the main road.
LINSLADE PARISH	In contrast to the undated lowering of the hill west of Wing, the hill in Linslade parish down from today's A505 roundabout to the bridge beneath the railway was recorded as having its gradient eased by the trust in 1828-29 at a cost of £205 2s 6d. Today the hill is on a gentle S-bend and it can be seen that 300 yards in the middle of the 'S' has been lowered into a cutting to reduce the gradient, with excavated spoil used to form an embankment across a hollow at the foot of the cutting.
LEIGHTON BUZZARD AND EGGINGTON PARISHES	The two miles of the present road – Hockliffe Road and Leighton Road – from the centre of Leighton Buzzard to the T-junction north-west of Eggington probably did not exist as a highway before the turnpike era. It appears that, previously, eastbound travellers left Leighton Buzzard southwards down Lake Street before turning off to the east just before Chain Bridge. From there they followed a winding course, which has today largely vanished, up to 500 yards south of the present road. The old and present routes converge briefly to cross Capshill Bridge, which today takes Hockliffe Road over Clipstone Brook, but only finally come together at the former cross roads – now a T-junction – at the north-west end of Eggington village. In 1815 the trust was discussing dealing with the waterlogging which bedevilled this section of road by diverting 1½ miles of it between Capshill Bridge and Eggington northwards on to the higher and drier route of the modern Hockliffe and Leighton Roads. No direct reference has been found to show that the trust actually built the present road, but the modern route of

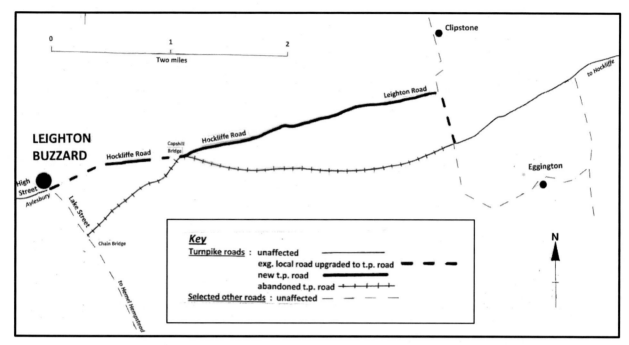

FIGURE 37:
A sketch plan showing the Leighton Buzzard to Eggington turnpike road, with an indicator of its predecessor route.
Although this is now largely a built-up area, most unaffected roads have been omitted for clarity

the A4012 had appeared on maps by 1825,[224] and this was not the doing of enclosure commissioners, because the open fields of Leighton Buzzard and Eggington parishes were not enclosed until the 1840s.

So this leaves the turnpike trust as the only other body likely to obtain the necessary parliamentary powers to acquire the land needed to build the new road across farmland in two parishes.

The reason for using a somewhat indirect route incorporating two right-angled bends was probably to minimise land-take in the open fields by following an existing headland east from Capshill Bridge and then taking over part of an existing north-south lane between Clipstone and Eggington. While these bends did not create problems in the days of horse-drawn wagons and coaches, they have become a serious nuisance in the motor age.

From the T-junction north of Hill Farm, Eggington *(at grid reference SP 950 254)* a linear mound can be seen in certain crop conditions extending westwards for at least 800 yards across fields. This could well be the remains of the pre-turnpike road.

Toll gates and tollhouses

The trust obtained its first Act in May 1810 and tolls began to be collected at Aylesbury, Wing, and Hockliffe gates on 25 August 1810. These three gates remained in use throughout the trust's life.

This was one of the trusts in Buckinghamshire which saw side bars across minor side roads as a worthwhile source of revenue. In its 14 miles it operated four or possibly five side bars at one time or another. But a decision in 1812 to erect two more at Linslade was quickly rescinded in the face of a hostile reaction from people in Leighton Buzzard.

AYLESBURY GATE
1810-1868

Sample annual toll income: £211 in 1813/14.

The gate stood across Cambridge Street on the east side of its junction with Dropshort, which is today renamed Park Street. The toll house was complete by August 1810, and may have been demolished and rebuilt in 1834 because a contract was offered for this work, but no details of the rebuilding have survived. There is no trace of this building today.

The trust was soon concerned with toll evasion by travellers who left the main road in Bierton and followed a tortuous string of minor roads via Burcot and Stocklake to come up Dropshort and rejoin Cambridge Street on the Aylesbury side of the tollgate. Therefore a side bar was placed across the top of Dropshort later in 1810 and kept there until about 1833. It seems to have been discontinued in that year, only to be reinstated in about 1851.

BIERTON SIDE BAR
from 1818
to around 1827
and 1835-37

No separate records of toll income have been found for this bar, which was presumably included in Aylesbury Gate's records.

The trust's worries about toll evasion on the east side of Aylesbury crystallised into a decision on 30 March 1818 to place a side bar across Burcott Lane in Bierton, at the eastern end of the unofficial diversion to avoid the Aylesbury gate.[225] By 25 May that same year the new side bar was in use,[226] although there was no mention of a shelter for the gatekeeper.

On the face of it this bar simply duplicated the work of the Dropshort side bar *(see above)*, which might explain why the Bierton side bar appears to have been discontinued in 1827. However it was reinstated in 1835 after the removal of the Dropshort bar. This provoked objections from Bierton residents and the lessee of the side bar soon complained that travellers were already finding a way around it, to the detriment of his toll collection.[227] There clearly was not an ideal place at which to catch determined toll evaders and the Bierton side bar was removed for a second time by 1837.

HULCOTT SIDE BAR
Dates unknown

No separate records of toll income have been found for this bar, which was presumably included in Aylesbury Gate's records.

Griffin and Thurston's 'Story of Bierton' states that a third side bar in the Aylesbury area was across the northern exit from Hulcott village on to the turnpike road *(which would have been at grid reference SP 846 168)*.

This author has not found any record of tolls being collected there, but Ordnance Survey maps for 1834 and 1880 do show an unlabelled building at this junction, standing on what is now part of the A418 carriageway, and this <u>could</u> have been a toll collector's cottage.

However an argument against there having been a side bar at this point is that there are two exits from Hulcott and anyone from the village who wished to avoid paying toll had simply to use the southern exit.

Honor Lewington of Hulcott recalls that the building beside the A418 was called 'The Dirt House' because it was built of cob – a mixture of clay, chalk, dung and straw – on stone foundations. It may be significant that the cottage, which was demolished in 1956 when the A418 bypass of the old Rowsham Road was being built, was not called 'The Tollhouse'.

WING GATE
1810-1868

Sample annual toll income: £171 in 1813/14.

The trust's initial Act of 1810 tried to placate objectors in Leighton Buzzard by stipulating that no toll gates or weighing engines could be placed between that town and the boundary between Wing and Linslade parishes.

The Wing gate was accordingly sited precisely on that boundary, which has also been the county boundary since 1974. The gate was at a minor crossroads *(at grid ref. SP 897 236)*.

From 1811 to 1828 a side bar was maintained on the south side of the turnpike road across the minor road which is now a cul-de-sac but which then led towards Ledburn and Grove.

The Wing toll house was built on private land at the south-east corner of the crossroads and nothing remains of it today. 'Tollgate House' on the other side of the road is modern.

PLANS FOR SIDE BARS
IN LINSLADE IN 1812

Trustees concerned about loss of revenue took counsel's opinion on whether side bars came within ban on toll gates between Leighton Buzzard and the Linslade-Wing parish boundary. They then agreed on 22 July 1812 to erect side bars in Linslade across the ends of what are now called Mentmore Road and Old Road. This provoked a furious backlash: opponents of the proposed side bars became trustees, and a packed meeting on 19 October 1812, attended by four times the usual number of trustees, rescinded the decision.[228]

CLIPSTONE SIDE BAR
1811-1868?

No separate record of tolls found for this bar, which was apparently included in Hockliffe Gate's records.

This bar appears to have stood across the turning from the turnpike road to the hamlet of Clipstone at the northernmost of two sharp bends in Leighton Road, now the A4012 *(at grid reference SP 948 258)*. Hockliffe Gate *(see below)* was situated just over a mile to the east, and although it did not stand at a road junction it was recorded with an unnamed side bar from 1811 onwards. The implication is that Clipstone was the anonymous side bar and that its toll takings were merged with those from Hockliffe.

In 1815 trustees agreed to erect a 'box' to shelter the gate keeper at Hockliffe Gate's side bar, without saying where that bar was. Then in 1832-33 a toll house was built at 'Clipstone Side Bar'.

Confusingly, an agenda item for the trustees' meeting on 27 April 1840 was to consider erecting a toll gate, side bar and toll house at Gipsy Lane, which was the name of the turning to Clipstone. In the absence of any minutes of the meeting this could indicate the intention to move the Hockliffe gate to Clipstone Side Bar. However no evidence has been found that this was approved and it certainly was not carried out.

On 8 November 1856 the Bucks Herald reported a burglary 'at a turnpike house between Leighton Buzzard and Hockliffe'. The intruders found so little money – three shillings – that this incident could well have been at the Clipstone Side Bar. The report mentioned that nobody usually spent the night in the toll house, which supports the idea that the burglary was not at the main gate.

HOCKLIFFE GATE 1810-1868	*Sample annual toll income for Hockliffe Gate and Clipstone Side Bar together: £320 in 1813/14, and £420 in 1844.*

The Hockliffe toll house was situated on the boundary between Eggington and Hockliffe parishes, just north-east of the village of Eggington. It stood on the north side of the road, with its main part in a field and its day room and porch on the highway verge. This was an above-average size of toll collector's garden, with more than ¼ acre cut out of the field.

Hockliffe Gate's toll takings included those from an un-named side bar from 1811 to at least 1854, but there was no side turning at Hockliffe gate on which that side bar could have been placed. So Clipstone Side Bar is therefore likely to have been the anonymous site.

Toll collection here seems to have been abandoned slightly prematurely. Although the trust's powers ended on 1 November 1868, the off-road part of the toll house site had already been sold for £70 on 4 February 1868 with the comment that the toll house had "recently been pulled down having become useless and no longer required".

Weighing engines

In 1812 a decision at one trustees' meeting to erect weighing engines at Aylesbury and Hockliffe gates (in order to identify and charge overweight wagons) was unsuccessfully challenged by some trustees at a later meeting.

Weighing engines and small brick offices were therefore built on the highway verge beside the Aylesbury and Hockliffe toll gates in 1814 by William Shepherd of Woburn at a cost of £165 each. Shepherd undertook to maintain the machines for ten years.

They were last recorded in use in 1833 at Aylesbury and 1834 at Hockliffe. Most unusually the engine at Hockliffe was recorded on Bryant's 1825 map of Bedfordshire, annotated "Hockliffe TB and Weighing Machine".

Milestones and mileposts

The Aylesbry and Hockliffe turnpike trust had been in business for about ten years before it decided in 1820 or 1821 to put cast-iron mileposts along its road. Maps of 1834 show 14 in place along the road, and many of these were still in place in the 1920s. Most were probably removed during the Second World War and today only one survives, at Bierton. However a post-turnpike pressed-steel 'Bucks Pressing' style of milepost – a replacement probably dating from the early twentieth century – stands in the cutting just west of the village of Wing.

1868: The Trust wound up

With the Aylesbury and Hockliffe Turnpike Trust's cross-country route not directly threatened by new railways, its total toll revenue actually rose from £641 a year in 1837 to £887 a year in 1846. This was presumably due to new traffic heading for the railway stations at Aylesbury and Leighton Buzzard. Tolls fell back in the 1850s as the railway network spread, but the trust, which had not reduced its original £2,400 debt at all by 1838, was able to start to reduce this and was among the first Buckinghamshire trusts to apply to Parliament to be wound up.

Under **31/32 Vic. c.99 (1868)** the trust's powers expired on 1 November 1868. However the trust did not wait until the bitter end and seems to have ceased toll collection, and therefore presumably road maintenance, late in 1867, using 1868 just to sell off property and wind up its legal affairs.

Road 22:
The Buckingham and Newport Pagnell Turnpike Road 1815

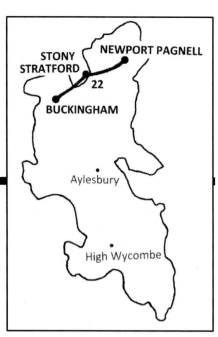

Identifying the road's route

The Buckingham and Newport Pagnell turnpike road consisted of two separate roads, one on each side of Stony Stratford, whose High Street was maintained by the town's bridge and street commissioners. Starting in the west the trust's road became the A422 from Buckingham to the west end of Deanshanger bypass, a C-class road – Buckingham Road and Stratford Road – through Deanshanger village, another short length of the A422, then an unclassified road - Deanshanger Road – which ended at London Road, Old Stratford in Northamptonshire.

Continuing from the south-east end of Stony Stratford High Street, the turnpike road has today become a series of C-class roads from there to Newport Pagnell: Wolverton Road in Stony Stratford, Stratford Road, Old Wolverton Road, Newport Road in New Bradwell, and Wolverton Road in Newport Pagnell. A ¼-mile section joining Old Wolverton Road with Newport Road north of Wolverton station has since ceased to be a highway.

Historic background

This trust's road, and its eastward continuation under the Bedford and Newport Trust *(Road number 10)*, formed part of the centuries-old Oxford–Bedford–Cambridge cross-country route. Between Oxford and Bedford the route split, with this road via Buckingham and Newport Pagnell forming the northern arm while a southern arm went via Aylesbury and Leighton Buzzard *(see Roads numbers 14 and 21)*.

By the late Middle Ages the Buckingham to Newport route was so much the preferred way that late seventeenth-century cartographers such as Ogilby in 1675 did not show the route via Aylesbury on their maps.[229] However, probably due to the deteriorating condition of the northern route between Newport and Bedford, the southern arm returned to favour for long-distance traffic during the turnpike era as the northern route went out of fashion.

Although the Buckingham and Newport Trust's road had medieval origins, its route for about 2½ miles on the west side of Stony Stratford had changed significantly not long before it was turnpiked. In 1675 Ogilby[230] mapped the route from Buckingham towards Stony Stratford to a point about one mile north of Thornton village. From there he showed it dropping down to cross the River Great Ouse just south of Beachampton Mill *(at grid reference SP 775 380)*.

Most of the route between the A422 and Beachampton Mill has since disappeared beneath arable agriculture. However the site of the 140-yard crossing of the valley's flat floor survives as a grassy lane between substantial earth banks topped by the stunted remains of hawthorn hedges, though it is no longer a public right of way. The most likely function of the banks was to protect the road from flooding and the failure of that protection was the most likely reason for abandoning this route in favour of the current high-level route of the A422 via Deanshanger and a crossing of the Great Ouse on Old Stratford Bridge, on today's A5.

In Ogilby's day the route, having crossed the valley floor to Beachampton Mill, continued along the present C-class road which came from Beachampton village to enter the southern end of Stony Stratford via Calverton Road and Horsefair Green, almost opposite where the road to Newport continued. Cartographic evidence suggests that the main route had moved from Beachampton Mill to its turnpike era route via Deanshanger not long before this trust obtained its first Act in 1815.

The limits of the trust's road	The trust's western section began at Buckingham Town Hall and ended at its junction with the A5 Holyhead Road in Old Stratford, north of Stony Stratford. Its eastern section began at the southern end of Stony Stratford at the junction of High Street with Wolverton Road, and ended at the south end of the North Bridge on the Northampton Road in Newport Pagnell.
Its length and maintenance districts	The Buckingham and Newport Pagnell turnpike road was 13½ miles long, of which 10 miles were in Buckinghamshire and the remainder in Northamptonshire. This distance excludes the connecting link along the High Street in Stony Stratford which was maintained in this trust's time by the town's bridge and street commissioners. Until 1824 the trust had one surveyor for the road west of Stony Stratford and another dealing with east of the town, after which a single surveyor managed both districts.
Initial Act of Parliament	The western end of the trust's road had been included in an earlier turnpike scheme. In 1769 Parliamentary approval had been given for the turnpiking of a cross-country route from Woodstock in Oxfordshire through Kirtlington, Bicester and Buckingham to Stony Stratford. That trust was slow to start work and didn't hold its first meeting until July 1770. By 1772 it was considering applying to Parliament for a change of route to bypass Bicester on its north side, but nothing else appears to have happened and the powers in the 1769 Act were allowed to lapse. The trust now under consideration was authorised 43 years later by **55 Geo.III, c.75 (1815).**
Continuation Act	**6 Will.IV, c.9 (1836).**

Control of the Trust TRUSTEES	The chairmanship of the trust seems to have rotated fairly freely, so no dominant trustees emerged.
CLERKS	From 1815 until 1847 the trust employed clerks in pairs, starting with Robert Miller of Buckingham and William Lucas of Newport Pagnell until the 1820s, then J F Congreve of Stony Stratford and W Lucas until 1832. From that year Congreve and H J Lucas of Newport continued these roles until 1846. Congreve was then sole clerk from 1847 until at least 1854 and Edward Harris of Stony Stratford from at least 1859 to 1878. Congreve and Harris were also clerks to the Hockliffe and Stony Stratford Turnpike Trust.
MEETINGS OF THE TRUSTEES	Meetings were held solely at the 'Cock Inn' in the High Street at Stony Stratford, near the mid-point of the trust's road.
Improvements to the road	This is a generally level route in the wide valley of the River Great Ouse, so the trust did not need to engage in lowering hills. It did not make any alterations to the route of the road between Buckingham and Stony Stratford and it initially planned only two minor realignments east of Stratford at Old Wolverton and New Bradwell Green. However in the 1830s the trust's route came to be crossed at Wolverton by the London and Birmingham Railway, and the railway company decided to build its locomotive works there. The resulting industrial and housing development from the 1840s onwards led to a significant realignment of the turnpike road.
IN WOLVERTON	Between 1815 and 1825 the trust built a 100-yard bypass on the south side of a sharp bend immediately east of 'The Galleon' public house and the canal bridge in Old Wolverton. Today the old road remains as an unmetalled track beside the grassy mounds which mark the lost village of Wolverton. When the trust was inaugurated in 1815 the turnpike road ran in largely open countryside through what is now Old Wolverton. In the mid-1830s, however, the London and Birmingham Railway started to build a locomotive works, station and housing for staff nearly a mile to the east of the old village of Wolverton. It therefore became desirable that the route of the turnpike road should go through the middle of the new town instead of lying to the north of it. In 1843-44 the trust built 1¼ miles of almost straight new road, the present Stratford Road, on railway-owned land between the new works and the workers' housing. It relinquished control of the old route, which remained a public highway and became known as Old Wolverton Road. Modern road widening and straightening has removed all vestiges of turnpike character from the old route, whose eastern end was lost in 1880 when a bypass railway line was built partly on the former turnpike road, causing a diversion on to the modern route of Wolverton Road.

The trust's 1815 Act authorised a 200-yard cut-off for what is now Newport Road, Wolverton, across the north side of New Bradwell Green. However the trust did not carry this out and it was left to highway authorities in the early twentieth century to do the work.

BUCKINGHAM TO STONY STRATFORD AFTER THE TURNPIKE	Today's A422 from the outskirts of Buckingham to the county boundary near the turning to Thornton still retains the character of a turnpike road, with a winding alignment and boundary hedges still at the distance apart set in the nineteenth century. But over the border in Northamptonshire the road was totally transformed in the 1980s. The road was straightened, its carriageway widened and given wide verges, and its turnpike character was completely lost. The old character returns on the sections of declassified road through Deanshanger and Old Stratford which were bypassed in the 1980s.
EAST OF WOLVERTON STATION AFTER THE TURNPIKE	Most of the turnpike character of this section has been lost due to urbanisation. A ¼-mile 1980s bypass has also been built on the north side of the turnpike road at the Black Horse, Stantonbury, and a 200-yard 1950s bypass on the same side immediately west of the bridge over the M1 motorway at Newport Pagnell.
Toll gates and tollhouses	The trust's 1815 Act prevented it from erecting tollgates within the parish of Buckingham and the town of Newport Pagnell.
	Three gates stood across the trust's road throughout its life and two more were added in the 1840s. Four side bars came and, in some cases, went in the 1820s-1840s.
	The several changes to gate and side bar distribution between Stony Stratford and Newport probably arose from the major changes in traffic flows to and from work which followed the development of Wolverton Railway Works and its associated housing in the 1840s.
HYDE LANE GATE probably 1815-1877	*Sample annual toll income for Hyde Lane and Passenham Gates together: £286 in 1835.*
	The Hyde Lane Gate was situated two miles west of Buckingham, just outside the Buckingham parish boundary at the junction of Stratford Road with the turning to Foscote. The toll house stood on the north side of Stratford Road, and was replaced after the turnpike trust closed by the present bungalow with its distinctively tall central chimney, which stands further back from the main road.
	This gate was usually let together with Passenham Gate and side bar.
PASSENHAM GATE 1815-77 AND SIDE BAR about 1825-45	*Usually let with Hyde Lane Gate, so no separate toll income found for this gate and side bar.*
	In spite of its name, the main Passenham gate was located on Deanshanger Road, just south of Old Stratford in what was then open country. It was about 350 yards from London Road, and the modern side turning called The

Meadows is close to the long-lost site. The toll house was probably on the north side of the road.

Passenham Lane Side Bar was erected between 1824 and 1827 across the west end of the minor road which then led from the turnpike road through the hamlet of Passenham. The side bar stood at a road junction *(at grid ref. SP 774 399)* more than ½ mile from its main gate, so must have been manned separately and therefore expensively. It would have made more sense economically to site the main gate at the same place as the side bar, so this suggests that the side bar was an afterthought to catch traffic avoiding the main gate by going through Passenham and past Calverton.

The junction at which the side bar had stood was re-sited westwards in the late 1980s during the construction of the Deanshanger bypass.

WOLVERTON GATE **1844-1877**	*No separate records of income for this gate because always let with Bradwell Gate.*

The Wolverton Gate stood on the Wolverton Road in Stony Stratford, roughly on the site of today's Queen Eleanor Street roundabout. It was erected in 1844, presumably to catch the growing traffic between Stony Stratford and the new railway community at Wolverton which had been expanding fast since 1838. The gate and toll house, probably just a hut, were moved here from Meads Mill Lane when the side bar there closed in 1844.

MEADS MILL LANE **SIDE BAR** **from about 1825** **to 1844**	*No separate records of income for this side bar are recorded because it was always let with Bradwell Gate.*

The Meads Mill Lane side bar, which was possibly not erected until about 1825, was placed beside what is now Old Wolverton Road across what was then the turning to Meads Mill and Haversham *(at grid reference SP 817 416)*. The site ceased to be a road junction in 1843-44 when the development of the railway works at Wolverton was changing the local landscape and road network *(as described above under 'Improvements')*. The road to Haversham, now called Wolverton Road, was moved eastwards to accommodate the new railway and the turnpike road through Wolverton was diverted southwards from the Old Wolverton Road to the newly-built Stratford Road, leaving the Meads Mill Lane side bar without any traffic to toll.

The trust therefore decided in December 1843 to abolish the side bar and re-use its gate and toll house, probably just a hut, at the new Wolverton Gate further west. The site of the side bar, although unrecognisable today, can be pin-pointed to the junction of Old Wolverton Road with Colts Holm Road, about 100 yards west of the nearest railway bridge across the old turnpike road.

BRADWELL GATE **1815-1877**	*Sample annual toll income for this gate and the gates and side bars on both sides of it: £236 in 1835.*

At first this was probably the trust's only gate east of Stony Stratford, but later it came to oversee the gates at Wolverton and Great Linford and the side bars erected across turnings off the turnpike road at Meads Mill Lane and Stantonbury.

Bradwell Gate stood in what was then open country at the junction of Newport Road and Bradwell Road, with its toll house standing on the highway verge on the south-west corner of the junction. A side bar across Bradwell Road was added between 1829 and 1832. In 1854 the trust considered moving this gate nearer to Wolverton Station but nothing has been found to indicate that this was carried out.

STANTONBURY SIDE BAR about 1832-1845	*No separate records of income for this side bar because always let with Bradwell Gate.*

The Stantonbury side bar, which did not appear in the records until 1832, presumably stood in open country on the east side of the canal bridge at Stantonbury Wharf *(at grid reference SP 845 423)*. It guarded the lane to Stanton church and Little Linford Mill. It is difficult to see the economic justification for employing a gatekeeper here, but the side bar continued to be let with Bradwell Gate well into the 1840s.

The 25-inch scale Ordnance Survey map of 1881 records a weighing machine on the west side of this canal bridge, but no evidence has been found for this trust weighing wagons, so it is assumed that the weighbridge was associated with the canal wharf.

GREAT LINFORD GATE 1840s and 1850s	*No separate records of income for this side bar because always let with Bradwell Gate.*

The Great Linford Gate stood just over a mile west of Newport Pagnell, across the main road at the turning to Great Linford, now called Marsh Drive. No record of the gate has been found before 1843, but the reported activities of its gate keepers[230] on other turnpike roads show that it was still operational into the 1850s.

Bizarrely, long after the trust had been wound up, the Great Linford Gate became commemorated on at least two twentieth-century editions of the Ordnance Survey one-inch map as 'Linford Toll Bar'.

Weighing engine	No mention has been found of a weighing engine at any of the trust's gates.

Milestones and mileposts	Mileage was measured from Buckingham Town Hall and rose to 'Buckingham 13¾' at the west end of Newport Pagnell High Street. Cast-iron mileposts were installed, to an unusual design with blank triangular top and destinations set in rectangular frames on the two faces below it. A further oddity is that the bottom place name on each milepost is the same on both faces. Only three have survived, all on the south side of the road, one near Foscote turn two miles east of Buckingham, one in Stratford Road, Old Wolverton, and one at New Bradwell. At the west end of Newport High Street a fourth cast-iron original has been replaced after the turnpike

era by a steel 'Bucks Pressing' style milepost with lettering painted on smooth surfaces.

1878: The Trust wound up

Between Buckingham and Wolverton the trust never had any direct rail competition, and east of Wolverton a branch-line railway to Newport Pagnell which closely followed the turnpike road was not opened until 1866. As a result the main early effect of railways upon the trust was a substantial rise in toll income after the opening of the London and Birmingham Railway through Wolverton in 1838. As traffic to and from Wolverton Station grew, total annual tolls rose from £447 in 1835 to £983 in 1846 before falling away slightly.

The impact of the 1866 opening of the Newport Pagnell branch railway was probably masked by the great growth in traffic to and from the railway works so that toll income remained high at £848 a year as late as 1877.

However trustees must have seen the writing on the wall and first applied for the trust to be wound up in 1875, nine years after the opening of the branch line. This application was unsuccessful, but in the following year **39/40 Vic. c.39 (1876)** authorised the trust to stop work on 1 May 1878 and this seems to have taken effect at the end of 1877.

Road 23:
The Buckingham and Towcester Turnpike Road 1824

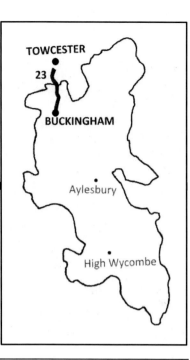

Identifying the road's route

The route of the Buckingham and Towcester turnpike road follows today's A413 from the centre of Buckingham through Akeley and Whittlebury in Northamptonshire to its junction with the A43 Oxford to Northampton road about two miles south-west of Towcester.

Historic background

This is not one of the historic main roads of Buckinghamsire. Its frequent and sharp changes of direction between Buckingham and Lillingstone Lovell, and again north of Whittlebury, reflect the fact that the present route was formed in the mid-eighteenth century by joining together a string of minor local roads to make a through route.

Between Buckingham and Lillingstone Dayrell the pre-eighteenth century route, which lacked the directness of a main road, had run up to 1½ miles to the west of the present A413. Then in the 1730s-1740s the second Earl Temple extended Stowe's landscaped park eastwards across the old road. He obtained a licence to close the road and today there are few traces of it except for grassy holloways north and south of Lamport. The earl did not create a new road to act as a replacement, which forced travellers to find their own way along existing minor roads outside the park's new eastern boundary.

By the time that this turnpike trust was formed, a string of lanes via Maids Moreton and Akeley had come into general use as the way between Buckingham and Towcester, and that was the route that the trust set out to improve.

The limits of the trust's road

The Buckingham and Towcester turnpike road starts from the junction of High Street and Moreton Road beside Buckingham Gaol, and ends at the junction of today's A413 and A43 some two miles south-west of Towcester.

Its length and maintenance districts

The road was eight miles long, of which 5¼ miles were in Buckinghamshire and the remainder in Northamptonshire.

The road was administered as one unit throughout the trust's life.

Initial Act of Parliament

5 Geo.IV, c.141 (1824).

Continuation Act	17 Vic., c.50 (1854).

Control of the Trust TRUSTEES	The chairmanship of this trust seems to have rotated fairly freely, so no dominant trustees emerged.
CLERKS	The legal firm of Elliotts of Towcester held the clerkship from the start of the trust in 1824 until the 1850s, after which Henry Hearne of Buckingham was clerk from at least 1861 until the trust was wound up.
MEETINGS OF THE TRUSTEES	The trust met solely at the 'Cobham Arms' in Buckingham until about 1850, when it moved to the 'White Hart Inn', also in Buckingham. Meetings thereafter were held in Buckingham but the actual venue was not recorded.

Improvements to the road	The trust made negligible changes to the route or gradients of its road, except for the realignment of its northernmost ¼ mile leading up to the future A43. The course of the A413 north of Buckingham today remains little changed from its course in turnpike days.
LAYBYS CREATED IN THE TWENTIETH CENTURY	During the 1960s four sharp bends were bypassed by Buckinghamshire and Northamptonshre County Councils, leaving the redundant sections of the old turnpike road as laybys. These were at the junction for Chackmore ¼ mile south-west of Akeley, the junction for Lillingstone Lovell, the junction for Heathencote north of Whittlebury, and north of Lords Field Farm in Whittlebury parish.
REALIGNMENT IN WHITTLEBURY	The northernmost ¼ mile of the trust's road, nearest to today's A43, was originally at a lower level. On the north-east side of the present road the grassy course of the old alignment can be seen in the shelter belt of trees. In the absence of trust records we cannot definitely credit it with having built the modern higher-level road, but cartographic evidence suggests that the present road was built during the turnpike era, so it is likely that it was built by the trust.

Toll gates and tollhouses	Throughout its life the trust only had two gates across the main road, one south of Akeley and one north of Whittlebury, but at its peak of activity it had no fewer than five side bars controlling turnings off the main road.
	Bearing in mind that levels of traffic on those turnings was probably very low, it is hard to see how it can have been worthwhile for the trust to employ anyone to man most of their side bars, which were let to toll contractors as part of a package with the nearest main gate. Surviving records, except for part of 1826, give only total annual toll income for the whole trust, so we have no way of judging the side bars' viability.
AKELEY GATE AND BISCELL SIDE BAR 1824-1877	*Sample annual toll income for Akeley Gate alone: about £88 in 1826. There is no data for the side bar.*
	The main Akeley Gate and Biscell side bar adjoined each other, so one gatekeeper could control both. He had a toll house to work from, but there is no indication of where it stood. The gate was ¼ mile south-west of Akeley

village, at the junction of the old turnpike road alignment – now a layby – with the road to Chackmore. The name of the side bar referred to Bycell Farm, which was reached by the same side turning.

The Stockwell and Lillingstone Dayrell side bars were let with the Akeley gate, but presumably were far enough away to need to be separately manned.

STOCKWELL SIDE BAR
1830s to at least 1850

No details of toll income from this side bar have been found.

The Stockwell side bar, which was always let to contractors as a package with Akeley Gate, is a mystery. Several advertisements to let it confirm that it existed, but there is no logical site for it.

About half a mile north of Akeley village Stock<u>holt</u> Farm lies at the end of its own track off the former turnpike road, and Stock<u>well</u> Wood was once further along the same track but has since been cleared. This farm track formerly doubled back to Akeley village but did not bypass Akeley Toll Gate, so is unlikely to have attracted toll evaders. It is highly unlikely that the trust could afford to man a side bar across a track leading to just one farm, and the advertisements did not mention a tollhouse, so perhaps the farm paid an agreed annual fee for passing through a notional side bar.

LILLINGSTONE
DAYRELL SIDE BAR
1824 to at least 1850

No details of toll income from this side bar have been found.

Only ¾ mile north of Stockholt Farm, in the hamlet of Lillingstone Dayrell, this side bar was across a minor side road which winds south to Maids Moreton. This route duplicated the turnpike road so was presumably viewed by the trust as a way of avoiding paying toll at Akeley Gate.

As at Stockwell, a toll house was not advertised to prospective contractors, so the unidentified building shown on the highway verge on the 1880 edition of the Ordnance Survey map was presumably a toll collector's basic shelter which has since vanished without trace. This side bar was the third in the group which was let as a package with Akeley Gate.

LILLINGSTONE LOVELL
SIDE BAR
1824 to at least 1850

No details of toll income from this side bar have been found.

The Lillingstone Lovell side bar was located only ¾ mile north of the Lillingstone Dayrell Side Bar, and stood across the turning into Lillingstone Lovell village *(at grid reference SP 706 407)*. Today the A413 bypasses the junction, leaving a triangular green between it and the old turnpike road. This side bar which had a toll house after about 1841 and was let to toll contractors as part of a package with Lord's Field Gate.

In 1841 Lillingstone Lovell Side Bar ceased to be mentioned in the trust's advertisements, but Whittlebury Forest Side Bar began to be listed in the same context, suggesting that the bar had been renamed. This may have heralded the replacement of the gatekeeper's roadside shelter by a proper toll house, which began to be mentioned in 1844. The area of woodland formerly called Whittlewood Forest lay half a mile to the north of this side bar, although now much reduced in extent.

WHITTLEBURY SIDE BAR 1824 to late 1860s	*No details of toll income from this side bar have been found.*

The Whittlebury Side Bar was located at the south end of Whittlebury village across the minor turning north-eastwards to Pury End, and had a shelter instead of a cottage for the gatekeeper. It was let as a package with Lord's Field Gate.

The minor road vanished in the late 1860s when it was closed and incorporated into a park that was being created around the newly-built mansion called Whittlebury Lodge. The need for a side bar would have ended with this closure.

The drive to the new mansion left the turnpike road where the Pury End road had formerly started and was provided with a splendid Italianate lodge cottage named Park Lodge which survives today even though the house that it guarded has gone, replaced by a housing estate. It is quite likely that Park Lodge stands on the site formerly occupied by the toll collector's shelter.

LORD'S FIELD GATE 1824 to probably 1877	*Sample annual toll income for Lord's Field Gate alone: £87 in 1826.*

The trust's initial 1824 Act indicated that this gate would be at the road's northern extremity. A plan of the road submitted by the trustees to Parliament in 1823 clearly showed Lord's Field Gate at the junction with the Towcester and Weston-on-the-Green Trust's road, now the A43.[232] This plan showed a toll collector's kiosk in the middle of the turnpike road from Buckingham with a gate on each side. It also showed that this gate would have stood less than 100 yards from the Towcester and Weston's Burcote Wood toll gate, which would have been unusual.

There is no evidence that this site beside the A43 was actually used for a toll gate, and by 1827 Bryant's map of Northamptonshire showed the Lord's Field gate standing one mile to the south at the junction of the turnpike road with the minor road to Heathencote. There it stayed, with its toll house in the angle between the diverging roads, on a site which is now part of a wide, grassy sight line. The original site of the junction was bypassed in the 1960s leaving the turnpike road as a layby.

Weighing engine	There is no indication that this trust ever had a weighing engine.

Mileposts	Cast-iron mileposts with raised capital letters were installed by the trust along the west side of the road. Today the only one to remain in place is in Maids Moreton village, where it has local fame through the misspelling of 'BUCKINGAHM' on one of its faces. The 'milepost' in use as a nameplate for two houses in Lillingstone Lovell village is a modern concrete replica which is deceptively realistic but not like the genuine surviving Buckingham and Towcester Trust milepost!

Financial matters	Emphasising what a minor route this was, the trust had no direct competition from a railway during the main turnpike years. Railways to which it could have fed traffic did not open until 1850 at Buckingham and 1866 at Towcester.
	Toll income for the whole trust in 1826-27 was £276 18s 9d, and as the road was improved this rose to a probable peak of £454 6s 8d a year in 1840, before declining to £396 a year in 1849-50.
1877: The Trust wound up	The trust made two attempts to cease work between 1875 and 1877, with the delay possibly due to difficulties in paying off the last of its debts. It was finally wound up on 1 November 1877 under **39/40 Vic. c.39 (1876)**.

Road 24:
The Northampton and Cold Brayfield Turnpike Road 1827

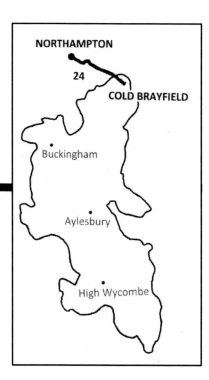

Identifying the road's route

The Northampton and Cold Brayfield turnpike road starts in Derngate in central Northampton, follows an unclassified road to the town's inner ring road, then today's A428 Bedford Road through Yardley Hastings to end at a junction with the B565 from Newport Pagnell ¼ mile west of Cold Brayfield. Exceptions to this route are at Little Houghton, Denton and Yardley Hastings, all in Northamptonshire, where the A428 now bypasses the villages but the turnpike road went through them.

Background

The county towns of Northampton and Bedford are only 20 miles apart, so one would expect the direct connection provided by the A428, which passes through the northernmost tip of Buckinghamshire, to have been a busy link.

But in 1675 Ogilby's atlas of roads in England and Wales did not mention the route, and in the eighteenth and nineteenth centuries traffic levels along it seem to have been so low that this was the last-but-one length of road in Buckinghamshire to attract the attention of the turnpikers. (The last, in 1833, was the Blackthorn branch of the Aylesbury, Thame and Shillingford Trust *(Road number 14).*

The first turnpike trust on this route between Northampton and Bedford took control of its eastern end, between Bedford and Lavendon, in 1754 *(see Road number 10).* That trust quickly failed, however, and it was 1790 before the Bromham & Olney Trust took over the road from Bedford as far as Cold Brayfield *(see Road number 16).*)

A further 37 years then passed before this Northampton and Cold Brayfield trust was formed to complete the job and take over the remainder of the road from Cold Brayfield to Northampton.

The apparently weak ties between Northampton and Bedford are emphasised by the fact that it took two trusts, one based at each end, to turnpike the road between them, which is unusual for neighbouring business and social centres. So with an unpromising history the Northampton and Cold Brayfield Trust started work with only 11 years to go until the opening of the first main-line railways spelled the beginning of the end for turnpike trusts.

The limits of the trust's road	The turnpike road started at the junction of Derngate with St Giles Street in Northampton and ended at the junction of today's A428 Bedford Road with the B565 from Newport Pagnell ¼ mile west of Cold Brayfield. In Lavendon village between Olney Road and Harrold Road the route was controlled by the Great Staughton and Lavendon Trust *(Road number 20)*, which had come on to the scene first.
Its length and maintenance districts	The trust controlled 12 miles of road, of which the eastern 3 miles were in Buckinghamshire and the rest in Northamptonshire. The road was never sub-divided into maintenance districts.
Initial Act of Parliament	**8 Geo.IV, c.71 (1827).**
Continuation Act	**16-17 Vic., c.61 (1853).**
Control of the Trust: TRUSTEES	At least 15 men took the chair of this trust's meetings during its short life. However while most were only active for between one and six years, William Tyler Smyth of Little Houghton in Northamptonshire, a parish through which the road passed, chaired many trust meetings between 1829 and at least 1852 and thus appears to have been the guiding influence on the trust. In 1827 Smyth was recorded as lord of the manor of Little Houghton and owner of about 80 per cent of the property in the parish.
CLERKS	The legal firm of Markham of Northampton held the clerkship throughout the trust's life. Charles Markham was appointed clerk in 1827 at £2 2s 0d per meeting and continued until he died in post in 1846. He was succeeded by Arthur Markham, still on £2 2s 0d per meeting. At some time between 1867 and 1876 Arthur was replaced by a second Charles Markham, by now on a salary of £20 a year, who was in post until the trust was wound up.
MEETINGS OF THE TRUSTEES	The Northampton and Cold Brayfield trust, in contrast to most turnpike trusts in Buckinghamshire which met in a small number of places throughout their existence, met at one time or another in its short life at seven inns spread through every village on their road.

The majority of meetings were held at Yardley Hastings, near the mid-point of the trust's road, in the 'Red Lion Inn' and 'Rose and Crown', but other venues were the 'Red Lion Inn' at Little Houghton, the 'Red Lion Inn' at Brafield-on-the-Green, the 'Quart Pot Inn' at Denton, the 'Red Lion Inn' at Denton, and the 'Horse Shoe Inn' at Lavendon. How often did trustees go to the wrong 'Red Lion'?.

For all this variety, this was a not-very-active trust, as instanced by the low frequency of its meetings after an initial flurry in 1827-28 while it got going. In the 1830s trustees only held two meetings per year, attended by between three and five people, and there was little discussion of the management or improvement of the road. Meeting frequency increased in the 1840s, with up to five per year, while trustees debated changing the location of the tollgates. |

| **Maintenance of the road** | The trust started road repairs with vigour in 1827,[233] although it seems that it was simply laying an extra layer of broken stone on the existing road surface, levelling it to minimise ruts, and spreading gravel into the horseway between the ruts made by wheels. The trust was clearly not going for a complete rebuilding of the road from its foundations, as recommended nationally by McAdam. |

Having got their road into more useable condition the trustees intended to give "constant attention" to keep it in trim, but this attention seems to have waned by 1840. The infrequency of trust meetings in the 1830s reduced trustees' opportunities to discuss the matter and question the surveyor. The inevitable result was that in 1840 the surveyor reported that some parts of the road were in such poor condition that he had ordered "a boat load and fifteen tons of hard stones" with which to carry out repairs.

| **Improvements to the road** | The trust's early concentration on bringing the surface of the existing road up to an acceptable standard, and building 700 yards of new road at Little Houghton *(see below)*, seem to have drained it of funds with which to build any further lengths of new road. When the trust was set up £4,640 had been raised by investors but more was needed to bypass the difficult gradients, narrow streets and sharp bends in three of the villages that the road passed through. |

In its 1826 application to Parliament the trust had proposed to build a mile-long bypass south of Little Houghton in Northamptonshire, a half-mile bypass on the south side of Denton, a 200-yard 'chord' to cut out a sharp bend at Broad Lane Spinney just west of Warrington crossroads – today a roundabout – and the straightening of some 600 yards west of Lavendon.

Trustees had a flurry of investigation into these projects in 1827-29 which led to the Little Houghton scheme being reduced in scope and the other three being abandoned, each found to be too expensive. In general, trustees stopped discussing major improvements after 1830 due to lack of funds and a growing concern about servicing the debts already incurred. Unpaid interest rose from £170 in 1828 to £1,731 in 1835.

Long after the turnpike era the two county councils carried out extended versions of all three of the above schemes in the twentieth century.

| **SOUTH-EAST OF LITTLE HOUGHTON** | Immediately south-east of Little Houghton village the pre-turnpike road described a sharp curve away from the unclassified part of the Bedford Road in order to drop into, cross, and climb out of a small but deep and steep-sided valley. |

In 1827-28 the trust built a new road 700 yards long – the present Bedford Road – south-eastwards from the sharp bend in the village to roughly where this road today joins the Little Houghton bypass. The new road was carried across the valley on an embankment and a substantial stone bridge. This was the biggest piece of new construction carried out by the trust. It was to be some 140 years before the village itself would be bypassed.

BRAFIELD-ON-THE-GREEN	Immediately west of the village of Brafield-on-the-Green the turnpike road made a sharp curve across a shallow valley to the south of the present road. Where it crossed the valley the old road was so soft in wet weather that in 1827 the trust agreed that this section should be bypassed. However nothing came of it until after the turnpike era, when the county council built the modern road on higher ground. The former road, now partly a public footpath, can still be seen.

DENTON	The old main road followed a sharp curve northwards in Denton village, descending into a narrow valley as far as the church before turning to climb out again. In 1827 the trust noted that the road was too narrow and steep for carriages to pass, and that the solution would be to bypass the village, but this was deemed to be unaffordable. Instead during 1827 and 1828 the road in the village was realigned on to a higher level in the hollow by the church at a cost of £300.

The trust's funds were exhausted before this work was complete and an appeal for more investment had to be made. It is not clear from the trust's minutes[234] whether all the intended work was finished, but what was done did not address the steep narrow street above the church.

Residents had to wait until the twentieth century for the county council to build the present bypass, and when it came it was slightly longer and to the south of the bypass that the trust had planned.

YARDLEY HASTINGS	At Yardley Hastings as at Denton the pre-turnpike road turned north downhill into a narrow valley in the village and back uphill out again. In 1827 the trust observed that the road within the village was too narrow, but decided that a diversion was not practical, so again the bypass was not provided until after the turnpike era.

In 1829 trustees were considering lowering Yardley Hill, immediately south-east of Yardley and up to the turning of the future B5388 to Olney, at a cost of £120. Again nothing was done until the twentieth century.

NEAR WARRINGTON HOUSE IN WARRINGTON PARISH	In 1828 the trust decided to shorten the road by bypassing the sharp bend between Warrington House (at grid reference SP 891 552) and Broadlane Spinney with a 200-yard section of straight road. Once again nothing happened until the county council carried out a bigger, ¼-mile-long improvement in the twentieth century, leaving the former turnpike road as an inverted 'W' of minor roads on the north side of today's A428.

Toll gates and tollhouses	Although the trust had three main gates for most of its existence, only one stayed on the same site. A period of upheaval between 1845 and 1850 saw one gate introduced, another abandoned, and a third gate re-sited.

GREAT HOUGHTON GATE AND SIDE BAR 1827-1880	*Sample annual toll income for this gate alone: £320 in 1836/37.*

Late in 1827 it was agreed to put gates across the main road and side turning just north-west of Great Houghton village, at the junction of the main road with the side road from Hardingstone *(at grid reference*

SP 788 592, now beside Martins Farm). The side road is no longer a public highway.

The toll house, which cost £80 to build in the spring of 1828, was the only one to remain in use throughout the trust's life and was sold by auction late in 1880. Today its site is probably within the garden of the farmhouse which replaced it.

BRAFIELD-ON-THE-GREEN GATE 1851-1880 AND SIDE BAR 1848-1880

Usually let together with Great Houghton Gate, so no separate toll takings available.

The trust was only a few years old when trustees began to be concerned about traffic from Newport Pagnell via Horton in Northamptonshire coming on to their road at Brafield-on-the-Green without paying toll. In 1834 the surveyor was ordered to report on the benefits of erecting side gates across the roads from Horton and Great Billing, but advised against.

The issue surfaced again in 1840 but was deferred until 1841, after which it was not mentioned until 1847, when the trustees agreed to erect a side bar across Horton Road and to spend not more than £60 on erecting a toll house beside it. The side bar was in use by 1848 and may have produced a disappointing income because in 1850 trustees began to think that it would be worthwhile to erect a gate across the main road beside the new toll house. This was done by August 1851.

These gates were always let as one lot with Great Houghton Gate. The takings for the two sites together suggest that the new gates at Brafield-on-the-Green did not significantly improve the trust's income. In turnpike days, unlike today, Horton Road and Billing Road faced each other to make a direct crossroads, with the toll house adjacent to Horton Road. Its site is now lost under the grassed visibility splays at the junction.

YARDLEY HASTINGS GATES 1827-1880

Sample annual toll income: £120 in 1836/37.

As soon as the trust started work a gate was placed across the turnpike road at the southern tip of Yardley Hastings village, a few yards east of today's crossroads with Chase Park Road. It was decided to rent an existing house beside the gate instead of building a new toll house and one was rented at £3 a year. Mr Carter, a tailor and the existing tenant of the house, was engaged as toll collector at four shillings per week, which seems a mutually convenient arrangement.

A stone-built house on the corner of High Street, then on the turnpike road, and Bedford Road East is old enough to have been the house in question, but no evidence has been found to confirm this.

By 1830 the rent had increased to £3 10s 0d a year but the trustees were beginning to worry about the condition of the toll house. By 1842 they were complaining about the its state of repair. They were also considering the replacement of this gate at Yardley Hastings and that at Lavendon three miles to the east with a single new gate located between the two.

By 1843 a site for the new gate was being fixed some 530 yards to the south-east at the top of Yardley Hill, where the side road to Olney diverged from the turnpike road.

Matters seemed to come to a head in 1844 with the death of the Yardley toll house's owner and, in 1845, a two-storey toll house was built for £110 11s 2½d at the road junction atop Yardley Hill. The existing gate was moved out from the village to the new site and an additional gate was placed across the turning to Olney.

As the new gates started work the tollgate at Lavendon was removed, leading to an increase of toll income at Yardley that settled down to about £40 a year extra. On the winding up of the trust in 1880 the toll house beside the new gates was sold at auction. Today its site is part of the wide, grassy visibility splay at the junction.

LAVENDON GATE 1827-1845	*Sample annual toll income: £86 in 1836/37.*

**LAVENDON GATE
1827-1845**

Sample annual toll income: £86 in 1836/37.

A gate was placed across the road at the west end of Lavendon village in 1827 and the gatekeeper was accommodated by renting an existing house from W B Higgins of Turvey, one of the road's trustees, for £3 a year. A terrace of existing stone-built cottages on the south side of the road is old enough for one of them to have been the house concerned, but no evidence has been found to confirm this. The maintenance problems with the rented toll house at Yardley *(see above)* were avoided here by the trust itself carrying out any repairs needed.

The justification for the Lavendon gate, only three miles from the trust's gate at Yardley, was presumably to catch traffic coming on to the road between the two gates by turning east off the Kettering and Newport Trust's road at Warrington crossroads. Experience presumably showed that such traffic was not significant, so the 1845 re-siting of the Yardley gate was the catalyst for the removal of the gate at Lavendon and surrender of the lease on the toll house there.

Weighing engine

The trust agreed in 1840 to erect a weighing machine at Great Houghton Gate, and twice advertised for a contractor to build it, but there is no indication that one was actually erected. 1840 was very late in the turnpike era to be acquiring such equipment.

Milestones and mileposts

For its first seven years the trust does not appear to have marked the miles on its road. Then in 1834 one of the trustees "liberally donated" six *mileposts*, which had been installed by 1838 when £1 16s 0d was spent on painting the *milestones* and toll gates. In 1852, after sixteen months of intermittent deliberations, the trust agreed to put up *mileposts* along the road, and to ask the town commissioners to put up one within Northampton. Whether the new mileposts included replacements for the original six stones or simply added to them was not made clear. Either way not one milepost survives along the trust's road today.

1880: The Trust wound up

The first flush of road repairs and new road construction in 1827-30 seems to have exhausted the trust's reserves and created difficulty in servicing its debts. This led to a period of careful spending in the 1830s and early 1840s, with toll income rising steadily until growth was suddenly reversed by the opening of the Bedford to Bletchley branch of the London and Birmingham Railway in 1846.

It is difficult to understand the direct impact of this, the first railway into Bedford, on the Bedford to Northampton road which went in a different direction – but it appears to have upset local travel patterns and led to the drop in the trust's traffic and income.

In November 1845, without waiting to assess the new situation, the renters of the Houghton and Yardley Gates abruptly terminated their contracts. It then became difficult to find contractors willing to take on the trust's toll gates due to low traffic levels. This was serious for a trust which in 1850 had annual toll income of around £500 and unpaid interest to investors totalling £3,656.[235]

The final straw came in 1872 when the Bedford to Northampton railway opened along a route which loosely paralleled the turnpike road. The trust thereupon petitioned in 1874 to be wound up. This was unsuccessful, probably due to difficulty in paying off its creditors, but when it applied again the trust was given until 1 November 1880 under **38-39 Vic., c.194 (1875)**, to wind up its affairs.

As a result, the trust was one of the last three with roads in Buckinghamshire to be wound up. As soon as the winding up date had passed the auctioneers moved in to dispose of toll houses, gates and other assets.

Appendix A:
Mileage and toll income of each trust in peak turnpike year 1836

Turnpike Trust	No.	Start	Mileage in Bucks [1]	Mileage outside [1]	Income in 1836 [2]	Income £ per mile	End
Aylesbury and Hockliffe	21	1810	8½	5½	£ 584	£ 41.70	1868
Aylesbury, Thame and Shillingford (Thame United after 1838): [2]							
Aylesbury to Shillingford	14	1770	8½	13¼	£1,183	£ 55.70	1880
Postcombe branch	14	1785	0	4	£ 164	£ 41.00	1880
Blackthorn branch	14	1833	8	4	£ 293	£ 24.40	1880
Wheatley branch	14	1838	0	5	0	0	1880
Banbury and Brackley	17	1791	6½	9	£ 658 [3]	£ 42.40 [3]	1873
Beaconsfield and Stokenchurch	4	1719	9¾	2½	£ 3,045	£ 248.60	1867
Bedford and Newport Pagnell	10	1754 /1814	5	6¼	£ 290	£ 24.20	1870
Bicester and Aylesbury	15	1770	12	4	£ 1,003	£ 62.70	1875
Bromham and Olney	16	1754 /1790	7	4½	£ 461 [3]	£ 40.10 [3]	1874
Buckingham and Hanwell	7	1744	3½	17	£ 1,693	£ 82.60	1871
Buckingham and Newport Pagnell	22	1815	10	3½	£ 621	£ 46.00	1878
Buckingham and Towcester	23	1824	5¼	2¾	£ 368	£ 46.00	1877
Colnbrook:							
Cranford to Maidenhead	6	1727	10	3½	£ 4,028 [4]	£ 236.90	1871
Datchet branch	6	1767	1¾	0	Included above		1871
Eton branch	6	1767	1¾	0	Included above		1871
Great Marlow and Stokenchurch	18	1791	5½	2½	£ 91	£ 11.40	?
Great Staughton and Lavendon	20	1802	2	16	£ 508 [3]	£ 28.20 [3]	1877
Hockliffe and Stony Stratford	1	1706 /1740	10½	3½	£ 3,525	£251.80	1867
Hockliffe and Woburn	2	1706 /1728	6½	6	£ 2,615	£ 209.20	1877

Turnpike Trust	No.	Start	Mileage in Bucks [1]	Mileage outside [1]	Income in 1836 [2]	Income £ per mile	End
Kettering and Newport Pagnell	11	1754	8	14½	£ 1,237	£ 55.00	1878
Newport Pagnell	3	1709 /1723	6½	7½	£ 2,335	£ 166.80	1870
Northampton and Cold Brayfield	24	1827	3	9	£ 526	£ 43.80	1880
Reading and Hatfield	13	1767	22½	32	£ 2,149	£ 39.40	1881
Red Hill and Beaconsfield	9	1751	7½	0	£1,347	£ 179.60	1867
Princes Risborough and Thame: [2]							
Stoke Mandeville to West Wycombe	19	1795	13	0	£ 513	£ 39.50	1871
Thame branch	19	1825	5	1¾	£ 136	£ 20.10	1871
Sparrows Herne	12	1762	5½	20	£ 3,440	£ 134.90	1873
Wendover and Buckingham	5	1721	21	0	£ 1,730	£ 82.40	1878
Wendover and Oak Lane	8	1751	17½	0	£ 957	£ 54.70	1866

Total mileage for 24 trusts:
231½ miles of turnpike road inside Buckinghamshire / 197½ miles outside.

Average length of road controlled inside and outside the county = 17.9 miles.

NOTES TO APPENDIX A:

1. Mileage inside and outside Buckinghamshire has been calculated using the county boundaries in 1836.
2. Toll income is for the whole trust, except where branch totals are given for the Princes Risborough and Thame, and the Aylesbury, Thame and Shillingford.
3. Toll income and income per mile are for the year 1836 but this was not found for all trusts. The exceptions are: Bromham and Olney 1835; Banbury and Brackley 1831; Great Staughton and Lavendon 1831/32.
4. No separate income was found for the Colnbrook Trust's branches, so the figures for the whole trust are given under the trust's main Cranford to Maidenhead road.

Appendix B:
Mileage of new-built road, toll gates, side bars and weighing engines in 1836, and the road status of each trust in 1919

Turnpike Trust	No.	Totsls inside and outside Buckinghamshire [1]								A-class road in 1919 [3]
		New-built mileage		Toll gates		Side bars		Weighing engines		
		In	Out	In	Out	In	Out	In	Out	
Aylesbury and Hockliffe	21	-	1½	2	1	1	1	-	-	YES
Aylesbury, Thame and Shillingford (Thame United after 1838):										
Aylesbury to Shillingford	14	¼	2¼	1	-	3	-	1	-	PART
Postcombe branch	14	-	-	-	1	-	1	-	-	NO
Blackthorn branch	14	½	-	1	1	-	-	-	-	NO
Chilworth branch	14	-	-	-	-	-	-	-	-	YES
Banbury and Brackley	17	¾	4½	2	2	1	1	-	-	YES
Beaconsfield and Stokenchurch	4	3¼	-	2	-	-	-	1	-	YES
Bedford and Newport Pagnell	10	¼	-	1	1	-	1	1	-	YES
Bicester and Aylesbury	15	-	¼	2	1	-	1	1	-	YES
Bromham and Olney	16	-	-	2	1	2	2	1	=	PART
Buckingham and Hanwell	7	-	1	1	3	-	1	-	-	PART
Buckingham and Newport Pagnell	22	1¼	-	2	1	3	1	-	-	YES
Buckingham and Towcester	23	-	¼	1	1	4	1	-	-	YES
Colnbrook:										
Cranford to Maidenhead	6	¼	-	-	1	-	1	-	1	YES
Datchet branch	6	-	-	1	-	-	-	-	-	YES
Eton branch	6	-	-	1	-	-	-	-	-	YES
Great Marlow and Stokenchurch	18	2	-	1	1	-	-	-	-	NO
Great Staughton and Lavendon	20	-	1	1	4	-	2	-	-	NO
Hockliffe and Stony Stratford	1	¾	-	1	1	1	-	-	-	YES
Hockliffe and Woburn	2	-	2½	1	1	1	-	-	-	YES
Kettering and Newport Pagnell	11	-	¾	2	2	-	1	1	-	YES

Turnpike Trust	No.	Totals inside and outside Buckinghamshire [1]								A-class road in 1919 [3]
		New-built mileage		Toll gates		Side bars		Weighing engines		
		In	Out	In	Out	In	Out	In	Out	
Newport Pagnell	3	-	¼	1	1	1	1	-	1	YES
Northampton and Cold Brayfield	24	-	½	1	2	-	-	-	-	YES
Reading and Hatfield [2]	13	5½	1¾	4	7	3	6	-	-	YES
Red Hill and Beaconsfield	9	¼	-	1	-	-	-	-	-	YES
Princes Risborough and Thame:										
Stoke Mandeville to West Wycombe	19	4	-	3	-	1	-	-	-	PART
Thame branch	19	-	2	1	-	1	-	-	-	YES
Sparrows Herne	12	1½	2	1	3	1	4	-	1	YES
Wendover and Buckingham	5	1¾	-	3	-	2	-	1	-	YES
Wendover and Oak Lane	8	2	-	2	-	1	-	-	-	YES
TOTAL FOR 24 TRUSTS		24¼	20½	42	36	26	25	7	3	

NOTES TO APPENDIX B:

1. Mileage, toll gates. side bars and weighing engines inside and outside Buckinghamshire has been calculated using the county boundaries in 1836.
2. The totals for the Reading and Hatfield trust include new turnpike road built between 1767 and 1881 by all agencies due to uncertainty about how much of this total was actually built by the turnpike trust.
3. This indicates whether or not the turnpike road became an A-class road when highway classification began in 1919. This is based on the Geographia 2 miles to 1 inch Road Map of England and Wales, published circa 1923.

Sources and references

Abbreviations   Local Record Offices and study centres:

BLARS :   Bedfordshire Archives Service.
CBS :   Centre for Buckinghamshire Studies.
HALS :   Hertfordshire Archives and Local Studies.
LMA :   London Metropolitan Archive.
NRO :   Northamptonshire Record Office.
OHC :   Oxfordshire History Centre.
PA :   Parliamentary Archives, (in the House of Lords).
RBLLS : Reading Borough Libraries and Local Studies.

Source references
in the text

1.   Paul Hindle, **Roads and tracks for historians** (Phillimore, 2001) page 91.
2.   Dorien Gerhold**, Carriers and Coachmasters; trade and travel before the turnpikes** (Phillimore, 2005), various pages.
3.   Gerhold, various pages.
4.   W Albert, **The Turnpike Road System in England** (Cambridge University Press. 1972) page 223.
5.   Albert, various pages.
6.   Sir Frank Markham, **History of Milton Keynes & District**, volume 2 (White Crescent Press, 1975) page 58.
7.   Peter Gulland, **Making the Road from Princes Risborough to Thame** (Buckinghamshire Archaeological Society, 2006) pages 29-31 and 34,
8.   Account book of surveyor to Risborough Road Trust 1795-97, CBS ref T/5/2.
9.   Report of a committee of the Beaconsfield and Stokenchurch Road's trustees into the conduct of their surveyor, 23 December 1811, Bodleian Library.
10. Colnbrook Trust minute books, LMA ref TP/COL/001, microfilm X/001/157.
11. Sparrows Herne Trust minute books, HALS ref TP4 / 1-6.
12. Albert, page 165.
13. Albert, page 166.
14. **Jackson's Oxford Journal**, 16 July 1791, OHC.
15. Richard Morris, **Roads: Archaeology and Architecture**, (Tempus Publishing 2005) pages 119-122.
16. Letter from J Higgins of Turvey, 1791, BLARS ref HG/12/4/58.
17. Letters from Rev J L Dayrell, Vicar of Lillingstone Dayrell, 1822-25, CBS refs D/22/25/129, D/22/25/131, and D/22/25/134-6.
18. Aylesbury & Hockliffe Trust, working papers, CBS ref T/1/10), and draft minutes 1810-21, CBS ref T.1.7.3/1-39.
19. **Bucks., Beds., & Herts. Chronicle,** CBS.
20. **Bucks., Beds., & Herts. Chronicle**, 13 December 1823, CBS.
21. **Bucks. Herald**, 20 February 1836, CBS.
22. Wendover and Buckingham Trust minute books, CBS ref T.3/8.
23. Risborough Road Trust minute books, CBS ref T/5/1.
24. Gerhold, page 50.
25. Michael Hallett and Grainne Farrington, 'A history of the Trinity Milestones: the work of William Warren of Trinity Hall, Cambridge' in **Milestones and Waymarkers**, Journal of the Milestone Society, volume 3, 2009.
26. 'Invasion measures' in the Milestone Society Newsletter, January 2006.
27. See http://inflation.stephenmorley.org

28. John Kersey Fowler, **Records of Old Times** (Chatto and Windus, 1898) pages 13-22.
29. **Northampton Mercury**, for example 7 July 1792 and 28 July 1810, BLARS and OHC.
30. Fowler, pages 13-22.
31. **Jackson's Oxford Journal**, 18 August 1792, OHC.
32. Wendover and Buckingham Trust minute books, CBS ref T.3/8.
33. 'Inrolment of turnpike statements by Clerk of the Peace' (1827 – 1879), CBS ref Q/RuT/1-2; see entries for Red Hill and Beaconsfield, and Beaconsfield and Stokenchurch Trusts.
34. Eric Pawson, **Transport and Economy : the turnpike roads of 18th century Britain**, (Academic Press, 1977) page 166.
35. Bromham and Olney Trust minute books, 1832 and 1844 BLARS ref GA 576/5.
36. Albert, page 181.
37. Pawson, page 133.
38. Newport Pagnell Trust minute books, NRO ref ML.26.
39. Sparrows Herne Turnpike Trust notice pasted into minute book, HALS ref TP4/3.
40. Arthur Parker, 'The Woburn Toll Road' (1975); typescript, BLARS and CBS.
41. Lavendon and Brayfield Enclosure Map, 1801, CBS ref IR/25.A.R.
42. Plan of Lavendon Rectory Lands, 1856, CBS ref PR/126.28/1.
43. Sparrows Herne Trust minute books, HALS ref TP.4/4.
44. Fowler, pages 13-22.
45. Colnbrook Trust minute books, entry for 5 November 1764, LMA ref TP/COL/001, microfilm X/001/157.
46. Sparrows Herne Trust minute books, HALS *ref TP.4/1*.
47. Justices' case notes from Midsummer Sessions, Aylesbury 1805, CBS ref Q/JC/1/11.
48. Colnbrook Trust books, entry for 4 September 1732, LMA ref TP/COL/001, microfilm X/001/157.
49. Sparrows Herne Trust minute books, entry for 2 July 1766, HALS ref TP4/1.
50. Sparrows Herne Trust minute books, entry for 11 April 1809, HALS ref TP4/3.
51. Fowler, pages 13-22.
52. Colnbrook Trust Trust minute books, entry for 21 October 1771, LMA ref TP/COL/001, microfilm X/001/157..
53. Sparrows Herne Trust Trust minute books, entry for 27 October 1818, HALS ref TP4/4.
54. Colnbrook Trust minute books, entry for 20 December 1729, LMA ref TP/COL/001, microfilm X/001/157.
55. Beaconsfield and Stokenchurch Trust's 1719 Act, PA ref 5 Geo I, c.1.
56. **Bucks Advertiser and Uxbridge Journal**, 19 August 1865, CBS.
57. Margaret March, 'Sparrows Herne Turnpike Road' (1969) dissertation manuscript. HALS.
58. Colnbrook Trust minute books, entry for 30 April 1781, LMA ref TP/COL/001, microfilm X/001/157.
59. John Steane, **Oxfordshire**, (Pimlico, 1996) page 132.
60. George Lamb, *'Aylesbury in the Civil War'* in **Records of Buckinghamshire**, volume 41 (Buckinghamshire Archaeological Society, Aylesbury 2001).
61. Steane, page 132.
62. Albert, page 58.
63. Letter from William Praed to Lord Sidmouth, October 1814, Devon Record Office, ref 152M / c.1814.
64. Newport Pagnell Trust minute books, NRO ref ML.26.
65 – 66. Kettering and Newport Pagnell Trust minute books, NRO ref X3472.
67. Colnbrook Trust minute books, LMA ref TP/COL/001, microfilm X/001/157.
68. Kettering and Newport Pagnell Trust minute books, NRO ref X3472.
69. Introductory notes on turnpike roads in subject catalogue at HALS.
70. *'Inrolment of turnpike statements by Clerk of the Peace'* (1827 – 1879), CBS ref Q/RuT/1-2; see entries for Banbury and Brackley Trust.
71. Albert, page 181.
72. Gerhold, various pages.
73. Joan Chibnall, 'The Roads of Bucks. 1675-1913, with particular reference to turnpike roads' (1963) MSc thesis, CBS ref L002 CHI.

74. Milestone Society Newsletter, January 2010.
75. Milestone Society Newsletter, July 2010.
76. Hockliffe and Stony Stratford Trust 1706 Act, PA ref 6 Anne c.4.
77 – 78. Hockliffe and Stony Stratford Trust bundle of petitions for and against renewal of its Act, circa 1736-37, CBS refs D-LE/C/5/12, 13 and 14.
79. Hockliffe and Stony Stratford Trust minute books, CBS ref T.8/1.
80. Hockliffe and Stony Stratford Trust annual statements to Buckinghamshire Clerk of the Peace, CBS ref Q/Rut.3/1-2 ms.TP a/cs.
81. *Paterson,* 'Roads' *(*1829) reprinted in C W Scott-Giles, **The Road Goes On**. (Epworth, 1946) page 169.
82. Daniel Defoe, **A tour through the whole island of Great Britain**, volume 2 (1720s) pages 118-9 and 123-4.
83. Hockliffe and Stony Stratford Trust minute books, CBS ref T.8/1.
84. Plan of several farms in Potsgrove parish, 1731, BLARS ref R1/268.
85. Hockliffe and Stony Stratford Trust bundle of petitions, for and against renewal of its Act, circa 1736-37, CBS refs D-LE/C/5/12, 13 and 14.
86 – 90. Parker, 'The Woburn Toll Road' (1975); typescript, BLARS and CBS.
91. Three maps: Surveys of estates at Broughton ... in 1779 and 1837, CBS ref D/X 85/1,2 and copy of 1837 map of Broughton parish held by Two Villages Archive Trust, Milton Keynes.
92. Reproduced in Parker, 'The Woburn Toll Road' (1975); typescript, BLARS and CBS.
93. D C Mynard, P Woodfield, and R Bailey, **Newport Pagnell's Bridges** (Phillimore 2009).
94. Parker, 'The Woburn Toll Road' (1975); typescript, BLARS and CBS.
95. **Northampton Mercury**, BLARS and OHC.
96. Newport Pagnell Trust's 1723 Act, PA ref 9 Geo I c.13..
97 – 99. Newport Pagnell Trust minute books, 1776 – 97, NRO ref ML 26, and 1797 – 1818, NRO ref ML 24.
100. For Horton compare Bryant's map of Northamptonshire,1827, with Ordnance Survey 1835.
101. **Northampton Mercury,** BLARS and OHC.
102. Newport Pagnell Trust clerk's account book 1788 – 1839, NRO ref ZA 369.
103. Newport Pagnell Trust minute books, 1797-1818, NRO ref ML 24.
104. Newport Pagnell Trust: 'A weekly account of tolls taken on Newport Turnpike Road' 1843, NRO ref X 3818.
105. Newport Pagnell Trust minute books, 1776 – 97, NRO ref ML 26, and 1797 – 1818, NRO ref ML 24.
106. **Ogilby's road maps of England and Wales, from Ogilby's Britannia, 1675, (**Osprey, 1971).
107. Beaconsfield and Stokenchurch Trust: Report of a committee of trustees into the conduct of the trust's surveyor and treasurer, 23 December 1811, Bodleian Library).
108. Clerk of the Peace's inrolment of conveyances of turnpike land, CBS ref Q/RX/3.
109. For eyewitness account see **Bucks, Beds and Herts Chronicle**, 1 September 1827, CBS.
110. **Ogilby's road maps of England and Wales, from Ogilby's Britannia, 1675, (**Osprey, 1971).
111. Estate map of West Wycombe, 1752, CBS ref Ma R 36/2.
112. Exchange of lands between Sir John Dashwood and the turnpike trust on 26 March 1783 in connection with the re-routing of West Wycombe Road, CBS ref D/D/6/335,336).
113. Arthur Bryant, 'Map of the County of Buckingham, 1825' in **Buckinghamshire in the 1760s and 1820s'** (Buckinghamshire Archaeological Society, 2000).
114. Thomas Jefferys, 'The County of Buckingham, surveyed in 1766-68' in **Buckinghamshire in the 1760s and 1820s'** (Buckinghamshire Archaeological Society, 2000).
115. 'Inrolment of turnpike statements by Clerk of the Peace' (1827 – 1879), CBS ref Q/RuT/1-2;.

116. **House of Commons Journal,** 1711, page 148, and 1712, page 186, PA.

117. Wendover and Buckingham Trust minute books, CBS ref T/3/10.

118. **Bucks Herald,** April 1845, CBS.

119. M Foulger, **A short history of Whitchurch to 1939,** (no date), Buckinghamshire Archaeological Society Library, ref P/5c.

120. Wendover and Buckingham Trust minute books, CBS ref T/3/8.

121. Plan of road widening at north end of Whitchurch, 1822, CBS ref T/3/71.

122. Plans, sections, and estimates for alterations to the turnpike road at Winslow and Swanbourne, CBS ref T/3/76.

123. **Bucks, Beds and Herts Chronicle,** 10 March 1827, 5 May 1827, and 27 October 1827, CBS.

124 – 126. Wendover and Buckingham Trust minute books, CBS ref T/3/10.

127. Wendover and Buckingham Trust: specification for erection of Hoggeston toll gate and toll house, CBS ref T.3/32.2.

128. Janet Kennish, **Datchet Past,** (Phillimore 1999), pages 44-48.

129 – 135. Colnbrook Trust minute books, LMA ref TP/COL/001, microfilm X/001/157.

136. Michael Dumbleton, *'The Bath Road'* , reprinted in **The two villages of Harmondsworth (**West Middlesex Family History Society, 1993).

137 – 139. Colnbrook Trust minute books, LMA ref TP/COL/001, microfilm X/001/157.

140. Colnbrook Turnpike: sale details, 1871, CBS ref D-SY/50.

141. Exchange of lands on Colnbrook Turnpike in 1845 recalled in 1872 sale details, CBS ref. Q/RX/9.

142. Colnbrook Turnpike: sale details, 1871, CBS ref D-SY/50.

143. Weeping Cross Trust: annual statement submitted to Oxfordshre Clerk of the Peace, OHC ref. QSD/T/10).

144. Alan Rosevear, **Turnpike roads to Banbury** (Banbury Historical Society, 2010) page 9.

145 **Ogilby's road maps of England and Wales, from Ogilby's Britannia, 1675** (Osprey, 1971) compare plates 12 and 82.

146. Adderbury Enclosure Act, 1766, OHC ref M1/1/H.

147. **Jackson's Oxford Journal,** 24 October 1871, OHC.

148 – 149. Wendover and Oak Lane Trust Treasurer's account book, CBS ref T/4/1.

150. Map titled 'A survey of the Manor of Brudenells in the parishes of Chalfont St Peter and Iver ... 1736/37', British Library ref Add Mss 11749.

151. Jefferys, 'The County of Buckingham, surveyed in 1766-68' in **Buckinghamshire in the 1760s and 1820s'** (Buckinghamshire Archaeological Society, 2000).

152 – 155. Wendover and Oak Lane Trust Treasurer's account book, CBS ref T/4/1.

156. **Bucks Herald,** 19 August 1865, CBS.

157. Aylesbury and Hockliffe Trust, working papers, CBS ref T/1/14/11.

158. Papers of House of Commons Select Committee, 17 May 1852, PA ref HC/CL/PB/2/20/19).

159. 'Map of the parish of Denham, 1783', CBS ref Ma/W/99R.

160. *'Diversion of footpaths and highways at Beaconsfield and Chalfont St Peter, 1805',* CBS ref Q/H/20.

161. Bedford and Newport Pagnell Trust: bundle of correspondence about the trust's work in 1765-73, BLARS ref R Box 772.

162. Bedford and Newport Pagnell Trust: bundle of correspondence in 1857/58 about tolls at Webb's Lane Side Bar in Bromham, BLARS ref P67/28/2/i-xxiv.

163. Bedford and Newport Pagnell Trust: bundle of correspondence about the trust's work in 1765-73, BLARS ref R Box 772.

164. Great Staughton and Lavendon Trust : bundle of correspondence about the union of Odell and Riseley Districts, BLARS ref Q.T. 18/C/1.

165 – 166. Bedford and Newport Pagnell Trust Minute book, BLARS ref Q/T/5/0).

167. Kettering and Newport Pagnell Trust minute books, NRO ref X3472.

168. Olney Bridge: Correspondence about its rebuilding, 1828-33, CBS refs Q/AB/32/1-3, 18-20, 30, 31, 35, 49, 59, 61, 66, 67 and 72).

169 – 171. Kettering and Newport Pagnell Trust minute books, NRO ref X3472.

172. Olney Bridge: Correspondence about its rebuilding, 1828-33, CBS ref Q/AB/32/4.

173. **Beds, Bucks and Herts Chronicle,** various issues, CBS.

174 – 181. Sparrows Herne Trust minute books, HALS ref TP4 / 1-6.

182. **Northampton Mercury**, BLARS and OHC.

183. Sparrows Herne Trust minute books, 4 July 1764, HALS ref TP4 / 1-6.

184. Sparrows Herne Trust minute books, 6 September 1803, HALS ref TP4 / 1-6.

185. Declaration by R A Ward, trust clerk since 1850s, on 1 December 1881, CBS ref D/CN/9/7/2/3. In fact Lord Salisbury was only an Earl in the 1730s, but the clerk may be forgiven this anachronism because the Earls of Salisbury had been made a Marquess in 1789, so in 1881 the Lord Salisbury the clerk knew was a Marquess.

186. Map, CBS ref D/30/127.

187. Photograph titled 'Plan of the Earl of Shelburne's estate at Wycombe, 1762', CBS.

188. Declaration by R A Ward, 1 December 1881, CBS ref D/CN/9/7/2/3.

189. **Reading Mercury**, 28 May 1859 and 3 September 1859, RBLLS.

190. Julian Hunt, **A History of Amersham,** (Phillimore, 2001).

191. **St Albans' Own East End,** booklet, HALS local studies library.

192. Painting dated 1882 by John Westall reproduced in **St Albans Own East End**, HALS.

193. Justices' case notes from Midsummer Sessions, Aylesbury 1805, CBS ref Q/JC/1/11.

194. **Jackson's Oxford Journal,** 28 July 1792, OHC.

195. 'Map of the north-western border of the ancient forest of Bernwood comprising Doddershall Mansion and Park ....', reproduced in Lipscombe, **History and Antiquities of the County of Buckingham,** volume 1, between pages 50 and 51.

196. **House of Commons Journal**, 1711, page 148, PA.

197. **House of Commons Journal**, 1712, page 186, PA.

198. Bicester and Aylesbury Trust: initial Act of Parliament, 1770, PA ref 10 Geo.3, c.72.

199. June Strong, 'Photographs shed light on old Waddesdon' in **Buckinghamshire Countryside** (October 1982).

200. Bicester and Aylesbury Trust: second Act of Parliament, 1791, PA ref 31 Geo.3, c.101.

201. **Jackson's Oxford Journal,** 25 June 1791, OHC.

202. **Bucks, Beds, and Herts Chronicle'**, CBS.

203. Bicester and Aylesbury Trust's accounts for 1862, CBS ref D/X 1425/14 and D/105/54).

204 – 06. Bromham and Olney Turnpike Trust minute book, 1832-75, BLARS ref GA 576/5.

207. Lavendon and Brayfield Enclosure map, 1801, CBS ref IR/25.A.R.

208. Estate map of Gayhurst and Stoke Goldington, base map undated but overdrawn with cropping arrangements for 1858/59, CBS ref D-CN/18/5/7.

209. Bromham and Olney Turnpike Trust minute books 1832-75 BLARS ref GA 576/5.

210. **Jackson's Oxford Journal,** 16 July 1791, OHC.

211. Rosevear, **Turnpike roads to Banbury** (Banbury Historical Society, 2010).

212. Great Marlow Tithe Map, 1843, CBS ref 259.

213. W Francis, 'Map of the Borough of Great Marlow', 1830, Marlow Museum.

214. Details of 18 March 1833 auction of properties in Dean Street, Marlow, CBS ref D/X 900/5.

215. 'Stokenchurch inclosure : schedule of public ways stopped up or diverted from 1 March 1858' in **Jackson's Oxford Journal,** 28 November 1857, OHC microfilm.

216. Thame and Risborough Turnpike Trust Minute book, CBS ref T/5/1.

217. Map of old and new routes between Little Kimble and Ellesborough churches, 1797, CBS ref QH/14,28.

218. For a fuller account see Peter Gulland, **Making the road from Princes Risborough to Thame** (Buckinghamshire Archaeological Society, 2006).

219. Letters dated 29 March 1801 and 19 April 1801 to Lady Lucas, of the Harrold Estate, from Joseph Pawson of Silsoe, Bedfordshire (who was possibly her land agent), BLARS refs L/30/11/215/110 and 111).

220. Great Staughton and Lavendon Trust: Bundle of papers on the merging of the Riseley and Odell Districts in 1855, BLARS ref Q.T. 18/C/1.

221. Harrold inclosure map and award, 1799, BLARS ref MA 12/2 and A, Book D.

222. Lavendon and Brayfield inclosure map and award, 1801, CBS ref IR/25.A.R. and IR/25/2 respectively).

223. **Northampton Mercury**, BLARS and OHC.

224. Bryant's 1825 map of Bedfordshire, BLARS.

225 – 227. Aylesbury and Hockliffe Trust miscellaneous papers, CBS ref T.1/13.

227. **Bucks Herald**, 8 August 1835, CBS.

228. Alesbury and Hockliffe Trust draft minutes, 1810-21, CBS ref T.1.7.3/1-39.

229 – 230. **Ogilby's road maps of England and Wales, from Ogilby's Britannia, 1675** (Osprey, 1971) see plate 80 for the northern route.

231. Bromham and Olney Trust minute book, entry for 4 December 1848, BLARS ref GA. 576/5), Bedford and Newport Pagnell Trust minute book, entry for 22 June 1852, BLARS ref Q/T 5/0.

232. 'Plan of the intended turnpike road from the town of Buckingham to the Oxford– Northampton turnpike road in the open fields of Silston', deposited 27 September 1823, CBS ref Pu.B/32 and NRO ref 6A.

233 – 235. Northampton and Cold Brayfield Turnpike Trust Minutes, NRO ref ML 19-32.

Index

Benwell, Joseph, treasurer, Colnbrook Turnpike
    Trust 113
Berkhamsted (Herts) 28,50,163-165,169,173
Berkley, Countess of 117
Bernard-Morland, Sir Scrope, landowner
    at Kimble 53,243,244; intending to build a
    mansion at Kimble 53,243-244; trustee and
    chairman, Risborough Road Turnpike Trust
    50, 245
Berril, Charles, surveyor, Bedford and Newport
    Pagnell Turnpike Trust 145
Bicester (Oxon) 101,122,127,193-
    195,199,202,205-212,265,276
Bicester and Aylesbury Turnpike Trust
    27,35,51,62,205-213,297,299
Biddenham (Beds) 143
Bierton Side Bar 270
Bignell, Richard,(3 generations) clerks,
    Buckingham and Hanwell Turnpike Trust 122
'Bird in Hand' ('Punch Bowl') public House,
    Colnbrook 117
Biscell (or Bycell Farm) Side Bar 284-285
Bisham 175,178,184; Gate 184,187
Black Boy, Bricket Wood,(Herts) Gate 187;
    toll house 187
Blackthorn (Oxon) 193-195,198-199,202-205
Blackthorn Hill 194,204-205,207,209
Bletchley 56,67,128,173,233,295
Bletsoe (Beds.) 257-259,261
Bloxham, Edward, clerk, Hockcliffe and Stony
    Stratford Turnpike Trust 65
Bodicote (Oxon) 122,124,127
Bolney Farm and Court (Henley) 183
Bolter End 238
Bolton, Thomas, gatekeeper, Chalfont St. Peter
    134
Boughton, Thomas, gatekeeper, Sparrows Herne
    Turnpike Trust 170
boundary markers 28,173
Bourne End 91,137,164,169
Bozeat Wold Gate 158; toll house 158
Brackley (Northants) 25,35,54,121,225-233
Brackley Consolidated Trust 226-227,233
Bradshaw, Daniel, surveyor, Kettering and
    Newport Pagnell Trust 53
Bradwell Gate 279-280; toll house 280
Brafield-on-the-Green (Northants.) 87,292; Gate
    and Side Bar 293; toll house 293
Brafield Road, Horton (Northants) 59, 61-62
Brandon's Wood 113
Brentford Trust 115,117
Bricket Wood (Herts) 187; Side Bar 187
Brickhill, Little 45-46
Brick Kiln (Thame, Oxon) Gate and Side Bar
    200-201; toll house 201
bridges *see under* place names
Bridgwater, Earl of, trustee, Sparrows Herne
    Turnpike Trust 164
Brill 27,59,202
Brockhampton (or Brookhampton) (Oxon) Gate
    200; toll house 200

Bromham (Beds) 143-147,215-219,222-223;
    Bridge 146,216; Gate 146-148,218-220; Side
    Bars 217-220; toll house 147,219-220; wooden
    watchbox 220
Bromham and Olney Turnpike Trust
    18,31,36,39,52,62,147,152,215-223,258,
    297- 299
Broughton (MK) 18,31,36,39,52,73-74,76-77,122;
    Gate 77-78; toll house 77
Broughton Lane (Aylesbury) Side Bar 170
Bryan, William, chairman, Kettering and Newport
    Pagnell Turnpike Trust 152
Buckingham 23-25,27,59,99-102,105,108-109,121-
    122,127,129,143,193,205-206,225-227,275-
    278,280,283-284,287; Gate 35,108; toll house
    108,230
Buckingham and Hanwell Turnpike Trust 62,
    121-128,297,299
**Buckingham and Newport Pagnell Turnpike
    Trust** 49,56,62,65,143,193,275-281,297,299
Buckingham and Towcester Turnpike Trust
    36,45,62,283-287,297,299
Buckinghamshire County Council
    23,85,96,102,154,167,268
'Bucks Pressings' 27,79,204
Buffler's Holt Gate and Side Bar 230;
    toll house 230
Bull and Morris, contractors, Sparrows Herne
    Turnpike Trust 166
'Bull Inn', Gerrards Cross 139
'Bull Inn', Olney 153,217
Bullshead Farm ('Bull's Head') Eakley Lanes
    86-87
Bunsty Side Bar 86
Burcote Wood, (Northants) Gate 286
Burnham, George Hodson, clerk, Kettering and
    Newport Pagnell Turnpike Trust 152
Burnham, James, Trustee, Wendover and
    Buckingham Turnpike Trust 100
Bushey (Herts) 163,165,169

C

Cadmore End 238
Caldecot (Tickford) Side Bar 78
Caldecot Mill, Newport Pagnell 78-79
Cambridge 143,150,193,265,275
Cambridge and Fowlmere Turnpike Trust 26
Camp Road, St. Albans (Herts), Side Bar 188;
    toll house 188
canals 5,29,57,61,67,166,168,266,277,280
'Capability' Brown, work at Chalfont House 131
Capshill Bridge, Leighton Buzzard (Beds) 268-269
carriages 9,32,43,45,69,101,104,118,172,252,292
Carter, Mr., toll collector, Yardley Hastings Gate
    293
carts 9,16-17,37,77,92-93
    see also water carts
'Cartwright Arms', Aynho 122
Cassiobury Park (Herts) 168,176
'Castle Inn', Salt Hill, 113-114; poisonings at
    113-114

Dunkley, William, toll collector, Bedford and Newport Pagnell Turnpike Trust 148
Dunstable (Beds) 11,64,74
Du Pré, James, chairman, Beaconsfield and Stokenchurch Turnpike Trust 92
Dupre, Rev., complaint about toll collector at New Ground Gate, Tring 43
dust control 19,70,93,112-115,130,139,165
    see also water pumps

E

'Eagle, The', Nash Mills 168
Eakley Lanes 81,85,86,88: Gates 33,86- 87; Side Bar 86-88; toll house 86
East Adderbury 123-124
Edgell, Mr., builder of Woburn weighing engine 78
Eggington 266-269,272; enclosure 269
Ellesborough Road 53, 244,250-251
Elliotts of Towcester, clerks, Buckingham and Towcester Turnpike Trust 284
Emberton 154,156,161; Gate and Side Bar 153,159-160; toll house 159-160
enclosure of open fields 15,23,221,259; Adderbury 124, Amersham 181, Eggington 269, Haddenham 15,196, Harrold 261,263, Lavendon 261,263, Leighton Buzzard 269, Marlow 240, Princes Risborough 245,249, Stokenchurch 239-240, Stoke Mandeville 243,Thame 15,250, Waddesdon 209, Whitchurch 18
Essex, Earl of 176-177,181
Eton 111-115,117,119-120; Gate 119; toll house 119
Eton College 112,114
Ewesdin, Thomas, clerk, Hockcliffe and Stony Stratford Turnpike Trust 65

F

'Falcon Inn', Bletsoe 259
Farthinghoe (Northants) 15,226-227,229-230; Gate 231-233; toll house 232
Fastnedge, James, clerk, Beaconsfield and Stokenchurch Turnpike Trust 92
Fawley Court 179,184
Fell, George, clerk, Risborough Road Turnpike Trust 243
Felmersham Lane (Beds) Side Bar 262; toll house 262
Fenny Stratford 64-67; Gate and Side Bar 44,68; toll house 69
Fiddle Gate , Hatfield 189-190
'Fiddle, The', Hatfield 189
Filgrave Lane Side Bar 159; box/shed 160
Filling Highway (Northants) Side Bar 60-61; toll house 61
financial matters, general background 9,11,13, 16,23,26,29-30,44,50,56
    further details are included with each trust
Finch, R., clerk, Bedford and Newport Pagnell Turnpike Trust 144
Finmere (Oxon.) (or Finemere Warren) Gate 125-126; toll house 126

'Five Bells', Riseley 259
Flackwell Heath 190
Fornhill , near Hockcliffe, Beds., 10,33,63-64,67-68; Gate 10,33,67 ; toll house 68
Fourne Hill Farm, near Hockliffe, Beds 64
Freeman family, Fawley Court 179
Fremantle, Thomas, trustee, Wendover and Buckingham Turnpike Trust 100
'French Partridge', Horton 83,85

G

Garrard, John, clerk, Bromham Olney Turnpike Trust 217
'Gate, The', PH, Chorleywood 187
Gawcott 104,108,125
Gayhurst 86,89,215-216; Bunsty Side Bar 86
Gell, Thomas, surveyor, Great Staughton and Lavendon Turnpike Trust 258
'George Inn', Aylesbury 101,165,196,207,266
'George Inn', Colnbrook 113
'George Inn', (Home Farm), Little Brickhill 65-66
'George Inn' ('Bedford Arms'; 'The Woburn Hotel'), Woburn 74
'George Inn' ('George Dragon'), Princes Risborough 243
Gibbard, John, clerk, Great Staughton and Lavendon Turnpike Trust 258
Goldsmith, Henry, clerk, Great Marlow and Stokenchurch Turnpike Trust 236
Goodwin, Matthew, surveyor, Colnbrook Turnpike Trust 113
Gould, Rev. John, chairman, Red Hill and Beaconsfield Turnpike Trust 138
'Gout Track' 175-176,190
Grant, John, chairman, Aylesbury and Hockliffe Turnpike Trust 266
Gravel Hill (Chalfont St Peter) 133-134
gravel in road maintenance 16-18,291; digging 17-18,114,133-134,208
Great Billing (Northants) 85,87,293
Great Harrowden Lane Gate (Northants) 155-156; toll house 156
Great Houghton (Northants) Gate and Side Bar 232-234; toll house 232; weighing engine 234
Great Kimble 20,241-242,244
Great Linford Gate 280
Great Marlow 28,138,178,238,247; Chapel Street Gate 184-185; obelisk 28
Great Marlow and Stokenchurch Turnpike Trust 47,52,62,178,235-240,257,297,299
Great Milton 197
Great Missenden 129,131-132; Gate 132-134; toll house 40-41,59,132; weighing engine 134
Great North Road 139, 205
Great Staughton (Cambs) 257-259; Gate 148,261; toll house 261
Great Staughton and Lavendon Turnpike Trust 47,54,62,148,257-264,290,297,299
Greaves, John, surveyor, Hockcliffe and Woburn Turnpike Trust 74
Green, John, clerk, Hockcliffe and Woburn Turnpike Trust 74
Green, Mr., toll collector, Datchet Gate 118

Green, William, Aylesbury, builder of Walton and Padbury toll houses 106-108
Greenlands Gate 184; toll house 184
Gregory, Dixie, clerk, Hockcliffe and Woburn Turnpike Trust 74
Grendon Underwood 27,59,205-206
'Greyhound Inn', Chalfont St.Peter 45,134
'Greyhound, The', Thame 196
'Griffin Inn', Amersham 130
Grimsbury Green Gate (Banbury) 232-233
Grover, Charles Ehret, clerk, Sparrows Herne Turnpike Trust 164-165
Grover, Harry, clerk and treasurer, Sparrows Herne Turnpike Trust 164
Grover, William, surveyor, Colnbrook TurnpikeTrust 113
Grubb, John, trustee and chairman, Risborough Road Turnpike Trust 50,243
Grundy & Co., Northampton, manufacturers of milestones 79,89
'Gunning Arms' ('French Partridge'), Horton 83
Gunning, Sir Robert, chairman, Newport Pagnell Turnpike Trust 82,85

H

Hackleton (Northants) 83,85,88
Haddenham, enclosure 15,196
Hagden Lane , Watford, Gate 187
Hampden Lane, Great Missenden, Side Bar 132
Handy Cross (south of High Wycombe) 242-243,246-248,253,257
Hanwell 121-122,127
Hardmead 143,146,159
Hardwick Bridge 102-103
'Hare and Hounds', Red Hill (Denham) 139
Harlington (Middx) 111,118,307; Gate and Side Bar 117-118
Harris, Edward, clerk, Hockcliffe and Stony Stratford and Buckingham and Newport Pagnell Turnpike Trusts 65,277
Harrison, William, clerk, Hockcliffe and Woburn Turnpike Trust 74
Harrold (Beds.) 257-259; enclosure 261-263; Gate 263
Harvey, Benjamin, gatekeeper, Colnbrook Turnpike Trust 43
Hatfield 4,175-177,181,183,189-190
Hayton, William, clerk and treasurer, Sparrows Herne Trust 51,164
Hayward, William, surveyor, Newport Pagnell Turnpike Trust 83
Hazlemere 181; Gate 184-186; toll house 186
Hearn, Thomas, clerk, Buckingham and Hanwell Turnpike Trust 122
Hearne, Henry, clerk, Buckingham and Towcester Turnpike Trust 284
Heath, Henry, clerk, Wendover and Oak Lane Turnpike Trust 130
Hedsor Wharves 91,137
Hempstead Road, Watford 164,168,171

Henley 15,25,137,177-179,184,194,235; Gate 183; toll house 183-184
Higgins, Charles Longuet, chairman, Bromham and Olney Turnpike Trust 216
Higgins, John, chairman, Kettering and Newport Pagnell Turnpike Trust and Bromham and Olney Turnpike Trust 152,216-217
Higgins, Thomas Charles, chairman, Kettering and Newport Pagnell and Bromham and Olney Turnpike Trusts 152,216,258
Higgins, William Bartholomew, chairman, Kettering and Newport Pagnell, Bromham and Olney and Northampton and Cold Brayfield Turnpike Trusts 152,216-217,220,294
High Wycombe 11,15,36,91-92,94,98,137,139, 141,175-177,180,186,190,193,235,241-242,247-248,254; Gate 96-97; toll house 40-41,96; weighing engine 97
Hill, Charles, chairman, Kettering and Newport Pagnell Turnpike Trust 152
'Hind,The', Wellingborough 153
Hockliffe 10,63-64,69,73-75,78,81,265; Gates and Side Bar 44,67,68,269,271-272; toll houses 68,272, weighing engine 272
Hockliffe and Stony Stratford Turnpike Trust 11-12,33,37,44-45,47,62-71,277,297,299
Hockliffe and Woburn Turnpike Trust 9,21,33,37,62,73-79,85,89,151,161,297,299
Hodson, Charles, Henry and John, clerks, Kettering and Newport Pagnell Turnpike Trust 152
Hoggeston 99,107; Gate 106-107,109; toll house 107
Hogshaw 23,101
Hollier, John, senior and junior, clerks, Aylesbury and Shillingford (Thame United after 1838) and Wheatley and Stokenchurch Turnpike Trusts 51,155,195
Holloway, R., clerk, Thame United Turnpike Trust 190
Holman's Bridge (Aylesbury) Gate 20,99,106-108, toll house 107; weighing engine 108
Holtspur 22,93,96,137; Gate 96; kiosk 96
Holyhead Road 10,18,63,65-66,69-70,73,89, 212,226,265,276
horse drawn transport 9-17,21,26,32,55,91,93, 101,115,139,169,269,291
Horseshoe Fiddle, Hatfield, (Herts), Gate 189-190, hut 189
Horseshoe Gate, Smallford, (Three Horseshoes Gate) 188-189
'Horse Shoe Inn', Lavendon 230
'Horton Inn' ('French Partridge'), Horton 83,85
Horton (Northants) 81-85,87,293
Howard, Thomas, clerk, Hockcliffe and Woburn Turnpike Trust 74
Hulcott 19,265,267-268,271; Side Bar 270 ; toll house 270
Hunton Bridge (Herts) 165,168
Hurdlesgrove Hill, gravel digging 18
Hyde Lane (near Buckingham) Gate 278; toll house 278

Pierce, Hester, widow of Joseph Pierce 45
Pierce, Joseph, murdered toll keeper, Colnbrook
Turnpike Trust 45
pikers *see* toll keepers/collectors
'Plough, The (Plowden Arms)', Henley 83
Postcombe 193-195,198,200-201,203,298,300
Potsgrove (Beds.) 64,69,76
Poyle (Middx) 16-118; water pump 20, 115
Preston Lane, New Hackleton, (Northants) 85-86;
Gate 86-88; toll house 88; weighing engine
88
Prickett, Edward, clerk, Risborough Road
Turnpike Trust 243
Prickett, Giles, clerk, Aylesbury and Shillingford
Turnpike Trust 195
Priest End Gate and Side Bar, Thame 199-200,
202-203; toll kiosk 199
Princes Risborough 23,201,241-243,245,248-249;
enclosure 245,249
Princes Risborough and Thame Turnpike Trust
s*ee* Risborough Road Turnpike Trust
Puddle Hill Turnpike Trust 64
'Punch Bowl', Colnbrook 117
Purefoy, Henry, Trustee, Wendover and
Buckingham Turnpike Trust 100

Q

'Quart Pot Inn', Denton (Northants) 290
Quinton (Northants) 86-88

R

Radclive Gate and Side Bars 125,230; toll house
230
Radnage 13,91
railway era, effect on the trusts
5,21,35,55-57,61,70,77,79,88-89,98,103,109,
112,114,116,119-120,128,135,141,150,156-158,
162,168,173,191,198,204,208,212,216-217,223,
233,251,254,273,277-279,281,289,295
railway stations: Bletchley 56; Burton Latimer
122 ; Didcot 200; Finedon 122; High
Wycombe 203; Slough 115,120; Stoke
Mandeville 242; Wellingborough 154;
Woburn Sands 77
Randall, Thomas, murderer 170
'Rat's Castle' St.Albans 188
Ravenstone Gate and Side Bar 218,221-222;
toll house 222; 'wooden watch box' 221
Reading and Hatfield Turnpike Trust
15,28,31,33,36,44,49,52,57,62,112,121,131,
175-191,193,218,236,247,297,299
Red Hill and Beaconsfield Turnpike Trust
19,27,51-52,54, 62,92-93,98-100,129-130,
132,134,137-142,298-299
Red Hill Gate 140; toll house 140
'Red Lion', Banbury 92
'Red Lion', High Wycombe 65
'Red Lion', Nash Mills 131
'Red Lion Inn', Brackley 181
'Red Lion Inn', Brafield-on-the-Green 230
'Red Lion Inn' ('Cartwright Arms') Aynho 91

'Red Lion Inn', Denton 230
'Red Lion Inn', Little Houghton 230
'Red Lion Inn', Yardley Hastings 230
'Red Lion', Thame 155
Reynolds, Thomas, clerk, Beaconsfield and
Stokenchurch Turnpike Trust 65
Rickford, William, MP for Aylesbury 169;
trustee, Wendover and Buckingham Turnpike
Trust 100; chairman, Bicester and
Aylesbury and Aylesbury and Hockliffe
Turnpike Trusts 207-208,265
Rickmansworth (Herts) 15, 175-178,182
Ridge Lane (Watford) Gate and Side Bar
42,169,172; toll house 171
Ridley, Rev. Henry Colbourne, chairman, Great
Marlow and Stokenchurch Turnpike Trust 236
Ringrove, Mr., builder of weighing engine 172
Rintoul, Alexander, surveyor, Kettering and
Newport Pagnell Turnpike trust 153
Risborough Road Turnpike Trust 13,15-16,
20,23,30,36,45,47,50,53,62,94,97,193,201,
241-256,298,300
Riseley (Beds) 257-259; Gate and Side Bar
148,261; toll house 261
rivers: Cherwell 122-124; Colne 100,116,129-130,
133-134,137-138,140-141,171; Crane 117;
Great Ouse 69,105,145,151,154,158,215,227,
231,276-277; Kym 261; Misbourne 131; Nene
81,154,157; Ouse 13,83,217,262; Ousel 67,78;
Ray 207,209; Thame 19,211; Thames 91,111-
112,119,137,179,194; Ver 172; Wraysbury 116;
Wye 19, 93-94
road classification 3,5-6,13,57-59,250,264
Robinson, Thomas, general and superintending
surveyor, Red Hill and Beaconsfield Turnpike
Trust 139
Roe, Thomas, senior and junior, surveyors,
Newport Pagnell Turnpike Trust 52,82-83
Rogers, Jonathan, creditor, Colnbrook
TurnpikeTrust 120
Rogers, William, surveyor, Great Staughton and
Lavendon Turnpike Trust 258
Roman roads 3,5,10,47,55,63,101,163,205,208-209
'Rose and Crown', Yardley Hastings 290
Rotherham, John, clerk, Hockcliffe and Woburn
Turnpike Trust 74
Rothschild, Baron S.N. de 171
Rotten Row, Whitchurch High Street 102
routes of the roads, general background 5,11,
13-15,22-23,25,27,56,59
further details are included with each trust
Rowsham Bridge 19, 267
Rumsey, John, clerk, Beaconsfield and
Stokenchurch Turnpike Trust 92
Rycote Lane, Thame 194-195,197-198,200
Ryder, Granville D., chairman, Sparrows Herne
Turnpike Trust 164

S

St. Albans (Herts) 15,175-178,182-183,188-190
St.Neots to Higham Ferrers turnpike road 257-258
Salcey Forest 33,86,88

Whielden Lane, Amersham, Gate 186; toll house 186
Whitchurch 99,101-102,107; enclosure 18
'White Hart Inn', Aylesbury 101,165,196,207,266
'White Hart Inn', Buckingham 122,227,284
'White Hart, The', Princes Risborough 243
White Hill, Holtspur 22,93,96
White Hound Pond Gate, Thame 200-201
White Lion Road (Little Chalfont) 181,186; Gate 186-187
Whittlebury (Northants) 25,283
Whittlebury Forest (or Lillingstone Lovell) Side Bar 285-286; shelter 286
Wilder & Sons, manufacturers of milestone 190
Williams, John, drover 43
Willis, Browne, trustee, Wendover and Buckingham Turnpike Trust 100
Wilton Park, Beaconsfield 92,139
winding up of trusts, general background 41,5,59
  further details are included with each trust
'Windmill Inn', Salt Hill 113
Windsor 111,113,119; Bridge 119
Windsor, Thomas, milestone manufacturer 119
Wing Gate and Side Bar 271; toll house 271
Winslow 99-103,109; Side Bars 56; abortive site for weighing engine 108
Woburn 73-74,76,81,272; Gate 53,55; toll house 53; weighing engine 37,78
'Woburn Hotel The', Woburn 74
Woburn Sands 74,76; Gate 76-77; toll house 77
Wollaston (Northants) 155-156
Wolverton 279,281; Gate 279; Railway Works 277-279; toll house 279
wooden watch boxes 36,39,220-221,253-254
Woolley, James, treasurer, Kettering and Newport Pagnell Turnpike Trust 152
Wootton (Northants) 86-88
World's End, Wendover 20,99,241-242
Wraysbury River 116
Wretchwick (or Chapel Lane) Gates , Bicester 210-211; toll house 210
Wright, John, clerk, Great Marlow and Stokenchurch and Reading and Hatfield Turnpike Trusts 236
Wyatt, Lancelot, clerk, Wendover and Buckingham Turnpike Trust 100
Wyatt, Rev. Charles F. chairman, Buckingham and Hanwell Turnpike Trust 122
Wycombe End, Beaconsfield 93,137
Wycombe Hill Gate 185; toll house 185
Wykeham, Philip, Tythrop House, trustee, Risborough Road Turnpike Trust 249

Y

Yardley Hastings (Northants) 289-290,292; Gates 293; toll houses 293
Yardley Hill 292,294
Yeates, Samuel, clerk, Wendover and Buckingham Turnpike Trust 100

Buckinghamshire Archaeological Society

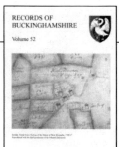

MEMBERSHIP OF THE SOCIETY

Members receive the annual *Records of Buckinghamshire* free every year, have the use of the society's Library and take part ina range of activities including active archaeology, lectures, outings, project groups, day schools and historical research.

Single membership is £18 a year, family £22, junior £12. TO JOIN, Contact the Membership Secretary at BAS, County Museum, Church Street, Aylesbury HP20 2QP

Some of our other publications

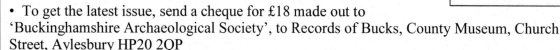

RECORDS OF BUCKINGHAMSHIRE

The Society's annual journal, **Records of Buckinghamshire,** publishes reports of archaeological excavations, historic buildings, local and industrial history, documentary research and fieldwork and all aspects of times past in Buckinghamshire. It is published in May every year.

• To get the latest issue, send a cheque for £18 made out to 'Buckinghamshire Archaeological Society', to Records of Bucks, County Museum, Church Street, Aylesbury HP20 2QP

THE CHILTERNS IN 1748
An Account by Pehr Kalm, Visitor from Finland

The botanist and agricultural economist Pehr Kalm wrote a unique account of life in the Chilterns when on a botanical mission in 1748. This new edition of Professor Bill Mead's translation is a valuable contribution to our understanding of the area's history.

To get a copy, send a cheque for £7.50 made out to 'Bucks Archaeological Society' to BAS, County Museum, Church Street, Aylesbury HP20 2QP

WINSLOW IN 1556: THE SURVEY OF THE MANOR by David Noy

Putting together the 1556 survey with other historical documents – wills, household inventories, parish registers and legal records – this book develops a panorama of the towns's people, properties, occupations, familes and relationships, petty crimes and long-term feuds.

To get a copy, send a cheque for £5.00 made out to 'Bucks Archaeological Society' to BAS, County Museum, Church Street, Aylesbury HP20 2QP

ILLUSTRATED HISTORY OF EARLY BUCKINGHAMSHIRE

This book covers the history of our county from the Ice Age to the Tudors, drawing on many recent discoveries by archaeologists and historians. Its seven specialist authors are all members of the society.

To get a copy, send a cheque for £18.50 made out to 'Bucks Archaeological Society' to BAS, County Museum, Church Street, Aylesbury HP20 2QP